THE CAMBRIDGE COMPANION TO

ANC

The Camb
to underst
cal though
of essays s
ing schola
brings the
the proble
Thucydid
issues, incl
munity fo
of several

Stephen S
at Bryn M
and Practic
articles an
research h
ment for t
has receiv
for Advan

THE CAMBRIDGE COMPANION TO

ANCIENT GREEK POLITICAL THOUGHT

Edited by

STEPHEN SALKEVER

Bryn Mawr College

CAMBRIDGE UNIVERSITY PRESS
Cambridge, New York, Melbourne, Madrid, Cape Town, Singapore, São Paulo, Delhi

Cambridge University Press
32 Avenue of the Americas, New York, NY 10013-2473, USA

www.cambridge.org
Information on this title: www.cambridge.org/9780521687126

First published 2009

Printed in the United States of America

A catalog record for this publication is available from the British Library.

Library of Congress Cataloging in Publication data

The Cambridge companion to Ancient greek political thought / edited by
Stephen Salkever.
p. cm.
Includes bibliographical references and index.
ISBN 978-0-521-86753-5 (hardback) – ISBN 978-0-521-68712-6 (pbk.)
1. Political science – Greece – History – To 1500. I. Salkever, Stephen G., 1943–
II. Ancient greek political thought III. Title.
JC73.C364 2009
320.0938 – dc22 2008049243

ISBN 978-0-521-86753-5 hardback
ISBN 978-0-521-68712-6 paperback

Contents

Contributors

RYAN K. BALOT is Associate Professor of Political Science at the University of Toronto. The author of *Greed and Injustice in Classical Athens* (Princeton University Press, 2001) and of *Greek Political Thought* (Blackwell, 2006), he specializes in the history of political thought. He received his doctorate in classics at Princeton University and his B.A. degrees in classics from University of North Carolina at Chapel Hill and Corpus Christi College, Oxford, where he studied as a Rhodes Scholar. Balot is currently at work on *Courage and Its Critics in Democratic Athens*, from which he has published articles in the *American Journal of Philology*, *Classical Quarterly*, and *Social Research*. Balot is also editor of the forthcoming *Companion to Greek and Roman Political Thought* (Blackwell, forthcoming).

SUSAN BICKFORD is Associate Professor of Political Science at the University of North Carolina at Chapel Hill. She is the author of *The Dissonance of Democracy: Listening, Conflict, and Citizenship* (Cornell University Press, 1996) as well as articles on feminist political theory, democratic theory, and ancient Greek political thought.

ERIC BROWN is Associate Professor of Philosophy at Washington University in St. Louis and is the author of several articles on Greek and Roman philosophy and of *Stoic Cosmopolitanism* (Cambridge University Press, forthcoming). Before moving to St. Louis, he studied classics and philosophy at the universities of Cambridge, Pittsburgh, and especially Chicago.

JILL FRANK is Associate Professor of Political Science at the University of South Carolina, Columbia. Her recent publications include *A Democracy of Distinction: Aristotle and the Work of Politics* (University of Chicago Press, 2005) and "Wages of War: On Judgment in Plato's *Republic*," *Political Theory* 35 (2007): 443–67.

DEAN HAMMER is John W. Wetzel Professor of Classics and Professor and Chair of Government at Franklin and Marshall College. He is the author of *The Iliad as Politics: The Performance of Political Thought* (University of Oklahoma Press, 2002) and of *The Puritan Tradition in Revolutionary, Federalist, and Whig Political Theory: A Rhetoric of Origins* (P. Lang, 1998). He is currently at work on the book *Roman Political Thought and the Return to the World.*

GERALD MARA is Executive Associate Dean, Graduate School of Arts and Sciences, and Professorial Lecturer, Department of Government, Georgetown University. His research interests are classical political philosophy, historical and contemporary liberalism, and democratic theory. He is the author of *The Civic Conversations of Thucydides and Plato: Classical Political Philosophy and the Limits of Democracy* (SUNY Press, 2008) and *Socrates' Discursive Democracy: Logos and Ergon in Platonic Political Philosophy* (SUNY Press, 1997) and joint editor of and co-contributor to *Liberalism and the Good* (Routledge, 1990). He has also published historical essays on Thucydides, Plato, Aristotle, Spinoza, Hobbes, Rousseau, Nietzsche, and J. S. Mill, and conceptual essays on virtue, pluralism, and autonomy.

FRED D. MILLER, JR., is Professor of Philosophy and Executive Director of the Social Philosophy and Policy Center at Bowling Green State University. He is the author of *Nature, Justice, and Rights in Aristotle's Politics* (Oxford University Press, 1995) and co-editor of *Freedom, Reason, and the Polis: Essays in Ancient Greek Political Philosophy* (Cambridge University Press, 2007) and *A History of the Philosophy of Law from the Ancient Greeks to the Scholastics* (Springer, 2007). He served as president of the Society for Ancient Greek Philosophy from 1988 to 2004.

S. SARA MONOSON is Associate Professor of Political Science and Classics and Director of the Classical Traditions Initiative at Northwestern University. Her book *Plato's Democratic Entanglements: Athenian Politics and the Practice of Philosophy* (Princeton University Press, 2000) won the Best First Book Award from the American Political Science Association in 2001. Her current project, *Socrates in American Life*, examines creative appropriations of Socrates in twentieth and twenty-first century North American popular media.

DAVID ROOCHNIK is Professor of Philosophy at Boston University. His most recent books include *Retrieving the Ancients: An Introduction to Greek Philosophy* (Blackwell, 2004), and *Beautiful City: The Dialectical Character of Plato's* Republic (Cornell University Press, 2003).

STEPHEN SALKEVER was educated at Amherst College and the University of Chicago and is Mary Katharine Woodworth Professor of Political Science at Bryn Mawr College. He is the author of *Finding the Mean: Theory and Practice in Aristotelian Political Philosophy* (Princeton University Press, 1990) and a variety of articles and chapters on ancient and modern political philosophy.

ARLENE W. SAXONHOUSE is the Caroline Robbins Professor of Political Science and Adjunct Professor of Classics at the University of Michigan. Her most recent book is *Free Speech and Democracy in Ancient Athens* (Cambridge University Press, 2006).

NORMA THOMPSON is Associate Director of the Whitney Humanities Center and Senior Lecturer in the Humanities at Yale University. She received her A.B. from Bowdoin College and her Ph.D. from The Committee on Social Thought at the University of Chicago. Her scholarship and teaching are in the humanities, with special interests in political philosophy and politics and literature. She is the Director of Undergraduate Studies for the humanities major at Yale College. Her latest book is *Unreasonable Doubt: Circumstantial Evidence and an Ordinary Murder in New Haven* (University of Missouri Press, 2006). She has published two books with Yale University Press: *Herodotus and the Origins of the Political Community: Arion's Leap* (1996) and *The Ship of State: Politics and Statecraft from Ancient Greece to Democratic America* (2001). She edited the volume *Instilling Ethics* with Rowman & Littlefield (2000) and has also published articles in *Arion*, *Nomos*, and *International Journal of the Classical Tradition*, and in the festschrift for David Grene, *Literary Imagination, Ancient and Modern.*

CATHERINE H. ZUCKERT is Nancy Reeves Dreux Professor at Notre Dame University. Her writings include *Postmodern Platos: Nietzsche, Heidegger, Gadamer, Strauss, Derrida* (University of Chicago Press, 1996); *Natural Right and the American Imagination: Political Philosophy in Novel Form* (Rowman & Littlefield, 1990); and most recently, *Plato's Philosophers* (University of Chicago Press, 2009).

Introduction

Stephen Salkever

This volume is a companion to Greek "political thought," rather than "political philosophy" or "political theory" – why? One reason will be apparent from the table of contents: the chapters have a broader scope than the terms "philosophy" and "theory" would suggest, and their authors have been trained and teach in a variety of fields, including philosophy, classical literature and history, and political theory. But there is a more substantial reason behind the choice of title. There are three propositions that unite these chapters and that define a central tendency in recent interpretive work on Greek political thought:

(1) Our consideration of fundamental questions about politics in the world of ancient Greece must be pursued in texts that cross the standard modern genre distinctions among philosophy, history, and literature. Taking these modern academic distinctions too seriously as a guide to inquiry is an anachronistic mistake and can result in serious distortions of the Greek texts. Treating Plato as a post-Kantian systematic and doctrinal philosopher is one important example of such a distortion; treating Thucydides as a proto-"scientific" historian is another.[1]

(2) But the purpose of studying these Greek texts and practices is not archival or antiquarian, nor is it a romantic longing to escape from modernity to a lost idyllic world; instead, the ultimate goal inspiring these studies is to bring voices embodied

[1] On Plato, contrast Kraut 1992 with Cooper 1997. See also Griswold 2001. On Thucydides, see the chapters by Thompson and Mara in this volume.

in these ancient texts into our contemporary discussions of political thought and action.

(3) At the same time, this attempt to bring ancient Greek voices into modern discussions will itself be anachronistic unless we are very careful to place the Greek texts in the context of debate and action in which they were written.

The major recent direction in the study of Greek political thought is the emergence of a variety of ways of interpreting Greek texts and institutions with an eye to *both* the ancient Greek political/discursive context *and* modern practice. We no longer see the field divided between scholars who show how Greek political theory fits into ancient Greece and scholars who show how such theory might be instructive for our own time. More and more, the presumption is that one must be able to do both at least adequately in order to do either well. There is widespread agreement that our job as interpreters of Greek political thought is to show how these texts speak to us *indirectly*, that is, through their response to the arguments and events of ancient Greek political life. Negatively put, we see a rejection of the agendas of both antiquarianism and presentism/progressivism – of both the idea that the study of Greek texts is an activity that has no purpose beyond that of accumulating as accurate as possible a record of the thoughts and deeds of ancient Greek civilization as an end in itself, and the idea that the modern world is so different from that of ancient Greece as to render any conversation between them impossible at best and a sign of reactionary politics at worst. Politically, this means a general reorientation around the project of bringing questions that arise in contemporary democracies to the study of Greek texts and institutions. This new focus has meant a healthy lessening of the influence of disciplinary boundaries among political scientists, classicists, and philosophers, and has provided a healthy counterbalance to the strong "modernist" bias of some influential modern political philosophers, such as John Rawls and Jürgen Habermas. All of the chapters in this volume are characterized by a present and future-oriented – though historically informed – interpretation of Greek political thought. One proposition runs through all the chapters: the texts and practices of ancient Greece can provide contributions to modern democratic discussion that are otherwise unavailable. Thomas Jefferson was wrong.[2] Our goal is in part to rebut an

[2] "The introduction of the new principle of representative democracy has rendered useless almost everything written before on the structure of government, and in a

all-too-common assumption among teachers and students of political theory that we can begin our study with Machiavelli or Hobbes and that we moderns no longer have anything to learn from thinking through the Greek texts.

Another way of characterizing this recent tendency of studies in Greek political theory is to say that they have aimed at broadening the "modern political imaginary" (Charles Taylor's[3] phrase), our sense of what is politically normal and possible. For example, thinking through Greek political theory might enable us to call into question the Hobbesian and Kantian idea that the job of political theory is to discover principles, whether formal or substantive, that will solve our deepest political problems. A number of students of Greek political thought, beginning with Hannah Arendt, have suggested instead that the job of political theory is to prepare citizens to make the best possible judgments by encouraging us to discern and reflect on the central problems of political life; not to tell us what we must do, but, in Arendt's phrase, to help us "think what we are doing."[4] Other scholars have used reflection

great measure relieves our regret if the political writings of Aristotle or of any other ancient have been lost or are unfaithfully rendered or explained to us" (Jefferson 1903, p. 66).

[3] Taylor's position on our modern relationship to Greek texts is complicated. On the one hand, he frequently asserts the neo-Hegelian view that modernity is sui generis and that it is not possible to understand modern freedom and democracy via the categories and methods of the ancient philosophers. On the other, he has been instrumental in establishing the position that ancient philosophy, and especially Aristotle, is right about certain key issues in ethics and politics that are generally misunderstood by modern moral and political philosophy. A good example is the following from *Sources of the Self*:

> [There is] a tendency to breathtaking systematization in modern moral philosophy. Utilitarianism and Kantianism organize everything around one basic reason. And as so often happens in such cases the notion becomes accredited among proponents of these theories that the nature of moral reasoning is such that we ought to be able to unify our moral views around a single base. John Rawls, following J. S. Mill, rejects what he describes as the "intuitionist" view, which is precisely a view which allows for a plurality of such basic criteria. But to see how far this is from being an essential feature of moral thinking we have only to look at Aristotle's ethical theory. Aristotle sees us pursuing a number of goods, and our conduct as exhibiting a number of different virtues. We can speak of a single "complete good" (*teleion agathon*) because our condition is such that the disparate goods we seek have to be coherently combined in a single life, and in their right proportions. But the good life as a whole doesn't stand to the partial goods as a basic reason. (Taylor 1989, pp. 76–77)

[4] Arendt 1958, p. 5.

on Greek political theory as a point of departure for thinking outside the categories of modern political theory by suggesting that politics is not simply about securing equal liberty and providing mutual benefits or a social minimum, but also has something to do with human well-being or the quality of life. Two important examples of this line of analysis are the "capabilities" approach to the study of political development initiated by Martha Nussbaum (2006) and Amartya Sen (1999, 2004) and the naturalism of Alasdair MacIntyre's *Dependent Rational Animals* (1999). This broadening of our conceptual repertory has been prompted by new readings of the big three – Thucydides, Plato, and Aristotle – but also by new studies of Homer, Herodotus, the playwrights, and the orators.

These new developments in the study of Greek political theory have implications for liberal education in the humanities that reflect more than a growth of interest in a particular scholarly specialty or historical period. The chapters in this volume represent a variety of orientations to the study of Greek political theory, but there is within that variety overall agreement that we need to reject both a narrow historicism that reduces text to context and an abstractly ahistorical approach that treats ancient authors as if they were our contemporaries. Speaking of his approach to Homer in the conclusion to the first chapter of this volume, Dean Hammer puts it this way: "The challenge of political thought is to remain attentive to the historical, cultural, and poetic context from which the epics emerged without, in turn, reducing interpretation to that context." The shared goal of all the chapters is to reconstruct Greek political thought as a conversation that matters to us because it is both like and unlike the political discourse of our own time.

The first four chapters in this volume address texts that are not typically regarded as political philosophy or systematic political thought: works of epic poetry, tragic drama, and narrative history – works by Homer, Aeschylus and Sophocles, Herodotus and Thucydides. One might call these "pre-philosophic" works, but all four chapters indicate that to say this would be to overstate the difference between these works and those of the political philosophers. This refusal to be guided by traditional genre expectations comes across strongly in all the chapters in this volume. Narrative history, imaginative literature, and self-conscious philosophizing need to be brought into dialogue with one another, a step precluded by the strict genre distinctions that are silently reinforced by the organization of specialized inquiry in the modern university.[5] To

[5] See Plato's Socrates in the *Gorgias* on *muthos* and *logos*. At 523a, Socrates prefaces his mythic account of death and judgment with the following: "Listen, as they say, to

use a convenient Greek term, there is a kind of *logos*, of articulate speech about human nature and its relation to nature as a whole, in all the texts we consider, and it is our job to bring these *logoi* out and to engage them with the *logoi* – both explicit ones and those implicit in our practices and institutions – about politics and human action that are familiar to us as members of our own political communities today. In all of these chapters, a refusal to be tightly guided by genre expectations about what counts as literature or history or philosophy yields substantively new interpretations of Greek politics and Greek reflections on political life.

Dean Hammer, in "Homer and Political Thought," begins by rehearsing the traditional view that Homeric epic and philosophy are entirely different kinds of discourse, and goes on to argue that this distinction is overstated. Hammer contends that the *Iliad* and the *Odyssey* are veridical, reflective, and political – rather than merely an artful expression of the folkways of a pre-political society. He challenges the standard view of a sharp rupture between the Homeric world and the emergence of the democratic polis. Instead, he argues, the poems give us a picture of politics as a "field" of contention over rights and leadership, "one in which charismatic and participatory elements are held in tension." According to Hammer, "the story Homer tells, like the story Achilles tells Priam, is one in which we are moved toward a recognition of a shared world, a recognition that arises not from outside, but from within a world constituted by experience." Properly understood, the Homeric epics give modern readers the opportunity to think of politics as an activity, and thus help liberate us from "the Weberian association of politics with the exercise of a monopoly of force." Hammer's very different understanding of politics owes an acknowledged debt to Hannah Arendt, but his chapter is no mere restatement of her position; instead, he puts us in a better position to read Homer as Arendt did, paying attention to both the political questions of our own time and the particular context and language of the ancient poet.

Arlene Saxonhouse's "Foundings vs. Constitutions: Ancient Tragedy and the Origins of Political Community" develops further this question of how to think about the emergence of political life in ways that are foreign to the modern social imaginary. She argues that the

this especially beautiful *logos*, which I think you will regard as a *muthos*, but which I regard as a *logos*." Distinctions among genres ought to be preserved and discussed, but treating them as rigid and deterministic leads away from liberal education and toward narrow scholarship. The chapters in this volume, taken together, express a turn in the opposite direction.

problem of the founding is brought into a surprising and valuable new perspective by several Greek tragedies, notably Sophocles' *Antigone* and *Oedipus* and Aeschylus' *Oresteia*. One significant potential gain from reading and discussing these plays as she suggests is a way out of the pervasive conceptual world of the modern social contract metaphor. As Saxonhouse reads them, "what the tragedies offer is a different understanding of the original grounding of cities – not as constitution writing moments of self-limitations, but as moments when human rationality faces the terrifying forces that limit it." What the tragedies can provide is not a new theory of the founding, but an opportunity to expand our political imagination and hence our powers of judgment.

The next two chapters turn to the work of the Greek historians, Herodotus and Thucydides. As they do, they continue to explore the possibility that the work of political thought, of whatever literary genre, and in modern times as well as ancient, is the project of opening the imagination beyond the limits of the prevailing culture as a way of educating practical reason. Norma Thompson ("Most Favored Status in Herodotus and Thucydides: Recasting the Athenian Tyrannicides through Solon and Pericles") shows that while the rejection of tyranny is a central feature of each writer's narrative of the two great wars of the fifth century BC, both aim to debunk the traditionally honored Athenian story of the tyrannicides Harmodius and Aristogeiton as the embodiment of the founding of democratic rule. Instead, they propose two figures – Herodotus' Solon and Thucydides' Pericles – whose lives and characters they present as heroic and exemplary, and yet at the same time as flawed and for that very reason open to continuous reinterpretation. As Thompson reads the two historians, their portrayal of non-tyrannical political leadership in this complex and even ambivalent way leads to two conclusions: that their work has more in common than has usually been thought; and that we must reject the stereotypes of Herodotus as the simple and uncritical transmitter of the prevailing myths of the day, and of Thucydides as a precursor of modern social scientific history who refuses to evaluate the phenomena he explains. What can we say, then, about their intention? According to Thompson, this:

> Both historians hold out the hope that in another time and place, the unlearned lesson from their age might get another review. The historians' purposes are political as well as literary, and revolve around making a tighter case against tyranny than their characters were able to effect. Herodotus and

> Thucydides identify with their characters, in other words, for the purpose of deepening their own testament to self-rule.

Gerald Mara's "Thucydides and Political Thought" approaches the question of Thucydides' intention in a similar spirit. In his analyses of the speeches of Pericles, the Melian debate, and especially the speech of the enigmatic Diodotus concerning the fate of the Mytileneans, Mara stresses the provisional and open-ended character of Thucydides' account of the events, both the spoken words and the deeds, of the Peloponnesian war: "The alternative readings that I offer suggest that Thucydides' narrative should be interpreted as contributing resources for the thoughtful judgments and practices of citizens, not simply within his own immediate political context but within political futures whose contours are necessarily indeterminate." As Mara reads it, Thucydides' artful logos is anything but directive and conclusive; the book achieves the status its author claims for it (as a "possession for all times") by presenting the inevitable open-endedness of political life and thus providing a contribution to democratic discussion, both ancient and modern, that is otherwise unavailable. This incitement to ongoing deliberation – and to coherently focused anxiety – about a vividly depicted and non-obvious set of political problems is what the book is about. Mara's Thucydides summons us to face and to worry about things we would not otherwise notice.

The next three chapters focus on the Platonic dialogues, and so concern themselves with self-consciously philosophical texts; all three, however, underline the continuities between Platonic philosophizing and the epic, theatrical, and historical works discussed in the first four chapters. Susan Bickford's "'This Way of Life, This Contest': Rethinking Socratic Citizenship" takes its title from the rallying cry Plato's Socrates addresses to "all human beings" at *Gorgias* 526e. Bickford's initial point is that just what the Socratic way of life involves is far from clear, especially concerning the relationship of this way of life to the politics of democratic Athens. Starting with the *Apology* and then working through critical passages in *Gorgias*, *Republic*, and *Laws*, she builds a case for thinking that the sort of "soul-shaping" that both Plato and Socrates practice is neither paternalistically antidemocratic (as many democratic critics of Plato have argued), nor only counterculturally aporetic (as for example, Plato's Cleitophon claims in the dialogue that bears his name). Nor does she accept the dubious easy out of regarding Plato as the arch-authoritarian and Socrates as at least a semi-democrat.

Plato's Socrates, for Bickford, is never *merely* aporetic – he also offers images, myths, and "the inspiration of his own practice and discourse." The dialogues themselves, she argues, are best understood as "summoners" – they provide us with a summons or exhortation to investigate, like those sense-objects that "don't declare any one thing more than its opposite" (*Republic* 7, 523b–25a). Such objects, according to Socrates in the *Republic*, cause us to see that sense perception isn't enough; analogously, the dialogues cause us to see that received opinions aren't enough. Thus the dialogues themselves, for Bickford, like these sense-objects, provide, when properly interpreted, both an aporetic moment *and* a call to rigorous inquiry. Is Socrates' kind of inspiration institutionalizable? Bickford concludes with an intriguing argument that in the *Laws*, in which Socrates is not a character, Plato indicates the indispensability of Socratic summoning for successful self-rule by sketching the institution of the Nocturnal Council as a site for Platonic/Socratic dialogue that includes political leaders as participants, but that promotes deliberation about fundamental questions rather than producing authoritative decisions and rules.

David Roochnik's "The Political Drama of Plato's *Republic*" addresses directly the charge that the *Republic* is a manifesto for undemocratic rule by philosophers. Roochnik acknowledges that the dialogue contains a radical critique of democracy, providing ample reason for critics of Plato, like Karl Popper in *The Open Society and Its Enemies*, to conclude that the *Republic* has no value for committed liberal democrats: Popper's "enormous distaste for Plato's *Republic* may appear well founded, but in fact it entirely neglects an essential feature of the dialogue," argues Roochnik. "Plato is a genius at throwing a monkey wrench into what initially seems to be a smoothly functioning piece of conceptual machinery, and thereby transforming it into something far more puzzling and provocative." Roochnik identifies five such "monkey wrenches" in the *Republic*, including the ambiguity of the dialogue's position on democracy and the extent to which the concluding myth of Er provides a defense of diversity. What the *Republic* seems to teach, on his view, is no straightforward doctrine, whether democratic or antidemocratic, but the necessity of asking certain questions, such as "What is the value of democracy and of diversity?" and "What form of authority ought to hold sway in a political community?" Roochnik concludes that what matters about this most famous of the dialogues is not whether it is pro- or anti-democracy: "The *Republic* expresses a tension. . . . It forces its readers to wonder about justice, the city, and the question of political authority, and it sets into motion a series of responses, both positive and negative, that becomes the history of political philosophy itself." A history, moreover, that calls for our participation.

The third chapter on Plato, Catherine Zuckert's "Practical Plato," presents a reading of the *Statesman* as perhaps the "strangest" of Plato's dialogues. On the one hand, it is intensely "practical," insofar as the Eleatic *xenos* (stranger or visitor), who is the principal speaker in this dialogue, seems bent on "gradually leading his interlocutors (and Plato's readers) toward an understanding of politics as arising not from human nobility, but from human need." The Eleatic, on Zuckert's reading, lowers the goal of politics from justice to preservation and protection – unlike both the *Republic* and the *Laws*. Moreover, there is no apparently ideal or nearly ideal polis imagined here, nothing to compare with Kallipolis in the *Republic* or even Magnesia in the *Laws*. And yet, a central theme of the dialogue is that the science of politics and the life of true political leadership, "properly understood, requires extraordinary intelligence and learning. Precisely for that reason, it is also extremely rare, if it exists at all." Politics, according to Zuckert's reading of the *Statesman*, thus seems both to require and to resist philosophical leadership:

> Politicians, properly speaking, are not contemptible. . . . The problem, on the other hand, is that individuals capable of acquiring the "science of the rule of human beings" will learn that they will not be able to exercise that knowledge without endangering their own survival. There is little, if any incentive for such individuals to perfect their knowledge, especially if they see that they will never be able to put it into practice for long, if at all.

Readers may wonder whether this deep and apparently insoluble problem indicates the essentially tragic character of political life. Like Plato, Zuckert steadfastly refuses to resolve or domesticate the dilemma her reading uncovers.

The three chapters on Plato are followed by two on Aristotle. Both chapters stress continuities between the two philosophers, but not in terms of principles; rather, these chapters argue that Aristotle, like Plato, follows a non-doctrinal and non-systematic mode of philosophizing about political life. My chapter, "Reading Aristotle's *Nicomachean Ethics* and *Politics* as a Single Course of Lectures: Rhetoric, Politics, and Philosophy," attempts to trace Aristotle's pedagogical aims in the *Nicomachean Ethics* (*NE*) and *Politics*. I treat the two works not as separate treatises, but as a single series of connected lectures on what Aristotle calls *politikē*, a term that corresponds in one way to our "political philosophy" and in another to our "social science." My argument is that these lectures do not intend to supply a systematic political theory, but rather to show auditors and readers how to address what Aristotle takes to be the central and permanent problems of political life – and indeed of human life as a whole. While it is true that Aristotle asserts a distinctly naturalist approach to politics, his introduction of the language of his version of natural science into political matters is not intended to replace political discourse, or to serve as a fundamental first premise from which political principles can be deduced; instead, his goal is to supply a point of view – a conceptual space – from which our particular political deliberations may be more successfully undertaken. "*Successfully* undertaken" here means undertaken in such a way that the potential benefits of the practice of politics for human virtue or excellence can better be achieved and that the degradation to which this same practice too often subjects humanity can better be avoided.

In their chapter "Lived Excellence in Aristotle's *Constitution of Athens*: Why the Encomium of Theramenes Matters," Jill Frank and Sara Monoson address the genre question directly: what kind of a work is the *Constitution of Athens* (*CA*)? Their answer, using categories from Aristotle's *Poetics*, is that it is a "poetic history," an account of Athenian events and institutions, from the distant past up to Aristotle's own time, that has the universalizing quality Aristotle attributes to poetry. They identify two major examples of such universalization in the *CA*, both of them aspirational norms, "lived excellences" in Frank and Monoson's phrase, that can serve as an incitement to good politics. The first is the story of an individual Athenian politician, Theramenes; the second, the story of the Athenian demos itself: "Aristotle uses his commentary on Theramenes and on the constitutions with which he associates Theramenes to open a course for both citizen virtue and Athenian constitutional development, a course of lawfulness and moderation absent from the regimes under which Theramenes lived, but available for the future through an understanding of Athens's past and present." These life-stories are no mere record of events, but a look at the qualities that, for Aristotle, identify these lives and ways of life as meaningful wholes. On this reading, Aristotle presents Theramenes as an embodiment of the key political virtue of *lawfulness* – a devotion to the norm of constitutional government that by no means rules out radical disobedience against a regime that transgresses its own laws. Such subtle lawfulness is also a kind of moderation, in the sense that it rejects commitment to extreme factions who want to use politics for their own extra-political ends. The life of Theramenes exemplifies this virtue for Aristotle, but so does the way of life of the Athenian demos. This conclusion will challenge those who regard Aristotle as deeply elitist, but on Frank and Monoson's careful reading of the *CA*, Theramenes and the Athenian demos are the characters through whom Aristotle celebrates "the difficult practices of lawfulness and moderation," the preeminent political virtues.

The final three chapters focus on broad themes in Greek political thought – virtue politics, individual rights, and natural law – rather than on individual authors or texts. They also take up more directly the relation of ancient Greek thought to the theory and practice of modern politics.

Ryan Balot's "The Virtue Politics of Democratic Athens" begins by noting the recent emergence of Aristotelian "virtue ethics" within modern moral philosophy. Contemporary virtue ethicists use Aristotelian ethical theory as a resource to overcome what they see as flaws in modern utilitarianism and neo-Kantianism.[6] Balot asks whether it is possible to develop an analogous idea of "virtue politics" from Athenian sources, a conception of political life that would allow us to avoid the dilemma of being forced to choose between two unsatisfactory alternatives, liberal individualism and civic republicanism. He thinks it is possible, but argues that Aristotle is the wrong place to begin, on grounds that Aristotle's political thought is too elitist to serve as a starting point for conceiving a democratic politics of the virtues. Instead, he uses the 150 speeches from the fourth century B.C.E. that make up the corpus of Attic oratory, especially the words of Demosthenes, to formulate a conception of democratic virtue politics: "We can find in the Athenian virtue politics a practical, largely successful, example of the attempt to square virtue politics with freedom. This alone should make the Athenian case good to 'think with.'" Arguing that criticizable talk about what constitutes human flourishing or happiness should be a part of contemporary democratic discourse, Balot makes the case for incorporating this composite Athenian voice into our own political imaginary: "Athens's politics of virtue was truly populist in that the democratic virtues applied to the entire citizen body and were evaluated by the entire citizen body. In no other non-democratic tradition do we find such an emphasis on practical reasoning, egalitarianism,

[6] For "virtue ethics," see Anscombe 1958, MacIntyre 1984, and Hursthouse 1999.

individualism, and freedom as we find in the democratic virtue politics of Athens."

Following Balot's call for a reconsideration of Athenian virtue politics, Fred Miller's "Origins of Rights in Ancient Political Thought" argues that we moderns have tended to exaggerate the distance between Greek political thought and our own by assuming that they have no concept of individual rights, a concept central to our sense of good democratic politics. Miller's goal is to correct that assumption so as to enrich our sense of what rights discourse is all about. Surveying a broad range of ancient political and philosophical texts, he argues that the absence of assertion of individual rights from ancient political discourse has been greatly exaggerated. Demosthenes has a prominent place in the story Miller tells, but in contrast to Balot, Miller sees the orator as a voice for individual rights, rather than as a virtue theorist: "Demosthenes' appeal to individual rights was an integral part of his democratic ideology. . . . His statements that all citizens have rights based on a higher universal law make him sound like a modern liberal." Miller acknowledges the difference between ancient rights locutions and modern ones, and in particular the fact that ancient theory and practice saw no contradiction between the politics of rights and the institution of slavery. Nonetheless, he contends that a concept of individual rights is more central for Aristotle, Demosthenes, and some other ancient thinkers than it is for early Christian thought, even though the Christian principle that any human being is worthy arguably provided an important inspiration for the modern theory of human rights.

The volume concludes with Eric Brown's wide-ranging study of "The Emergence of Natural Law and the Cosmopolis." Brown traces the development of these "two influential metaphors" – "right reason" as a metaphorical "law" of nature, and this natural "law" as the basis for a metaphorical world state or cosmopolis – through a variety of texts, from Heraclitus through Cicero. By treating these two concepts as metaphors, as works of the political imagination rather than as impersonal doctrines, Brown enables us to see the recurrent problems they are meant to clarify. The metaphor of natural law is more basic, as well as older. Reading him as a political thinker and writer, Brown argues that for Heraclitus "there is a standard for human laws manifest in the order of the cosmos and open to discovery by successful human inquiry." At the same time, Heraclitus, like Plato and Aristotle who follow him, is unwilling to characterize the universal logos he identifies as a *law*. The reason for this restraint seems to be persistent doubts about the extent to which these natural norms can be codified into statements of law-like clarity and universality. In Plato's *Gorgias*, it is Callicles, and not Socrates, who explicitly appeals to a natural law as a basis for criticizing conventional laws and customs. For Aristotle, to speak of natural laws amounts to claiming to know precisely things that can be known only in outline, a position already asserted by Plato's Eleatic in the *Statesman*. Nonetheless, according to Brown's narrative, there is over time a steady drift in the direction of codifying natural norms. Assertions of non-codifiability are also found in Stoics such as Zeno and Chrysippus, and even in Cicero – though stoicism moves in the direction of codifiability and the idea that there is one and only one best codification of natural law, especially with Cicero.

What are we to make of this semantic drift from natural law as metaphor to natural law as actual law? Perhaps it represents a powerful temptation to answer difficult problems in a clear and categorical way. Is the lesson of Greek political thought that such temptation should be resisted? Brown's response captures the drift of this volume as a whole:

> The Greek metaphors of natural law and the cosmopolis have exerted tremendous influence through Cicero's writings, Roman law, and Christianity, and many have found them irresistible. But a glance at their emergence is enough to show how flexible they are and how difficult it is to translate the metaphors in their richest, most suggestive form into persuasive non-metaphorical claims. These two lessons are related, and they encourage some skepticism.

Brown concludes that "the skepticism called for is ancient: the skeptic keeps on inquiring." To generalize: both the interpretive chapters in this volume and the texts they engage aim at improving our theoretical sense and our capacity for practical judgment – by supplying not a roadmap, but a push in the right direction.

It is my pleasure to acknowledge the support of several individuals and institutions. Beatrice Rehl, my editor at Cambridge University Press, oversaw the project with considerable patience and wisdom. I am indebted to Edward Whitehouse, a graduate student in classics at Bryn Mawr, whose energy and erudition in checking quotations and citations substantially improved the quality of the volume. I also thank Peggy Rote and the staff at Aptara, Inc., for their expertise and care in moving the project from typescript to print. Professor E. J. Hedley of Bryn Mawr is a source of perpetual correction (see Aristotle,

Nicomachean Ethics 9.12, 1172a11–14). Part of my work on the book was completed during an energizing term at the National Humanities Center. Finally, I am grateful for the resources of various kinds provided by Bryn Mawr College.

Works Cited

Anscombe, G. E. M. 1958. "Modern Moral Philosophy." *Philosophy* 33: 1–19.

Arendt, H. 1958. *The Human Condition*. Chicago.

Cooper, J. M. 1997. "Introduction." In *The Complete Works of Plato*, ed. J. M. Cooper. Indianapolis, IN.

Griswold, C. L., Jr., ed. 2001. *Platonic Writings, Platonic Readings*. University Park, PA.

Hursthouse, R. 1999. *On Virtue Ethics*. Oxford.

Jefferson, T. 1903 [1816]. "Letter to Isaac Tiffany," 8/26/16. In *The Writings of Thomas Jefferson*, ed. E. Lipscomb, 20 vol. Vol. 16, p. 66. Washington, DC.

Kraut, R. 1992. "Introduction to the Study of Plato." In *The Cambridge Companion to Plato*, ed. R. Kraut. Cambridge.

MacIntyre, A. 1984. *After Virtue*, 2nd ed. Notre Dame, IN.

MacIntyre, A. 1999. *Dependent Rational Animals: Why Human Beings Need the Virtues*. Chicago.

Nussbaum, M. 2006. *Frontiers of Justice: Disability, Nationality, Species Membership*. Tanner Lectures on Human Values. Cambridge, MA.

Sen, A. 1999. *Development as Freedom*. New York.

Sen, A. 2004. "Elements of a Theory of Human Rights." *Philosophy and Public Affairs* 32: 315–56.

Taylor, C. 1989. *Sources of the Self: The Making of the Modern Identity*. Cambridge, MA.

Taylor, C. 2004. *Modern Social Imaginaries*. Public Planet Books. Durham, NC.

1: Homer and Political Thought[1]

Dean Hammer

Plato did Homer no favors. When Plato banished Homer from his republic, he posited a split between epic and philosophic knowledge that would remain a part of a Western philosophical tradition. For Plato, the problem with the Homeric epics was that they were imitations of phenomenal appearance because they depicted the shadowy world of human action and emotion. Though tempered in recent years by examinations of both the philosophic contributions of literature and the literary basis of philosophy, what has often emerged is a distinction, made both implicitly and explicitly, between political thought – which is depicted as a systematic, reasoned, reflective, and critical account of the political world – and the epics – which are often characterized as uncritical appropriations of myths, legends, stories, and superstitions. As evidence, commentators point to a seemingly irrational cosmology alive with divine forces, inconsistencies in the stories that comprise the epic, and the oral nature of epic verse in which the aim was to tell a particular story and not to analyze the foundations of thought.

In this chapter, I approach Homer as a political thinker. By this I mean both that the epics are engaged in critical reflection and that this reflection is political in nature.[2] The chapter will proceed in several

[1] This chapter is dedicated to the memory of Walter Donlan. I thank Vincent Farenga for his helpful comments on an earlier draft of this chapter and Craig Harris for his research assistance. I follow Lattimore's translations of the *Iliad* and *Odyssey* unless otherwise noted.

[2] I use Homer as shorthand for the poet or poets who composed the epics. My belief is that the epics assumed their current form in the second half of the eighth century (perhaps as late as the first half of the seventh century). For an overview of what is known as the "Homeric question," which now appears as questions about both the authorship and dating of the epic, see Schein 1984: 1–44; Powell 2004; and

parts. First, I will examine two major obstacles to approaching the epics as works of political thought: the ideas that oral poetry lacks a critical dimension and that Homeric society is pre-political. I end these sections by making an argument about what is critical and what is political in the epics. In the subsequent sections, I engage in a series of forays into Homeric political thought, taking up contending notions of power, rights, the people, gender, and ethics.

Oral Poetry and Critical Reflection

Homeric studies owe a great debt to the pioneering work of Milman Parry, and the continuation of his work by Albert Lord, that explored how the method of "composition *during* oral performance" imposed a structure on Homeric verse.[3] Parry provided a way of understanding how a single poet, working within an oral tradition, could compose such a monumental poem. One could imagine a range of analogies – to modern jazz and blues, for example – in which traditional formulas and themes provide the foundation for a composer's improvisation that, in turn, alters how we hear those formulas. But Parry tended more to emphasize how each formula was fixed in its meaning, how formulaic phrases were chosen because they fit the needs of rhythm and meter, and how, when added together, the meanings of each discrete formula defined the totality of the poem's meaning.[4] Others, taking Parry still further, have examined the conceptual limits placed on the Homeric epics by an oral consciousness. Havelock, for example, characterized the Homeric epics as a "compilation of inherited lore," a "tribal encyclopedia" of conventions, practices, and procedures that cannot conceive of or reflect on the world around it.[5] We should not be surprised, then, when political relationships in the epic, including debate and council, are seen as "composed summarily and formulaically" and offered "only as the story prompts their intrusion."[6]

Graziosi and Haubold 2005: 15–34. Though Homer draws extensively from an oral poetic tradition, the unity of its structure and images, as well as the creative reshaping of this tradition in the development of a unified plot, suggest (though it does not prove) the work of one poet or a poet of the *Odyssey* who learned from and inherited the themes and techniques of the poet of the *Iliad*.

[3] Lord 1960: 5.

[4] Parry 1987: 370. Parry (304) distinguishes between formulaic and ordinary language.

[5] Havelock 1963: 66.

[6] Havelock 1963: 69.

An extraordinary amount of scholarship has been devoted to modifying Parry and Lord, whether by rescuing Homer through recourse to aesthetics, by suggesting that the epics actually evince traces of literacy, or by viewing orality and literacy as forms of textualization. More promising has been growing interest in viewing orality as a form of communication and interaction between poet and audience. Bakker, for example, in seeking both to remind us that orality is all around us and to provide a language for analyzing what is distinctive about oral poetry, emphasizes the "crucial importance of the human voice in the production, transmission, and reception of poetry whose essence lies in performance."[7] Cognitive psychology has joined with discourse theory to explore how oral communication draws upon mental models of cultural knowledge and experience that are critical for both composition and comprehension. These cognitive models of episodic memory, which are variously called "scripts," "frames," scenarios," or "schemas," are comprised of "stereotypical representation[s] of knowledge incorporating a sequence of actions, speech acts and situations."[8] The narrative arrangement of these episodes creates a "shared seeing" that expands beyond the immediate words to draw upon a more complex set of cultural images and experiences.[9] Examples of such episodes include battle and funeral scenes, but can also be extended to scenes of debate, deliberation, and decision. Indeed, Ong's suggestion that orality embeds knowledge in human struggle serves as a useful way for viewing the epics not only as a means of cultural transmission, as Ong suggests, but also as a way of raising questions about the organization of human experience.[10] The epics, as they were composed in performance, appear as public poetry that was engaged in a reflection on the activity of organizing community life. There are several implications of these performance approaches that help us understand how epic composition introduces a critical dimension to epic poetry.

First, where the epic world is often seen as unconnected to any historical time, the public activity of performance ties the epics back to a broader set of cultural issues contemporaneous with their telling. In the development of plot and characters, as Redfield argues, the poet "employs and persuades us to certain assumptions about the sources and

[7] Bakker 1997: 32; see also Martin 1989; Foley 1999; Minchin 2001; Scodel 2002; and Farenga 2006.

[8] Farenga 2006: 8.

[9] Bakker 1997: 76.

[10] Ong 1982: 44.

conditions of action."[11] Although the poet likely archaized, exaggerated, and made-up components of the heroic past, the composition of the poems, as they convey both coherence and meaning to its audience, rests upon a comprehension of culture – upon the attitudes, assumptions, and material conditions that make the plot believable.[12]

Second, the boundaries, values, beliefs, tensions, and ambiguities of the culture emerge and are given shape dialogically as characters constitute themselves and their world through language. That is, characters, as they enact, extend, and manipulate cultural patterns and codes, are as much performers as the poet. Through what is said and done, as well as what (as narratology has explored) is unspoken, stories "dramatize values."[13] Questions of the criteria for the distribution of prizes, the bases of recognition, the responsibilities of leadership, the role of deliberation, and the reasons for fighting, let alone the encounters of the different voices of class and gender, all become subject to examination.

Finally, though the epics may tell us something about social ideals, these idealizations can serve to bring into sharper relief the struggles of community life. The city at peace on Achilles' shield, for example, stands in dramatic contrast to both the turmoil of the Achaean camp and the imminent destruction of Troy. And the idealized polis of Phaeacia brings into dramatic relief the "anti-Paradise in the heart of the Ithacan polis."[14] Placed in their social context, the epics present breaches in and inversions of accepted norms, actions, beliefs, and social structures, introducing a "performative reflexivity" in which the artist raises "problems about the ordering principles deemed acceptable in 'real life.'"[15] Set against the backdrop of war, the *Iliad* exposes divisions within the community that demand resolution at the price of corporate destruction. And the *Odyssey* explores both the disintegration of the social fabric and the encounter with alternate visions of community life.

WHAT IS POLITICAL ABOUT HOMER?

A second obstacle to reading the epics as works of political thought is the view of the epic world as pre-political. Finley, for example, who has

[11] Redfield 1994: 58, 23.

[12] See Redfield 1994; Raaflaub 1998: 178–84.

[13] Redfield 1983: 219.

[14] Cook 1995: 146.

[15] Turner 1988: 27. This is consistent with scholarship that has noted elements of tension, dissonance, and even ideological conflict within the Homeric epics.

argued persuasively for viewing the Homeric world as a functioning social system, concludes, nonetheless, that neither Homeric poem "has any trace of a *polis* in its political sense." For Finley, "political decisions" must be "binding on the society" and "political units" must have a "governmental apparatus."[16] Homeric society appears as pre-political because it lacks institutional forms and roles that emerge later: notions of citizenship, a system of governance, and politics, as an autonomous sphere, that defines human life.

These conceptions of the Homeric world are united by a set of assumptions about the nature of politics, assumptions that entered classical scholarship by way of the structural-functional anthropology of Radcliffe-Brown, Fortes, and Evans-Pritchard, and the evolutionary approaches of Service, Sahlins, Fried, and Cohen. Social anthropology provided Homeric scholarship with a powerful tool for viewing the Homeric world as a functioning social system – a fundamental departure from earlier analytic approaches that attempted to identify the inconsistencies, incoherence, and historical layering of the different parts of the poems. The question that emerged from the study of the Homeric epics, as it was guided by this anthropological tradition, was, not surprisingly, largely a taxonomic one: what type of pre-state society is reflected in the epics and does this reflection correspond to an actual historic period (and which one)? Scholars largely (though not completely) have abandoned earlier attempts to locate the epics in a Mycenaean past and more convincingly have identified a historical analogue with the stage of a ranked society out of which more stratified or state societies may develop. The *basileis*, or political leaders, appear as anthropological types of the big man and the chief who possess authority but not much coercive power.[17]

But these approaches take us only so far. The absence of formal governmental institutions almost invariably led to a view of the Homeric world as pre-political. Scholars interested in the politics of the epics, then, turned to identifying traces of polis organization, however embryonic, in the epics. In looking for the material conditions that gave rise to the polis, scholars point to the growth in population, density, and social complexity of settlements in the eighth century, which placed greater demands on community organization and coordination and necessitated more refined qualities of leadership and mediation.[18] Important,

[16] Finley 1979: 34; 1983: 9.

[17] Donlan 1979, 1985, 1989, 1997.

[18] For an overview of the archaeological evidence, see Crielaard 1995; Hammer 2002: 29–43; and Farenga 2006: 38–46.

as well, for finding traces of the polis is identifying a shared sense of a past, a common belief system and set of values, jointly enacted rituals, a common sense of a future, and shared responses to new and threatening challenges. Evidence of such communities of territory and identity, as *poleis* are often defined, can be found in references to shrines and altars for public worship that are tied back to civic organization and identity, a town layout with streets, an *agora*, communal washbasins, references to founders, and walls that enclose the entire city and demarcate the "flat land" from "the city" (*Il.* 22.456; also *Od.* 6.3, 177, 191).[19]

Viewing the epics against the backdrop of the nascent *polis* has been helpful in providing a context for interpreting the common understanding of both the poet and the audience. But these approaches leave us with a perplexity: institutions are political but the activity of creating those institutions is not. This is a particular problem for Dark and Archaic age politics since, as Raaflaub observed, "Institutions and constitutions and the corresponding terminology had to be newly created, and the political sphere itself had to be discovered and gradually penetrated by thought, understanding, and explanation."[20] To what extent, then, can we talk about the epics as political without defining politics in relationship to particular institutional arrangements?

In developing this language of analysis, we can identify politics not with static structures but with the "flow" of "social processes" – the succession of events, the seeking of goals, the ordering of relations, the emergence of conflict and tensions, the upsetting of norms, the creation of alliances, and attempts at redress and resolution.[21] Politics, from this perspective, appears as an activity in which questions of community organization are raised, determined, and implemented. There is a corresponding change in the unit of political analysis from a focus

[19] Generally, see Scully 1990 (though rejecting the epics as political); Raaflaub 1991, 1997, 1998; Crielaard 1995; and Hölkeskamp 2002: 324–27. Public worship: *Il.* 1.39, 440 (Achaean camp); 2.303–7, 549–51, 603–4; 6.297–310; 7.83; 8.47–48; 9.404–5; 10.414–16; 11.166–69; 22.169–72; 23.144–48; *Od.* 6.9–10; streets and town planning: *Il.* 2.12; 4.52; 5.642; 6.391; 20.254; agora and public spaces: *Il.* 2.788–89; 7.345; 18.497; *Od.* 1.272; 2.7; 6.266–67; 9.112 (absence); wash-basins/springs: *Il.* 22.153–55; *Od.* 6.291–92; 10.105–8; 17.205–6; foundings: *Il.* 7.452–53; 11.166, 371–72; 20.216–18; 24.349; *Od.* 11.260–65; walls: *Il.* 2.559 (Tiryns), 646 (describing Gortyn, which was not walled until the eighth century), 691; 3.141–55; 6.373; 7.449–53; 12.28–32, 36, 121–23, 258–66, 390, 397–99, 424, 453–62 (gateway); 16.57, 702–3; 18.274–76, 514–15; 21.446–47, 515–17; 22.4, 35–89, 455–65; *Od.* 6.9, 262–67; 7.44–45, 112–13; as a collective entity: *Il.* 21.584–88; *Od.* 2.154.

[20] Raaflaub 1989: 5.

[21] Turner 1974: 37.

on structure and function to a field. The *political field* is constituted by groups who are engaged in issues of identity and organization rather than defined by institutional and territorial boundaries. This adds fluidity to our understanding of politics since the boundaries of the political field can change as activities cut across old boundaries and create new ones.[22]

In thinking about what we mean by a political field, it might be helpful to imagine a battlefield. A battlefield is not defined by particular boundaries but is constituted by the activity. The boundaries of the battlefield can expand and contract and the composition of the field can change as new groups enter and exit. That it is the activity that defines the boundaries of a political field, and not the field that defines the activity, is not altogether different from Alcaeus' words in the late seventh and early sixth centuries, "for warlike men are a city's tower," or Nicias' words to his troops, "you yourselves, wherever you settle down, are a city already" (Alc. fr. 112 Campbell; Thuc. 7.77.4).

Through this conception of a field, one might identify a number of activities as political. These would include questions of authority and legitimacy, the exercise of persuasion and force, the emergence of demands or claims on the community, issues of conflict that threaten community organization, and ethical questions of our relationship, obligations, and responsibilities to others. It may well be that in the study of such activities we encounter institutions. But these institutions should be regarded as instances of political processes – particular formalized relationships that emerge from, are constituted by, and continue to be altered through political activity.

Violence, Force, and Power

Far from being pre-political, the epics provide an opportunity to explore the operation of politics in its elementally human, rather than its institutional, form. In our political age that is dominated by institutions, there is a tendency to mistake procedural order with political health, imagining politics as regularized processes that exist apart from the power of people to raise questions about the organization and purpose of community life. Power, in fact, appears as the ability of the state to compel obedience. Thus, the exercise of any real political power in the epics is

[22] On political fields, see Hammer 2002: 19–48.

seen as compromised by the absence of a governing authority that possesses the "right to exercise force."[23] To release us from the Weberian association of politics with the exercise of the monopoly of force, I want to suggest that Homer actually invites a reflection on how the intrusion of violence and force, rather than its absence, threatens to sap the political field of its power. In this pre-institutional setting, the "power" of the political field, what keeps this realm of speech and action intact, exists only as people constitute themselves together. "Power is actualized," writes Arendt, "only where word and deed have not parted company, where words are not empty and deeds not brutal, where words are not used to veil intentions but to disclose realities, and deeds are not used to violate and destroy but to establish relations and create new realities."[24] Deception and violence prevent the development of power by denying the condition of power; namely, people acting and speaking together. Fraud and violence, on the contrary, foster the conditions for isolation, rendering in people either weakness and passivity (which is contrary to acting together) or "self-sufficiency and withdrawal from the world."[25]

In the opening of the *Iliad*, Agamemnon poses just such a threat to the public realm. His intimidation of Kalchas prevents the seer from speaking truthfully about the cause of the plague. He is both forceful and deceptive toward Achilles, leading the best of the Achaeans to withdraw from the public space. But Achilles' withdrawal points to more than the discontent of one warrior; it reveals the depletion of power that constitutes this space when the only people who will submit to Agamemnon's leadership, as Achilles claims, are "nonentities" (*outidanoisin*), those who no longer speak or act (*Il.* 1.231). Agamemnon's test of his troops gives visual testimony to this depletion of public power and the dissolution of the political field: the troops flee to their ships, possessing neither the will nor the desire to act together in war. In the place of power is force as Odysseus must use the scepter as a weapon to beat back the soldiers. By the ninth book, the implications of the substitution of force for power have become all too clear: the Achaean community faces imminent destruction. Even Agamemnon seems to recognize how inextricably his power is tied to the maintenance of his own people when he laments that he will lose his honor since he "lost many of [his] people" (*Il.* 9.22).[26]

[23] Finley 1983: 8–9.

[24] Arendt 1958: 200.

[25] Arendt 1958: 203.

[26] See Haubold 2000.

The *Odyssey*, too, opens with a vivid depiction of the depletion of power: Telemachus is able to reconstitute (if only temporarily) with Athena's help a public space that has been vacant for twenty years. Telemachus looks to the people precisely because he does not have the "power" to defend his household (*Od.* 2.62). The suitors, like Agamemnon, enforce passivity and silence on the seer who speaks of justice (*Od.* 2.177–80) and the people (*Od.* 2.239–41, 244–51). Like Agamemnon, who feeds on his people (*dēmoboros*) (*Il.* 1. 231), the suitors also use the public forum to justify their own devouring of Odysseus' household (*Od.* 2.74–79, 85–88). And unlike Agamemnon, who inadvertently dissolves the political field and must find a way to reestablish its power, the suitors end by deliberately dispersing the people, "each to his own holdings," so that they will pose no threat (*Od.* 2.252; also 2.257–59).

The absence of institutions makes the play of power all the more dramatic because there is little to hold things together apart from the activity of the people. That is why Mentor, as much as Achilles, assails the quiet complicity of the people. But this fragility of the political field also points to a paradoxical aspect of the epics. Force, violence, and deception permeate the Homeric world. Indeed, Odysseus' ability to deceive (as opposed to engage in outward violence) is seen as representing a new Archaic hero who possesses the skills to adapt and endure in a new world that demands "change and innovation."[27] But the actual survival of these Homeric communities, a concern with durability that was likely an ongoing concern of early Iron Age settlements, is continually imperiled when that violence and deception become modes of political action. As an exploration of power, the Homeric epics appear to us as more than the palimpsest of political forms: they are a more fundamental exploration of the human forces that threaten to destroy a community from within.

Leadership and the Politicization of *Themis*

The epics explore, as well, the forces that bind a community together. One such political force is claims of leadership. A long-standing and still-employed perspective views the authority of the Homeric *basileus*, or leader, as premised on his unique power to interpret and enforce *themis*, or customary right and law. Scholars holding this view have

[27] Dougherty 2001: 162; also Foley 1978: 8–9.

sought to develop their case by identifying etymological associations between the *basileus* and the divine, noting the privileged position of the *basileus* as holder of the scepter of Zeus. Authority, from this perspective, flows downward from Zeus, to the *basileus*, to his followers. Not surprisingly, this has often led to an emphasis on the coercive aspects of kingly rule exemplified in the possession of the scepter. Even those who have rejected these divine associations with Homeric leadership have still emphasized the foundation of rule, and the defense of *themis*, as originating in the household. From this perspective, the *basileus* rules by personal prerogative and arguments about *themis* appear as a "purely private matter."[28]

The *basileus* cannot act unilaterally, though. Limits on Homeric leadership have been seen generally as derived from the need of the leader to attract and maintain a loyal following. The result is a *basileus* who is at the center of an exchange system that is organized into a weak redistributive system. Understood as an aspect of this exchange system, *themis* emerges "as a dynamic effort to share resources." Even though the historical trajectory of decisions about *themis* was toward increasing civic arbitration, *themis* in the epics is still viewed as a form of "oracular knowledge" that "endowed [the leader's] speech with an illocutionary force unavailable to other participants." When articulated, judgments of *themis* "rested on reasons that were not open to discussion."[29]

I do not disagree with the view that the performance of *themistes* is both linked to a comprehension of a cosmic order and restricted to an elite. In fact, the oracular basis of these claims ties into my argument (discussed later) about the persistence of charismatic claims to authority by leaders. But these claims exist in uneasy tension with what I would describe as the politicization of the performance of *themistes* that encompasses both a critique of judgments of *themis* as a prerogative of the king and a broadening of *themis* as a public claim (albeit one restricted primarily to the elite).

The danger of the notion of *themis* as a prerogative of the leader, a view articulated both by Agamemnon (*Il.* 1.135–38; also 9.160–61) and Nestor (*Il.* 9.98–102; 11.702–4), arises when one is unable to separate one's private desires from public claims to the distribution of resources. This is ultimately the basis of Achilles' critique of Agamemnon. Thus, Achilles employs a language of venality to characterize Agamemnon's motivations: greedy (*Il.* 1.122, 149, 171), vindictive (*Il.* 1.230), and

[28] Finley 1979: 110.

[29] Farenga 2006: 124, 125, 110.

devouring (*Il.* 1.231). Even Nestor seems to revise his earlier stance, later claiming that Agamemnon took Achilles' war prize by force "against the will of the rest of us" (*Il.* 9.107–8). When the political space becomes subject to the whim of the leader, then, as Achilles points out, no one will be left who will readily (*prophrōn*) obey (*Il.* 1.150). The ultimate consequence of such rule is borne out in the land of the Cyclopes where each man is the law (*Od.* 9.114–15). Or, closer to Odysseus' home, the lawlessness of the suitors exemplifies the rule by prerogative not of one man, but of the elite acting (and devouring) each by his own rule.

As works of political thought the epics play out a notion of *themis* as a political and public claim. *Themis* is neither formalized nor is it a right in the contemporary sense of an individual possession or entitlement protected in law. Furthermore, judgments of *themis* are not available to all members of the community, but remain very much an aspiration of the elite. What the epics convey is the process by which *themistes*, as a set of claims (however limited) about one's share in the life of the community, are themselves products of ongoing, negotiated relationships. Applied to issues of leadership, *themis* is tied to the maintenance of a collegial space among the elite in which there is a separation between public responsibilities and private affairs.[30] That is to say, we see in the epics a critique of leadership as premised on personal prerogative.

Themis emerges as a public claim on the leader rather than a claim of the leader. There are several aspects of this politicization of *themis*. First, both young and old men of the community, and not just the *basileus*, can invoke *Themis*, the goddess who summons and breaks up assemblies (*Od.* 2.28–32, 68–69; *Il.* 20.4–5). By way of historical comparison, one of the earliest written law codes, the Gortyn law code, begins with an invocation to the gods as a basis for constituting a political and legal space in which good judgments can be formed. Second, in such a public space the community "deal[s] out rights" (*Il.* 11.806–7). Among these actions is the apportionment of resources, for which the assembly is responsible (and is held responsible) (*Il.* 1.126; 2.227–28; 11.806–7; 16.387–88). Third, the assembly becomes the way in which *themistes* can be made part of a "corporate political memory"

[30] Mention of shared decision making among the elite appears at *Il.* 2.53–86, 402–40; 3.146–60; 4.322–23, 344; 7.323–44; 9.70–178, 422; 12.210–50; 13.726–47; 14.27–134; 15.283–84; 18.243–313, 497–508, 510–11; 22.99–110; *Od.* 3.127; 11.509–11; 16.242, 419–20; 22.230.

and not simply the result of the private interpretation of the leader.[31] Agamemnon's own claim to authority based on a divine lineage, and his belief that it is *themis* for him to test his troops (*Il.* 2.73), is dealt a serious blow when, leaning upon the scepter inherited from Zeus, he lies about a dream that was itself falsely planted by Zeus. Agamemnon subsequently loses complete control over the men.

Diomedes, later in the *Iliad*, points to a fourth aspect of *themis* as a public enactment when he claims his right to speak in assembly. Responding to Agamemnon's suggestion to retreat, Diomedes says that he "will be first to fight with your folly" and phrases his argument with an unconditional "is": "as is my right, lord, in this assembly" (*Il.* 9.33). This claim is noteworthy because it reflects a change in Diomedes' own understanding of a political space from his earlier silence when he is portrayed as standing "in awe before the majesty of the king's rebuking" (*Il.* 4.402; also one of the "nonentities" [*Il.* 1.231]). Diomedes appeals to a notion of *themis* as impersonal, not as a possession of the *basileus* that is exercised over others but as a public claim that the leader must administer.

Rights are not born of philosophy nor, for that matter, are they born of contracts. Rather, the framing of rights consists of two ongoing processes: the process of regularization and the process of situational adjustment. Whereas the first process derives from an attempt to create stability by establishing laws and institutions, the second process emerges from the interpretation and redefinition of rules to cover new situations, concerns, and interests, or to create new relationships. Rights, from this perspective, are not restricted to codified or abstract expressions. Rather, rights are defined by, and in turn define, a set of enacted relationships between actors within a public field.

The funeral games, which are often seen as ritualized enactments of the values and crises of a society, play out this alternate role of the political leader. The leader, in this case Achilles, does not act by personal prerogative but is implicated in issues of exchange and compensation that revisit the earlier crisis of distribution, extend beyond family and kin groups, and involve negotiation between groups about the terms and basis of apportionment. In such transactions, Achilles acts within traditional norms of gift exchange. But he also displays an important aspect of a deliberative mentality by anticipating and recognizing the claims of others. In such recognition Achilles goes some distance toward

[31] Cook 1995: 98. See *Od.* 9.106–7, 112–15, and lack of assembly with suitors.

answering his own question of how a leader can obtain ready obedience. But Achilles' seemingly limitless access to prizes sidesteps a more pressing issue: how do political systems cope with resource scarcity?

Enter the People

An increasing number of scholars have taken note of the role of the people (variously referred to as the *laos*, *dēmos*, and *plēthos*) in the epics.[32] This role, though, is by no means clear. The people do not initiate action, but they are not simply quiet, either. Scholars have often depicted the people as a "docile tool" who "neither voted nor decided."[33] Seaford, for example, sees the Homeric assemblies as "embody[ing] the ineffectiveness or foolishness of the mass."[34] Yet, the leaders appear at times to be interested in the tide of public opinion. Furthermore, leaders continually imagine judgments and face the judgments of the people.[35] Difficulties of interpreting these judgments politically are exacerbated both by the nature of epic poetry, which seeks to tell a story rather than convey history or social change, and by the paucity of knowledge about the role of the people in the eighth and seventh centuries B.C.E.

Royal models of divine kingship and *oikos* models of the leader as ruling by a household form of might do not take us very far in explaining the role of the people. More helpful have been attempts to place leadership in the context of an emergent, and increasingly self-conscious, *dēmos*. Two approaches have been particularly prominent for interpreting what the epics are saying about the role of the people. The first is to view the epics as ideological productions that play an active

[32] Though *laos* and *dēmos* are not synonymous, their meanings overlap (e.g., *Il.* 18.301; *Od.* 16.95–96, 114). Both terms refer to the people of a community. *Laos* and *laoi* often refer to the followers of a leader whereas *dēmos* refers to both a named territory and the people of the territory (see LfgrE 275-78, 1633-44; Donlan 1970, 1989; Haubold 2000). *Plēthos* seems to refer frequently to an undifferentiated multitude (see *Il.* 2.488; 11.305, 360, 405; 15.295; 17.31, 221; 20.197; 22.458; *Od.* 11.514; 16.105). *Plēthos* is not used as a pejorative term for *dēmos* or *laos*, though. *Plēthos*, *dēmos*, and *laos* are all used to refer to the mass of disorderly people (compare *Il.* 2.143, 198, and 191). And the *plēthos* are sometimes portrayed sympathetically (*Il.* 2.278; 9.641; 15.305).

[33] Andreyev 1991: 342; Finley 1979: 80.

[34] Seaford 2004: 182.

[35] Imagined judgments: *Il.* 6.460–61, 469; 7.87–91, 299–302; 22.106–7; 23.573–78; *Od.* 6.275–84; 21.253–55, 323–29, 331–33. See Haubold 2000; Scodel 2002.

role in the stratification of society. For Morris, the epics appear as an "ideological device" that legitimates the "class interests" of an exploitative aristocracy. The *basileis* are "glorified" and the *dēmos* are "ignored" almost "to the point of total exclusion."[36] Thalmann also reads the epics as an aristocratic strategy to legitimize its economic and political position. The textual strategy of the epics, as they are "composed for and conditioned by the interests of a military and landowning elite," is to show how challenges to an aristocratic ideal lead to social disruption that can be repaired only by a restoration of hierarchical bonds.[37]

No doubt the epics express elite ideals, and I would not want to understate the elements of conflict between different groups. But, as Scodel has recently observed, whether there was a "single, uniform, Panhellenic aristocratic ideology to promote" is questionable, especially since the epics appealed to different local audiences that were comprised of different groups, including the people.[38] Moreover, such views overlook the frequent, often critical, voice of the people. A second approach, attentive to this voice and articulated by Raaflaub, has posited a more interactive model of *polis* development in which the people and aristocracy developed alongside each other as those who owned land and fought to defend the territory of the community also participated in decisions of the community.[39]

Raaflaub's argument challenges notions of a sharp rupture between a Homeric world and the emergence of democracy. But in positing this evolutionary trajectory, there is a danger in smoothing out the extraordinary volatility both of the Archaic Age and of Homeric politics in which, at various points, oligarchic, tyrannical, demagogic, and democratic elements seem to have been present. We can still view the epics as a reflection on emergent authority relations, but they are relations that contain within them both authoritarian and democratic implications.

On the one hand, Homeric leaders make claims to privileged status: claims of divine favor and lineage, extraordinary prowess, wisdom, wealth, and might. In Weber's language, we see aspects of charismatic authority, in which authority is considered valid because the leader is seen as having some extraordinary personal, heroic, or divine traits that justify his leadership.[40] On the other hand, these charismatic attributes

[36] Morris 1986: 123–24.

[37] Thalmann 1998: 13, 284.

[38] Scodel 2002: 180.

[39] Raaflaub 1991: 222–30.

[40] *Od.* 2.12–13, 703–10; 8.19; *Il.* 1.54–55; 3.181, 224; 7.403–404, 418.

and authority undergo a reinterpretation when they are seen as derived from the people's recognition. Leaders, though retaining charismatic elements, come to premise their personal authority on recognition by the ruled. The people do not vote, nor do they make binding decisions. Furthermore, there are not formalized rules for succession to office, for responsibilities of office, for proposing and enacting legislation, for articulating interests, or for organizing the polity. Decisions are "enacted," instead, with minimal, and inconsistently applied, rules or procedures. The term "enacted" is useful because it draws attention to the public aspects of the activity without, in turn, stating that there is a formalized or democratic process. Within the public space, we see the emergence of a form of plebiscitary politics in which leaders play to the audience, seeking to persuade, cajole, or elicit support.[41] But this alters the nature of authority as leaders draft their appeals in anticipation of a response.

We see, for example, leaders assemble the people for important decisions that affect the entire community. There is evidence not only of the formalization of public assemblies, but also of the importance of the people in witnessing, and even influencing, decisions about public matters, the distribution of goods, the adjudication of disputes, and the conduct of foreign relations.[42] Both epics open with the people called to assembly, an assembly that is associated with some "public matter" that a member of the community may want to put forward and argue (*Od.* 2.32).[43] Even the infrequency of the meetings in Ithaca, suggestive of the near breakdown of the community, is juxtaposed to their frequency and formalization elsewhere (see *Od.* 10.114–15; 15.468).

More than just affirming decisions, the people seem to play a part in legitimating decisions and even directing action.[44] The assembly

[41] See Hammer 2005.

[42] Instances of calling assemblies for public matters: *Il.* 2.73–75; 7.345–378; 18.245–314; 18.497–503; *Od.* 8.10–45; contrast to Cyclops: *Od.* 9.114–15; formalization (role for heralds): *Il.* 2.99; 9.11; *Od.* 2.6–7; formalization (proper seating): *Il.* 2.96–97, 99; 9.13; *Od.* 2.14; 8.5–7; public matters: *Il.* 1.54–305; 2.84–398; 2.788–808; 7.345–79, 381–411, 414–20; 9.9–79; 11.806–7; 18.243–313; 19.34–237; *Od.* 3.126–50; 8.5–45; 16.361; 20.146; distribution of goods: *Il.* 1.125–26; 2.227–28; 11.704; *Od.* 13.14–15; adjudication: *Il.* 18.497–508; foreign relations: *Il.* 3.205–24; 3.245–345; 7.66–205; 11.122–42; *Od.* 21.15–21; other mentions: *Od.* 10.114–15; 15.468. See Raaflaub 1991, 1997, 1998; Schofield 1986; Hölkeskamp 2002: 311–18.

[43] There is a distinction made between public (*dēmion*) and private (*idion*) matters (*Od.* 4.314, 3.82).

[44] Legitimating decisions: *Il.* 1.22, 376; 2.72–73; 18.310–12; directing action: *Od.* 21.17; 14.239; 16.424–27.

is described as the "voice of the people" (*Od.* 15.468, trans. modified). Interestingly, this voice is sometimes depicted in the language of the heroic war cry, as when the people "shouted" their support for Diomedes' proposal (*Il.* 7.403; see also *Il.* 2.149). In the competitive world of the warrior, the cry corresponds to strength, courage, and individual distinction.[45] By depicting the people as shouting their approval, Homer not only reveals the force of the people, but also lends their voice some legitimacy by associating it with the agonistic, heroic world. Conversely, Mentor expresses anger with the people precisely because they sit "in silence" and do not try to stop the suitors through words, "though they are so few, and you so many" (*Od.* 2.239–41; also *Il.* 1.231).

Leaders might be able to play to the people, they might even be able to incite them, but they can hardly control them. Thersites provides perhaps the earliest example of the challenge of *parrhēsia*, or frank speech, in his public critique of Agamemnon's leadership. Along these same lines, Bakker has identified how *phēmis*, which is connected to openness (often unwanted), is associated with the people and the assembly.[46] But in such openness is potential turmoil. Agamemnon gives some sense of the tumult of the public assembly when he asks how, with the "great murmur" of the crowd, anyone can listen or speak (*Il.* 19.81). Although the people are able to recognize good counsel, they are also easily swayed by demagogic appeals, owing to the charismatic elements that are still associated with leadership. In playing to the people to demonstrate their own political prowess, leaders can imperil the good of the community.[47]

Both epics, as Donlan has observed, exhibit a "conscious perception of the social dangers which attend deterioration of the integrity of the [social] structure."[48] The competition for power – whether of leaders battling for the applause of the people or the suitors competing for rank – threatens to tear the community apart. One can see articulated in the epics a political ethic that seeks to join the competitive

[45] Comparison to noise: *Il.* 14.393–401; *Od.* 9.392; personal prowess: *Il.* 5.297–302; 8.321; 16.784–85; 18.160, 1228–29; 20.285; *Od.* 4.454; communal strength: *Il.* 13.834–35; 15.312–13; 16.78–79; 17.262–66; divine terror: *Il.* 5.784–92, 859–63; 11.10–14; 14.147–52; 15.321–27; 20.48–53.

[46] Bakker 2002: 139–40. Examples: *Il.* 10.207; *Od.* 6.273–75; 14.239; 15.468; 16.75; 19.527; 24.201.

[47] See *Il.* 2.142, 149, 155, 337; 12.211–14, 229; 14.84, 92–93; 18.311–13; *Od.* 3.137–40, 148–50.

[48] Donlan 1979: 59; also Wilson 2002: 251–53.

excellences of the warrior with these activities of the public assembly.[49] What emerges is a form of political heroism in which greatness consists of public speech actions (or *muthoi*) that involve a "performance" and a claim to authority "before an audience."[50] One wins glory through one's words in assembly as one speaks for, and persuades others of, the community good (*Il.* 1.490; 9.441; *Od.* 8.169–73). And one risks bringing ruin to the people.[51] As Schofield comments in discussing the counsel that Diomedes offers in Book 9, "the crucial point for the present is that Diomedes' speech is in its own way as much a feat of prowess as one of his exploits on the battlefield."[52] One sees a notion of distinction and acclaim that corresponds to the words of the elite in the assembly of the people (and, in turn, a model of deliberation that the people might emulate).

The picture of politics here is one in which charismatic and participatory elements are held in tension. We do not have to read the people out of the evidence any more than we have to impute to them a consciousness that is unwarranted by the evidence. The evidence we have, and that is certainly limited, points to not just a belief in the leader but an interaction between leaders and led that would fuel historically both demagogic excess and democratic reforms. Plebiscitary politics provided a public space, often volatile, in which a vocabulary of democracy could develop.

Gender

Scholarship has continued to broaden our understanding of the political depth of the epics by viewing them through the lens of gender. Feminist scholarship focuses largely on the dynamics of power by examining the ways in which politics constructs and reinforces social categories of gender. As Nancy Felson and Laura Slatkin write, "Inasmuch as Homeric epic conjures up a total world, the gendering of its conflicts, contradictions and values inform both the social order represented (and disturbed) within the poems and the metaphysical – indeed ideological – orders there limned."[53] One approach has been to read the epics (and

49 Competitive excellences: Adkins 1960. Cooperative virtues: Long 1970.

50 Martin 1989: 37.

51 See Haubold 2000. Examples: *Il.* 1.117; 2.115; 6.327; 7.345–53; 9.641; 14.83–102; 22.104–7; *Od.* 3.126–29.

52 Schofield 1986: 14.

53 Felson and Slatkin 2004: 92.

ourselves, in our enjoyment of the epics) as complicit in the construction of gender relations. Murnaghan, for example, sees Penelope as bowing ultimately to a world that will not allow her *mētis*, or cunning, to equal Odysseus'.[54] Doherty employs narratology to reveal an "interpretive hierarchy" in the *Odyssey* that invites women to identify with women who rival male heroes in cunning, but are rewarded for subordinating their purposes to male goals.[55] And Wohl argues that the *Odyssey* explores alternate political arrangements, from the primitive pastoral individuality of the Cyclopes to the royal model of the Phaeacians, only to give to Ithacan political arrangements "an air of inevitability" by making these arrangements look natural.[56] Control over women is reestablished to counter their potentially dangerous sexual and politically subversive power.

Others have explored how gender provides a more critical perspective on the heroic world. A gendered reading of the *Iliad* views Achilles' response to Agamemnon and the Embassy as "a critique of the broader exchange-logic animating war and a meditation on its apparent cause – traffic in women as a medium of contended honour among men."[57] The women, whether in mourning or in response to the warriors, continually evince a critical consciousness that war, however noble, threatens to destroy the familial institutions that it is intended to protect. The tension between the battlefield and the household is cast poignantly into relief with Andromache's final words: where Hector desires to perform some great deed so that he will be remembered forever, Andromache longs only for some small word by which she can remember him (*Il.* 24.743–45).

The *Odyssey*, perhaps not surprisingly given the centrality of Penelope and the range of female characters, has drawn more attention than the *Iliad*. A dead Agamemnon warns Odysseus of the treachery of women. But Penelope points to a more ambiguous statement about the role of women – as matching the cunning and restraint of Odysseus, as pointing to the narrative indeterminacy of the epic (and of identity generally) that reveals the constructed nature of social relationships, as a sign that refuses to be mute, as able to shape her own life, as prefiguring emphasis on "ethical norms such as justice and on the quieter values that promote social cohesion" that lead to the restoration of Ithacan order, as a bardic figure, and perhaps even as a critique of (or a way

[54] Murnaghan 1987.

[55] Doherty 2001: 127; 1995: 192.

[56] Wohl 1993: 19.

[57] Felson and Slatkin 2004: 96–97.

to imagine alternatives to) the male world.[58] Other female characters, such as the Sirens and Helen, are seen, as well, as subverting the truth claims of the epics because of their ability to use the language of epic culture while speaking truth and lies and contributing to benefit and harm.[59] As Foley writes in her seminal article on reverse similes, the comparisons (of men to women, women to men, fathers to children, swineherd to father, etc.) "seem to suggest both a sense of identity between people in different social and sexual roles and a loss of stability, an inversion of the normal." Odysseus' recovery of the household is "symbolic of a wider restoration of his kingdom on the same pattern." The politics of this restoration not only suggest the interdependence of male and female roles, but also that success "must be won with a special form of gentle, uncoercive negotiation."[60]

POLITICAL ETHICS

A common refrain in scholarship has been to view the *Odyssey* as portraying a more advanced ethical conception of human action than the *Iliad*. This view is premised on the overwhelming sense, captured in Achilles' encounter with Priam in the *Iliad*, that the gods are the cause of mortal suffering whereas in the *Odyssey* humans are seen as responsible for their own suffering. Even with this distinction, the values depicted in the epics are seen as decidedly inferior to notions of morality that developed later, which are premised on abstract and universal principles rather than cultural norms. Homeric individuals are seen as functioning unreflectively, conforming to external cultural norms and guided by honor and shame, rather than acting and reflecting upon internal motivations regarding what is morally right and wrong. That scholars would use terms from two different linguistic traditions – ethics from Greek, morals from Latin – to suggest the evolution of moral thought should raise some questions about retrofitting moral categories onto ethical practices. But even accepting the conventional distinction that ethics are articulated in practices and morals by reference to universal norms, we can still follow Ricoeur in arguing for "the primacy of ethics

[58] Matching cunning: de Jong 1994; Winkler 1990; narrative indeterminacy: Katz 1991; sign: Zeitlin 1996: 19–52; shape life: Felson-Rubin 1994: 3; quieter values: Foley 1995: 105; Vetter 2005: 33–34; bardic figure: Clayton 2004: 24; alternatives: Felson-Rubin 1994; Felson and Slatkin 2004: 105.

[59] Doherty 1995.

[60] Foley 1978: 8, 19.

over morality," or "the aim over the norm."[61] This aim, furthermore, is examined in one's dialogic and narrative relationship with others as one develops a conception of one's own worth in relationship to the worth of others.

From this perspective, the *Iliad* shows how desires can become subject to reflection and reevaluation, not because there is a non-desiring self who can look at the desiring self, but because these desires – and the implications of these desires – are seen as impacting one's own sense of worth. Briefly stated, in the Homeric world honor and shame operate as judgments (or anticipated judgments) of one's value, not only by society, but also by individuals as they see themselves through the eyes of society. We can think of this valuation of the self as "self-esteem."[62] Esteem, in the sense used here, does not denote some authentic inner self but is *an image of oneself in relationship to others* that necessarily involves questions of how this self relates to "the demands, needs, claims, desires, and, generally, the lives of other people."[63] The ethical self is an enacted self that must interpret and apply the standards of a community as well as encounter occasions in which community expectations are ambiguous, contradictory, or unsatisfactory. That is to say, the *Iliad* points to how esteem – as a sense of one's worth – can serve as a basis for ethical reflection.[64]

With the death of Patroclus, Achilles experiences a diminished sense of himself, a loss of worth. That sense of injury is not reducible to a simple failure of Achilles to live up to the social standards of a warrior culture, if for no other reason than the standards are quite ambiguous on this point. Achilles' initial reaction to the violation of his worth, as well as his later refusal of gifts, all seem consistent with the norms of a warrior society, yet come into conflict with Achilles' sense of failure to stand by Patroclus. The stimulus for Achilles' restatement of what counts as a worthwhile life is the immediacy of the pain that results from acting on his desires; namely, his desire to restore his esteem by humiliating Agamemnon. What is clarified for Achilles is what he desires most – not the humiliation of Agamemnon but the return of Patroclus. As Achilles' sense of worth appears implicated in

[61] Ricoeur 1992: 170–71.

[62] Cairns 1993: 16. On the reflective aspects of honor and shame, see Hammer 2002: 170–87.

[63] Williams 1985: 12. See also Ricoeur 1992: 172.

[64] Helpful explorations of the *Iliad* as engaged in ethical reflections, including discussions of wrath and pity, are made by Schein 1984; Crotty 1994; Muellner 1996; Zanker 1994; Hammer 2002. Applied to the *Odyssey*, see Farenga 2006: 195–205.

his attachments to others, his desires, too, must be brought into line with these broader considerations. Achilles' meeting with Priam reflects these considerations as his desire to mutilate Hector's corpse gives way to pity. The story Achilles shares with Priam in Book 24 arises from recognition that human attachments render us vulnerable to loss and responsible for care.

The importance of the epic is that it invites reflection on the exigencies of human enactment. The epic moves us to a comprehension of ethical relationships with others, relationships that are grounded in contingency, particularity, and vulnerability. As we are drawn into this world, we come to see ourselves as another, not in an empathetic moment in which we become the Other, but in an act of initiative in which, as we share a world of human enactment, we come to see ourselves as both doers and sufferers.[65] Hannah Arendt has pointed to the political implications of this recognition, a recognition that rests on two actions: releasing (or what Arendt refers to as forgiveness) and promising.[66] Releasing points to the possibility of projecting the world into the future by freeing oneself from a confinement (whether through the desire for vengeance or inconsolable grief) to the past. And promising points to the ways in which individuals, recognizing their connectedness, can bind themselves to each other and project themselves into the future. The story Homer tells, like the story Achilles tells Priam, is one in which we are moved toward a recognition of a shared world, a recognition that arises not from outside but from within a world constituted by experience.

Encountering the Other

For Levinas, Odysseus' travels chart the path of western philosophy: the "adventure in the world was but a return to his native island – complacency in the Same, misunderstanding of the Other."[67] Odysseus' travels mark, for Levinas, the refusal to engage the Other as an ethical being who cannot be subsumed into one's own self-knowledge. In seeking to revise this conception of Odysseus' travels, Hartog interprets these voyages as a series of encounters with the Other that map out the boundaries of identity and, in turn, point to the ambiguities

[65] Arendt 1958: 190.
[66] Arendt 1958: 236–47.
[67] Levinas 2003: 26.

and confusion of those boundaries. There is an encounter with different practices: lands without cultivation, without boundaries, without sociability, and without memory.[68] But there are also encounters with oneself as something different. Odysseus encounters himself in song, becomes "no-man," returns to an Ithaca that now seems foreign and dangerous to him (*Od.* 13.200–3), and takes on the form of a marginalized, itinerant beggar. He is "both present and absent, self and other at the same time."[69] As Hartog writes, "Odysseus, in his travels, through the very movement of a return journey that is constantly blocked or deferred, sketches in the outlines of a Greek identity, encompasses it. He marks out frontiers (between the human and the divine, for instance) or rather, he, the One who Endures, tests them out, at the risk of losing himself altogether."[70] Austin argues in this same vein that Odysseus progresses through increasingly complex systems of order as a "preparatory education" for his return to Ithaca.[71]

Others have sought to provide a historical context to this question of identity by showing how the epics emerge at a time when Greek conceptions of space and time are being altered by commerce, colonization, and mobility.[72] For Rose, the *Odyssey* plays out, by way of a "psychological profile" that includes "fearful ambivalence toward females and pervasive oral anxieties," the concerns of a colonizing aristocratic class that is both aware of the "crimes" they have committed in their "aggressive acquisitiveness" and yet proud of and aiming to validate their achievements.[73] Dougherty casts the *Odyssey* as a more forward-looking enterprise. To theorize, as Dougherty writes, is to leave home.[74] Homer theorizes about a new Archaic world, one that Odysseus, in some sense, re-founds in his return to Ithaca. Cook similarly notes that *mētis*, more than force, relies on the restraint of one's "physical appetites" – something not accomplished by Odysseus' crew, Polyphemus, and the suitors – that becomes "aligned with Greek culture and cultural values."[75] Deneen argues, as well, that Odysseus' ability to act with both moderation and violence gives him the qualities necessary to establish a new community, but adds that such qualities

[68] Also Foley 1978: 8; Cook 1995: 56–59.
[69] Clayton 2004: 65.
[70] Hartog 2001: 4.
[71] Austin 1975: 132.
[72] See Malkin 1998: 10, 14.
[73] Rose 1992: 140.
[74] Dougherty 2001: 4.
[75] Cook 1995: 64, 48.

are not suitable for rule over the long term. Such a limit on violence is "motivated and ultimately secured through the people's devices," a call for justice suggestive of the seeds of democracy.[76] And Farenga suggests that the encounter with cultural and social Others reflects "the development of moral consciousness" necessary for a democratic and deliberative self in a heterogeneous *polis*.[77]

Yet, Levinas raises a troubling question: what ultimately is Odysseus' objective? The terrifying part, as Buchan provocatively suggests, is not that Odysseus nearly fails in his return, but that he "comes all too close to succeeding" in fulfilling his fantasy of a return of Ithaca to his paternal power.[78] The fantasy is unfulfilled because he is prevented ultimately from massacring the remaining adult males on the island. Like in the *Iliad*, the *Odyssey* presents us with characters who imagine themselves as self-sufficient, Achilles of Book 9 and Odysseus (through his trickery).[79] Each of these expressions of invulnerability is, interestingly enough, associated with individuals who place themselves, at some point, outside human community. Achilles seeks to demonstrate his worth by killing, rather than saving, Achaeans. And Odysseus' *mētis* is a "tool of deceit" that, while necessary for civilization, can appear as "criminal" when directed against one's own community.[80] But both poems confront the audience with the untenability of this illusion: Achilles experiences a loss of a part of himself with the death of Patroclus and Odysseus' wiliness is purchased at the price of the death of every comrade with whom he set sail. So potentially disruptive is the chaotic violence at the end of the *Odyssey* that the gods impose a forgetting so that the deeds of either side will never be publicly debated or performed (*Od.* 24.481–86).[81]

The last several decades have witnessed a transformation in our understanding of the epics as works of political thought, from a view of the epics as a compilation of myths and legends that speak more to the irrationality of the cosmos than the possibility of politics to an increasing attempt to locate the epics in their historical context. Even that historicity has undergone substantial revision. The epics are no longer seen as referring to a Mycenaean past; rather, the political backdrop has been slowly pushed forward, from a view of the epics

[76] Deneen 2000: 66, 69.

[77] Farenga 2006: 229.

[78] Buchan 2004: 3; also Bakker 2002: 137.

[79] Buchan 2004: 14; also Hammer 2002: 93–113.

[80] Cook 1995: 9.

[81] See Farenga 2006: 258–59.

as depicting a functioning, Dark Age social system, to attempts to identify references to the emergent Archaic *polis*. Against this historical backdrop the epics emerge not just as a record of these embryonic political institutions and functions, but also as a reflection on the new demands of community organization. The political brilliance of the epics lies in the intensity with which the contours of political life emerge through the interaction – often the collision – of beliefs, goals, interests, assumptions, and aspirations: the challenge of authority, the near dissolution of the political field, the encounter with and potential incorporation of different groups, and the emergence of public claims that would play out in the tumultuous politics of Archaic Greece. The challenge of political thought is to remain attentive to the historical, cultural, and poetic context from which the epics emerged without, in turn, reducing interpretation to that context.

WORKS CITED

Adkins, A. W. H. 1960. *Merit and Responsibility: A Study in Greek Values*. Oxford.

Andreyev, Y. V. 1991. "Greece of the Eleventh to Ninth Centuries B.C. in the Homeric Epics." In *Early Antiquity*, ed. I. M. Diakanoff. Trans. A. Kirjanov. Chicago.

Arendt, H. 1958. *The Human Condition*. Chicago.

Austin, N. 1975. *Archery at the Dark of the Moon: Poetic Problems in the* Odyssey. Berkeley, CA.

Bakker, E. J. 1997. *Poetry in Speech: Orality and Homeric Discourse*. Ithaca, NY.

2002. "Polyphemos." *Colby Quarterly* 38: 135–50.

Buchan, M. 2004. *The Limits of Heroism: Homer and the Ethics of Reading*. Ann Arbor, MI.

Cairns, D. L. 1993. *Aidōs: The Psychology and Ethics of Honour and Shame in Ancient Greek Literature*. Oxford.

Clayton, B. 2004. *A Penelopean Poetics: Reweaving the Feminine in Homer's* Odyssey. Lanham, MD.

Cook, E. F. 1995. *The* Odyssey *in Athens: Myths of Cultural Origins*. Ithaca, NY.

Crielaard, J. P. 1995. "Homer, History and Archaeology." In *Homeric Questions*, ed. J. P. Crielaard. Amsterdam.

Crotty, K. 1994. *The Poetics of Supplication: Homer's* Iliad *and* Odyssey. Ithaca, NY.

Deneen, P. J. 2000. *The Odyssey of Political Theory: The Politics of Departure and Return*. Lanham, MD.

Doherty, L. E. 1995. *Siren Songs: Gender, Audiences, and Narrators in the* Odyssey. Ann Arbor, MI.

2001. "The Snares of the Odyssey: A Feminist Narratological Reading." In *Texts, Ideas, and the Classics: Scholarship, Theory, and Classical Literature*, ed. S. J. Harrison. Oxford.

Donlan, W. 1970. "Changes and Shifts in the Meaning of Demos in the Literature of the Archaic Period." *Parola del passato* 25: 381–95.

1979. "The Structure of Authority in the Iliad." *Arethusa* 12: 51–70.

1985. "The Social Groups of Dark Age Greece." *Classical Philology* 80: 293–308.

1989. "The Pre-State Community in Greece." *Symbolae Osloenses* 64: 5–29.

1997. "The Relations of Power in the Pre-State and Early State Polities." In *The Development of the Polis in Archaic Greece*, ed. L. Mitchell and P. J. Rhodes. London.

Dougherty, C. 2001. *The Raft of Odysseus: The Ethnographic Imagination of Homer's* Odyssey. New York.

Farenga, V. 2006. *Citizen and Self in Ancient Greece: Individuals Performing Justice and the Law*. Cambridge.

Felson-Rubin, N. 1994. *Regarding Penelope: From Character to Poetics*. Princeton, NJ.

Felson, N., and L. M. Slatkin. 2004. "Gender and Homeric Epic." In *The Cambridge Companion to Homer*, ed. R. Fowler. Cambridge.

Finley, M. I. 1979. *The World of Odysseus*, 2nd ed. New York.

1983. *Politics in the Ancient World*. Cambridge.

Foley, H. P. 1978. "'Reverse Similes' and Sex Roles in the *Odyssey*." *Arethusa* 11: 7–26.

1995. "Penelope as Moral Agent." In *The Distaff Side: Representing the Female in Homer's* Odyssey, ed. B. Cohen. New York.

1999. *Homer's Traditional Art*. University Park, PA.

Gill, C. 1996. *Personality in Greek Epic, Tragedy, and Philosophy: The Self in Dialogue*. Oxford.

Graziosi, B., and J. Haubold. 2005. *Homer: The Resonance of Epic*. London.

Gschnitzer, F. 1991. "Zur homerischen Staats- und Gesellschaftsordnung: Grundcharakter und geschichtliche Stellung." In *Zweihundert Jahre Homer-Forschung: Rückblick und Ausblick*, ed. J. Latacz. Colloquium Rauricum, 2. Stuttgart.

Hammer, D. 2002. *The Iliad as Politics: The Performance of Political Thought*. Norman, OK.

2005. "Plebiscitary Politics in Archaic Greece." *Historia* 54: 107–31.

Hartog, F. 2001. *Memories of Odysseus: Frontier Tales from Ancient Greece*, trans. J. Lloyd. Chicago.

Haubold, J. 2000. *Homer's People: Epic Poetry and Social Formation*. Cambridge.

Havelock, E. 1963. *Preface to Plato*. Cambridge.

Hölkeskamp, K.-J. 2002. "Polis and Agore: Homer and the Archaeology of the City-State." In *Omero tremila anni dopo*, ed. F. Montanari. Rome.

Jong, I. J. F. de. 1994. "Between Word and Deed: Hidden Thoughts in the *Odyssey*." In *Modern Critical Theory and Classical Literature*, ed. I. J. F. de Jong and J. P. Sullivan. Leiden.

Katz, M. A. 1991. *Penelope's Renown: Meaning and Indeterminancy in the* Odyssey. Princeton, NJ.

Levinas, E. 2003. *Humanism of the Other*, trans. N. Poller. Urbana, IL.

Long, A. A. 1970. "Morals and Values in Homer." *Journal of Hellenic Studies* 90: 121–39.

Lord, A. B. 1960. *The Singer of Tales*. Cambridge, MA.

Malkin, I. 1998. *The Returns of Odysseus: Colonization and Ethnicity*. Berkeley, CA.

Martin, R. P. 1989. *The Language of Heroes: Speech and Performance in the* Iliad. Ithaca, NY.

Minchin, E. 2001. *Homer and the Resources of Memory: Some Applications of Cognitive Theory to the* Iliad *and the* Odyssey. Oxford.

Morris, I. 1986. "The Use and Abuse of Homer." *Classical Antiquity* 5: 81–138.

Muellner, L. C. 1996. *The Anger of Achilles: Mēnis in Greek Epic*. Ithaca, NY.

Murnaghan, S. 1987. *Disguise and Recognition in the* Odyssey. Princeton, NJ.

Ong, W. 1982. *Orality and Literacy: The Technologizing of the Word*. London.

Parry, M. 1987. *The Making of Homeric Verse: The Collected Papers of Milman Parry*, ed. A. Parry. New York.

Powell, B. B. 2004. *Homer*. Blackwell Introductions to the Classical World. Oxford.

Raaflaub, K. A. 1989. "Homer and the Beginning of Political Thought in Greece." *Proceedings of the Boston Area Colloquium Series in Ancient Philosophy* 4: 1–25.

1991. "Homer and die Geschichte des 8.Jh.s v. Chr." In *Zweihundert Jahre Homer-Forschung: Rückblick und Ausblick*, ed. J. Latacz. Colloquium Rauricum 2. Stuttgart.

1993. "Homer to Solon: The Rise of the Polis, The Written Sources." In *The Ancient Greek City-State*, ed. M. Hansen. Copenhagen.

1997. "Politics and Interstate Relations in the World of Early Greek *Poleis*: Homer and Beyond." *Antichthon* 31: 1–27.

1998. "A Historian's Headache: How to Read 'Homeric Society'?" In *Archaic Greece: New Evidence and New Approaches*, ed. N. Fisher and H. van Wees. Cardiff and London.

2000. "Poets, Lawgivers, and the Beginnings of Political Reflection in Archaic Greece." In *The Cambridge History of Greek and Roman Political Thought*, ed. C. Rowe and M. Schofield. Cambridge.

Redfield, J. M. 1983. "The Economic Man." In *Approaches to Homer*, ed. C. Rubino and C. Shelmerdine. Austin, TX.

1994. *Nature and Culture in the* Iliad: *The Tragedy of Hektor*. Durham, NC.

Ricoeur, P. 1992. *Oneself as Another*, trans. K. Blamey. Chicago.

Rose, P. W. 1992. *Sons of the Gods, Children of Earth: Ideology and Literary Form in Ancient Greece*. Ithaca, NY.

Schein, S. L. 1984. *The Mortal Hero: An Introduction to Homer's* Iliad. Berkeley, CA.

Scodel, R. 2002. *Listening to Homer: Tradition, Narrative, and Audience*. Ann Arbor, MI.

Schofield, M. 1986. "Euboulia in the *Iliad*." *Classical Quarterly* 36: 6–31.

Scully, S. 1990. *Homer and the Sacred City*. Ithaca, NY.

Seaford, R. 2004. *Money and the Early Greek Mind: Homer, Philosophy, Tragedy*. Cambridge.

Thalmann, W. G. 1998. *The Swineherd and the Bow: Representations of Class in the* Odyssey. Ithaca, NY.

Turner, V. 1974. *Dramas, Fields and Metaphors: Symbolic Action in Human Society*. Ithaca, NY.

1988. *The Anthropology of Performance*. New York.

Vetter, L. P. 2005. "Women's Work" *as Political Art: Weaving and Dialectical Politics in Homer, Aristophanes, and Plato*. Lanham, MD.

Williams, B. 1985. *Ethics and the Limits of Philosophy*. Cambridge.

Wilson, D. F. 2002. "Lion Kings: Heroes in the Epic Mirror." *Colby Quarterly* 38: 231–54.

Winkler, J. J. 1990. "Penelope's Cunning and Homer's." In *The Constraints of Desire: The Anthropology of Sex and Gender in Ancient Greece*. New York.

Wohl, V. 1993. "Standing by the Stathmos: The Creation of Sexual Ideology in the Odyssey." *Arethusa* 26: 19–50.

Yamagata, N. 1994. *Homeric Morality*. Leiden.
Zanker, G. 1994. *The Heart of Achilles: Characterization and Personal Ethics in the* Iliad. Ann Arbor, MI.
Zeitlin, F. I. 1996. *Playing the Other: Gender and Society in Classical Greek Literature*. Chicago.

2: Foundings vs. Constitutions: Ancient Tragedy and the Origins of Political Community[1]

Arlene W. Saxonhouse

The characters who inhabit ancient tragedy continue to burn themselves into our consciousness. Oedipus, Antigone, Clytemnestra, and Electra all offer us visions of heroes and villains, personalities and psychologies caught in the labyrinthine consequences of their own characters and of fate. Yet, ancient tragedy goes well beyond the portrayal of the actions and choices of these commanding figures. Through the presentation of an Antigone or an Oedipus or an Orestes, it explores as well the challenges entailed in the founding of political communities. Today, whether we turn to the newly democratizing states or the issues surrounding the creation of a political union in Europe, our understanding of political beginnings and communal life often resides in the process of constitution making, the creation of institutions, and legal safeguards intended to provide for the security and protection of individual freedom. The ancient Athenians, writing long before the legalistic language of constitutions came to define political foundings, grappled with a range of issues that force us to reflect on the beginnings of political communities and to take those concerns well beyond the abstract legalistic focus that dominates the contemporary process. The tragedians recognize the myths, the gender-laden choices, the exclusions at the base of assertions of political order. They put on stage the potential tragic consequences that undermine the optimism often present at the foundational moments of political communities.

[1] I dedicate this chapter to the memory of my husband Gary Saxonhouse who died of leukemia in November 2006. Work on this piece began in Seattle where we spent our last weeks together.

While there is much to be said on this topic by looking at the philosophers of ancient Athens – comparing, for example, the *Republic* and the *Laws*, or considering Protagoras' speech in Plato's *Protagoras* or Book 2 of Aristotle's *Politics* – I will focus my discussion on three ancient tragedies[2] in order to address just those issues that are often ignored today in the theoretical and practical work surrounding the establishment of political institutions. The ancient tragedies allow us to raise questions about the consequences of the abstractions that emerge in a modern world that identifies political foundings with constitution writing, alerting us to the limits of our own perspectives – and the dangers of ignoring those limits.

INTRODUCTION TO THE ISSUES

Thomas Paine, in celebrating the emerging American nation, envisions the empty page on which the new nation will be built: "A situation, similar to the present, hath not happened since the days of Noah until now. The birthday of a new world is at hand. . . . " So he exults in 1776.[3] Later, in *The Rights of Man*, he will censure Edmund Burke who fails to understand that: "The vanity and presumption of governing beyond the grave, is the most ridiculous and insolent of all tyrannies" as he heralds this new world by dismissing the "manuscript assumed authority of the dead."[4] The world Paine envisions, the world that the social-contract theories of Hobbes and Locke had theorized, is one open to the creative powers of human reason and human speech. It is a world that exalts the human freedom that creates by itself the conditions under which we live. At the same time, as some have recently written, the writing of a constitution becomes a challenge to freedom, a self-limiting activity that arises from the foreknowledge of the actions of humans driven by self-interest.[5] Sheldon Wolin is one of those scholars who have focused on the oxymoronic nature of a constitutional democracy in order to underscore how constitutions are antithetical to the freedom envisioned by the democratic model.[6] But these constitutions come

[2] There are a multitude of possible plays that would be relevant for discussion. I think most specifically of Euripides' *Ion* (see Saxonhouse 1986), but one could just as easily engage his *Bacchae* or Aristophanes' *Birds* or *Ecclesiazusae*.

[3] This is from the appendix to *Common Sense* in Paine 1995: 52–3.

[4] Paine 1995: 438–39.

[5] See, for example, Elster 2000.

[6] See Wolin 1994.

from the sense of openness, the open field suddenly created by the opportunity to construct a new state. The ancient tragedians recognized this celebration of the new, but even as they celebrated it, they also feared the forgetfulness that underlies the act of constitutional creation. They ask us to reflect on what is lost with the novelty of what we today have come to call constitution writing, what in their world we might say would be the celebratory reliance on the creative powers of speech and reason.

Leo Strauss in *Natural Right and History* distinguishes ancient and modern political thought, in part, by saying that the moderns focus on the beginnings of cities while the ancients focused on their ends, or in Strauss' language, the "nonteleological" perspective of modern science versus the teleological foundation of "[n]atural right in its classic form."[7] The classic statement of this perspective comes when Thomas Hobbes so cavalierly dismisses the *summum bonum*: "[T]here is no such *Finis ultimus* (utmost aim) nor *Summum Bonum* (greatest good) as is spoken of in the books of the old moral philosophers" (*Leviathan*, Chap. 11). With the rejection of an "end" came the focus on origins, the creation of the political community through speech and science. And, the focus on beginnings meant the focus on the freedom of the individual as the starting point for political formation. The natural condition of mankind was understood as a condition of freedom for Hobbes and for Locke; abandonment of that freedom was possible only as an act of individual will or consent. In the final lines of his book, Strauss writes: "The quarrel between the ancients and the moderns concerns eventually, and perhaps even from the beginning, the status of 'individuality.'"[8] Given the polity's origins in individual choice, the evaluative focus of the modern world is the degree to which that "individuality" and freedom can be preserved. For example, Strauss writes: "According to Locke, the best institutional safeguards for the rights of the individuals are supplied by a constitution that, in practically all domestic matters, strictly subordinates the executive power (which must be strong) to law, and ultimately to a well-defined legislative assembly."[9] Here the understanding of political power emerges from an articulation of the origins of that power in the self-interested focus on individual rights.

[7] Strauss 1953: 7–8.

[8] Strauss 1953: 323.

[9] Strauss 1953: 233.

In the ancient world, in contrast, according to Strauss in his chapter "Classic Natural Right," speech is not the creator of political institutions, but the marker of sociability: "Man is by nature a social being. He is so constituted that he cannot live, or live well, except by living with others. Since it is reason or speech that distinguished him from the other animals, and speech is communication, man is social in a more radical sense than any other social animal: humanity itself is sociality."[10] Speech here does not create *ex nihilo*. It binds the human community together through debate concerning the just and the good, not through the construction of the bonds that will limit freedom so that members of the community can live together in peace rather than war. To develop his understanding of classic natural right, Strauss emphasizes the ancients' concern with the perfection of human nature, which is compatible with the end of the city, "peaceful activity in accordance with the dignity of man."[11] Thus, his reading of the ancients highlights their concern with ends and the understanding of the relation between the ends of the city and of the individual – their concern, in other words, with the *summum bonum* so summarily dismissed by Hobbes. It is Aristotle, however, not the playwrights, who lies behind Strauss's reading of the ancients here.

The ancient writers and especially the playwrights I discuss were also concerned with beginnings, how cities emerged and the consequences of those origins. Those origins, for sure, did not reside in contracts with individuals thinking in terms of cost-benefit analyses, but they did address the consequences of efforts to construct afresh and they offered a quite different reading of the place of reason in the polity – one hardly so sanguine as Strauss' portrait of the regime as the realm in which the human being can find his or her humanity.

Hannah Arendt, in many of her writings but especially in *On Revolution*, writes powerfully as well about the generation of political regimes. In *On Revolution* she quotes in a footnote the constitutional theorist and historian Edwin Corwin, who writes: "The attribution of supremacy to the [US] Constitution on the ground solely of its rootage in popular will represents . . . a comparatively late outgrowth of American constitutional theory. Earlier the supremacy accorded to constitutions was ascribed *less to their putative source than to their supposed content*, to their embodiment of essential and unchanging

[10] Strauss 1953: 129.
[11] Strauss 1953: 134.

justice."[12] Arendt, through Corwin, here suggests that the older view of constitutions could satisfy Strauss's reading of the goal of the ancient *politeia* or regime; it is only with the emergence of constitutions derived from "popular will" that there is the radical shift from ends to beginnings, not with constitutions themselves. Arendt's interest, however, is mainly with that constitution-writing moment. "[T]he end of rebellion is liberation," the source of our freedom, "while the end of revolution is the foundation of freedom," in other words, the constitution-writing moment when freedom is protected. Or, as she continues, "[T]he political scientist at least will know how to avoid the pitfall of the historian who tends to place his emphasis upon the first and violent stage of rebellion . . . on the uprising against tyranny, to the detriment of the quieter second stage of revolution and constitution."[13] But she, too, understands the constitution as the source of freedom understood as government limited by law and as the safeguard of civil liberties.[14] Quoting Paine, she remarks: "A constitution is not the act of a government, but of a people constituting a government."[15] Ever since 1789, constitution writing has been seen as a radical founding moment.[16]

Those of us interested in the ancient world cannot write of constitutions, nor even of a legitimizing popular will as Arendt does; such language simply was not part of the conceptual framework of the ancients. Nor do founding moments characterized by the adoption of constitutions capture the beginning point of regimes. Instead, what the tragedies offer is a different understanding of the original grounding of cities – not as constitution-writing moments of self-limitation, but as moments when human rationality faces the terrifying forces that limit it. Foundings are not the glorious moments of human creativity, but rather they highlight the community's debts to history and to ancient pieties. The optimism of the modern world of constitution writing is moderated by the weight of the past and of biology, neither of which reason and the imagination can escape. "Foundings" come not as the grand, free moment of constitution writing, but rather when the limits to our freedom are acknowledged.

[12] Arendt 1990 [1963]: 304–5 n. 32, italics added.

[13] Arendt 1990 [1963]: 142.

[14] Arendt 1990 [1963]: 143.

[15] Arendt 1990 [1963]: 145.

[16] Carl Freidrich 1963: 404–5, distinguishes acts of foundations which create groups as opposed to acts of institution that create order. I am blurring those distinctions here.

Antigone: The Impiety of Human Speech[17]

Antigone has defied the orders of the king of Thebes, Creon. She has performed the burial rites for her brother Polyneices. He had led an invading army against Thebes and had been declared an enemy of the city, denied burial by the city with his corpse left outside the city walls to be eaten by birds and wild animals. Creon believed he was bringing civil order to a shaken city by so marking Polyneices as an enemy. This clarification of friend and enemy would set the ship of state aright. But Antigone, brought before him as the one who has defied his decrees and performed the burial rites for her brother, confronts him with the weakness of his decrees, his human speech before those unwritten laws that come from Zeus. In a justly famous ode, Antigone scorns Creon's decrees and sings:

> Yes, it was not Zeus that made the proclamation;
> nor did Justice, which lives with those below, enact
> such laws as that, for mankind. I did not believe
> your proclamation had such power to enable
> one who will someday die to override
> God's ordinances, unwritten and secure.
> *They* are not of today and yesterday;
> they live forever; none knows when they first were. (450–57)[18]

The beauty of the translation by David Grene hides some of the antinomies that are at the heart of her ode – and of the argument here. Antigone gives this speech to set herself apart from the decree of Creon and in so doing she undermines both speech and writing. The laws of Zeus are not known through the language of men. They resist the grounding that writing would entail.

Creon had gloried in the power of the speech of man to create order. Man's capacity for speech is, for him, the source of political stability. In his effort to secure the safety of his city, he proclaims that his nephew Polyneices, who threatened the city with his army of Argive warriors, "shall no one honor with a grave and none shall mourn" (203–4). When Creon is confronted with Antigone, who has honored Polyneices with a grave and mourned him as well, he expresses

[17] This section draws to some degree on the discussion of the *Antigone* in Saxonhouse 1995.

[18] I use the translation of Grene 1991 with some modifications.

bafflement that she would have performed such an act: "Now, Antigone, tell me shortly and to the point, / did you know the proclamation against your action?" (446–47). How could she perform these acts, knowing the decree that was spoken before the city? How could she have so blatantly ignored in deed the power of his speech? For Creon, the speech of the ruler controls and limits the actions of others; how then could Antigone have resisted that power and performed the deeds the messenger reports and to which she admits?

From the opening moments of the play, Antigone has denied the efficacy of human speech, scornfully dismissing the spoken decrees of the city's leader, mocking Creon as a tyrant who imagines himself a free man who can say and do whatever he wishes, unrestrained by a people whose "tongue fear confines" (505–7). The inability to speak means powerlessness, as Antigone's less daring sister Ismene understands so well. Ismene had urged Antigone not to act against the speech of Creon and of the city, equating Creon with the freshly saved city. How can the two sisters perform the burial rites when "Creon has forbidden it" (47),[19] she asks. But Antigone scorns the orders that come from human speech even if they are to intended reassert an order that has been lost. The orders that she follows are worthy of obedience precisely because they are unwritten, beyond the realm of the political life of any city. She speaks haughtily to Creon of those unwritten laws knowing full well that Creon functions in a world of spoken decrees, proclaimed before the city through the voice of its leader and followed precisely because they have been spoken by the man who imagines himself holding the city (like a ship) upright through his speech.

Antigone in her memorable language has established an opposition between the natural order set out by the gods, an order that is not captured through human speech, and the man-made order that governs Creon's world, an order expressed through words and the letters engraved on stone stele. In Sophocles' play, Creon is initially not portrayed as an evil king; he presents himself as focused on the welfare of his city: "anyone thinking / another man more friend than his own country, / I rate him nowhere. For my part . . . I would not be silent / if I saw ruin, not safety, on the way / towards my fellow citizens" (182–87). When Antigone is identified as the perpetrator of the forbidden deed, he focuses on the city's need to define clearly friend and enemy

[19] The Greek is even stronger than Grene's translation: *anteirēkotos*, to have spoken against it. Three lines earlier Ismene had associated Creon's decree with the city as a whole: "Would you bury him, when it is forbidden by the city as a whole?" (44). The Greek in this instance is *aporrhēton polei*.

and dismisses the family ties – after all, Polyneices is his nephew, the son of his sister – that would call for compassion and leniency. And not only is Antigone Creon's niece, she is affianced to his son Haemon. Creon rises above such attachments and considers the whole city. He identifies with the city, not the family out of which the city is composed.

The welfare of the city that he is so eager to establish and preserve depends specifically on speech that denies the emotions that might lead him to soften before his son's beloved or his sister's child. His speech affirms the necessity of firmness and most especially of rationality against emotion. The devotion of Antigone to her brother, in contrast, depends on their common beginning in their mother's womb. That common birth evoking familial and emotional ties, not reason, binds them together beyond life. When much later in the play Antigone relies on reasoning to explain her actions, her language sounds hollow, shorn of the passion that motivated the earlier speeches; indeed, it borders on the absurd:

> Yet those who think rightly will think I did right
> in honoring you [Polyneices]. Had I been a mother
> of children, and my husband been dead and rotten,
> I would not have taken this weary task upon me
> against the will of the city. . . .
> If my husband were dead, I might have had another,
> and child from another man, if I lost the first.
> But when father and mother both were hidden in death
> no brother's life would bloom for me again. (905–7, 909–12)

When she tries to speak in the same language of Creon, assessing the status of "brother" versus "husband," she no longer speaks in her own voice drawn from the bonds of familial ties. She is, in fact, parroting a speech given by a Persian noblewoman, the wife of Intaphernes in Herodotus' *Histories* (3.119). So close to death, she justifies her actions in a speech so rhetorical that Aristotle considers it worthy of analysis in his *Rhetoric* (1417a). The strange rhetoric and emotional emptiness of this speech underscore the limits of human reason when confronted with a devotion to the unwritten demands of familial justice.

Creon, so certain in his assertion of the rightness of his actions and in his dependence on speech, stands forth as the male. He will not allow himself to be ruled by a female; he demands attention to what is built on speech, not the ties of the natural or the emotional. Antigone, despite her efforts to unsex herself and affirm the meaning of her name (*anti-gonē*: opposed to generation), from the beginning defends the priority of a unity dependent on birth, on the natural processes that bring forth life. Affirming in the first lines of the play that it is their common womb that ties her to her brother, she turns to the natural forces of generation to ground her world. Haemon's status as her fiancé is dependent on agreements based on speech and thus becomes irrelevant for her life. Ismene, not Antigone, reminds Creon of the engagement of Antigone and Haemon (568). In response, Creon crudely notes: "[T]here are other fields for him to plough" (569). A husband/fiancé is not born; he does not come from nature, but from convention. The ties to a brother, in contrast, are not constructed by speech.

In the early lines of the play, the chorus of Theban elders sings its justly famous choral ode about "the wonders of man." The audience hears of this creature:

> A cunning fellow is man. His contrivances
> make him master of beasts of the field
> and those that move in the mountains.
> So he brings the horse with the shaggy neck
> to bend underneath the yoke;
> and also the untamed mountain bull . . .
> He has a way against everything,
> and he faces nothing that is to come
> without contrivance. (347–52, 360–61)

These wonders, though, carry with them the threat of excess and of arrogance. Yet still the power of the gods and of nature remains in the form of death: "Only against death / can he call on no means of escape," concludes the chorus (361–62). The forces of the natural world limit human craft, however much that craft can tame the land and the seas and the wild animals. The divine and the natural retain their power despite human reason. Creon's speech alone cannot re-establish the upright city in defiance of the unwritten laws of Zeus. Despite all his contrivances, man cannot conquer nature.

Sophocles' tragedy turns his audience to a reverence for the gods over man. God is the creator of a natural order, the source of the unspoken, unwritten laws that can only be known through looking into our own hearts, not by listening to the spoken decrees by the likes of Creon. As Strauss (1953) develops in the third chapter of *Natural Right and History*, political philosophy emerges from the discovery of the opposition between the natural and the conventional. In the conflict between Antigone and Creon, we see the dramatic and tragic playing out of this conflict – the resistance to the founding of the city that depends on human reason and the natural order perceived in the ties that come from familial connections. In Sophocles' version, the failure to listen to Antigone's (and others') warnings about the imagined freedom of human action through the creative power of convention-creating speech leads to tragedy and loss beyond measure. With his wife and child dead, Creon learns that cities are not founded on nor held upright by human speech. He learns that attention to the unspoken and the ancient, the bonds that exist independently of the conventions created by speech, must be given their place in the city he tries so miserably to lead through reason and speech.

THE *ORESTEIA*: THE REASON OF THE GODS / THE PASSIONS OF MEN[20]

The *Oresteia*, written and performed several decades before the *Antigone*, affirms the priority of reason combined with obedience to the gods over the ties of birth. In some ways we can see the *Antigone* as a response to the *Oresteia*, for in the final play of Aeschylus' trilogy, the *Eumenides*, the ties of family arising from the processes of birth from the female's womb are banished to the dark caves below the city of Athens. Meanwhile, the shining brilliance of the goddess of wisdom, Athena – she who was born full grown from the head of Zeus – grounds the founding of the beautiful new city of Athens. This city arises from the goddess-imposed judicial system that attends to the city's need for political order, not to the needs of family members working out their complex ancestral and domestic relationships. In the final play of the trilogy, the theme of motherhood is openly argued and rejected. The common birth from the womb of Jocasta that tied Antigone to her brother is diminished by the assertion of the priority of the ties based on reason and craft, as opposed to those of nature. The *Oresteia* is the ancient expression of Arendt's "constitution-writing" moment – the old gods have been overthrown and the new world is about to be created. This moment, though, is marked by the ominous undertones that Aeschylus weaves into his trilogy and that Arendt seems to ignore.

The first two plays of Aeschylus' grand trilogy are plays of revenge for harms done to members of the same family. Clytemnestra kills

[20] The discussion of the *Oresteia* draws in part from Saxonhouse 1984.

Agamemnon, she claims, because "He thought no more of it [sacrificing Iphegenia] than killing a beast / . . . he sacrificed his own child, our daughter / the agony I labored into love / to charm away the savage winds of Thrace" (*Agamemnon* 1440, 1442–44).[21] Orestes kills his mother Clytemnestra because she has killed his father and has sent Orestes himself into exile. The harms are carried out within the family though the consequences spread well beyond into the lives of the inhabitants of the city of Argos.

At the end of the second play of the trilogy, The *Libation Bearers*, Orestes is being driven mad by the emissaries of his mother's ghost, the Furies who are avenging the mother's murder. He describes these Furies for the chorus of libation bearers who do not understand his screams and cannot see these visions in his head: "Women – look – like Gorgons / shrouded in black, their heads wreathed, swarming serpents! . . . No dreams, these torments, / not to me, they're clear, real – the hounds / of my mother's hate" (1048–50, 1053–55). Resolution will only be possible when those executors of familial justice are subdued, when the bonds of the family yield fully to the power of the city that has been constructed by the wisdom of the goddess, when the city can dismiss the ties that Antigone had so desperately wanted to affirm and for which she had found support in the unwritten laws of Zeus – and, indeed, in the action of the tragedy Sophocles sets on the Athenian stage. In the final play in Aeschylus' trilogy, the resolution of the terrible cycle of vengeance appears possible only when Orestes arrives in Athens to be tried for matricide in the courtroom over which Athena presides. It is here that Athens is founded by the actions of the goddess of wisdom; thus, I focus primarily on the *Eumenides*.

The beginning lines of the *Eumenides* recall some of the themes of the ode on the wonders of man from the *Antigone*, except that insofar as civilization arrives at this point in the trilogy, it comes not by human will and craft, but as the result of the visit by Apollo. The play begins with the speech of the priestess at the temple of Apollo in Delphi; she sings of the sequence of priestesses who have served at Delphi and then remarks on Apollo's arrival with an escort of "highway-builders, sons of the god of fire who tamed / the savage country, civilized the wilds" (13–14). The desolate land was transformed and what was once a wilderness with its succession of priestesses is a wilderness no more. The heralded transformation, though, comes at the expense of the female

[21] I use the translation of Fagels 1979. Line numbers, which are variable in different texts, here refer to Fagel's edition.

rulers who had served as the prophetic voice at Delphi. Apollo's arrival marks their departure.

Orestes comes to Athens for his trial searching for the civilized world that will end the natural cycle of vengeance of which he has been a part. And Apollo, he who has dismissed the female to tame the wilderness, along with the virgin goddess Athena, stands there at the foundation of the city of the Athenians, transforming it into that civilized world and providing for its security. The order they establish is predicated, however, on denying the forces of nature and replacing them with reason. Thus, Apollo in his oft-cited speech at the trial of Orestes says:

> The woman you call the mother of the child
> is not the parent, just the nurse to the seed,
> the new-sown seed that swells and grows inside her.
> The man is the source of life – the one who mounts.
> She, like stranger for stranger, keeps
> the shoot alive . . . (666–71)

Knowledge that the male is the father of the child, of course, depends on abstract reasoning, moving beyond what is empirically observed, the growing belly of the female and the processes of birth, to the speculative world of the invisible seed that can only be assumed, not seen. Nature does not identify the father;[22] reason, calculation, and custom perform that task.

Athena supports Apollo's views and she casts the vote necessary to tie the verdict and acquit Orestes. Relying only on the vote of the human jurors, Orestes would have been condemned by a margin of one.[23] The majority of the humans in this play side with the mother, the nature we observe, the female bearing the child in her belly. But the gods in the form of Athena intervene to move humans beyond the natural world of sight to the unseen, conjectured connection between father and child. Humans are forced by the gods to reject the simple

[22] Though see Aristotle's fine comeback to Socrates' proposals for a community where children are held in common in ignorance of their parents; Aristotle suggests that nature does identify the parents, even giving priority to the female (*Politics* 2.3.9).

[23] There is controversy over how exactly we are to read the vote of Athena – as a tie breaker or as creating the tie. In the former case, the vote among the mortals was even, in the latter Athena casts the vote that by creating the tie rejects the majority vote among the mortals. I read the vote in the latter fashion, though the argument is strong on both sides. See the discussion in Gagarin 1975.

observation and the sentiments of maternity in order to turn themselves over to the rule of rationality, speculation, and masculinity. The founding of the city requires divine intervention; it is, however, an intervention directed specifically at affirming the priority of reason and not the natural bonds at the base of the city.

Orestes is exonerated by the gods' strange argument that the mother is not the parent, that observable nature cannot be relied on. The gods' arguments themselves are based on the curious assumption that Athena, an immortal sprung fully formed from the head of Zeus, is an appropriate model for the birthing patterns of humans, who are necessarily born from the commingling of opposite sexes and emerge from the womb, not the head. "No mother gave me birth. / I honour the male, in all things but marriage. / Yes, with all my heart I am my Father's child," Athena announces just before casting the vote to acquit the matricide Orestes (751–53). The Athenians, whose citizenship laws had been put into force just around the time that Aeschylus wrote this play, demanded Athenian mothers as well as Athenian fathers for their citizens. They understood procreation as more than the flowerpot theory of generation that Athena and Apollo propound.

Though the setting for these speeches marking the founding moments of the city of Athens is a trial, specifically the trial of Orestes for the murder of his mother, there is nothing in the debate that addresses the guilt or innocence of Orestes. No one denies that Orestes has killed Clytemnestra. The question before the Athenians guided by Athena is whether punishment serves the interests of the city, whether the city can be grounded on the value of assessing guilt and innocence or whether there must be other principles at the foundation of the city and of the very trial itself. The issue of guilt and innocence only leads to the chaos of the continued bloodletting that dominated the earlier plays, as one family member after another executed justice by the killing of the one who killed previously. The *Eumenides* explores how to escape that world of endless revenge, how to arrive at a world of political stability, how to give the city a founding that transcends the personal vendettas, whether of kings and queens or of the everyday citizens. As the speeches suggest, this founding avoids the issue of justice that underlies demands for revenge, the giving of what is due to the malefactor, and instead looks forward to what will serve the interests of the political body as a whole – the subjection of the Furies and their transformation into gods friendly to the city (Eumenides) who, from their perch deep within the earth below the city, become the gods of wedlock fostering birth, not vengeance, looking forward, not backward.

Throughout the latter part of the *Eumenides* the Furies who had been eager to execute the vengeance of the ghost of Clytemnestra on her murderous son express horror at Athena's overthrow of their power. They complain repeatedly that the laws of younger time have ridden down the old laws. The Furies are the gods of old, as they describe themselves, the gods that come from the earth in their efforts to affect their own form of justice. Though Athena says, "I love Persuasion; / she watched my words, she met their wild refusals" (981–82), she also warns the Furies that if they are not persuaded there is the thunderbolt of Zeus to which she has easy access. Mollified in part by Athena's efforts to enlist them in the preservation of the new city through their attention to familial ties but also aware of the force of Zeus' thunderbolt, the Furies retreat into the depths of the earth and celebrate the birth of the city. Athena understands how much the city depends on the Furies, how they cannot be excised from the life of the city, even as they are "sped beneath the earth . . . home to the core of Earth" (1015, 1033). Reason cannot eliminate them without suffering sterility and civil wars. It is the true wisdom of Athena to acknowledge their importance to city even as she tries to hide them from the city's sight. The arc of Aeschylus' trilogy reminds us of how profoundly they remain part of the structure of the city.

A question mark that remains in Aeschylus' grand trilogy is why Apollo in organizing this trial and defending the matricide leaves aside the question of justice. Clytemnestra in the first play had portrayed herself as the perpetrator of justice, saying to the chorus of weak old townspeople: "Here is Agamemnon, my husband made a corpse / by this right hand – a masterpiece of Justice" (1429–30). She repeats later that she has repaid her husband for the evil he did her (1557). Likewise, Orestes is urged to repay his mother for the evil she has done. Justice must be served. Yet, instead of showing us a city built on the principles of a justice where evil is repaid, where crimes are punished, and where the power of the family bonds persist, Aeschylus shows us a city that is built on the conquest of what is according to the natural passions – the tortured love and revenge that marks the family of Argos. As recounted in the beginning of the *Eumenides,* Apollo, introducing civilization, had built roads where none had been before. He had civilized the wild, natural world of the priestesses when he arrived at Delphi; his civilizing journey preceded his Athenian venture when he civilizes the city with the denial of maternal and familial ties.

The gods at Orestes' trial are like Creon, who had tried to subdue the attachment Antigone had for her brother, to conquer those emotions that demanded justice for him irrespective of the needs of the constructed city dependent on human. In the *Antigone*, the city based on human decrees denied Polyneices the burial rites justly due him from his family members. In their willingness to hear the voice of maternity despite the arguments of the gods, the majority of human judges in the *Eumenides* recognized those same commitments that Antigone had so feistily urged on Creon. The Olympians deny the claims of maternity and present the goddess with her virgin birth as a model for human judgment. The story of the *Eumenides* introduces an order and stability that is based on a false conception of birth and thus of justice across the generations.

Further, it illustrates the city banishing its past to the depths of the earth and looking primarily to a glorious future unbound by the history of its citizens. The founding of Athens marks a new conception of time, a time present and future, but not a time past that recognizes generational ties. The Furies had tried to enforce a justice that looked to the past, but in the new city there is to be the abstraction from the past and the processes of generation. There must be, Aeschylus seems to suggest, the transcendence of justice as backward looking. The goal is to ignore history in order to found the brilliant new city, and so the past is banished to the caves at the earth's core.

This is not to suggest that Aeschylus denigrates the foundation of the city and the civilization to which the gods have led the Athenians. Participation in the city may require transcending the natural world that unites the human being with the life forces characteristic of all animals.[24] But Aeschylus does not ignore what is lost in this process of building up the city. As the old gods protest their suppression, the powerful images of the earlier plays in which the familial ties of birth could not be so easily tossed aside remain. There was the anguish of Clytemnestra as she described the sacrifice of her daughter, the child she "labored into love" (1443). There was Orestes' resistance to committing the actual murder of his mother though urged on by Apollo himself and his friend Pylades. The sight of her bare breast stops him: "What will I do, Pylades – dread to kill my mother?" (886). He resists, though we have just seen the nurse warmly welcome him with reminiscences of him suckling at her – not Clytemnestra's – breast. That recollection does

[24] Cf. Aristotle who makes this point powerfully when he presents man as the political animal who only becomes fully human once he moves beyond the family of procreation and the village of bodily satisfactions to life in the polis.

not undermine his understanding of the depravity of what he is about to do to the woman who bore him. These images do not or should not disappear as the brilliant Athena presides over the trial proclaiming the irrelevance of motherhood.

Perhaps the old justice was executed by dark, vile women with swarming snakes for hair, as Orestes sees them at the end of the *Libation Bearers* and as they appear on stage at the beginning of the *Eumenides*. But that justice found its source in the powerful attachments that were fostered in the womb and are now denied. Gods must push humans toward this new conception of the city. Humans do not go there easily; they were born from human mothers and did not spring full grown from a god's head. They remain bound by the familial ties that attend to those who have preceded them and not only to those who will follow. The gods introduce the future-focused reason that forgets birth and the maternal breast.

Within the structure of the city newly founded on principles of rationality, the crimes of the father as father become the crimes of the citizen. The murder of one's child for the sake of an aggressive war may become legitimate, while the revenge of the mother for that murder may not. The city portrayed in Aeschylus' trilogy forces the family to abstract from particularistic ties and even praises deeds that the justice of the family would seek to avenge. Within the framework of the city grounded on rationality, the murder of a child may become a positive act.[25] Within the justice of the family, it never could be. The gods' exploitation of such arguments in the *Eumenides* signifies the acceptance of a new concept of justice, where justice comes from the impersonal definitions of the city. The family must remain blessed; procreation must continue to ensure the physical survival of the city, but the family with its particularistic ties and emotional bonds can no longer remain the seat of justice. The city now, as in Creon's speech in the *Antigone*, defines who are friends and foe – not the common womb.

When Athena brings the abstraction from particularity into the founding of the city, she undermines the central force of the familial relations. We may not resonate as powerfully to these connections in the tale of the family of Agamemnon as we do when they provide the core of Antigone's appeal in Sophocles' play. In the *Oresteia* the glory

[25] One might think here of the Brutus who killed his sons that surfaces prominently in the Machiavellian construction of the founding of the Roman Republic, *Discourses on the first Ten Books of Titus Livy*, I.16 and especially III.3, entitled "That It is Necessary to Kill the Sons of Brutus to Maintain a Newly Acquired Freedom."

of Athena's new city overwhelms the force of Antigone's appeal. While Creon's harshness may be hard to connect to Athena's stature in the *Eumenides*, I would suggest that they are uncomfortably similar in their common effort to give their cities a grounding in a forward-looking reason rather than in the familial connections rooted deeply in the past.

Oedipus Tyrannus: History and the Limits of Rationality[26]

The *Oresteia* tells the tale of the founding of the city that emerges from a forward-looking justice, a justice that denies history, one's parents, one's birth. In Sophocles' *Oedipus the King* we find again this tension between the past and the future, between family and city. In this play Oedipus, convinced of the power of his own intellect and its own capacity for creation, learns the power of history and the limits that that history places on what rationality can achieve.

Oedipus' status as ruler in Thebes comes, Oedipus believes, from his intellect. He alone could answer the Sphinx' riddle and thus he alone saved Thebes from the suffering the monster had inflicted on the city. We, the audience of the play, know that it is his birth that brings him from Corinth to Thebes and makes him the ruler there. Oedipus understands – at the beginning of the tragedy – the source of his status in the city very differently. Emphasizing his own powers of rationality and dismissing the powers of augury, Oedipus taunts the seer Teiresias when he cannot get the prophet to say what he claims to know: "For, tell me, where have you seen clear, Teiresias, / with your prophetic eyes, where were you with the prophet's wisdom? When the dark singer, / the sphinx was in your country, did you speak / words of deliverance to its citizens?" (390–92).[27] Moments later, he snaps at the priest: "But I came, / Oedipus, who knew nothing, and I stopped her. / I solved the riddle by my wit (*gnōmē*) alone. / Mine was no knowledge got from the birds" (396–98). In the late moments of the play, the chorus sings of the former glory of Oedipus:

> In as much as he shot his bolt
> beyond the others and won the prize
> of happiness complete –
> O Zeus – and killed and reduced to nought

[26] This section builds on Saxonhouse 1988.

[27] I have used the translation of Grene 1991.

the hooked taloned maid of the riddling speech,
standing a tower against death for my land." (1197–1201)

The "bolt" he shot had only the force of his intellect.

Oedipus believes that he relied on no one and on nothing except his own mind. Oedipus who knows nothing of his own history and the limits that that history may set – indeed has set – on his actions sees all as free and open. Rule in Thebes has come to him because of intellectual skills. He does not understand that he rules because of the gods, because of his history, because the world is hardly as free and open as he envisions. His tyranny is to see himself as free from the past, relying only on his intellect to interpret and construct the world in which he lives. Oedipus is an ancient version of Paine, imagining the birthday of a new world opening up for him to fashion through his mind, freed from disastrous choices made by others (his parents, the servant who did not leave him to die on the hillside) in the past. This imagined freedom from the past that Oedipus glories in is the source of the deepest tragedy and suffering.

In response to the oracle's injunction that the city of Thebes pursue and punish the murderer of Laius if they wish to end the plague that sickens all the city, Oedipus begins his investigation only to discover, of course, that he is the murderer, that the freedom for the human intellect in which he had so gloried earlier does not exist, that what he thought was an independence of action is no independence at all. Instead, his own history determines where he is and what he has done. Born from the parents who were warned not to have children, he lives as a slave of their violation of the decrees of the gods. When Creon returns from Delphi to report that the sickness plaguing Thebes comes from the failure to find and punish the man guilty of killing their king Laius, Oedipus immediately commits himself to discovering and punishing the killer, an intellectual challenge that he feels ready to meet. It is this search, of course, this sense of intellectual purpose that reveals the chains that history has placed on him and on the city that he now rules.

As Oedipus pursues the clues that will lead to himself as the object of his own investigation, his wife-mother Jocasta understands the truth of his origins before he does. At first, she appears the female analogue of Oedipus, using argument and calculation, reasoning through the evidence, insisting that many cannot be one. The lone witness to the murder of Laius had reported that it was a band of robbers who killed Laius at the crossroads. "Be sure, at least, that this was how he told the story. He cannot / unsay it now," she tells him (848–50). But this is only a straw at which Jocasta grasps as she begins to realize who her husband is and who the murderer of Laius was. Unlike Oedipus, though, Jocasta, awakening to the truth of the impieties with which she is living, chooses to dismiss all limits on human actions, consciously to ignore the past that Oedipus had unconsciously disregarded. "Why should man fear since chance's rule is all in all / for him. . . . Best to live lightly, as one can, unthinkingly" (977–79). She who had earlier dismissed the gods' forewarning about bearing a child now asserts that man "can clearly foreknow nothing" (978). There is no naturally constituted order. Therefore all the prophecies of the gods are merely a source of fear for those who do not see the total openness of a world without limits. Jocasta's speech reveals a desperation, a longing for total freedom, a living in the moment. The randomness she posits denies any foundation – even that which might emerge from the human intellect. She longs to escape from any order, even one founded on reason, for fear of the limits it might set and the horrors it might reveal.

The chorus, frightened by the deep impiety of Jocasta's language, asks: "May destiny ever find me / pious in word and deed / prescribed by the laws that live on high: / laws begotten in the clear air of heaven" (863–67). The chorus retreats to an unchanging order decreed from above, not subject to human manipulation or control by speech. Jocasta is willing to live with the apparent impiety of her current life, to scorn the gods, to live in complete freedom in a world in which the son-husband is neither shameful nor lawless. Oedipus cannot match his mother-wife in her audacious vision of self-liberation and self-creation. He plunges himself into the self-mutilation that bears witness to the vanity of his efforts to find in the creations of the mind the source of political authority and order.

Oedipus rejects Jocasta's pleas to cease his search and view the world as random, without the causal connections that would tie the impiety of his marriage to the plague of sterility that infects Thebes. He concludes incorrectly that Jocasta, a queen, must be ashamed of the lowly birth that may lie in her husband's past, that she – unlike he – is bound by the conventions of the society in which she lives. How blind he really is! He sings now of his status as "a child of Fortune, / beneficent Fortune" (1080), but refuses to revel in the chaos that would have freed him from any restraints, ascribing only to the human world the disorder that Jocasta claims for the divine world as well.

Oedipus embodies the individual who attempts to disregard his paternity – his bounded origins – in his movement toward an individual freedom that allows him to be great on his own. It is a drunken man's taunt about his parents that precipitates his trip from Corinth to Delphi where he will encounter Laius at the crossroads. While he was still in Corinth he was concerned with his origins, so concerned that it is simply that drunken man's mocking question that makes him pursue the truth about his past. But once in the open road between cities, he becomes free. The story of his birth matters no longer as he remains content in his assumption that his Corinthian parents are indeed his parents; the only limits on him then are that he not return to Corinth lest he kill his father and sleep with his mother. As he plays the detective in Thebes, however, he begins to wonder about his parentage and the uncertainties he uncovers make him at first suspect that he was born on the mountainside – that child of Fortune. Such a birth opens the way to the greatest freedom, the opportunity to be anything. As a wild child of the mountain, he demonstrates in his person, he can become king of Thebes through his wit.

Of course, from such optimism that envisions this marvelous freedom, Oedipus will crash into the realization that he is not Fortune's child at all, but is bound ever so tightly by the nature of his birth. He is a man of history and place, the forbidden child of Laius and Jocasta. When Oedipus initially exults in his false sense of freedom as Fortune's child, the audience knows well how ill founded this belief is and that Oedipus' world, far from being free, is profoundly circumscribed. The limits of biology and history lie at the heart of the tragedy of Oedipus. He came as the savior to Thebes, re-founding Thebes in a sense as he freed the city from the stranglehold of the Sphinx and replaced the murdered king. Freely, he walked into the city and, in Creon's language, set it straight. The freedom at the heart of contemporary constitution making exemplifies Oedipus' imagined freedom, Fortune's child, the opportunity to create greatness from the unstructured or the oppressed beginnings. Oedipus arrived at Thebes as its savior acting through reason, but in the process of ruling he brought pestilence to it, most particularly the pestilence of sterility for the animals and the crops on which the city depended for its livelihood. The tragedy of the *Oedipus* presents both the glory and the failure of the individual attempt of the political actor to rise above the mere body and build a world where reason, released from the defective body, alone is power.

The revelation that his birth and not his reason is the basis of his claim to rule is at the core of the tragic uncovering of this play. A political optimism that envisions a world of infinite possibilities, subject only to the imagination and reason, meets its match in the last crushing moments of the play. The play is an exploration of the necessary grounding of power and authority in the direct experience of the world of physical birth. The tragedy of Oedipus is not the fall of a helpless and faultless ruler or the weakness of man subjected to divine laws, but the dashed hopes of the power of the mind to rise above the limits imposed by nature, by our biology, and by our past. Sophocles offers his play as a warning. Humans attempting the transformation of the world on the basis of abstract, calculating reason alone without regard to the limits of history or piety will call forth the Furies, enforcing limits on our creations and actions. In some sense, we are all like Oedipus, not in Freud's psychosexual terms, but in our desire to theorize and build from that theorizing, to impose an order on the world in which we live while rejecting Jocasta's attempt to view the world as completely random. When Oedipus appears on stage bloodied and blinded groping for his daughters, he incorporates the tensions between the limits that condition all our actions and the freedom our intellect imagines. Sophocles' play becomes a commentary on the modern assumptions of intellectual and political freedom to create, to build a grand new world through speech, to sing along with Paine "Happy Birthday" to this new world. The openness of constitution writing, the ancient tragedies suggest, must pay heed to the historical and physical grounding that they recognized as central to the success of political foundings.

Conclusion

Where do these great tragedies leave us – simply pawns of the gods, subject to their laws and their world, and subject as well to the biology of our past? Such "beginnings" do not sit easily in the contemporary imagination, so fond are we of forward-looking constitution writing. Attention to these tragedies is not intended to diminish the significance and power of such moments of creative speaking. But they do temper the optimism and remind us that such optimism marks a modern arrogance in the capacity of self-creation and liberation.[28] Thucydides

[28] Arendt reminds us in a footnote in *On Revolution* of Locke's constitution for Carolina "perhaps the first such constitution framed by an expert and then offered to a people" and then quotes from William C. Morely: "It was created out of nothing, and it soon relapsed into nothing" (Arendt 1990 [1963]: 300 n. 6). This obviously was not the fate of all such proposals, but consider the famous language of *Federalist* No. 1: "It has frequently been remarked that it seems to have been reserved to the people of this country . . . whether societies of men are really capable or not of establishing good government from reflection and choice, or whether they are forever destined to depend for their political constitutions on accident and force."

includes in his *History* a remarkable speech by the Corinthians to their Spartan allies urging them to attend to the threat that the Athenians pose. There the Corinthians describe the Athenians as a people who "are addicted to innovation (or what is revolutionary – *neōteropoioi*) who once they think of something (*epinoēsai*) swiftly accomplish it in deed . . . they alone are enabled to call a thing hoped for a thing got, by the speed with which they act on their resolutions" (1.70).[29] Though spoken by the Corinthians as a warning to the Spartans, the speech captures the Athenians self-conception, one which is so appealing to the modern mentality, but about which the ancient playwrights also want to warn the city. The powerful Books 6 and 7 of Thucydides recall the disastrous consequences of this love of novelty and this daring in the portrayal of the failure of the Sicilian expedition as the troops expire in the marshes and the salt mines outside Syracuse. The terrifying endings of *Antigone* and *Oedipus*, with the bloodied bodies and souls of Creon and Oedipus, serve as a harsh reminders to the Athenians (and us) of the limits of what speech and thought can accomplish. The shining goddess Athena can only demand that the city look forward and forget through harsh repression those powerful emotions that were born of just those limits that Oedipus and Creon were so eager to escape.

WORKS CITED

Arendt, H. 1990 [1963]. *On Revolution*. London.

Crawley, R., trans. 1982. *Thucydides: The Peloponnesian War*, rev. T. E. Wick. New York.

Elster, J. 2000. *Ulysses and the Sirens: Studies in Rationality, Precommitment, and Constraints*, rev. ed. Cambridge.

Fagles, R., trans. 1979. *Aeschylus: The Oresteia: Agamemnon; The Libation Bearers; The Eumenides*, rev. ed. Penguin Classics. Harmondsworth.

Friedrich, C. J. 1963. *Man and His Government: An Empirical Theory of Politics*. New York.

Gagarin, M. 1975. "The Vote of Athena." *American Journal of Philology* 96: 121–27.

Grene, D., trans. 1991. *Sophocles I: Oedipus the King; Oedipus at Colonus; Antigone*, 2nd ed. Chicago.

Paine, T. 1995. *Collected Writings: Common Sense, The Crisis, and Other Pamphlets, Articles, and Letters; Rights of Man; The Age of Reason*. New York.

Saxonhouse, A. W. 1984. "Aeschylus' Oresteia: Misogyny, Philogyny, and Justice." *Women and Politics* 4: 11–32.

1986. "Autochthony and the Beginnings of Cities in Euripides' Ion." In *Greek Tragedy and Political Theory*, ed. J. P. Euben. Berkeley, CA.

Saxonhouse, A. 1988. "The Tyranny of Reason in the World of the Polis." *American Political Science Review* 82: 1261–75.

[29] I use the translation of Crawley 1982 here with minor adjustments.

1995. *Fear of Diversity: The Birth of Political Science in Ancient Greek Thought*. Chicago.
Strauss, L. 1953. *Natural Right and History*. Chicago.
Wolin, S. 1994. "Norm and Form: The Constitutionalizing of Democracy." In *Athenian Political Thought and the Reconstruction of American Democracy*, ed. J. P. Euben, J. R. Wallach, and J. Ober. Ithaca, NY.

3: Most Favored Status in Herodotus and Thucydides: Recasting the Athenian Tyrannicides through Solon and Pericles

Norma Thompson

Tyranny and the Emergence of Historical Thinking

Herodotus and Thucydides, jointly responsible for the invention of history in the West, suggest an intriguing connection between historical thinking and the overcoming of tyrannical aspiration. On this topic, the historians should be regarded as fundamentally like-minded. Both object to the conventional tale of how Athens freed herself of her tyrants, the story of Harmodius and Aristogeiton and their alleged overthrow of the Peisistratid ruling family in 514 B.C.E. In the process of contesting this cherished tradition and replacing the tyrannicides with their own favored characters, Herodotus and Thucydides carve out a role for the historian in defining political identity. Herodotus, the Father of History, steps into the shoes of Solon, famed wise man of Athens, while Thucydides, often referred to as the Father of Objective History, assumes a Periclean role, *his* character of choice.[1] Presumably each seeks to maintain control over the interpretation of these figures in a way that was not the case with the iconography

[1] Herodotus and Thucydides identify with more than *one* of their characters, of course; my interest here is in accounting for the most favored. Among other works that are germane, see Carolyn Dewald on Herodotus vis-à-vis the "savant" and the "trickster" (Dewald 1985: 49, 60), and Fornara 1971: 64–69, on Pausanias and Themistocles. Cleisthenes is not even a contender. As for Thucydides, David Grene and others have

of Harmodius and Aristogeiton. The historical accounts preclude any mere celebration of self and require, instead, an immersion in a complex set of particular details. Ultimately, Athens was to receive the heroes she deserved: the Herodotean Solon and the Thucydidean Pericles.

The popular story of the Athenian tyrannicide was deeply entrenched during the time of Herodotus and gathered even more force in the generations to follow. It was immortalized in the tyrannicide statue group sculpted by Critius and Nesiotes, which depicts Harmodius and Aristogeiton in the moment just before they fatally struck Hipparchus, son of Peisistratus and brother of the tyrant Hippias. The youthful, beardless Harmodius is shown in mid-stride with his sword raised, resolute and fierce as he prepares to cut down his adversary ("the Harmodius blow"). Next to him is Aristogeiton, older and bearded, with a cloak draped over his left arm and a sword held in his right, ready for the attack. The composition is all vigor and manliness. This monument stood prominently in the Agora as an aggressive reminder to the Athenian demos of how the two men courageously attacked the tyrant and brought down the regime, paying for this act with their lives. This was the second such statue group; the original (sculpted by Antenor) was stolen from the city by Xerxes during the Persian War in 480/79, "in the ancient Near Eastern tradition of sapping an enemy's strength by carrying off his most important symbols."[2] From time to time the Athenians themselves would acknowledge that this depiction was not accurate – so Thucydides informs us – but that seemed not to affect the endurance of the narrative. And the scene was represented not just in statuary but in vase paintings, coins, and drinking songs: "the texts and iconography of tyrant killing are mutually implicated and in a variety of ways."[3]

The received wisdom on Herodotus and Thucydides on the matter of the tyrannicide story is that they lost the battle with the demos. In vain did the historians protest that the victim of the assassination was the tyrant's brother, not the tyrant himself; that the regime continued in power after the assassination and even became much harsher; or that four full years passed before the tyranny was overthrown, and then with the significant intervention of the Spartans. As Herodotus tells it, the rival Alcmaeonidae family, "men of wealth and of great distinction from of old," came to Delphi as suppliants and "bribed the

noted the "real coincidence" of his theory of causation and that of Diodotus. See Grene 1967: 66.

[2] Taylor 1991: xiv.

[3] Ober 2003: 216.

Pythia, whenever Spartiates . . . came to consult the oracle, to urge on them the freeing of Athens."[4] It was they, Herodotus concludes, "far more than Harmodius and Aristogeiton" (6.123), who were responsible for driving out the Peisistratidae. Thucydides' corrections go considerably further, as he discloses that "the daring action of Aristogeiton and Harmodius was undertaken in consequence of a love affair."[5] Thucydides then spells out the lurid details, even switching the usual order of the names Aristogeiton and Harmodius, as if to anticipate the thoroughgoing rearrangement of the elements of the story.

Thucydides informs us that Harmodius was "in the flower of youthful beauty" when Aristogeiton, "a citizen in the middle rank of life," possessed him. The stress on his inferior class is pointed. Meantime, the historian continues, Hipparchus solicited the young Harmodius, and Aristogeiton grew enraged. Aristogeiton became increasingly fearful of the power of Hipparchus and the Peisistratidae, especially after Hipparchus repeated his solicitations. Thucydides interjects that in point of fact Aristogeiton had no cause to be afraid of Hipparchus wielding power – such was the benevolent role of the Peisistratidae: "Indeed, generally their government was not grievous to the multitude, or in any way odious in practice; and these tyrants cultivated wisdom and virtue as much as any" (6.54.5). When Hipparchus actually attempted to exact revenge after his advances had been spurned, he did so by publicly insulting the sister of Harmodius, at the Panathenaic Festival. Outraged, Harmodius and Aristogeiton plot to kill Hippias and to overthrow the family. The plot falls apart when chance, emotion, and panic overtake them. As Rawlings observes, in this rendering, the murder of Hipparchus is a wholly sordid affair, "an audacious act . . . plotted by a commoner crazed with sexual jealousy and fear, and perpetrated against one of Athens' greatest and most beneficent families."[6] But the simpler version persisted: the Athenians kept telling the same old story of their heroes Harmodius and Aristogeiton. Taylor concludes: "By 400 B.C.E., the fame of Harmodius and Aristogeiton had become impervious to attack, even an attack as strong as that of Thucydides."[7]

The factual inaccuracies of the tyrannicide story, however, may well have had the beneficial effect of provoking the historians to invent their own methods of portraiture. In attempting to refute the iconography spawned by the sculptures of Critius and Nesiotes, Herodotus and

[4] 5.62–63, trans. Grene 1987.

[5] 6.54.1, trans. Crawley in Strassler 1996.

[6] Rawlings 1981: 105.

[7] Taylor 1991: 97.

Thucydides formulate an innovative historiography, answering "the Harmodius pose" with heroic representations of their own in the figures of Solon and Pericles. Some basic historiographical principles are at issue here, particularly in regard to the nature of the historical voices. Significantly, the historians do not cease to anchor themselves in common knowledge, despite its manifest unreliability. And for the historical figures Solon and Pericles, the common knowledge represents a sizable tradition. Before Herodotus and Thucydides could employ their characters for their own interests, they first had to make them credible, remaining at least broadly consistent with what everybody already "knew." Their recognition is that far from speaking from above, the historian is significantly restricted to the inherited testimony of his generation. His power comes from shaping, not inventing, this material, and his judgment arises through these particulars.

Many of the caricatures of Herodotus and Thucydides as historians seem to have come about because they identify so closely with their characters and seem to invest in them so personally. Generations of Herodotean critics have mocked him as credulous, garrulous, and a little out of touch, not unlike the picture that has come down to us of Solon. To his audience, Thucydides has looked matter-of-fact, humorless, and driven by a single idea, much in the way of Pericles. But these impressions have a way of fading with closer study, and in this generation no serious reader of either historian fails to detect his discerning gaze behind the character portrayals. Once it became established that the historians do not identify *completely* with their exemplary characters, scholars better appreciated the multidimensional character portrayals. The space between the historian and character is of the highest critical interest, revealing the heroic figures as both chastening and flawed.

Indeed, for both Herodotus and Thucydides, it appears that the condition of their own success in impugning tyrannical ways is tied to the partial failures of their most prominent characters. The lessons of Solon and Pericles either go unlearned or are themselves misguided. Herodotus and Thucydides may agree about the futility of the wise advisor and assume this as a basic condition of their writing, but it is not a terminal state. The historians find different ways to assure a continued existence for their heroes. They thereby suggest similar insights about how best to appropriate evidence for edifying purposes. This is where they improve upon the Harmodius and Aristogeiton narrative. That iconography is all assertion and closes off conversation, whereas the historians' portrayals are open-ended and never give up the fight. It appears that the historians breathe life into their historical figures in a manner that proves more enduring than the striking images of the tyrannicides.

Even Solon and Pericles can be improved in the telling. This insight underlies the accomplishment of Herodotus and Thucydides in transforming a historical individual into a political figure who might conceivably help define the Athenians. And the question of how free historians are to take a proactive role in shaping political identities has lost none of its relevance since Herodotus and Thucydides first opened the issue. Edmund Burke, in his *Reflections on the Revolution in France*, suggests that leaders have a surprising degree of creative control over political identity, with the ability to select from various past "performances" of a people the one most suited to a prosperous political future. Thus in the midst of chastising the French Revolutionaries for their wholesale rejection of their immediate past, as if they "had everything to begin anew," Burke claims: "If the last generation of your country appeared without much luster in your eyes, you might have passed them by – and derived your claims from a more early race of ancestors."[8] Herodotus and Thucydides similarly encourage the Athenians to reconsider from whom they are deriving their claims. The conventional heroes and the stories that celebrate them turn out to be poor role models for the democratic citizenry.

The juxtaposition of the dramatically dissimilar literary forms of the two histories adds to the interest of this issue of political formation. There was a world of difference in the wars of Herodotus and Thucydides, and doubtless each conforms his writing to his times to some degree. In the *History*, Herodotus offers up cinematic-quality displays of nobility and unexpectedly heartening events: the Athenians at Marathon in 490 B.C.E., the Spartans at Thermopylae in 480. Storytelling appears to be the appropriate mode of communication, as Herodotus makes manifest immediately with his paradigmatic tale of Solon and Croesus. No doubt the *History* contains very serious undertones regarding the direction that Athens is taking in world events, but the Persian war still represents a pinnacle for Athenian democracy, as well as a rebuke to the absolutism of the Persian monarch. A display of the good and surprise ending seems called for, since the story is eminently worth telling. The *Peloponnesian War*, in contrast, transmits only the darkest messages, as Athens slips from its highpoint of democratic glory to what Thucydides calls "a total destruction" in Sicily in

[8] Burke 1987: 31.

413 B.C.E. (7.87.6). Here the teachings are cautionary, powerfully transmitted through the literary form of speeches and their steady devolution. The self-induced ruin of Athens is chronicled in the distance between the smooth, sophistic language of Pericles' Funeral Oration through the later more jarring expressions of imperial longing. Before the Athenians are decimated physically, they relinquish their self-definition and lose their spiritual hold. Eventually they become the type of overreaching imperial power that they had once vanquished during the Persian War. Thucydides locates the decline firmly in the Athenian speeches.

Despite the gulf that exists between these worlds and the disparate literary forms that seem appropriate for each to capture his respective era, Herodotus and Thucydides share an antityrannical posture that is more basic than their differences. If the character appropriations by ancient historians occur matter-of-factly, there is nothing naïve about them. Nor do Herodotus and Thucydides subscribe to a mouthpiece theory whereby they assimilate a character's words and their own "real" opinions. Thus it seems like the most ordinary move in the world when Herodotus steps into the shoes of Solon, famed wise man of Athens, or when Thucydides assumes something of a Periclean role, *his* character of choice. Only in contrast to historiographical practices today does this seem an unusual strategy for a historian. Perhaps this is due to the different considerations of democratic historians (de Tocqueville claims that we see "the actors much less and the acts much more"[9]), or perhaps it is due to our understanding of an objectivity based on the model of modern science. Whatever the reasons, what looks natural to ancient Greek historians appears peculiar to us today and gives us cause to reflect on their propensities and ours.

The historians standing behind these flawed characters devote such intense energy to making clear the futility of human knowledge that they can be assumed to be exceedingly sensitive to the question of their own impact.[10] They well know that absent the historian's construct, the message would simply vanish. If, as we shall see, Solon's advice giving is marred by his distance from the shared stories of the Athenians, Herodotus offers the corrective workings of his own fighting stories, the "diverse amplifications about an event of time past that begin immediately to fight their way into the discourse, and that persist over time in this discourse."[11] The "fight" in question concerns transmission.

[9] de Tocqueville 2000: 471.

[10] On this topic, H.-P. Stahl has written brilliantly on both historians; see Stahl 1975, 2003.

[11] "Fighting stories" are defined and further elaborated in Thompson 1996: 28 ff.

The kind of story sought by the Father of History is one that captures something sufficiently meaningful as to warrant its repetition. Like the *bon mot*, it wends its way into common parlance. The fighting stories of Herodotus have a communal authority in the sense that they are recognized as the accounts that define a particular community by embodying its aspirations or exhibiting its cultural presuppositions or perhaps simply by embodying its anxieties. Factual veracity is not the point for a story to qualify as a significant memory. It may be an illusion that such stories come wholly intact and ready-made, depending only on a willing raconteur like Herodotus to preserve them. But it does seem important that such stories or *logoi* have an independent existence that a historian may tap into; a very great historian will do more.

Meantime Pericles reveals the propensity to embrace the sophistic worldview with a confidence that is unearned. Thucydides imitates the Periclean voice to set up what eventually comes crashing down. War, Thucydides reminds us, is *biaios didaskalos*, a rough master (3.82.2). Both historians hold out the hope that in another time and place, the unlearned lessons from their age might get another review. The historians' purposes are political as well as literary, and revolve around making a tighter case against tyranny than their characters were able to effect. Herodotus and Thucydides identify with their characters, in other words, for the purpose of deepening their own testament to self-rule.

Herodotus and Solon

The Herodotean Solon takes the stage early in Book 1, after the historian has "put his mark" on Croesus, as the man who initiated unjust acts against the Greeks (1.5).[12] Solon appears in Sardis in the midst of his ten-year travel abroad ["that he might not be forced to abrogate any of the laws he had laid down" in Athens (1.29)]. Sightseeing, Herodotus comments, was an added attraction. And so from Egypt and the court of Amasis, Solon travels to Sardis and the great palace of Croesus. There Croesus eagerly displays the fabulous wealth of his Lydian kingdom before putting the infamous question to Solon of "whether, of all men, there is one you have seen as the most blessed of all" (1.30). Solon does not take the royal cue and pronounce *Croesus* as that blessed man, even

[12] Sage 1985: 52, observes that Croesus' "first mention by Herodotus is as *tyrannos* (1.6), and his connection with the first known tyrant, his ancestor Gyges, is emphasized."

when he is given two chances. Instead, Solon lists "Tellus the Athenian," and then the Argives "Cleobis and Biton" – and in elaboration, establishes the literary genius of Herodotus for all time.

Solon's response elicits the potential of the politics that is gradually emerging in Athens. Tellus is his choice for most blessed man because "his city was in good condition when he had sons," sons who survived to have children of their own. This was combined with the glorious ending Tellus (*telos*) had in battle, such that he was honored by the Athenians in a public funeral. The city is first, but the city is constituted by the family, more primal still; the ideal has the old soldier honored in front of his young descendants. Cleobis and Biton, the brothers who elicited the second prize from Solon (perhaps on account of dying young), also transform a favorable physical inheritance ("sufficiency of livelihood and strength of body" [1.31]) into a reputable accounting by their countrymen ("the following story is told of them . . . "). Lucky in ordinary ways, they constructed their own honorable ending. The fact that Solon tells this pair of stories together is significant, as he evokes a range of possible understandings of virtue, from political to religious. The great potential of Athenian politics would ever be in its capacity to prosper within such a range. Public and private commitments might be balanced in a way that enhances both; the tensions could be productive.

Solon's response to Croesus also suggests the dividing line between character and historian, specifically in the depiction of the divine in the Cleobis and Biton story. Cleobis and Biton display their filial piety by transporting their priestess mother to the temple in time for a festival. Congratulated on her sons "who had honored her so signally," the mother prays to the goddess "that she should give them whatsoever is best for a man to win." And that was the end of Cleobis and Biton: "they never rose more" (1.31). Solon interprets this story to mean that "in them the god showed thoroughly how much better it is for a man to be dead than to be alive." He reiterates this view in direct conversation: "Croesus, you asked me, who know that the Divine is altogether jealous and prone to trouble us, and you asked me about human matters" (1.32). This is Solon, not Herodotus, whose religiosity is never so off-putting. "When I do mention the gods," Herodotus asserts in his own voice, "it will be because my history forces me to do so" (2.3).

The picture that is sketched of the Herodotean Solon is of a reliably judicious and far-seeing man, *ahead* of his time politically, but also persistently *separate* from his contemporaries. His view of the divine comes across as disturbingly assured ("holier than thou"), and his manner of expression is stiff and not easily abided. Croesus thought him "assuredly a stupid man" (1.33). Without a doubt, Croesus will have cause to reconsider that evaluation, and it is the perennial fate of the wise advisor to be unheeded. Yet the reaction is nonetheless a telling one. Solon appears to be more straight-laced, less in touch with the common parlance, than the historian who depicts him. All this is conveyed by Herodotus in a few light touches, with hardly a hint of how consequential this proximity to the view "on the ground" is to his historiography.[13]

Still, there is very much more to connect the historian and character than to disconnect them. By now most readers of Herodotus accept some variation of Solon as "alter ego" of the narrator of the *History* on account of the way Solon's moralizing advice to Croesus echoes and reverberates in events recounted thereafter. Among other notable reiterations, this includes Amasis' advice to Polycrates (3.39–43) and Artabanus' explanations to Xerxes (7.10–12), and continues through the closing chapter, where Cyrus is shown warning his men that "it is not possible that from the same land stems a growth of wondrous fruit and men who are good soldiers" (9.122) – good counsel that they are pictured as accepting, contrary to all preceding events that Herodotus has recounted. Some readers continue to object to this characterization of the Herodotean Solon, however, since they regard any literary patterning as detracting from the mission of a serious historian.[14] Accordingly it is worth stressing how light the Herodotean touch is in these literary maneuvers, such that the levels of meaning discerned by readers depends on the knowledge brought to the text; the narrative itself works smoothly on multiple levels. And of course the historian frequently utilizes oblique methods to draw the parallels and lessons that are germane. As Shapiro notes, Herodotus employs literary devices like analogies, juxtapositions, and modified repetitions to encourage his

[13] Benardete 1969: 17, suggests that Solon is "still Greek" in his understanding: "He has Solon use the word *atē*, 'doom,' which often occurs in Solon's poetry but never again in Herodotus. The word is almost entirely poetic, endowed with the meanings which Greek poets have given it, and Herodotus makes it clear in Book II that he does not always agree with them." And on the Solon-Croesus encounter: "He emphasizes the Greek and hence partial view of Solon by attributing to him a mistake in calculation."

[14] See Waters 1971: 46 and 7: "A historian deals with events and with complexes of events, not with moral questions. . . . " See also Lang 1984: 3. The term "alter ego" is applied to Solon by Redfield 1985: 102.

readers "to consider the broader similarities that link [different] contexts together."[15] Thus from the moment that Herodotus sets out the Solon-Croesus *logos* in Book 1, it is evident that its issues – the envy of the gods and the instability of human happiness – are going to frame the whole of the history, without that frame becoming a straitjacket. The literary means are neither labored nor heavy handed. The fit is loose and allows for maneuverability; after all, the Solonian ideas that course through the Herodotean narrative oftentimes reduce to sound common sense, especially, as Harrison notes, for any historian worth his salt.[16]

Herodotus is no fool: the historical character with whom he aligns himself most pointedly is one of the Seven Wise Men of Greece. Plutarch relates the relevant tale of the golden tripod, a story that underlines the unassuming temperaments of the wise. The story goes that the golden tripod was thrown into the sea by Helen of Troy upon her return from the war. When the tripod eventually is recovered by some fishermen, there are bitter quarrels about its ownership. The issue is brought to Apollo. Finally the decree comes down from above: the tripod is to be presented to the wisest man. Thereupon the tripod is sent off to Miletus, to be offered to Thales. But Thales demurs, and sends the honored object to Bias at Priene. Bias in turn directs it to another of the Seven Wise Men, "and so, going round them all, it came to Thales a second time" – eventually to be dedicated to Apollo Ismenius.[17] It is noteworthy that the intellectual modesty associated with the Seven Wise Men here anticipates the Socratic understanding of the limitations of human knowledge: "that which I do not know, I do not think to know."[18] If that understanding suggests an impossibly high standard for ordinary folk, still, there is something generally appealing about that deprecation of self and the disposition that refuses to claim honors for wisdom. At any rate the Greek sages concur in conceiving of wisdom

[15] Shapiro 1996: 349. Similarly, Raaflaub 1987: 238–48, traces the "pointers" in Herodotus that meaningfully connect past and present events.

[16] Harrison 2000: 63. The place of Solon's advice to Croesus in the Herodotean narrative is captured perfectly well by Pelling's 2006 term 'benchmark': "These remarks certainly do not represent Herodotus' last words on human experience, but they are prominent among his first, and provide the benchmark against which we measure much of the subsequent narrative" (143).

[17] Plutarch, *Life of Solon* 4.3, trans. Dryden 1992: 109. In other renditions, Solon responds "the god is the wisest" and it is he who sends the tripod to Apollo. See Martin 1993: 120.

[18] Plato, *Apology* 21d, trans. Kremer 2006.

through privation: to be wise is *not* to overextend, *not* to presume too much, prefiguring another Socratic dictum "an unexamined life is not worth living" (38a).[19]

For his part the historical Solon's self-examinations led him to see much farther than his contemporaries, beyond the satisfaction of immediate desires to their long-term consequences. This is the preeminent Solonic virtue and a key reason he is the character of choice for Herodotus. Solon was constantly identified as "the father of democracy" (wrongly, but interestingly) and as a staunch opponent of tyranny, since he apprehended its long-term repercussions. Thus Plutarch attributes the following saying to Solon: "it was true a tyranny was a very fair spot, but it had no way down from it." Plutarch goes on to cite from a poem in which Solon characterizes himself as "a dreamer, and a man of simple mind": "When the gods would give him fortune, he of his own will declined; / When the net was full of fishes, over-heavy thinking it, / He declined to haul it up, through want of heart and want of wit" (115).

In his various poems, Solon, this "simple-minded dreamer," circles around formulations of the same theme, and always in a way that we could imagine Herodotus approving.[20] Solon appeals to the "court of Time," for example, where his actions will eventually be justified, even if they are not appreciated in the present: "others here in ugly serfdom at their masters' mercy I set free. These things I did in power, blending strength with justice."[21] Herodotus articulates a similar preoccupation with how the passage of time alters meaning, and he takes on the Solonic role of looking to the end in all things when he states in his own voice that he will treat alike "the small and great cities of mankind" in his inquiries. "For of those that were great in earlier times most have now become small," Herodotus writes, "and those that were

19 There remains an unbridgeable gap between Socrates and the different contenders for the archaic Seven Wise Men. Socrates eschews the performative role of the sages and does not honor the public stage on which they operate, as Martin 1993: 124, humorously notes: "No archaic sage invented the *elenchos;* it was the specialty of a man who constantly broke the frame of the performance by confronting his audience in dialogue and refusing to rely on the power of emphatic, unidirectional self-presentation."

20 Chiasson 1986: 261: "Herodotus consciously and explicitly evokes the memory of Solon's verse . . . the conceptual affinities between them are sufficiently striking to suggest that Herodotus knew Solon's poetry well and attempted, with remarkable historical conscientiousness, to incorporate its most prominent themes into the speeches he composed for the Athenian."

21 Solon fr. 36 West. The poem cited by Plutarch is fr. 33 West.

great in my time were small in the time before. Since, then, I know that man's good fortune never abides in the same place, I will make mention of both alike" (1.5). Elsewhere the overlap between themes in the extant poetry of Solon and the Herodotean Solon are precise, as in: "But as to wealth, no limit's laid down clear for men, since those among us who possess the most strive to earn double" (fr. 13 West), not to mention the overarching theme of *koros* leading to *atē* and *hubris*. The line in Solon's poetry "surplus breeds arrogance" (fr. 6 West) is an abbreviated form of the pattern that underlies the biography of every Great King in Herodotus' *History*, culminating in the crazed wish of Xerxes to wish to eradicate all boundaries altogether from the Persian empire: "we shall show to all a Persian empire that has the same limit as Zeus's sky. For the sun will look down upon no country that has a border with ours, but I shall make them all *one* country, once I have passed in my progress through all Europe" (7.8).

Connected to the historical Solon's visionary perspective is the practical quality of judiciousness. "Hard to please everyone in politics," Solon remarks in his understated way, and his political career bears this out (fr. 7 West). He appeared to his fellow Athenians to be eminently fair-minded, and considering the times of tumult in which he lived, this was an exceptional status, and one that might have been put to excellent use. According to Plutarch, "the wisest of the Athenians, perceiving Solon was of all men the only one not implicated in the troubles, that he had not joined in the exactions of the rich, and was not involved in the necessities of the poor, pressed him to succour the commonwealth and compose the differences" (114). Thus began Solon's career as political reformer. Elected archon in 594 B.C.E., Solon attempted to restore civil order by softening the edges of class warfare. He faced the age-old political problem of factionalism, the Athenian version of which reduces simply to "rich versus poor." Solon's reforms were appropriately economic, most notably the cancellation of debts, the *Seisachtheia*, or the "Shaking-Off of Burdens." He took the occasion to reorganize the whole political structure of Athens, aligning different levels of property ownership with different levels of political participation. In a self-description preserved in poem 36, Solon writes of his attentions to both sides in the conflict: "I wrote laws for all, for high and low alike, made straight and just" (fr. 36 West).

But Solon's good deeds did not go unpunished (or at least unremarked) by either creditors or debtors. Both parties complained bitterly about being betrayed, the wealthy because Solon cancelled debts and abolished debt bondage for all time, and the poor because he resisted their demands to redistribute land. Aristotle (or his student) in *The Athenian Constitution* details how a slander spread about Solon allowing his friends to profit from foreknowledge about the *Seisachtheia*, and then adds the rejoinder: "Solon was so moderate and impartial in other respects that, when he could have got the rest of the people into his power and made himself tyrant over the city, he instead accepted the hatred of both sides and set a higher value on honour and the safety of the city than on his own advantage."[22] The price to be paid for Solon's moderation was the hostile resentment of everyone.

For better or worse, then, the historical Solon's reputation was for being able to articulate the middle position, even in an environment that was vitriolic. Above the fray and incorruptible, Solon inculcated respect for the law by his own example and was able to induce in the Athenians a greater self-consciousness of themselves as a political entity. Plutarch comments approvingly that Solon "gave general liberty of indicting for an act of injury," the point being that once the habit was instilled in the citizenry of sensing injustice as a collective transgression, each would begin "like members of the same body, to resent and be sensible of one another's injuries" (118). From perceived injustice to conceived justice: under Solon (perhaps for the first time), a political order was based "on a distinct idea of justice under enforced written laws, promoted by persuasion rather than divine commandment, and legitimated by a claim to have set its inhabitants free."[23]

Despite the malcontents, the historical Solon was selected to be lawgiver by his fellow Athenians. According to Plutarch, he was entrusted with complete power "to new-model and make laws for the commonwealth, giving him the entire power over everything, their magistracies, their assemblies, courts, and councils; that he should . . . dissolve or continue any of the present constitutions, according to his pleasure" (117). Once Solon had procured the agreement from the Athenians that no one but he could modify the laws for a period of ten years, he assured the existence and unchangeability of the code by simply removing *himself* from Athens (Hdt. 1.29). As lawgiver, then, Solon took on a role that was categorically distinct from that of a political mediator. A new dimension for reform was opened, one that brings to mind the *Social Contract* in which Rousseau delineates the uncanny characteristics of a Lawgiver. "Anyone who dares to institute

[22] [Aristotle], *The Athenian Constitution* 6.2–3, trans. Rhodes 1986.

[23] Lewis 2006: 122. Lewis concludes that Solon's is the first statement of political freedom in the West.

a people must feel capable of, so to speak, changing human nature; of transforming each individual who by himself is a perfect and solitary whole into part of a larger whole from which that individual would as it were receive his life and his being."[24] Rousseau's favorite example of Lawgiver is Lycurgus, someone who clearly has "recourse to an authority of a different order" and could "persuade without convincing."[25]

The legendary nature of Lycurgus is testified to elsewhere, including in the *History*, where Herodotus reports that the Pythia addressed him as a god (1.65). But how was Solon, a flesh and blood historical figure, to acquire this kind of authority? He would need his full persuasive powers, since the Athenians had self-consciously put themselves in his hands, without any supporting myth of divine origins. No analogue to Lycurgus existed in Athens. Certainly Solon seems to cultivate his own founding story in the tradition of Lawgivers, but that did not mean that it would be picked up in popular legend. As McGlew observes, the figure of Solon remained distant from the collectivity: "Any political figure could write his own story, as Solon did more deliberately than most, but none could himself make that story into a collective possession."[26]

One clue to Solon's failure to connect with the populace is mentioned by Plutarch: he seems to have promulgated a law against tyranny. The suspicion is raised through this instance that Solon was too naïve or idealistic to capture the imagination of the ordinary Athenian. In the "Comparison of Poplicola with Solon," Plutarch ranks Poplicola as the more intense opponent of tyranny and writes, "any one who attempted usurpation could, by Solon's law, only be punished upon conviction" (144). Even the guileless Plutarch knows better than to expect the despot to abide by ordinary regulations. The difficulties of prosecuting a tyrant through legal means are confounding, and McGlew concludes on this point that Solon's law against tyranny simply undercuts itself: "As an extrapolitical form of power, tyranny could not be eliminated by political means, since a man whose success proved him guilty of the charge of tyranny was not likely to allow the Areopagus to prosecute him."[27] It seems that Solon may have been too detached from political realities

[24] Rousseau 1997: II.7 (69). McGlew 1993: 106–7 perceptively notes that "Solon's laws were not *nomoi* (a word that Solon does not use) but *thesmoi*," which indicates a higher source of authority; his aim ultimately was "to prevent tyranny by establishing law (*thesmos*) in the place he himself had held as the mediator/lawgiver of Athens."

[25] Rousseau 1997: II.7 (70).

[26] McGlew 1993: 121.

[27] McGlew 1993: 114–15.

to be a lasting catalyst for change. For whatever reason, his reforms did not have the impact he wished, and he was to suffer the indignity of being succeeded by the tyrant Peisistratus. Aristotle's criticism of Solon in the *Politics* is relevant: despite the Solonic reforms, the Athenians did not cease to identify themselves by classes and so remained ill-suited to consider the claims to justice of others.[28]

Other more unpredictable dangers of tyranny were revealed in Solon's very act of abdicating personal rule in favor of the written law. Solon was justifiably proud of having "written down" the law such that it applied equally to all, yet as Socrates would argue famously in Plato's *Phaedrus,* it turns out that replacing the living ruler with inscribed law introduces its own perils of rigidity and reification.[29] Independent of their author, the laws might become despotic in their own right. "Paradoxically, Solon's disappearance has elevated the laws to the very position of preeminence that he himself refused to occupy," Steiner observes. "[T]he *thesmoi* have become effective masters of the city, unassailable and answerable to none."[30] Thus at the same time that Solon succeeded in making himself superfluous as the particular ruler, he also created a space for a potential tyrant, someone who did not possess his vision or share his restraint. Peisistratus was waiting in the wings.

Here is where Herodotean literary correctives come into play since the despotic possibilities that are opened up with the Solon's inscriptions apply equally to all writing. Herodotus faces reifying dangers in his history that are comparable to that of the lawgiver. In many respects the historical Solon serves as an excellent touchstone for the historian in dealing with such challenges. And that Herodotus heeded well Solon's mediating and impartial ways is borne out in the fact that among interpreters of the *History*, there is no consensus about whether the historian is pro-Athenian or pro-Spartan. While F. D. Harvey may be correct to label the view that Herodotus favors Athens the traditional one ("There seem, therefore, to be no good reasons for abandoning the traditional view that Herodotus was an admirer of Pericles and of the Athenian democracy"), others insist just as strongly that he supports Sparta ("Herodotus greatly admires Sparta in general, regarding her leadership in the Persian War as natural and inevitable").[31] Then there

[28] For further elaboration, see my account in Thompson 2001: 38–40.

[29] Thompson 2001: 53–61.

[30] Steiner 1994: 230–31.

[31] Harvey 1966: 255; Hart 1982: 68. For a fuller list of such examples, see Lateiner 1989: 263 nn. 17, 18.

is Plutarch, who believes Herodotus to be both anti-Athenian and a barbarian lover (*philobarbaros*).[32] Plutarch accuses Herodotus of a barely concealed malice and concludes that many people "have been deceived by the style (*lexis*) of Herodotus" (854e). More likely, the historian resembles Solon in his detachment, making his political sympathies difficult to identify.

But Herodotus does more. With the help of the historian, Solon taps into something larger than his mere self-representation. His transmutation from historical figure to Herodotean character is marked by his ability to encase his arguments in narratives suitable for generalization. Like the historian, Solon delivers proverb-like kernels of wisdom. "Herodotus' audience would have recognized his generalizations as *gnomai*," as John Gould writes in describing how Herodotus typically "explains and pigeonholes" some fact, action, or event, and brings it within the bounds of meaning: "The Greek word *gnōmē* is not quite what we call a proverb (since it can be the creation of an individual on the spur of the moment), but like a proverb it will have the form of generalization, a summing up of human experience ('divinity is envious'); it will be offered as a truth to be acknowledged by its hearers."[33] The Herodotean Solon is master of the *gnōmē*. In his own right, Solon becomes a fighting story, which wears its authority on its face.

The Herodotean Solon outlasts Harmodius and Aristogeiton, as a more deserving hero than either of them. In comparison, the tyrannicides are flat, and, despite the statuary, they come across as single-dimensional actors. The Herodotean Solon is ready to fight back as penetrating storyteller.

Thucydides and Pericles

By the time Thucydides is finished with Book 6 of the *Peloponnesian War*, the tyrannicides are finished as Athenian heroes as well. For the long term, and as a result of Thucydides' portrait, Pericles – not Harmodius and Aristogeiton – is associated with the formative political identity of Athens.[34] He is credited with the cultural enhancement of

[32] Plutarch, *The Malice of Herodotus* 857a, trans. Bowen 1992.

[33] Gould 1989: 81, continues: "What the proverb does not do . . . is require all subsequent experience to bear it out."

[34] Who remembers the valiant tyrannicides now? "Herodotus' digression is in its way as brilliant a stroke of diminution as Thucydides', but only Thucydides had the

Athens and the articulation of new democratic possibilities in the still-emerging political order: "Pericles thus met the challenge of the heroic tradition by showing that democracy would bring to all the citizens of Athens the advantages heretofore reserved for the well-born few. The Athenian democracy would encourage merit in its traditional form and reward it with victory, glory and immortality."[35] But for all of the positive characterizations of Pericles as statesman, orator, and general, his legacy is surprisingly ambivalent. Only gradually in the *Peloponnesian War* do readers apprehend that Pericles and his sophistic propensities lead to the same willful and morally bankrupt world as the one that embraced the adolescent story of the tyrant slayers.

This lesson is slow in coming because of the historian's close connection with his character. In the *Peloponnesian War*, the identification between Thucydides and Pericles is tighter even than that of Herodotus and Solon in the *History*.[36] The most emphatic evidence for this conjoinment occurs in Books 1 and 2, where the historian aligns his voice in the Archaeology with that of Pericles in the Funeral Oration. In turn, both Thucydides and Pericles appear to reflect the influence of the sophists. The last word is the historian's, however, and it is a cautionary one: Thucydides shows himself finally to be *in*, but not *of*, the sophistic world of Pericles. He may well have come to regret making the original identification so close. In any case the only lasting model of an antityrannical posture is not found in Pericles, the doer of deeds, but in the historian who shapes his memory. "Not Periclean Athens but the understanding which is possible on the basis of Periclean Athens is the peak."[37] Apprehending the statesman in his full worth and in his shortcomings, Thucydides is able to devise an improved statecraft.

Appropriately enough, readers of the *Peloponnesian War* credit the historian with an enormously complex narrative stance. Rood recalls the long-time warning about Thucydides: "the author and the man

intelligence to conceive and the skill to execute what is possibly the most subtle and effective disparagement of ancient times" (Fornara 1968: 406).

[35] Kagan 1991: 145.

[36] Parry 1972: 48, calls Thucydides "a passionate admirer of Periclean Athens" and cites Wade-Gery on the historian's relation to his character: "The devout disciple." Though many scholars believe that Thucydides does not maintain this passionate admiration, it is undeniable that many of his superb readers believe that he does. This impasse is disturbing, since the terms of Thucydides' approbation are necessarily at the crux of any interpretation.

[37] Strauss 1964: 229. Orwin suggests that Thucydides himself was once "afflicted by Athenianism," an affliction he hoped his history might serve to cure in others. Orwin 1994: 205.

may not be the same person."[38] Scholars have utilized the tools of narratology to explore Thucydides' so-called "focalization," the layering of points of view from which events are viewed and understood: "The narrator is the person narrating. The focalizer is the person who orders and interprets the events and experiences which are being narrated."[39] In the critical literature a consensus exists regarding the changes of meaning that are effected in some prominent examples of Thucydides' focalization. Such is the juxtaposition of Pericles' Funeral Oration, with its buoyant accounting of Athenian versatility ("all this ease in our private relations does not make us lawless as citizens" [2.37.3]), and the baleful Plague, when "men now did just what they pleased. . . . Fear of gods or law of man there none to restrain them" (2.53.1, 4). In other examples, the lack of comment by the historian speaks volumes, as when Thucydides describes the brutal actions of the Spartans against the Plataeans in 427. After the Spartans had set up a mock trial, they "slew them all without exception" (3.68.1). The reporting of this massacre is followed by Thucydides' careful description of the temple that the Spartans constructed on the site to honor the goddess Hera. Here the facts truly are allowed to speak for themselves.[40]

More controversial among Thucydides' readers is the issue of where the focalizer leaves off in Book 8 of the *Peloponnesian War*. Might the ending of a work of history that stops in mid-sentence and in a chaotic clutter actually be *intentional*? Greenwood theorizes that "the convoluted narrative in Book 8 is a reflection of the intricate plots that it describes, as opposed to the incomplete state of the work,"[41] and accepts the claim that Thucydides repudiates the voice with which he began his account. That possibility has been entertained over the years.[42] But even if we reserve final judgment on the status of Book 8, a prior question remains: why did Thucydides allow for the uncertainty,

[38] Rood 1998: 10 n. 8, citing Syme 1962: 52. Rood continues: "A dichotomy of story and discourse is no longer adequate; one must also allow for a referential level, and beyond that for the extra-textual level of the words and deeds of real people, even if this level is itself only accessible through other stories."

[39] Hornblower 1994: 134.

[40] As Jordan 1986: 142, remarks, the contrast of information is "so stark that it leaps from the page, revealing the Spartans for the religious hypocrites that they on this occasion prove to be."

[41] Greenwood 2006: 89.

[42] Connor's work has been pathbreaking: "We can already detect that [Thucydides'] treatment of this war will not fully reproduce the initial austere but confident approach to the Greek past but will break new ground and grow into a new form" (Connor 1984: 32).

such that serious scholars cannot agree about this most fundamental matter of interpretation? If Thucydides wanted to renounce his earlier voice, he could have done so more unambiguously. Why assume such an authentic-sounding Periclean voice, only to disclaim it later, if that, in fact, is what occurs?

In resolution I posit a very "Herodotean" Thucydides who anchors himself in the stories of his contemporaries to establish his credentials and his worthiness to debate – accepting what is perhaps the only conceivable basis from which to think historically. And if the inescapable voice of Thucydides' generation was sophistic, the inescapable orator was Pericles, who announces his own worth on the public stage. The greatness of Pericles was ever to be found in his irrepressible combination of unlikely qualities: "what was nominally a democracy was becoming in his hands government by the first citizen" (2.65.9). As "first citizen" Pericles had powers to shape the polity that were reminiscent of Solon's, the original lawgiver.

> Pericles indeed, by his rank, ability, and known integrity, was enabled to exercise an independent control over the multitude – in short, to lead them instead of being led by them; for as he never sought power by improper means, he was never compelled to flatter them, but, on the contrary, enjoyed so high an estimation that he could afford to anger them by contradiction. (2.65.8)

Thucydides conveys the "given" nature of Periclean power by reproducing his paradoxical genius on the page, and leaving him (uniquely) unopposed in his three speeches. Further, Thucydides supplies means for readers to *test* this prerogative of Pericles, pulling them into the rhetorical scene, to experience firsthand its default nature.[43] In this way the sophists supply the terms of understanding for ancient and contemporary readers alike.

Background description of the sophistic world comes to us most fully from the works of Plato. Protagoras in the Platonic dialogue of that name describes his sophistic expertise thus: "What I teach is sound deliberation (*euboulia*), both in domestic matters – how best to manage

[43] Debnar 2001: 22: "Thucydides' skill in accommodating rhetorical speech to his contemplative work has ensured that even readers are in danger of falling prey to the rhetorical guile of his speakers. Thus we are 'transformed into spectators' not only of his actions . . . but of speeches, which are also composed with the aim of having 'a similar effect on those who read about them.'"

one's household, and in public affairs – how to realize one's maximum potential for success in political debate and action."[44] Through Plato's various accounts we discern that with the spread of democracy (not to mention other political unrest), sophists like Protagoras and Gorgias presented themselves as the cutting-edge professional educators capable of teaching young students the techniques of political success. And as Plato's Socrates always hastened to add, in contrast to his own free exchange of ideas, the sophists charged a fee for their teachings. Sophists claimed proficiency in the art of persuasive speaking such that according to many scholars, "the whole teaching of the sophists is summed up in the art of rhetoric."[45] Substantively, sophists asserted human self-sufficiency, independent of religious truth or idealism and committed to the mechanistic view that human behavior follows observed laws of nature. As Protagoras famously remarked, "Concerning the gods I cannot know either that they exist or that they do not exist, or what form they might have, for there is much to prevent one's knowing: the obscurity of the subject and the shortness of man's life."[46] Faced with the unknowable, the sophists showed the capacity to suspend judgment at will on ethical conundrums, and tended to circumscribe evidence in favor of things that could be measured.

One ethical conundrum mentioned by Plutarch in his account of Pericles places the statesman in the forefront of the changing times. Plutarch reports that the eldest of Pericles' lawful sons, Xanthippus, was on poor terms with his father. In one moment of particular bitterness, Xanthippus attempted to ridicule him by imitating the typical discourses Pericles would have with the sophists who visited his house. Pericles, the son recounted, once spent an entire day in debate with Protagoras, pondering the theoretical question of who was responsible in an accidental death case: "whether the javelin, or the man that threw it, or the masters of the games who appointed these sports, were, according to the strictest and best reason, to be accounted the cause of this mischance."[47] This tame anecdote nevertheless brings to mind more caustic representations of the sophists elsewhere, such as in Aristophanes' *Clouds*. In that comedy, Socrates (pictured as a typically shameless sophist) heads the Thinkery, a school that specializes in the newest teachings while condemning everything old-fashioned: religion, filial piety, and all established law. And in a scene particularly relevant

[44] Plato, *Protagoras* 318e–319a, trans. Lombardo and Bell 1992.
[45] Guthrie 1969: 20.
[46] DL 9.51 = Protagoras fr. 4 DK (Sprague 2001 [1972]: 20).
[47] Plutarch, *Pericles* 36.3, trans. Dryden 1992: 232.

to Thucydides' *Peloponnesian War*, Aristophanes squares off Just Speech and Unjust Speech in a contest, with the result that Just Speech cannot defend itself. Aristophanes and Thucydides seem to have been in full agreement about the vulnerability of conventional virtues to sophistic mockery. "The ancient simplicity into which honor so largely entered," Thucydides would report in his first full account of *stasis*, "was laughed down and disappeared, and society became divided into camps in which no man trusted his fellows" (3.83.1).[48]

The Archaeology, however, is set before the downturn of the Athenians is evinced, and Thucydides' intersection with the sophists still looks innocent enough. Elsewhere as well, he shares the sophistic tendency to argue from the likely to the true; throughout, his speakers highlight "expediency" as one of their primary motives. And while Protagoras may have made famous the general method of inquiry through "antilogy," or the posing of opposite arguments, no one took this method further than Thucydides, as Finley argues: "the habit of grasping ideas by pairs and in contrast was fixed in his mind. . . . [It was] the most instinctive, necessary clothing of his thought."[49] This habit of grasping ideas by pairs results in Thucydides' uncanny ability to distance himself from the subject at hand. In the Archaeology, the materialist posture he assumes seems to be directly aligned with the Athenian mentality that made her an imposing imperial power. But he goes out of his way to praise the longevity of Sparta, as well as to stress her tradition of putting down tyrannies. Sparta "at a very early period obtained good laws, and enjoyed a freedom from tyrants which was unbroken" (1.18.1). This is not widely testified to elsewhere.[50] More off-putting, perhaps, is the abrupt rendition of the Persian War that has the Spartans assuming command of the confederate Hellenes "in virtue of their superior power," whereas the Athenians, "having made up their minds to abandon their city, broke up their homes, threw themselves into their ships, and became a naval people" (1.18.2). The vision is somewhat disquieting: "it is part of the text's ideology to withhold what many contemporary audiences wanted to hear and to approach the historical present from a future, historicizing vantage point."[51]

48 Price 2001: 88–89, 145, takes note of the unsuccessful record of conventional Hellenic values in the reported speeches: "Shared meanings dissolved under pressure of internal war."

49 Finley 1942: 46.

50 Price 2001: 128.

51 Greenwood 2006: 17.

At the same time, the materialist worldview of the Archaeology appeals in its Athenian guise because it suggests that at least some human beings have progressed to the point of being able to control large forces of history. From inauspicious beginnings (the "poverty of its soil"), Attica enjoyed freedom from faction such that Athens became the destination of "the most powerful victims of war or faction from the rest of Hellas" (1.2.5–6). Thucydides traces a path from the earliest stages of Greek history when homes were insecure to the later stage when governments were unstable; the progress evident in this historical development is aligned with political unity and boosted by naval power. "Money, commerce, naval power, and large-scale centralization are the necessary steps on the road which leads from a condition of simple barbarism to the developed and sophisticated empire of Athens."[52]

Characterized by the physically manifest, the Archaeology leaves little room for interpretation: the materialist reckoning is grounded in an immoveable reality. Thus a new and promising standard for historical evidence emerges as well.[53] By the close of this section, Thucydides writes confidently of his evidence that it might be useful to "those inquirers who desire an exact knowledge of the past as an aid to the understanding of the future" (1.22.4). Accordingly, lasting expressions of power are sought out, rather than symbolic signs of civilizational greatness. "For I suppose that if Sparta were to become desolate," Thucydides imagines, "and only the temples and the foundations of the public buildings were left, that as time went on there would be a strong disposition with posterity to refuse to accept her fame as a true exponent of her power" (1.10.2). He can assure posterity of a more reliable index of power.

Pericles reproduces the materialist tone from Thucydides' early chapters when he connects the observed power of the state to the Athenian character, "equal to so many emergencies, and graced by so happy a versatility" (2.41.1). He pictures Athens as the enviable center of interest to all Hellas ("we are rather a pattern to others than imitators ourselves" [2.37.1]), an image already prefigured by Thucydides in the Archaeology: "where Attica is a static point (*astasiastos*) in the midst of surrounding upheaval, cherished as a refuge by talented exiles who had fallen victim to *stasis* (civil unrest) in their own city-states (1.2.6)."[54] But for those who will hear, Herodotean echoes intrude to disrupt

[52] Grene 1967: 49.

[53] Edmunds 1993: 848: "Words formed on the base *dēl* are central to the argument of the Archaeology, where they constate manifest, inescapable evidence."

[54] Greenwood 2006: 48.

the static picture. Not that Pericles raises the question of the happiest man in anything like the directness of Croesus, but he *is* anxious to claim the highest degree of self-sufficiency for the Athenian citizen. Scanlon identifies Pericles as "a new Solon,"[55] but the self-sufficiency that Pericles holds up for inspection leans more toward Croesus than to that of his wise advisor. Athenian success, Pericles assures us, is all measurable: "we have not left our power without witness, but have shown it by mighty proofs" that will not "melt at the touch of fact" like some Homeric eulogy (2.41.4). Prompted by Pericles to view Athens as an unchanging paradigm, readers may be put in mind of the Great King Croesus and his futile efforts to secure oracular "promises" in his attempt to expand his empire. From the beginning, we recall, Croesus was hostile to Solonic storytelling, impatient with its open-endedness and desirous of staying with "just the facts." After all, he had a system to guarantee his future happiness, which he equated with imperial acquisition. That equation goes underground in the case of Pericles – happiness is not his trade – but for all that the assumption remains fully operative.

Thucydides' identification with Pericles has the effect, however, of dissuading too much watchful criticism on our part. For in the Archaeology, Thucydides, with his steely gaze and unsentimental approach, establishes as a new and authoritative standard for history his own judgment and his own deliberations. "Thucydides, an Athenian, wrote the history of the war between the Peloponnesians and the Athenians, beginning at the moment that it broke out, and believing that it would be a great war, and more worthy of relation than any that had preceded it. This belief was not without its grounds" (1.1.1). Henceforth to be historical is to be able to enumerate the grounds for argument. His authority "comes from his own demonstrated willingness to think, to argue with himself, to draw reasonable conclusions, and to deliver to us the result of his internal cogitations."[56] Thus may a historian be the measure of all things. Mythical digressions have no place in these cerebrations. Thucydides' devastating way of treating his forbears in the Archaeology is to treat legendary figures as if they were historically known. Minos, for example (1.4.1), is brought into line with human

[55] Scanlon 1994: 143. The echoes that Scanlon brings to the surface, particularly concerning the language of self-sufficiency, are indisputable. Once again, however, there are deep divisions among readers about whether these echoes are meant pejoratively or not. Scanlon's view that Pericles is being "ennobled"(156) by this allusion is doubtful; cf. Macleod 1983: 151.

[56] Dewald 1999: 236.

nature as the historian knows it – goaded by fear and attracted by profit. Thucydides' austere reasoning process is also at odds with the poet's world. Individual *kleos* or glory no longer seems to announce its own significance; those heroics pale next to "the large movements of power, by aggression or alliance," where the *locus* of power "is found in states and their resources rather than in individuals."[57] Thucydides draws attention to his distance from the poet, disallowing himself "the exaggeration which a poet would feel himself licensed to employ" (1.10.3). As Rutherford comments, thinking back to Herodotus: "This seems a narrower and more sombre world."[58]

Pericles elicits a similar non-poetic picture of a man who establishes authority based on his reasoning process and his ability to persuade others. There is no gainsaying the attractive features of the city he describes: "We cultivate refinement without extravagance and knowledge without effeminacy. . . . Our public men have, besides politics, their private affairs to attend to" (2.40.1–2). He discloses his own thought process in a way analogous to that of the Athenians presenting themselves to the rest of Greece: "We throw open our city to the world, and never by alien acts exclude foreigners from any opportunity of learning or observing, although the eyes of an enemy may occasionally profit by our liberality" (2.39.1). But when we look more closely at the education that Athens (and Pericles) offers, the details are elusive. For all of Pericles' mastery of how to manage the citizenry, he gives the Athenians very little in the way of ideals to attach to themselves. As stirring as the Funeral Oration or his other speeches might be in terms of their calls to forsake one's private good for the benefit of the state, we look in vain for a statement about justice or morality in general – the subject matter of old-fashioned storytelling.

For a disenchanted age like our own, the question of how long the non-poetic language of Pericles could induce great acts of self-overcoming is of no small interest. The sacrifices he calls for are ultimate ones. The Athenians are to subsume all under the collective power of the state: "you must yourselves realize the power of Athens, and feed your eyes upon her from day to day, till love of her fills your hearts" (2.43.1). But for these Athenians, another uncomfortable echo from the past might make itself felt, this time with Herodotus' Persians, among whom the individual counted only insofar as he was part of the whole. To Herodotus this mattered decisively in the outcome of the Persian

[57] Pouncey 1980: 10.

[58] Rutherford 1994: 64.

War, for at crucial junctures, the Persians had to be whipped into battle, evidently lacking a sense of self-worth sufficiently compelling to spur them on in times of mortal danger. With the Greeks it was different, or at least it became so; the Athenians in particular took on the storied role of defenders of political freedom and self-rule. But Pericles fears dwelling upon these old themes, already "too familiar" to his hearers, and instead honors their ancestors for passing down the country "free to the present time," complete with imperial acquisitions (2.36.1–4). Acquisitions were welcome, of course, but as "hedonism" could not stand alone as an inspiring factor, Pericles suggests that the Athenians were both rich in material goods and above them (2.40.1). His rhetoric seemed inspiring enough at the time, or was it the charismatic appeal of his own person?[59] It appears that the Athenians needed a fuller account of themselves, stories that could be retold in earnest and in pride, especially during this time when the traditional narratives were faltering. Thucydides notes that everything changed with his successors: "More on a level with one another, and each grasping at supremacy, they ended by committing even the conduct of state affairs to the whim of the multitude" (2.65.10).

What remains in force after the death of Pericles was the notion that the Athenians of the era during the Peloponnesian War lived in an age like no other. Thucydides inaugurates this line of thinking when he sets out the unique features of the war: "Never had so many cities been taken and laid desolate . . . never was there so much banishing and bloodshedding . . . there were earthquakes of unparalleled extent and violence; eclipses of the sun occurred with a frequency unrecorded in previous history . . . and that most calamitous and awfully fatal visitation, the plague" (1.23.2–3). Similarly, the sophists were quick to attach all forms of novelty to themselves. Relying on the fact of the matter and judging solely by the "weight" of evidence has the discernible effect of encouraging observers to conclude ("from the numbers") that a complete break in time has occurred. History becomes no guide at all, traditions lose their force, and "the new" tends to win out. Lloyd writes about the various "contests of wisdom" that occurred frequently during this time period in which participants would stress their own

[59] We are put in mind of Solon again; like him, Pericles may have underrated the importance of the leader actively working out the narrative that identified the people politically. Palmer 1992: 41, asks "whether Pericles' treatment of the political problem in his speeches took too much for granted, and whether he had reflected sufficiently on the fundamental beliefs that are necessary to keep a political community bound together in some kind of harmony." See also Monoson and Loriaux 1998: 289, 292.

innovative positions as a means to undermine those of their opponents: "the occasions for display that occurred . . . did not just permit, but must sometimes positively have *favoured* open, indeed ostentatious, claims to originality."[60] The trouble is that in such an atmosphere it is difficult to justify the continued existence of even the most basic identity traits. It seems to be Thucydides' special skill to denote convincingly how this rhetoric encourages those involved finally to *lose* their voices and, eventually, their political identities.

Pericles' language already betrays a shift in this direction as he encourages a thoroughgoing presentism. In the Funeral Oration Pericles famously claims that "our constitution does not copy the laws of neighboring states," and avers similarly that "we present the singular spectacle of daring and deliberation . . . in generosity we are equally singular" (2.37.1; 2.40.3–4). Such pronouncements are so particularized to Athens as to remove them from any potential cautionary lessons of the past. The Athenians thereby free themselves of the implicit criticism of prior ages. The new measure of their actions is the future, not the past, as Price concludes, with the result that the Athenians actually began to lose contact with the everyday language around them: "the Athenians in general had developed a peculiar – one could almost say private – way of speaking, of representing themselves and others to both themselves and others, which made perfect sense to them but was not heard in the same way by others."[61] Equally interesting is what they did not allow into their speech at all.

Pericles goes so far in his third speech as to acknowledge publicly to the Athenians that "what you hold is, to speak somewhat plainly, a tyranny; to take it perhaps was wrong, but to let it go is unsafe" (2.63.2). We recall Solon's competing slogan, "it was true a tyranny was a very fair spot, but it had no way down from it." Much can be read in the distinction between these two expressions. The *gnome* that Solon favors universalized the lesson being illustrated, inviting the listener to receive the lesson or not, either by prudence, in advance, or by experience, after the fact. Pericles' admission, in contrast, suggests the bad conscience of the Athenians and locks them into a predetermined end: there is nothing to be done about their situation now. Thus it will be jarring, but not altogether surprising, when Cleon ("the most violent man at Athens" [3.36.6]), himself takes on a Periclean tone when he warns his fellow Athenians against "forgetting that your empire is a despotism"

[60] Lloyd 1987: 90.

[61] Price 2001: 195, 181.

(3.37.2). With that kind of memory, the softer, traditional elements in the Athenian identity did not stand a chance.

Stuck with their despotic empire, Athenian leaders are equally doomed to make decisions based on the lowest common denominator, in the competing expressions of desire. The phenomenon recurs, again and again, of the most radical expression winning out in circumstances when all the measuring is done in quantitative terms. As Plato's Socrates details so unforgettably in the *Republic*, in the tyrant's soul, desire feeds on itself, promoting ever more desires, allowing reason a role only in aiding their satisfaction and perhaps to rationalize their existence. When desire becomes *the* generating cause of action, the most radical outcome begins to trump every less radical one, without a thought, as it were. Socrates' rendition of the tyrannical soul in the *Republic* and Thucydides' rendition of Athenian statesmen in the *Peloponnesian War* have much in common – moderating, statesmanlike voices are overridden by ever more strident self-assertions.

The phenomenon of politics devolving in this way to the bluntest, most self-promoting spokesmen has special resonance in our time. It goes back at least as far as the Athenian national legend of Harmodius and Aristogeiton. Stahl observes trenchantly of the Athenian legend that it completely reverses cause and effect to suit Athenian inclinations, and that the very same falsehood will incite their action in the future, even a whole century later: "Thucydides shows historical *misconception as a direct cause* of action which has jumped the rails of rational control."[62] For Thucydides' account of the tyrannicides in Book 6 serves as an excursus (514 B.C.E.) in the midst of his description of the catastrophic moment when Alcibiades is summoned home from Sicily for his alleged role in the desecration of the Herms (415 B.C.E.). The connection is in the Athenian habit of dealing in conspiracy theories, always "preferring to sift the matter to the bottom," as Thucydides writes: "instead of testing the informers, in their suspicious temper welcomed all indifferently, arresting and imprisoning the best citizens upon the evidence of rascals" (6.53.2). For a people to allow a conspiracy theory to stand at the center of the national legend corrodes its integrity for the long term. The historian offers the Athenians the occasion to reconsider their roots: the national symbol should be eminently transportable to the world, rather than the matter of a sordid private affair.

If the seductive lure of tyranny is ever present – in rulers, political entities, and individual thinkers – Herodotus and Thucydides show us

[62] Stahl 2003: 8.

the way to resist. After the Persian War, the Athenians became victim to their own imagination, opting for the simplistic and despotic line, feigning an openness to the world, and losing contact with what was said. The historians reestablish the critical contact with the vernacular. Thucydides stays with the sophists long enough to appreciate the claims of hard evidence, but he also apprehends how a materialist bent can take on its own momentum and become a destructive force. He surely appreciated the virtue of complexity and the value of hard fact, using them relentlessly to undermine the inaccurate traditions of the Athenians: "That Hippias was the eldest son and succeeded to the government is what I positively assert as a fact upon which I have had more exact accounts than others" (6.55.1). The point is not for him to become free from a point of view, much less to substitute "the whole truth, for a collective error," as Loraux charges.[63] Instead, he might be seen as attempting to insert an opening into the self-representations that were overdetermined, to leave room for individuals to reflect for themselves. Thucydides turns out to be supremely interested in the "soft touch" – the openness of a polity to the past, to cultural traditions, to the proverbs of everyday people who are willing to sum up human experience in search of truths universally recognized.

Like Herodotus before him, Thucydides established a new model of writing that could stand up the challenges of the day without being dictative. The genre of history becomes their exemplary act of newly founding and preserving the political order – the greatest theme of statecraft. Both transform the most pointed of national stories into generalizable, cautionary lessons. They thereby illustrate in action what Edmund Burke called for when he urged the French to pass by their ancestors who "appeared without much luster" in order to identify themselves with more noteworthy predecessors. This means precisely *not* living in accordance with a fantasy of one's own construction and wishful desire – *not* memorializing the likes of Harmodius and Aristogeiton in vain and superficial admiration – but holding up to a critical gaze heroes that the whole world can admire.

WORKS CITED

Benardete, S. 1969. *Herodotean Inquiries*. The Hague.

Bowen, A., trans. 1992. *Plutarch: The Malice of Herodotus (de Malignitate Herodoti)*. Warminster.

[63] Loraux 2000: 79.

Burke, E. 1987. *Reflections on the Revolution in France*, ed. J. G. A. Pocock. Indianapolis, IN.

Chiasson, C. C. 1986. "The Herodotean Solon." *Greek, Roman and Byzantine Studies* 27: 249–62.

Connor, W. R. 1984. *Thucydides*. Princeton, NJ.

Debnar, P. 2001. *Speaking the Same Language: Speech and Audience in Thucydides' Spartan Debates*. Ann Arbor, MI.

Dewald, C. 1985. "Practical Knowledge and the Historian's Role in Herodotus and Thucydides." In *The Greek Historians: Literature and History: Papers Presented to A. E. Raubitschek*. Saratoga, CA.

1999. "The Figured Stage: Focalizing the Initial Narratives of Herodotus and Thucydides." In *Contextualizing Classics: Ideology, Performance, Dialogue*, ed. T. M. Falkner, N. Felson, and D. Konstan. Boston.

Dryden, J., trans. 1992. *Plutarch's Lives*, vol. I, ed. and rev. A. H. Clough. Modern Library Classics. New York.

Edmunds, L. 1993. "Thucydides in the Act of Writing." In *Tradizione e innovazione nella cultura greca da Omero all'età ellenistica. Scritti in onore di Bruno Gentili*, ed. R. Pretagostini. Roma.

Finley, J. H., Jr. 1942. *Thucydides*. Cambridge, MA.

Fornara, C. W. 1968. "The 'Tradition' About the Murder of Hipparchus." *Historia*: 400–24.

1971. *Herodotus: An Interpretative Essay*. Oxford.

Gould, J. 1989. *Herodotus*. London.

Greenwood, E. 2006. *Thucydides and the Shaping of History*. London.

Grene, D. 1967. *Greek Political Theory: The Image of Man in Thucydides and Plato*. Chicago. Originally published as *Man in His Pride: A Study in the Political Philosophy of Thucydides and Plato* (Chicago, 1950).

Trans. 1987. *Herodotus: The History*. Chicago.

Guthrie, W. K. C. 1969. *A History of Greek Philosophy*, vol. III: *The Fifth-Century Enlightenment*. Cambridge.

Harrison, T. J. 2000. *Divinity and History: The Religion of Herodotus*. New York.

Hart, J. 1982. *Herodotus and Greek History*. New York.

Harvey, F. D. 1966. "The Political Sympathies of Herodotus." *Historia* 15: 254–55.

Hornblower, S. 1994. "Narratology and Narrative Techniques in Thucydides." In *Greek Historiography*. Oxford.

Jordan, B. 1986. "Religion in Thucydides." *Transactions of the American Philological Association* 116: 119–47.

Kagan, D. 1991. *Pericles of Athens and the Birth of Democracy: The Triumph of Vision in Leadership*. New York.

Kremer, M., trans. 2006. *Plato and Xenophon Apologies*. Focus Philosophical Library. Newburyport, MA.

Lang, M. L. 1984. *Herodotean Narrative and Discourse*. Cambridge, MA.

Lateiner, D. 1989. *The Historical Method of Herodotus*. Toronto.

Lewis, J. 2006. *Solon the Thinker: Political Thought in Archaic Athens*. London.

Lloyd, G. E. R. 1987. *The Revolutions of Wisdom: Studies in the Claims and Practice of Ancient Greek Science*. Sather Classical Lectures 52. Berkeley, CA.

Lombardo, S., and K. Bell, trans. 1992. *Plato/Protagoras*. Indianapolis, IN.

Loraux, N. 2000. *Born of the Earth: Myth & Politics in Athens*, trans. S. Stewart. Myth and Poetics. Ithaca, NY.

Macleod, C. 1983. *Collected Essays*. Oxford.

Martin, R. P. 1993. "The Seven Sages as Performers of Wisdom." In *Cultural Poetics in Archaic Greece: Cult, Performance, Politics*, ed. C. Dougherty and L. Kurke. New York.

McGlew, J. F. 1993. *Tyranny and Political Culture in Ancient Greece*. Ithaca, NY.

Monoson, S. S., and M. Loriaux. 1998. "The Illusion of Power and the Disruption of Moral Norms: Thucydides' Critique of Periclean Policy." *American Political Science Review* 92: 285–97.

Ober, J. 2003. "Tyrant Killings as Therapeutic Stasis: A Political Debate in Images and Texts." In *Popular Tyranny: Sovereignty and its Discontents in Ancient Greece*, ed. K. A. Morgan. Austin, TX.

Orwin, C. 1994. *The Humanity of Thucydides*. Princeton, NJ.

Palmer, M. 1992. *Love of Glory and the Common Good: Aspects of the Political Thought of Thucydides*. Lanham, MD.

Parry, A. 1972. "Thucydides' Historical Perspective." *Yale Classical Studies* 22: 47–61.

Pelling, C. 2006. "Educating Croesus: Talking and Learning in Herodotus' Lydian Logos." *Classical Antiquity* 25: 141–77.

Pouncey, P. R. 1980. *The Necessities of War: A Study of Thucydides' Pessimism*. New York.

Price, J. J. 2001. *Thucydides and Internal War*. Cambridge.

Raaflaub, K. A. 1987. "Herodotus, Political Thought, and the Meaning of History." In *Arethusa: Herodotus and the Invention of History* 20.1–2: 221–48.

Rawlings, H. R., III. 1981. *The Structure of Thucydides' History*. Princeton, NJ.

Redfield, J. 1985. "Herodotus the Tourist." *Classical Philology* 80: 97–118.

Rhodes, P. J., trans. 1986. *Aristotle: The Athenian Constitution*. New York.

Rood, T. 1998. *Thucydides: Narrative and Explanation*. New York.

Rousseau, J.-J. 1997. *The Social Contract and Other Later Political Writings*, ed. V. Gourevitch. Cambridge Texts in the History of Political Thought. Cambridge.

Rutherford, R. B. 1994. "Learning from History: Categories and Case-Histories." In *Ritual, Finance, Politics: Athenian Democratic Accounts Presented to David Lewis*, ed. R. Osborne and S. Hornblower. New York.

Sage, P. W. 1985. *Solon, Croesus and the Theme of the Ideal Life*. Ph.D. diss., Johns Hopkins University. Baltimore, MD.

Scanlon, T. F. 1994. "Echoes of Herodotus in Thucydides: Self-Sufficiency, Admiration, and Law." *Historia* 43: 143–76.

Shapiro, S. O. 1996. "Herodotus and Solon." *Classical Antiquity* 15: 348–64.

Sprague, R. K., ed. 2001 [1972]. *The Older Sophists. A Complete Translation by Several Hands of the Fragments in Die Fragmente der Vorsokratiker Edited by Dielz-Kranz with a New Edition of Antiphon and of Euthydemus*. Indianapolis, IN.

Stahl, H.-P. 1975. "Learning Through Suffering? Croesus' Conversations in the History of Herodotus." *Yale Classical Studies* 24: 1–36.

2003. *Thucydides: Man's Place in History*. Swansea.

Steiner, D. T. 1994. *The Tyrant's Writ: Myths and Images of Writing in Ancient Greece*. Princeton, NJ.

Strassler, R. B., ed. 1996. *The Landmark Thucydides: A Comprehensive Guide to the Peloponnesian War*. New York.

Strauss, L. 1964. *The City and Man*. Chicago.

Syme, R. 1962. "Thucydides." *Proceedings of the British Academy* 48: 39–56.

Taylor, M. W. 1991. *The Tyrant Slayers: The Heroic Image in Fifth Century* B.C. *Athenian Art and Politics*, 2nd ed. Salem, NH.

Thompson, N. 1996. *Herodotus and the Origins of the Political Community: Arion's Leap.* New Haven, CT.

2001. *The Ship of State: Statecraft and Politics from Ancient Greece to Democratic America.* New Haven, CT.

Tocqueville, A. de. 2000. *Democracy in America*, trans. and ed. H. C. Mansfield and D. Winthrop. Chicago.

Waters, K. H. 1971. *Herodotos on Tyrants and Despots: A Study in Objectivity*. Wiesbaden.

West, M. L., trans. 1993. *Greek Lyric Poetry: The Poems and Fragments of the Greek Iambic, Elegiac, and Melic Poets (Excluding Pindar and Bacchylides) down to 450* BC. Oxford.

4: Thucydides and Political Thought

Gerald Mara[1]

While the works of Plato and Aristotle draw universal attention from students of political philosophy, Thucydides' reception has been more limited and localized. Most frequently, he is sought for his contributions to international relations theory, often accessed through a small number of set pieces such as the Melian dialogue. Whatever the reasons for this relative lack of attention, it is unfortunate, for Thucydides is an important conversation partner not only with more familiar voices within the so-called Western tradition of political philosophy but also with modern political theorists who discuss the functions and disorders of political institutions and political cultures. In this connection, Thucydides may have more to contribute to democratic political theory than is often supposed. Appreciating his contributions means taking him at his word when he writes early in Book 1 of the *History* that he has composed "a possession forever, and not a competitive entry to be heard for the moment" (1.22).[2] Yet the precise meaning of this very ambitious claim is unclear. Interpreting it is inseparable from coming to grips with the kind of work this is.

Assessments of the genre of Thucydides' work proliferate. He has been read as a historian who narrates and explains the most striking events of his time, as a social theorist who discovers the deepest causes of political disorder, and as a memorializer of the civic leadership

[1] I am particularly grateful to Jill Frank and Stephen Salkever for their comments and criticisms on earlier drafts. Significant portions of this chapter draw on much longer discussions in *The Civic Conversations of Thucydides and Plato: Classical Greek Political Theory and the Limits of Democracy*, State University of New York Press (2008).

[2] My central resources for translations of Thucydides are the editions of Lattimore 1988 and Smith 1962–88, though I have made changes when they seemed appropriate.

of Pericles. To the extent that we are convinced by one or more of these judgments, however, Thucydides' voice is heard as conclusive and monologic and the political thought that emerges from the pages of his work stands apart from the immediate context of political life. In what follows I will try to suggest that none of these interpretations fully succeeds in capturing the complexity of Thucydides' book. My goal goes beyond commenting on these other views, however. The alternative readings that I offer suggest that Thucydides' narrative should be interpreted as contributing resources for the thoughtful judgments and practices of citizens, not simply within his own immediate political cultural context but within political futures whose contours are necessarily indeterminate. I therefore read the contention that this work is a possession forever as an invitation for a reflective and critical appropriation of the text and as an acknowledgment that the outcomes of such engagements are unpredictable and risky. Consequently, Thucydides' book is not a distant and conclusive series of pronouncements but a speech act that is embedded in political interaction. As such, it stimulates a form of political thought that is critical and discursive, a way of thinking about politics that is particularly appropriate for and possible within democracies.

Narrative and Time

Thucydides' book appears most frequently under the title *History of the Peloponnesian War.* For the classical Greeks, a *Historia* signified an investigation, a "learning by inquiry," as one of Liddell and Scott's translations puts it. Thus understood, a "history" presumes a complex, puzzling, and significant field of phenomena that can be made clearer through careful scrutiny. The professionalization of the academic disciplines, particularly in the nineteenth and twentieth centuries, both sharpened and narrowed this intellectual focus to construct the writing and teaching of history as we have come to know it. Consequently, a number of modern scholars read and evaluate Thucydides' work according to professional standards of historical research. Such readings have asked if Thucydides' account of the causes of the Peloponnesian War is consistent with the available evidence, if his treatments of the events he narrates and the figures he represents are objective and unbiased, and so on.[3] Asking these questions can provide valuable guidance for further

[3] See Kagan 1969; Hanson 1996.

historical inquiry into the period and events that occupy Thucydides. However, this perspective can be ironically anachronistic in its conception of the book's genre. Thucydides begins simply by stating that he has "written about" or "brought together by writing" (*sunegrapsē*) the events of the war, a characterization of his project that continually repeats. Construing this "writing" as a history in more familiar disciplinary terms may limit the questions we ask about the work and undercut the extent of its contributions to the ways in which we think seriously about politics.

Admittedly, Thucydides encourages readers to treat his book as an explanatory and narrative history, particularly in his methodological comments in chapter 26 of Book 5. Responding to those who contend that the Peace of Nicias interrupted the course of the war, and who thus deny that the war was a single event, Thucydides underscores the continuities linking the truce with preceding and succeeding periods of outright war and concludes that this was indeed one conflict, lasting twenty-seven years (431–404 B.C.E. from beginning to end. He writes about these events "as they each came to be in the order of summers and winters." These comments seem to imply that we should read his "writing" as a linear narrative whose order follows the sequence of events as they occurred in time.

Yet while this periodization circumscribes the core of Thucydides' narrative, it does not define it. Even casual readings make clear that there is far more to the book than a report of these events "as each of them came to be." At the outset, the structure of what later editors have organized as the first book of the *History* unsettles senses of linearity. Thucydides begins with an explanation of why he chose to write about the war. Its scope and power suggested immediately that it would be "most worthy of being spoken about" (*axiologōtaton*). He follows this claim with an account of the construction of the Hellenic culture (within a set of chapters – 1.2–19 – known as the Archeology), focusing particularly on the two principal regimes of Athens and Sparta (1.2, 6, 10, 18, 19), and then steps back once again to comment more synoptically (1.20–23) on the character of his work. These last statements include a different reason for believing that the war was an *axiologōtaton*, not sweep and energy but the suffering and dislocation that resulted (1.23). He also offers (1.23) his own belief about the "truest causes" of the war, the greatness of the Athenians and the fearfulness of the Spartans, reinforcing the sense that commentary on the character of these two very different political cultures will be central to what follows. He then begins a substantial account (1.24–88) of the events leading up to the beginning of the war itself, the bases of the "most openly spoken accusations [against Athenian aggression]" (cf. 1.23). This is followed by an extended narrative (1.89–117, the *Pentecontaetia*) that selectively describes the fifty years between the end of the Persian Wars and the prelude to the Peloponnesian War. He then resumes (1.118) the account of the events immediately prior to the war. However, the linearity of this last narrative section is in itself interrupted by considerations (1.128–38) on the careers of the foremost Athenian (Themistocles) and Spartan (Pausanias) of that time.

Departures from linear time horizons are not confined to the first book. Perhaps most notably, in the midst of the description (in Book 6) of the events following the mutilation of the statues of Hermes and the alleged profanation of the Eleusinian mysteries that took place prior to the massive Athenian invasion of Sicily, Thucydides offers a long (6.54–59) excursus on the historically distant (514 B.C.E.) events surrounding the deaths of the famous tyrannicides, Harmodios and Aristogeiton, whose heroism is alleged to have marked the end of the Peisistratid tyranny and the beginnings of Athenian political freedom.

Though earlier commentators often read such gaps within linear history as lapses on Thucydides' part, it is now more generally recognized that they play deliberately crafted roles in his writing. The *Pentecontaetia* closely follows a speech given by unnamed Athenians at Sparta to the members of the Peloponnesian coalition who assemble to make a decision that will move the two sides closer to war or peace. The Athenians offer an account of the beginnings of Athens' empire following the Persian wars, ultimately attributing its creation to the influence of the compelling and conquering forces of fear, honor, and interest (1.75–76). As Thucydides' account of the empire's beginnings given in his own name, the *Pentecontaetia* serves as a commentary on this partisan Athenian statement. The Thucydidean account of the empire's beginnings prompts a more direct engagement with the question of the relative influence of the three alleged compulsions (which are listed twice by the Athenians, the second giving first place to honor rather than fear), the adequacy of accepting the Athenian thesis (Clifford Orwin's phrase[4]) that the creation of the empire was in fact compelled, and the meaning or meanings of compulsion (*anankē* and its variations) within the work generally.

The comparative biographies of Themistocles and Pausanias can likewise be read as playing significant and complicating roles with

[4] Orwin 1994: 44–56.

respect to portions of the work that immediately surround them. The example of Themistocles, who moves from being champion of Athenian interests (1.90–93) to traitor (1.137–38), problematizes the closely following Periclean statement (1.144) that the well-being of cities and individuals harmonizes in the pursuit of honor in the face of the greatest risks. The career of Pausanias undercuts the valorization of the Spartan culture of discipline and deference to the laws proclaimed earlier by the Spartan king Archidamus (1.84). More generally, these biographies reinforce the *History*'s focus on the role of political culture in shaping individual practice. The actions of Themistocles and Pausanias are both of and not of their respective cities; both their dependence upon and challenges to their own regime's priorities are provocative reflections of the complexities of the regimes themselves. Themistocles exhibits a pursuit of individual renown that is distinctly Athenian even as it compromises Athenian interests; Pausanias gives himself over to luxury and arrogance in a way that both defies and presupposes Spartan severity. Numerous readings of Thucydides have emphasized that his treatment of political interactions focuses heavily on the influence exerted by political cultures or regimes. Some of these interpretations have gone further to argue that Thucydides' understanding of regimes is essentialist or reductive.[5] Juxtaposing the stories of Themistocles and Pausanias with statements made by other figures in the work who do, in fact, essentialize the Athenian and Spartan regimes complicates this judgment. The Corinthians overgeneralize when they characterize (1.68–71) the Athenians as energetically public spirited and the Spartans as restrained stay-at-homes. Thucydides' broader perspective suggests that regimes need to be understood in terms not only of coherence and power but also of contradiction and contestation.

The tyrannicide excursus plays heavily into a broader treatment of how political memory functions to strengthen or disrupt forms of political action. The extended treatment of 6.54–59 is both continuation and revision of a much more compressed reference (1.20) offered as part of the synoptic methodological remarks in Book 1. In the first passage, Thucydides criticizes the erroneous Athenian memory that enshrines the liberation achieved by the tyrannicides. Here memory fails to fulfill what Paul Ricoeur calls its truthful function;[6] the Athenians did not realize that those they call the tyrannicides killed only the tyrant's brother Hipparchos, leaving the tyrant himself, Hippias,

[5] Cf. Sahlins 2004: 46–49.

[6] Ricoeur 2004: 88.

alive and in power. However, when, in Book 6, he considers how the tyrannicide symbol influenced reactions to the mutilations, Thucydides claims that the Athenians knew that the Peisistratids were put down "not by themselves and Harmodios but by the Spartans." Possessing truthful memory does not, however, ensure the appropriate response. Here memory fails in the context of Ricoeur's pragmatic function,[7] for the anxiety stemming from a correct memory of the facts surrounding the tyranny's overthrow leads the Athenians to reenact a politics of fear and violence. Knowing that Hippias' rule became harsh in the end, the Athenians still fail to understand the reasons for it. In a way, the tyranny's lapse into violence is traceable to the thoughtless daring (*alogistos tolma*) of the tyrannicides themselves (6.59.1). They were motivated not by a public-spirited love of freedom, but by more personal disputes and resentments (6.56). And it was the murder of Hipparchos that caused the onset of Hippias' truly "tyrannical" rule (6.59). Haunted by vulnerability and a fear of new subversions prompted by the mutilations and the alleged profanations, the democracy turns to violence in a way that parallels the harshness of the last of the Peisistratids (6.60).

From this perspective, recalling the deficiencies of the tyrannicide story clarifies two ways in which political memory can contribute to healthy political activity. The first is to know the factuality of events so as to resist impulses for cultural romanticization and self-congratulation. The second is to respond to a knowledge of the facts in an appropriate way. To the degree that Thucydides' *History* is an attempt to provide resources for both functions, it must be seen as more than simply a narrative of events as they have come to occur. It is, instead, a *historia* in its richer and more complicating sense, part of an ongoing and interactive investigation concerned with civic conduct and direction.

Action and Speech

Thucydides' concern to provide resources for both truthful and pragmatic memory may help to interpret his provocative comments (1.22) on how he has framed his distinctive treatments of the actions (*erga*) and the speeches (*logoi*) that together constitute his narrative. He notes that he has been as accurate as possible with respect to the *erga*, "neither crediting what I learned from the chance reporter nor what seemed to me [to be credible], but [writing only] after examining what I was involved

[7] Ricoeur 2004: 88.

with myself and what I learned from others" (1.22). With respect to the speeches, "recalling precisely what was said was difficult"; consequently, he represents what "seemed to me each would have said [as] especially required (*ta deonta malist' eipein*) on the occasion, [yet] maintaining as much closeness as possible to the general sense (*gnōmēs*) of what was truly said" (1.22). At first blush, this distinction seems to reflect the concerns of a writer who approaches his field of investigation in a way that strives to achieve the greatest degree of factual accuracy. Josiah Ober interprets this comment as reflecting Thucydides' suspicion of speeches that are not tested against the reality of deeds. Heard in contexts that do not allow for such verification, speeches are too susceptible to manipulation or misunderstanding to serve as adequate guides to practice. For Ober, the suspicion of unverified speech is one of the bases for Thucydides' strong critique of democracy.[8] Yet Thucydides' treatment of events and speeches can be interpreted in a way that reflects a more complicated concern to provide resources for both truthful and pragmatic memory. Striving to be as accurate as possible with respect to *erga* acknowledges the importance of truthful memory, while presenting the *logoi* most required by each situation critically inscribes a variety of pragmatic efforts to respond to – to understand or to control – the order of political events within the narrative as a whole. In this respect, Thucydides' speakers become conversation partners among themselves, with Thucydides and for an indefinite range of potential readers.

While the thematic consideration of deeds and speeches is one of the central concerns of the *History* as a whole, the possibility of establishing either a clear hierarchy or even a firm separation between them is less apparent. Thucydides himself suggests that the criteria for distinguishing between speech and action are not as definite as this preliminary methodological framework implies. The war as a whole is called an *ergon* (1.22.2) and the entire narrative that represents it is a *logos*.[9] The collection of narrated speeches includes not only directly quoted statements but also many indirect discourses. While the choice between direct and indirect forms of representation may seem arbitrary or incidental, Thucydides' resorting to one mode or the other seems intentional. The only speech that qualifies as a (kind of) direct speech in Book 8 – 8.53.3 – presents the language of a planned statement before

[8] Ober 1998: 57.

[9] On the relation between *logos* and *ergon* in Thucydides, generally, see also Parry 1981: 9; Price 2001: 74–75; and Strauss 1964: 163.

it is uttered. This speech is to be delivered in the context of attempts to persuade the Athenian *dēmos* to make the city's governance more oligarchic. Thus, one consequence of the success of this speech will be to censor the content of future speeches – "In our deliberations [we must] take less heed of the regime and more of safety." The silencing of political speech by the temporarily ascendant oligarchy is therefore reflected in the style of the narrative itself. Some indirect speeches are significant because of their practical consequences, as when Alcibiades persuades the army on Samos not to sail against oligarchically governed Athens (8.86). Others deserve attention because of what they reveal about political cultural conditions, as when Boeotian and Athenian heralds give competing views on the relation between piety and military power in an exchange reported within the account of the Athenian defeat at Delium (4.97–99). Though the direct speeches are specifically marked as such within the text and therefore separated from deeds or actions, they must also be understood as deeds in the form of speech acts.[10] The pragmatic character of these utterances is sometimes set by institutional or cultural contexts, Pericles' funeral speech, for example.[11] Others have more dramatic and immediate outcomes, for example, Diodotus' success in pleading for mercy toward the Mytilene democrats (3.41–49) or the Melians' fatal defiance of the Athenian demand for submission (5.84–116). However, others – the hopeless pleas of the defeated Plataens as they attempt to escape capital punishment (3.53–59) or the formulaic exhortations of Nicias during the retreat from Syracuse (7.77) – are notable precisely because they are completely without consequence.

Another reason to question sharp distinctions between speeches and actions within the narrative is Thucydides' statement that much of what he learned about the war's *erga* depended on reports provided by others.[12] As reports, such speeches are indeed susceptible to error and misrepresentation. Yet this is more than a methodological problem for a serious historian. It seems to be a clear recognition that no facts can ever speak for themselves. However, on some occasions Thucydides seems to say quite clearly that they can, particularly (at 1.1 and 1.23) when they decisively show the war's importance, as a coherent series of deeds worthy of speech. While this might not eliminate the need for the historian, as Ober speculates, it may reinforce Connor's observation

[10] On the varieties of speech acts, see for example Butler 1997: 44.

[11] See for example, Loraux 1986: 180–93.

[12] Noted by Ober 1998: 59–60; cf. Saxonhouse 2004: 64–65.

that the historian's primary role is to make the facts plainly visible to the readers.[13]

As suggested above, however, in these two passages the facts "say" very different things. In his first statement, Thucydides indicates that he began writing about the war because he believed that it would be "great and more worthy of being spoken about than any previous war." In this connection, he emphasizes the war's power and scope. "For this was the greatest motion (*kinēsis . . . megistē*) that had come to be among Greeks and even [among] portions of the barbarians, indeed one may speak of [the involvement of] most of humanity" (*pleiston anthrōpōn*) (1.1.2). This war is thus truly worthy of being spoken about because of its spectacular displays. Yet this contention itself presupposes a valorization of particular criteria of worth, scope, motion, and energy, all of which would be prized within an Athens that the Corinthians describe (1.70) as obsessed with daring, even reckless, motion. These same evaluative standards are given pride of place by Pericles in the funeral speech where the fact of greatness itself makes linguistic representations of greatness unnecessary. "With the great display and asserting power that has not gone unwitnessed, we will be the wonder of both those now living and those who follow, needing no Homer to praise us nor any other whose phrases might please for the moment, but whose claims the truth of [our] deeds (*ergōn . . . hē alētheia*) will destroy" (2.41.4). This statement extends to his broader characterization of Athens as a city remarkable for deeds, not words. It uses all of its resources "more for critically timed action (*ergou mallon kairō*) than [for] boastful speech" (2.40.1). Yet in spite of Pericles' express contentions, Athens' deeds do in fact require more than a simple perception of their power. Their inspirational significance depends upon Pericles' ability to persuade the Athenians about the criteria that should be applied within any exercise of civic judgment.

In appealing (1.1) to energy and motion as signs of the war's importance, Thucydides appears to validate a Periclean sense of what makes deeds or practices notable. Yet those criteria are challenged within Thucydides' second explanation of the reasons behind the war's importance. At 1.23, the facts communicate not only energy and daring

> but also such sufferings as came to afflict Hellas unlike those [experienced] in any [length of] time. For never had there been so many cities seized and abandoned, some by

[13] Ober 1998: 56; Connor 1984: 29.

> barbarians and others by the Hellenes warring against each other (and some even changed population after they were overpowered), nor were there so many human beings dislocated or slaughtered, both on account of the war itself and because of factional fighting.

These ugly sufferings and hatreds are consistently concealed or diminished in Pericles' own direct speeches (2.43–44, 64). What he represents as most important for human beings is a love of honor that is fulfilled by the anticipation of an eternal remembrance for one's name (2.64.5). In underscoring the sufferings caused by the war, Thucydides reinstates criteria of significance that Pericles' *logos* had effectively diminished. Thus, the facts cannot simply speak for themselves. They are given very different significances, first by the Periclean affirmation of daring and reputation, and then by the challenging and problematizing narrative of Thucydides. Consequently, one could read these claims that the facts speak for themselves as introducing a question that recurs within the narrative as a whole: What truly makes events most worthy of being spoken about (*axiologōtaton*)?[14]

Since facts speak only through *logoi* that may signify and evaluate *erga* very differently, what does Thucydides mean when he claims to have represented the speeches as they were "especially required in the given situation"? Against this more complicated backdrop, it is unlikely that the narrated speeches provide reliably verified reports of what was factually stated on the various occasions. However, Thucydides certainly has not replaced the voices of the speakers with his own, correcting their statements with an authorial version of what they should have said if they were him. I believe that representations of these speeches within the narrative reveal how the speakers in question (individuals or regimes) would have articulated their responses to political dilemmas if they were to speak completely in character, in ways consistent with their most fundamental identities or firmest commitments. As such, the speeches of the various participants are embedded in psychological and cultural networks of calculation and desire, ambition and fear. To this extent, the narrated *logoi* offer a body of pragmatic responses to the war's *erga*. By including these speeches within the encompassing *logos* of the *History* as a whole, Thucydides both takes them seriously and subjects them to potential criticisms, inviting his readers to consider the values and limitations of the forms of political thought and practice that they reveal.

[14] The importance of this question is implied also by Forde 1989: 4–5.

What, then, is the character of Thucydides' own *logos*? Two interpretations are particularly pronounced within the scholarly literature. The first sees Thucydides as a social theorist who maps the dynamics of power relations as they occur within and among regimes.[15] The second treats his writing as an appreciative recognition of the leadership of Pericles.[16] Initially, these two views seem to extend in different, even opposite, directions. Seeing Thucydides as a general theorist of power elevates his perspective above that of particular regimes or individuals, while interpreting his *logos* as homage to Pericles situates it within the political debates of a single political culture. Moreover, synoptic theorizing would expose the Periclean encomium to renown as limited and self-deceptive, while affirming the Periclean ethic would reveal the inadequacies of reductive theoretical categories that pretend to be guideposts to the heart of human aspiration. For all of their differences, however, both interpretations imply that Thucydides' *logos* is conclusive and directive in tone. To this extent, both tend to diminish the importance of political thought as a discursive and interactive enterprise, the one view deferring to the penetrating insights of theory, the other to the effective exhortations of political leadership. Yet while Thucydides dramatizes both synoptic and rhetorical modes of political intelligence in his narrative, I believe that neither represents his own position and that neither of these assessments does justice to Thucydides' work, understood as a possession forever. Critical scrutiny of these interpretations suggests that Thucydides' practice of political thought acknowledges more ambiguity and requires more discursive and more critical interaction.

The Imperatives and Restraints of Power

A number of Thucydides' speakers certainly offer generalized visions of how power relations play out, allegedly according to nature. In different ways, the Athenians at Sparta (1.76.2–4), the Syracusian statesman Hermocrates (4.61.5–7), the Athenian envoys to the Melians (5.105.2), and the Athenian negotiator at Camarina in Sicily, Euphemos (6.85.1–2, 87.4–5), all acknowledge the universal imperative that the strong control the weak. This dynamic can be expressed in different

[15] See, for example, Crane 1998: 146–47.

[16] For example, Edmunds 1975: 193, 211; Farrar 1988: 163; Parry 1981: 188; Wohl 2002: 71; Yunis 1996: 79–80.

ways. It can arise from a calculated (Euphemos) or anxious (the Athenian envoys on Melos) pursuit of interest, or it may simply be what human beings do (the Athenians at Sparta, Hermocrates) when opportunities arise. Those speakers implicated in the most violent action (the envoys to the Melians) give what seems to be the deepest and most structured account. What they know about gods and human beings (and thus about the cosmos, generally) tells them that the strong are naturally compelled (*anankaias*) by a kind of law (*ton nomon*) to rule when they are empowered.[17] All of these cases lead Jacqueline de Romilly to see this position as that of Thucydides as well. "In the final analysis Athenian imperialism is the only perfect example of a common experience whose nature is governed by universal laws."[18]

Yet it is hardly obvious that the speeches of Thucydides' characters are simply intended to transmit his own beliefs.[19] All of those who affirm the universality of a supposed law of nature validating domination speak from positions within powerful regimes. Consequently, all may represent cultural priorities or advantages as confirming natural imperatives. Thucydides' own statement on nature seems to communicate a very different set of conclusions. In his commentary in Book 3 on the significance of the devastating civil war (*stasis*) in the city of Corcyra, he represents nature not as order but as turbulence. Within this turbulence, it is no longer clear what the categories of strength and weakness mean.[20]

> The meaner in intellect were more often the survivors; out of fear of their own deficiencies and their enemies' intelligence, that they might not be overcome in words (*logois*) and become the first victims of plots issuing from the others' intelligent deceptions, they daringly embraced deeds (*erga*). And those who contemptuously believed they would know all in advance, and that they need not seize by deed what would come to them by intelligence, were taken off their guard and perished in greater numbers. (3.83.3–4)

From this perspective, a generalizing theory asserting the universal control of the weaker by the stronger should now be understood as a discourse emerging out of a particular kind of political culture. Insofar

[17] Compare with Plato's *Gorgias* 484a–c.

[18] de Romilly 1963: 312.

[19] As Price 2001: 197, warns as well.

[20] See also Price 2001: 47, 57.

as it is treated as a mandate for practice, it is shown in the *History* to be illusory and self-defeating. Thucydides must be read, then, as separating himself from that culture and offering a critical perspective, though hardly an impartial one, on its content. I believe that this conclusion emerges within the portion of the *History* that is often read as making the strongest case for a universal theory of power, the Melian dialogue.

The occasion is Athens' attempt to coerce the independent island city of Melos into subjection during a period of supposed peace between the warring sides. Earlier, the Athenian general Nicias (after whom the peace is named) had led an unsuccessful expedition to Melos for the same imperial purpose (3.91.1–3). Athens presses the agenda again in part because of the hollowness of the negotiated peace (5.25–26, 69–74) and in part because of growing ambitions toward Sicily (6.1). The episode ends with Melos' destruction; the men are killed and the women and children enslaved (5.116). As horrible as this act is, however, it is no different from the punishment imposed on the defecting Chalchidean city of Scione after the peace agreement (5.32.1–2) or from the first decision about the fate of rebellious Mytilene (3.36.1–3). What is unique in the Melian episode is what is said,[21] the "dialogue" between representatives of Athens and Melos' "leaders and the few" (5.84.3).

This is hardly a dialogue, of course, if dialogue means a discursively open conversation that is settled by what Jurgen Habermas calls the forceless force of the stronger argument.[22] Any rational interchange is distorted at the outset by two expressions of power, the first by the Melian leadership's exclusion of the city's populace from the conversation (5.85), the second by the Athenian exploitation of the military imbalance between the two cities. Consequently, the Athenians demand that the conversation be limited to a consideration of the issues they themselves raise and that the Melian contribution be confined to responses. This will also exclude appeals to justice as pointless ("for just things are only decided through human speech [when directed by] equal compulsions – *isēs anankēs* – [consequently] the powerful do what they can, while the weak give way to them" [5.89]) and will focus the discussion squarely on questions of advantage. The Athenians treat the interchange as a narrow form of bargaining, urging the Melians to purchase safety with submission.

[21] Cf. Connor 1984: 150.

[22] Cf. Habermas 1996: 541 n. 58.

Resisting these constraints, the Melians do not see the terms of the exchange as settled because of their continued attachments to certain beliefs about the structure of the political cosmos they inhabit. The Athenians dismiss the Melians' assessments as wishful thinking, grounded in hopes in things inscrutable or invisible (*ta aphanē*) (5.103, 113). They represent themselves, on the other hand, as quintessential realists, taking their bearing from "things right before their eyes" (*tōn horōmenōn*) (5.113). Echoing de Romilly, a number of commentators have read the Athenian position as stating Thucydides' own.[23] However, this conclusion ignores the extent to which the Athenians are also driven by highly problematic beliefs in invisible things, a perspective that we might call a certain political imagination.

The Melian leadership retains hope for their city's independence because of the unpredictability of war and especially because they anticipate assistance from both the gods and the Spartans. "We trust that, regarding fortune, through the influence of the divine, we shall not suffer, since we stand as pious men against those who are unjust, and regarding power, that the Lacedaemonians our allies will necessarily provide us with resources, if for no other reason than out of kinship and respect (*aischunē*)" (5.104). The Melians continue to rely on a kind of justice not simply because the desperateness of their situation leaves no other recourse, but also because their vision of the world as ordered by patterns of lawfulness and reciprocity seems to obligate the Spartans and even the gods to come to their aid. Calling this coherent picture a kind of imagination need not dismiss it as illusory. It seems rather to be an interpretation of experience that is testable against and to a degree verifiable by practical outcomes. The continuing care of the gods or fortune can be inferred by the city's long-standing independence (5.112). Trust in Sparta is reinforced by the Lacedaemonians' reputation as enemies of tyranny, shown most recently by Brasidas' apparent (though badly misunderstood) liberationist expedition in the north (5.110). Precisely because the political cosmos is envisaged as a stable order, the Melians remain attached to conventional beliefs about shame and nobility (5.100) and they insist that they be accorded a recognition equal to that which Athens demands from them (5.92).

However, for all its supposed clear-sightedness, Athens, too, proceeds on the basis of a distinctive political imagination rooted in beliefs

[23] Other commentators who have read Thucydides as accepting the validity of claims that the rule of the strong reflects a certain kind of natural standard or order include Ostwald 1988: 38, 55, and Pouncey 1980: 104.

in things that are also in a way invisible. Its demands presume an image of Athens as a powerful, yet vulnerable, imperial city within an unforgivingly competitive cosmos. The envoys say they can accept nothing short of complete submission from the Melians because anything less will be seen as Athenian weakness, particularly by those cities that are currently their subjects. "[A]side from extending our rule, you would offer us security by being subdued, especially since as islanders, and weaker than the others, you should not have prevailed over the masters of the sea" (5.97). While this vision of the cosmos seems altogether different from the order structured by justice and piety that the Melians imagine, it also supposes a coherent frame of reference where those strong enough to rule do so and where the continuation of both strength and rule must run in parallel.

> For of the gods we hold the belief and of human beings we know, that by a necessity of their nature, where they are stronger, they rule. And since we neither laid down this law, nor, when it was in place, were the first to use it, we found it in existence and expect to leave it in existence forever, so we make use of it, knowing that both you and others, taking on the same power we have, would do the same. (5.105.2)

Athens is therefore conceived as playing its own necessary role in an ordered world. They must comply with imperatives set not by reciprocity but by power. Consequently, the Athenians seem as constrained by their surrounding cosmos as the Melians are by theirs. While the remarkable political success of the empire may be reassuring evidence of the reality of such an order, the accompanying pressure demands that the Athenians work ceaselessly to maintain their position of advantage. Within this world, the only alternative to continuously active political energy is servitude or disintegration (5.91, 99).

The Athenian political imagination is said to reflect the nature of things. The envoys' reliance on what they call the natural law as a validation of the stronger's rule (5.105) assumes that there are obvious and unambiguous measures of strength and weakness that can determine political relationships in clearly accessible ways, the manifest power of the Athenians as opposed to the "invisible things" that reassure the Melians. From this perspective, different forms of political imagination could be comparatively tested against the demanding but definite natural standard. Understanding the content and implications of this standard would thus constitute the truest political wisdom. Yet while this may be the envoys' position, for reasons I have indicated it is not at all obvious that it is Thucydides'. The Athenians' own language thus collapses differences between natural standards and political or cultural constructions. Their appeals to natural necessity are elaborated by references to decision and legislation. Yet if this allegedly natural law is one that has been, so to speak, laid down (*keimenōi*), it is not clear that it has been in place, as they say, forever (*aiei*). When the Athenians' infer beliefs (*doxē*) about the gods from what is known clearly (*saphōs*) about human beings, they rely on a kind of political wisdom or political imagination that constructs rather than defers to natural imperatives.[24]

If conceptions of the cosmos or nature can be traced to forms of political imagination, such conceptions should therefore be subject to criticism and revision as alternative images arise. However, because both the Athenians and the Melians maintain allegiances to dogmatic extra-political foundations, whether theological or anthropological, they reject alternative formulations as unintelligible. The Melians willfully resist Athenian pressure because they do not envisage a political order wherein justice disappears. The Athenians contemptuously dismiss the Melians as suicidal fools because the envoys reject any measure of regime strength beyond the exercise of material power. When challenges are encountered from whatever quarter, some dogmatic belief in "things invisible" silences.

While these powerful beliefs are treated by their advocates as both sources of political strength and conditions for political rationality, in the end they foster irrationalities and disasters. Melos' disaster comes first. Yet this seeming validation of Athenian realism is followed by Athens' own disaster in Sicily, the sources for which are the same political imaginaries that underlie the campaign against Melos (6.1.1–2). The catastrophic end of the Sicilian campaign is marked by the reappearance of the voices discounted by the envoys as the defeated Athenian general Nicias, who was ironically the leader of the first assault against Melos (3.91.1–3), irrationally hopes for assistance from the gods and the Spartans (7.77.1–4, 85.1–2).[25] And the invasion creates the very crisis that it was allegedly initiated to prevent, the frightening prospect of Athens' domination by others (6.18.3; 8.1–2).

[24] Thus, Palmer's 1992: 70, comment: "What the Athenians believe they know about men determines what they believe about the gods."

[25] Cf. Connor 1984: 155.

Thus interpreted, the statement that nature requires the strong to rule and the weak to submit emerges within Thucydides' narrative not as a penetrating insight but as a dangerous illusion. Its dangers are caused by two deficiencies that are intimately connected with attempts at conclusive and synoptic theorizing more generally. First, framing priorities are specified so rigidly as to eliminate challenges or alternatives before the fact. Second, beliefs that these forms of political imagination are founded on cosmic standards of necessity mask their political-cultural origins and frustrate possibilities of rational critique and pragmatic change. These observations may begin to provide a clue as to *one* meaning of *anankē* as represented in Thucydides' claims (1.23; 5.25) that the Athenians and Spartans were compelled to wage war. Here, *anankē* may point to the presence of what might be called unexamined obsessions that demand even as they resist the scrutiny of a more critical political thought. In pairing Melian and Athenian obsessions, Thucydides does not proclaim the necessity of domination, but instead displays the need for critically examining synoptic pretensions of whatever sort.

Periclean Leadership and the Valorization of the Noble

Pericles' project seems very different from the envoys' recognition of sweeping cosmic imperatives. He consistently appeals not to a universal and compelling nature but to the distinctiveness and agency of Athens. Far from rising to the heights of a theory that stands above individual regimes, Pericles practices a culturally embedded political judgment, expressed through pragmatic speech and sensitive to changing circumstances. Moreover, Periclean aspirations ennoble the exercise of power not as confirming natural law but as marking an excellence that will achieve lasting renown for those daring enough to run the required risks. This passion for the noble is extended into a vision of civic well-being, where the concern to foster the name of one's city becomes a guiding priority. All of the three direct Periclean speeches presented by Thucydides inspirationally urge a harmonization of private well-being and the common good (1.144; 2.43; 2.60, 64). For these reasons, many commentators read Pericles' speeches as attempts to foster public spirit and thoughtful judgment among the Athenians and interpret Thucydides as preserving and valorizing the Periclean example as the proper response to political challenges, a prudent blending of speech and action that strives to create better citizens.[26] Perhaps the most compelling textual support for the validity of this reading is Thucydides' encomium to Pericles' leadership and harsh condemnation of those who competed for preeminence after his death.

> Whenever he perceived that [the people] were arrogantly bold against what the times warranted, he confounded them into fearfulness by his speaking, and again, when they were irrationally afraid, he restored them to confidence. And what was said to be a democracy was in fact a rule by the first man (*protos anēr*). Those who came in later, in contrast, since they were much more like one another and each was extending himself to become first, [they] gave over the affairs [of the city] to the pleasure of the *dēmos*. (2.65.9–10)

Yet read within the broader context of the *History* there are aspects of Pericles' leadership that Thucydides himself seems to criticize.[27] For all of his appeals to the common good, Pericles is consistently guided by priorities informed by his own singular vision of human well-being. This vision is most forcefully revealed in his final speech (2.60–64) in which an anticipation of how Athens will be remembered takes pride of place. Though it is in the fate of all things to be diminished (*ellassousthai*), what is to be valued most is reputation or the great name (*onoma megiston*) that is won by daring action and competitive achievement. Though Athens' constant motion may well end with the diminution of its material accomplishments and perhaps even the disappearance of its political existence under the ravages of time (cf. 1.10.2–3) and while it will also certainly encounter the hatred of rivals and subjects, "hatred does not persist for long, but the brilliance of the instant and repute (*doxa*) thereafter remain in eternal memory (*aieimnēstos*)" (2.64.5). In affirming this conception of political success, Pericles thus disregards the crass material ambitions for profit and status that motivate cities such as Corcyra (cf. 1.33–36). In reality, such achievements are simply signs of the truly valuable psycho-cultural resources of energy and virtue that Athens uniquely and continuously replenishes. Pericles' Athens is therefore driven to pursue the enduring reputation that defeats death. This

[26] Note especially Farrar 1988: 163.

[27] For those who read Thucydides as also offering a critique of Pericles, see the different presentations of (for example) Monoson and Loriaux 1998: 285–97; Orwin 1994: 25–28; Strauss 1964: 193–94; Balot 2001: 148–49.

ambition further extends the funeral speech's anticipation (2.43.3–4) of the boundless fame that awaits those conspicuous individuals who have the whole earth as their monument into a vision of civic glory, unbounded by space or time. While this vision seems to integrate the individual love of reputation with the city's achievements, therefore opposing those who would treat the city's good as simply instrumental to selfish purposes,[28] it also represents Athens as a civic image of the conspicuous man, valorizing the agenda of the daring individual as the good of the political community as a whole.

For these reasons, the Periclean visions of the human good and thus of Athens' political well-being are represented by Thucydides in ways that underscore their political contestability. Pericles' explanation for why Athens will eternally possess its shining reputation is that "we as Hellenes ruled over the most Hellenes, sustained the greatest wars against them, both individually and united, and lived in a city that was in all ways best provided for and greatest" (2.64.3). This praise of Athens' boundless energy and imperial sweep encounters opposition from a variety of voices, ranging from families of the fallen (2.44–45) to those opposing this project in the name of either their own political integrity (1.143.5) or a different version of Athenian interest (2.64.4–5). Periclean rhetoric combats such dissent at every turn. In his first speech, he preemptively absorbs all conceptions of individual well-being within an expansive and controversial vision of the public good. "[O]ut of the greatest dangers (*megistōn kindunōn*) emerge the greatest honors (*megistai timai*) for both city and individual" (1.144.3), as if the promise of the greatest honors would induce every individual to run the greatest risks. When the funeral speech exhorts all citizens to "really pay regard (*theōmenous*) each day to the power of the city and become her lovers (*erastas*)" (2.43.1), it simultaneously recognizes and rejects as useless (*achreia*) any attachments to private goods that might challenge or dilute enthusiastic citizenship (2.40, 44.4). Though his final speech begins with an acknowledgment of the city's crucial role in ensuring personal security, it ends, as previously noted, with an eloquence that praises Athens' power and brilliance precisely because of the magnitude of the sacrifices that it demands from its citizens (2.64.4–5).

Pericles' commitment to strengthening those bases of Athens' eternal reputation significantly affects his treatment of what *logos* and democracy mean within Athenian political culture. In the funeral speech, he links his appreciation of Athens' unique blending of speech

[28] A position some commentators (Forde 1989; Palmer 1992) ascribe to Alcibiades.

and action with his characterization of the city as a democracy (2.37.1, 40.1–3). Yet speech eventually plays its most important role as handmaid or witness to the power of Athens' deeds (*erga* [2.41.1–3]). The exhorted response to the city's accomplishments is a sense of amazement (cf. 7.28.3) that displaces any serious attention to the contributions of the poets or culture, generally (2.41.4). The appropriate sensory response to Athens' accomplishments is, therefore, sight ("pay regard [*theōmenous*] each day to the power of the city and become her lovers" [2.43.1]), rather than speech or listening ("we use wealth for critical action not for boastful speech" [2.40.1]). While the influence of Athens' deeds certainly depends on the rhetorical success of Periclean speech (*logos*), without which the fact (*ergon*) of power would be hidden, the *logos* is itself a speech act, a powerful *ergon* whose character is measured by its success in forging emotional unity among the individual citizens. From this perspective, Pericles' rhetoric seems intended not to develop judgment (*gnōmē*) as a democratic good but to elicit participation in the project of creating a political identity that will live (forever – *aiei*) in memory, which construes the selective development of civic judgment as instrumental. Similarly, the funeral oration's characterization of the democratic culture as the establishment of equality before the law quickly gives way to the praise of democracy as the regime that gives individual excellence the opportunity to shine (2.37.2). Thucydides' own contention that Periclean Athens was a democracy in name, while being in fact the rule of the first man (2.65.9–10), is anticipated in the representation of Periclean rhetoric in the narrative.

We might detect reservations about Periclean leadership even within Thucydides' apparently explicit statement of praise. In spite of the dramatically different judgments about Pericles and his successors, there is an unsettling continuity between Pericles' being the city's "first man" and the politically destructive competition among those who followed. When Thucydides assesses the regime of the five thousand as the "Athenians' . . . best government at least in my lifetime" (8.97.2) he may not be imagining an institutional approximation to Periclean leadership,[29] but instead offering an implicit comment on the limitations of Periclean brilliance. As described by Thucydides, the regime of the five thousand is no democracy in name, but it is also far from the rule of a single *protos anēr*. It is, strangely, a regime whose distinction lies in its moderation (8.97). Finally, notwithstanding the appreciation of Pericles' foresight in opposing expansion of the empire in wartime, the eulogy

[29] As in Farrar 1988: 186.

ends with the implication that Pericles' own prediction about Athens' success in the war may have been radically distorted by impressions that he himself helped to create. "So great were the resources Pericles had at that time, enabling his own forecast that the city would easily prevail in the war over the Peloponnesians alone" (2.65.13).[30] In offering the basis of an appreciative but critical assessment of Pericles, Thucydides performs an exercise in political thought that is less directive and more discursive; indeed, one that is potentially more democratic.

Diodotus and the Unpredictability of Agency

Thucydides' implicit criticisms of the leadership of Pericles have led some scholars to suggest that traces of Thucydides' own voice are more pronounced within the speech of the character Diodotus, the Athenian citizen who succeeds in persuading the assembly to reverse its own previous harshness toward the democrats of the city of Mytilene (3.35–50).[31] In the fourth year of the war Mytilene's oligarchs have led an unsuccessful revolt against Athens. The rebellion has been suppressed with the aid of the Mytilene *dēmos*. Incensed, the assembly first decides to kill all of the adult males, including the democrats. Once their anger softens, the citizens opt for a reconsideration. The demagogue Cleon (the orchestrator of the previous day's decision) argues again for the severest punishment. Diodotus opposes him and the relatively more merciful course of action prevails, though only by a small majority (3.49). Diodotus appears nowhere else in the *History* or any other known classical source.[32] Arguably, his speech is the most complex of all of those represented by Thucydides. The speech is given with a view to an immediate political decision that must be confronted by the democratic assembly. Yet it is also surrounded by a broader reflection on the contributions of political speech in a democracy and by an

[30] Moreover, Thucydides is provocatively silent about how success against the Peloponnesians would have affected the quality of the Athenian regime thereafter.

[31] I agree with Strauss's 1964: 231, assessment that "Diodotus' speech reveals more of Thucydides himself than does any other speech." See also Orwin 1994: 204–6; Saxonhouse 2006: 214. My view of exactly what is revealed differs somewhat from Strauss's and Orwin's and is closest to Saxonhouse's.

[32] Leading some commentators (Forde 1989: 40 n. 34; Palmer 1992: 125 n. 22; Saxonhouse 1996: 75) to suggest that Diodotus is a product of Thucydides' literary imagination.

even deeper psychological assessment of human motives and human educability. As such, the speech is informed by the structure of a certain kind of political philosophy. However, Diodotus treats none of these questions straightforwardly.

In opposition to Cleon, who has attacked logos as trivializing whimsy and dangerous obscurantism, Diodotus contends that logos and the thoughtfulness behind it are the most important resources for political communities (3.41). Yet as much as Athens needs rational and interactive political speech, its institutions discourage it by creating a hostile and distorting environment for honest speakers. Consequently, any proposal offered to the assembly must deceive to succeed (3.43). These criticisms are followed by a case for leniency toward the Mytilene *dēmos* that is framed exclusively in terms of Athenian interest (3.44), and some commentators have on this basis assailed Diodotus for stripping all considerations of justice from public deliberation.[33] Yet since this appeal to interest has been preceded by an acknowledgment of the necessarily deceptive nature of political speeches, it is questionable whether it is really all there is to Diodotus' case. Some scholars have in fact traced a parallel justice-based argument for leniency in Diodotus' presentation.[34] Yet if this is valid, his speech has immediate success only by continuing and reinforcing the structural pathologies that distort democratic political speeches altogether.[35] This dire outcome is, however, softened by the fact that Diodotus had already warned his audience to be alert for such distortions. He therefore can be read as arguing for a kind of thoughtful care on the part of democratic citizens, especially when deciding issues of the highest moment. If so, he attempts to foster the democratic political good of thoughtfulness through a rhetorical deception made regrettably necessary by the damaging aspects of democracy itself. In so doing, Diodotus complicates the sort of judgment that is so prevalent among modern democratic theorists that the cure for the ills of democracy is simply more democracy.[36] Instead, he prompts a more critical attention to both the strengths and the dangers of democratic regimes.

Yet these more positive implications seem to be overridden by Diodotus' highly depressing assessments of human motivations. Part

33 As in, for example, Johnson 1993: 107–10, 135; White 1984: 75.

34 See, for example, Strauss 1964: 233; Orwin 1994: 152–53; Mara 2001: 825–32; Saxonhouse 2006: 160–63.

35 The criticism of Euben 1990: 182, and Ober 1998: 102–3.

36 Good statements of this position can be found in Warren 2001: ch. 7, and Young 1997: 402–4.

of his argument for sensible leniency hinges on the powerlessness of capital punishment in the face of the passions. The suggestion that the Mytilenes cannot really be blamed for their revolt is grounded in a deeper diagnosis of what seems to be an inevitable human inclination to overreach. "[E]ither poverty, which brings about boldness through compulsion; abundance, which brings about ambition through insolence and pride; or other circumstances because of human passion . . . will lead human beings to run risks" (3.45.4). No matter how dangerous or destructive the enterprise, *erōs* leads and hope (*elpis*) follows (3.45.5). But this pessimistic conclusion is also softened by Diodotus' own practice. Because the harshest punishments have failed to prevent the commission of crimes, he infers the general impotence of punishment as a strategy for moderating the passions (3.45.4–7). Yet he does not expressly deny the possibility of educating the passions through a cultural reliance on *logos*. In fact, the practical futility of capital punishment becomes a part of his case for the rationality of moderation. Thus, while the express content of Diodotus' speech acknowledges the overwhelming power of passions, his speech act performatively legitimates the possibility of education and therefore the pragmatic value of a kind of rationality.[37]

Nonetheless, Diodotus' success in saving the Mytilene democrats has a more ambiguous pragmatic position within the *History's* succeeding narrative. In the context of Diodotus' own speech, we have found that his complex rhetoric turns (so to speak) back on itself in two ways. The first of these turnings occurs when his claim to focus only on Athens' interests is complicated by the earlier statement that successful proposals to the assembly must deceive. The second happens when his seemingly damaging reliance on deception is offset by its contribution to the democratic good of critical *logos*. However, a third, and much darker, turn occurs when an appeal to interests overwhelms both justice and *logos* in the speech of the envoys to Melos. Through connections to a range of previous Athenian speakers, including Diodotus, the envoys' speech displays the problematic complexities of Athens' political culture. The envoys' insistence that the parties attend only to their interests dismisses the relevance of a justice that only holds when equal powers confront one another (5.89.1). However, tracing the abuses of the envoys' speech to Diodotus would, in my view, be a

[37] In a way, this sort of effect can be described as a performative contradiction (Butler 1997: 83–84), though the effect of the contradiction is not to create conditions for contestation but to prompt further inquiry by showing the limits of summary judgments on the human condition.

misreading.[38] A different insight is that the path from Diodotus' speech to that of the envoys reveals the impossibility of assuring that political actions justifiable on one occasion will not be misused or perverted on another. While Diodotus may invite one reconsideration of the good of the Athenian empire (If Athens should concern itself with guarding against the defections of the subject cities, what good is such rule for a city with Athens' ambitions?), the envoys' speech presumes a different reassessment of the empire's condition, one that retains the ambition behind the Sicilian invasion while confessing the fear of a reputation for weakness. Diodotus' speech can no more control the speeches and practices of the Athenians with regard to Melos than it can prevent the killing of the Mytilene oligarchs at the instigation of Cleon (3.50). In spite of his careful sensitivity to political circumstance, Diodotus as political agent cannot eliminate the unpredictabilities and risks of political practice.

POLITICAL THOUGHT AND POLITICS

Thus interpreted, Diodotus' political speech may be an important clue to the character of Thucydides' *History* as a whole. Thucydides, too, points repeatedly to the characteristics of human beings that overwhelm thought and turn expressions of political energy and innovation into the greatest suffering and bloodshed. This darker sense of the human prospect has led numerous commentators to conclude that Thucydides' vision of politics is overwhelmingly bleak, diagnosing the inevitable paths of political disintegration and destroying any expectations for improvement. His characterization of the devastating *stasis* in Corcyra seems key.

> And there fell upon the cities many hardships on account of *stasis*, events that take place and will recur always as long as human beings have the same nature, worse or gentler in their types (looks), depending on the changes presenting themselves in each instance. In times of peace and goodness, cities and individuals are better disposed because they are not overthrown by the constraints of necessity. But war, depriving [human beings] of daily resources is a violent teacher, making the dispositions of most like that [harsh] condition. (3.82.2)

[38] As, for example, in Johnson 1993: 135.

Building on this statement, Jonathan Price has argued that the dynamics of internal war constitute the frame of reference for the *History* as a whole.[39]

That this projection of the looming catastrophe of political *stasis* is validated in a great deal of the *History* cannot be questioned. Yet, like Diodotus, Thucydides often softens the impact of his speech with the speech act that is within the *History* itself. In this sense, the *logos* of Thucydides is also an *ergon* whose pragmatic presupposition is not the amusement stimulated by a competition piece for the moment, but the kind of education that can be provided by a possession forever. As practiced through the *History*, this education is not didactic but interactive and indeterminate. This means that the value of this possession is contingent on its being used well, an outcome that Thucydides as author cannot simply control. The *History* can only fulfill the promise that Thucydides sets for it if the events narrated are understood in ways the text, through eliciting and engaging thoughtfulness among its readers, itself tries to encourage. Yet readings of Thucydides have more often presented him as the quintessential political realist, the first systematic theorizer of the dynamics of political power, or the most sobering political pessimist.[40] Like Diodotus' speech, Thucydides' *History* can invite an engagement with its insights only if it accepts possibilities that they will be misunderstood or misused. In this respect, Thucydides' treatment of his own *logos* is a reverse image of his presentation of the speeches of his characters. While he respects the importance of these speeches by representing them in ways most appropriate to speaker and circumstance, he tempers any sense of deference – or neutrality – by inscribing them within a larger critical narrative. Conversely, the magisterial character of Thucydides' education as a possession forever[41] is offset by the vulnerabilities and risks that it accepts. In its parallel gestures of respect and challenge, confidence and vulnerability, the tone of Thucydides' political thought reflects characteristics that mark democratic speech and

39 Price 2001: 11–19.

40 See for example, Crane 1996: 208, 1998: 99–100; de Romilly 1963: 336–37, 357; Price 2001: 11–22. There are of course important exceptions, see especially Euben 1990; Saxonhouse 1996, 2006; and several commentaries (Forde 1989, Orwin 1994, Palmer 1992) informed by the interpretations of Strauss 1964, but they have been exceptions.

41 Underscored in the interpretations of Strauss 1964: 229–30; Bruell 1974: 17; and Orwin 1994: 204–5.

Thucydides becomes a potential partner in a certain kind of democratic conversation.[42]

For these reasons, I am not convinced by arguments that Thucydides' regime preference lies with the disciplined restraint and moderation of the Spartans.[43] As Sparta displays its practice of moderation in the narrative, we find a regime that relies heavily on forms of social coercion that discourage the sort of critical *logos* that is more endemic to democracies. Ultimately, this deficiency compromises even the virtues that allegedly lie at the heart of the Spartan ethic. In the trial of the defeated Plataeans that is narrated in close proximity (3.52–68) to the Mytilene debate, the Spartan regard for justice is exposed as formal and manipulative. What is valorized as justice (3.52) is simply the execution of the Plataeans as justified by their inability to respond adequately to a question whose damning answer is altogether obvious. The executions are ordered to placate Plataea's long-standing enemy Thebes, whose support is seen as vital to the Spartan cause. This misuse of justice is paralleled by a refusal to take *logos* seriously. The extended speeches of the Plataean and Theban representatives (covering more chapters than the Mytilene debate) are pointless exercises in the shadow of a sentence already passed (3.68). Though democratic speech is clearly vulnerable to distortion and abuse, democracy remains the realistically achievable regime in which *logos* and judgment have the best chances of being taken seriously. It is Athens and not Sparta that is the appropriate home of political thought and of the political action that may be so informed.

The indeterminacy and thus the politicality of the *History* are reinforced if we entertain the *possibility* that the text we possess is, as understood by the author, essentially complete.[44] As partial evidence one could emphasize that the outcome of the war is both narrated (5.26) and explained (2.65) within the text as we have it. The last portion of the work (organized as Book 8) includes a large number of claims made in Thucydides' own name on matters of fundamental import. The virtual absence in Book 8 of any direct discourse ascribed to the *History's* characters suggests, among other things, that this last part of the *History*

[42] For an interpretation that discovers democratic elements in Thucydides' treatment of the *erga*, rather than the *logoi* of the war, see Saxonhouse 2006: 149–51.

[43] For a good statement and defense of this position see Orwin 1994: 183, 204.

[44] A possibility suggested as well by Strauss 1964: 227 n. 89, and Forde 1989: 171–72 n. 53, though on somewhat different grounds and with different implications. Forde's comments are particularly valuable because they suggest that "completeness" can be understood in a variety of ways.

might be read, more than any other portion of the work, as the direct speech of Thucydides. The principal claims within this speech include an account of the hollowness of the Athenian empire's claim to good order (*eunomia*) (8.64), the praise of Alcibiades' most distinctive service to the city on the basis of his serving as a peacemaker (8.86), the statement that Athens' success in the war (already read against its eventual defeat) depended significantly on the good fortune of having the cautious Spartans as opponents (8.96), and the judgment that the rule of the five thousand constituted the best Athenian regime of Thucydides' time (8.97).

In spite of what seem to be decisive tones, however, none of these statements is simply conclusive. All prompt further reflections that enrich and deepen the indeterminacy of the *History* as a whole. Calling the Athenian regime's *eunomia* hollow suggests that the discourse enabled by Athenian power (as in 1.76) can be turned against the ways in which that power is exercised. The praise of Alcibiades as peacemaker valorizes distinctiveness on grounds different from Periclean daring and energy. Yet Alcibiades' restraining influence also connects his most distinctive action with Pericles' ability to tame the *dēmos* (2.65), potentially prompting a deeper examination of how Pericles and Alcibiades might be both similar and different. The criticisms of Spartan dilatoriness implicitly challenge the validity of Athens' reputation for greatness (cf. 7.27). The endorsement of the regime of the five thousand has more than a tinge of irony, since that regime's effective existence and certainly its duration over time are matters of serious question.[45]

If the *History* is in fact Thucydides' completed text, it also urges rethinking of how and why time horizons are constructed, a problem that is continuous with both the writing of history and the pragmatics of agency. Thought as *historia* and politics as *praxis* must order and cohere. The war lasted twenty-seven years and had a beginning, middle, and end. Yet Thucydides may well offer, from his point of view, a complete *historia* of the war without narrating its final six years in the order of summers and winters. In this connection, it is also worth noting that the text of the *History* recognizes a variety of periodizations that open different apertures on the narrative. While this conflict lasted nearly twenty-seven years, its patterns of violence can also be mapped by tracing the events spanning its first beginning (2.1) and its second (8.5), when Athens shows remarkable resolve in the face of the Sicilian disaster. Here, the shape of the war is not linear but circular; yet the

[45] Cf. Aristotle, *Constitution of Athens* 41.

(different) closures of linearity and circularity are interrupted by the abrupt ending of the *History* as we have it. The text also frames the beginning and (temporary) end of Athens' democratic governance, from the expulsion of the Peisistratids (6.53–59) to the oligarchy of the Four Hundred (8.68). The construction of the league and the empire, blurred almost to indistinguishability in 1.97, ends as the subject cities rebel or defect (2.65). And Thucydides tracks how the Hellenic defeat of the Persians (1.89) spawns a Hellenic war that reinvolves the Persians (8.6). The last event narrated in the *History*, that the Persian satrap Tissaphernes sacrificed to Artemis at Ephesus, not only signals the return of the Persians, but also reaffirms the constructed and blurred character of cultures, problematizing, as in the Archeology (1.5–6), any permanent distinction between Greeks and barbarians and thus refocusing on a more expanded and complicating vision of the human.[46] All of this is offered within the encompassing horizon of eternity, extending the text indefinitely in space and time.

If this is a plausible interpretation, the work's authorial completeness is offset by deeper incompleteness, a recognition that attempts to impose closure on how we understand and cope with human events are, while needful, inevitably unstable and fleeting. If this is in fact the Thucydidean view, it sharply departs from the stance of Pericles within his final speech (2.64). Though everything naturally diminishes, Athens' name is projected to live in "eternal memory" (*aieimnēstos*), honored according to criteria that remain – oddly – permanent. Within a realm that demands immediate attention even as it offers constant reminders of its own transience, Thucydides neither deludes himself about the prospect of providing some sort of final lawlike judgment on the dynamics of political action nor surrenders his intelligence to the turbulence of uncontrollable *stasis*. Instead, his *History*, understood as narrative and practice, *logos* and *ergon*, is a form of political thought that both engages and reflects the permanent qualities of political life.[47]

[46] For a further treatment of Thucydides' engagement with the cultural distinction between Greeks and barbarians see Mara 2003.

[47] In this respect, Thucydides' response to political turbulence differs significantly from those of two of his greatest modern admirers within the tradition of Western political philosophy. Unlike his eloquent translator Hobbes, Thucydides does not envisage an institutional context that would respond to political disorder by managing hubris into submission (*Leviathan*, ch. 28). And unlike his passionate advocate Nietzsche (*Twilight of the Idols*, "What I Owe to the Ancients," 2), he does not simply confront the world disclosed by that harshest teacher, war, with a redoubled energy aimed at overcoming.

WORKS CITED

Balot, R. K. 2001. *Greed and Injustice in Classical Athens*. Princeton, NJ.

Bruell, C. 1974. "Thucydides' View of Athenian Imperialism." *American Political Science Review* 68: 11–17.

Butler, J. 1997. *Excitable Speech: A Politics of the Performative*. New York.

Connor, W. R. 1984. *Thucydides*. Princeton, NJ.

Crane, G. 1996. *The Blinded Eye: Thucydides and the New Written Word*. Greek Studies: Interdisciplinary Approaches. Lanham, MD.

Crane, G. 1998. *Thucydides and the Ancient Simplicity: The Limits of Political Realism*. Berkeley, CA.

Edmunds, L. 1975. *Chance and Intelligence in Thucydides*. Loeb Classical Monographs. Cambridge, MA.

Euben, J. P. 1990. *The Tragedy of Political Theory: The Road Not Taken*. Princeton, NJ.

Farrar, C. 1988. *The Origins of Democratic Thinking: The Invention of Politics in Classical Athens*. Cambridge.

Forde, S. 1989. *The Ambition to Rule: Alcibiades and the Politics of Imperialism in Thucydides*. Ithaca, NY.

Habermas, J. 1996. *Between Facts and Norms: Contributions to a Discourse Theory of Law and Democracy*, trans. W. Rehg. Studies in Contemporary German Social Thought. Cambridge, MA.

Hanson, V. D. 1996. "Introduction." In *The Landmark Thucydides: A Comprehensive Guide to the Peloponnesian War*, ed. R. B. Strassler. New York.

Johnson, L. M. 1993. *Thucydides, Hobbes, and the Interpretation of Realism*. DeKalb, IL.

Kagan, D. 1969. *The Outbreak of the Peloponnesian War*. Ithaca, NY.

Lattimore, S., trans. 1998. *Thucydides: The Peloponnesian War*. Indianapolis, IN.

Loraux, N. 1986. *The Invention of Athens: The Funeral Oration in the Classical City*, trans. A. Sheridan. Cambridge, MA.

Mara, G. 2001. "Plato and Thucydides on Democracy and Trust." *Journal of Politics* 63: 820–45.

2003. "Democratic Self Criticism and the Other in Classical Political Theory." *Journal of Politics* 65: 739–58.

Monoson, S. S., and M. Loriaux. 1998. "The Illusion of Power and the Disruption of Moral Norms: Thucydides' Critique of Periclean Policy." *American Political Science Review* 92: 285–97.

Ober, J. 1998. *Political Dissent in Democratic Athens: Intellectual Critics of Popular Rule*. Martin Classical Lectures. Princeton, NJ.

Orwin, C. 1994. *The Humanity of Thucydides*. Princeton, NJ.

Ostwald, M. 1988. *ANAΓKH in Thucydides*. American Philological Association American Classical Studies. Atlanta, GA.

Palmer, M. 1992. *Love of Glory and the Common Good: Aspects of the Political Thought of Thucydides*. Perspectives on Classical Social and Political Thought. Lanham, MD.

Parry, A. M. 1981. *Logos and Ergon in Thucydides*. New York.

Pouncey, P. 1980. *The Necessities of War: A Study of Thucydides' Pessimism*. New York.

Price, J. J. 2001. *Thucydides and Internal War*. Cambridge.

Ricoeur, P. 2004. *Memory, History, Forgetting*, trans. K. Blamey and D. Pellauer. Chicago.

Romilly, J. de. 1963. *Thucydides and Athenian Imperialism*, trans. P. Thody. Oxford.

Sahlins, M. 2004. *Apologies to Thucydides.* Chicago.

Saxonhouse, A. W. 1996. *Athenian Democracy: Modern Mythmakers and Ancient Theorists.* Notre Dame, IN.

2004. "Democratic Deliberation and the Historians Trade: The Case of Thucydides." In *Talking Democracy: Historical Perspectives on Rhetoric and Democracy*, ed. B. Fontana, C. Nederman, and G. Remer. State College, PA.

2006. *Free Speech and Democracy in Ancient Athens.* Cambridge.

Smith, C. F., trans. 1962–88. *Thucydides*, 4 vols. Loeb Classical Library. Cambridge, MA.

Strauss, L. 1964. *The City and Man.* Chicago.

Warren, M. E. 2001. *Democracy and Association.* Princeton, NJ.

White, J. B. 1984. *When Words Lose Their Meaning: Constitutions and Reconstitutions of Language, Character, and Community.* Chicago.

Wohl, V. 2002. *Love among the Ruins: The Erotics of Democracy in Classical Athens.* Princeton, NJ.

Young, I. M. 1997. "Difference as a Resource for Democratic Communication." In *Deliberative Democracy: Essays on Reason and Politics*, ed. J. Bohman and W. Rehg. Cambridge, MA.

Yunis, H. 1996. *Taming Democracy: Models of Political Rhetoric in Classical Athens.* Rhetoric & Society. Ithaca, NY.

5: "This Way of Life, This Contest": Rethinking Socratic Citizenship

Susan Bickford

When I teach Plato, I begin, as many of us do, with the dialogues surrounding the trial and death of Socrates. And I find that for the most part my students enthusiastically embrace what they take to be Socrates' urging – to continually question our beliefs and our claims to know. Indeed, they understand this to be what their college education involves, and to a point I agree with them. But surely that is not all education involves. As Eva Brann says, "the claim, so often made in prose and poetry that the quarry is nothing and the quest everything, turns the pursuit of truth into a mere exercise, which is, for all its strenuousness, rather idle. Why look when one does not mean to find?"[1]

Whatever else we can say about Socrates, it is surely the case that for him the pursuit of truth was no "mere exercise." Yet my students' view of Socrates as emphasizing questioning above all has its echoes in contemporary scholarship. Let me take as one example Dana Villa's conception of "Socratic citizenship," which emphasizes the critical, dissident force of Socratic interaction.[2] Here Socratic *elenchus* is not so much a method of philosophical investigation as a method of inducing perplexity; no one ever figures out what justice or piety really is. Socrates' activities, Villa argues, are best characterized by the notion of "dissolvent rationality," where what is dissolved through the use of reason is the lazy or dogmatic assumption that the beliefs we hold

[1] For Brann 1979: 143, genuine questioning involves both "a receptive openness, a defined ignorance," and also "a *directed desire of the intellect*" (italics in original). This strikes me as very Socratic, as will be clear from what follows.

[2] Villa 2001.

are true. The point of the perplexity that results is a slowing down, a "greater hesitancy in action" that may help us avoid injustice.[3]

This is a familiar portrait of Socrates – the gadfly, puncturing the certainty of those who think they know – but it is also a partial one. By focusing on Socratic citizenship as a negative, critical force, Villa leaves us with a curiously one-sided Socrates, one who lacks any sort of affirmative project. Indeed, following Vlastos[4] and many others, Villa attributes any positive project to Plato. According to this approach, there are early dialogues that represent the views and approaches to philosophy of the "historical" Socrates, while in later dialogues Socrates is best regarded as a character through which Plato presents his own more programmatic views.[5] In accepting this view, Villa misses two crucial things (things I also try to persuade my students to consider). First, the project of even the "historical" Socrates is more complicated than Villa's reading allows. Socrates aimed to provoke those who settled for conventional wisdom or thoughtless dogmatism, to be sure, and thus submitting unthinkingly accepted cultural beliefs to scrutiny was part of Socrates' characteristic activity. But another part of Socrates' characteristic activity was to insist that there is a good that is worth pursuing – that ethical norms are not simply cynical artifice or cloaks for power – for he was also arguing against the sophistic claim that nothing is true. In other words, dogmatism was one challenge, but cynicism or relativism was another. So Socratic "citizenship" was particularly complicated – to continually question our claims to know, while paradoxically affirming the purposeful *pursuit* of knowing. If we don't recognize that paradox, then we are missing something crucial about the practice of reason that Socrates summons us to.

Second, the claim that the early gadfly Socrates is different from the later, more positive Plato rests on the unexamined assumption that what the character of Socrates says in the dialogues is what Plato means to advocate. This neglects the insights we gain from keeping in view the artfulness of the dialogues. As Michael Frede argues, there is a philosophical point to Plato's use of the dialogue form in that it allows

[3] Villa 2001: 2–5, 30, 39.

[4] Vlastos 1991.

[5] The earlier "Socratic" dialogues in Vlastos' chronology include *Gorgias*, *Euthyphro*, *Apology*, and Book 1 of the *Republic*, while the "middle" period includes the rest of the *Republic*, *Symposium*, *Phaedrus*, and the "late" period includes *Laws*, *Sophist*, and *Statesman*. But note that even the first group of dialogues involves positive claims by Socrates to know something at least provisionally (e.g., *Apology* 29b–c, *Gorgias* 508e–509a).

him to pursue arguments that he thinks deserve consideration, without in fact endorsing them as true. Since Plato doesn't present his own views in an authoritative way, the reader of the dialogue can't defer to the "expert" but has to think for herself.[6] The dialogue form, then, prevents the reader from accepting an argument just because Plato says it – because it's not clear what Plato in fact says.

What Plato *does* in the dialogues is show Socrates asking questions about living well and insisting on taking those questions the most seriously, without ever offering a final or complete answer.[7] By almost always using Socrates as a dramatic character, Plato keeps the necessity of questioning directly in front of us even in seemingly less aporetic dialogues. But the existence of these seemingly less aporetic dialogues suggests that we can take the question seriously-and-as-a-question not only by dissolving answers, but by attempting them. One way Plato does this is by examining the way political practices and institutions – real or imagined – sustain or impede living well, especially in terms of how they cultivate and condition citizen desires. Now, to consider these political modes of soul-shaping is to raise a specter of "legislating desires" that makes us democrats uneasy. But Plato draws our attention to the inevitability of this "shaping," the inescapable impress of our practices on who we are. In other words, soul-shaping happens one way or another, and there are challenges for both philosophers and democrats – and democratic philosophers – in the realization.

I turn, then, to three of Plato's dialogues in which the political shaping of souls takes center stage: the *Gorgias*, the *Republic*, and the *Laws*.[8] By exploring ways of humans acting upon one another and pursuing various arguments about "making citizens good," these dialogues raise questions about what kind of "making" is appropriate to what kind of "material." They do so in ways that open up for examination particular conceptions of freedom and of reason. And that leads us to a final reason why Plato's dialogues cannot be understood as simply presenting logical arguments or positive position statements: what the dialogues dramatize is precisely the insufficiency of reason and of rational certainty – and Socrates' response to that challenge.

[6] Frede 1992: 214–17. An argument might "deserve consideration" either because it has a plausible claim to be true, or because it is particularly prevalent in the political culture in which Socrates is engaged.

[7] This is Salkever's 1993: 135, nice description of "Platonic and Socratic philosophical politics."

[8] Unless otherwise stated, translations of the *Gorgias*, the *Republic*, and the *Laws* are based on Zeyl 1987, Grube 1992, and Pangle 1980, respectively.

The *Gorgias*: Pastrymakers and Politicians

The *Gorgias* begins as a dialogue about rhetoric and about those who make a living teaching rhetoric to aspiring politicians. More exactly, it begins with Callicles (who we later learn is an aspiring Athenian politician) making a dig at Socrates for arriving only when the "battle" is over, referring to a public performance just completed by Gorgias, a renowned visiting rhetorician. Socrates' seemingly innocuous reply implies that it was a "feast," a meaningless gorging, rather than a battle of any significance.[9] This opening sets up an opposition between Socratic practice and political rhetoric, and indeed Socrates goes on to criticize rhetoric and, by extension, the politics of democratic Athens. Yet Socrates' own practice has many rhetorical aspects, and the terms of his criticism turn back on themselves in a way that makes the dialogue much more than a straightforward critique of Athenian political practice.

As Socrates talks with three defenders of rhetoric (Gorgias himself, then Polus, a brash and not-too-bright follower, and, finally and most extensively, Callicles), the dialogue moves back and forth between two sets of related questions. First, there is the discussion of what rhetoric as a political practice can accomplish, which leads to the question of what the aim of politics should be. Second, there is the debate about whether it's better to do or to suffer injustice, which leads to the question of what counts as living well. These questions are related because Socrates asserts that politics truly is the craft of caring for the soul, or "making the citizens themselves as good as possible" (513e–514a, 464b ff.).

Socrates early on (463a–466a) disparages rhetoric as something that "guesses at what's pleasant" rather than knowing what's good – a successful rhetorician is someone who has a talent for unhealthy "flattery" of the soul in the same way that a pastrymaker tempts the body with sweets. But Socrates cares more about whether rhetoric has a *logos* than do his interlocutors, so his scornful designation of it as flattery and a mere "knack" may not affect its status in others' eyes. For they are concerned with power in the city. As Gorgias first puts it, rhetoric produces freedom for orators by enabling control over others (452d–e).[10]

[9] My thinking about the opening of the dialogue owes much to the insights of my student Ben Peterson.

[10] Cf. the comments by Wardy 1996: 62–63.

But in the arguments of its proponents, rhetoric transmogrifies into or calls up something darker and often more violent. Gorgias' "proof" of the power of rhetoric includes his ability to persuade patients to take their medicine when his brother the doctor has failed. But in the very next sentence the rhetorician is no longer assisting the doctor, but fraudulently claiming to *be* a doctor (456a–d); persuasion turns into outright deception about who is the expert in health. For Polus, the power of orators in the city is evident in their ability to deal death, poverty, or banishment to "anyone they see fit" (466b–d). But surely this is an indication of the *limits* of persuasion (if one could persuade others to go along, one wouldn't have to kill them).[11] By these lights, Callicles has more faith in the power of persuasion than does Polus; although Callicles ominously raises the possibility of death more than once (485e–486c, 511a–b, 521b–d), it is rhetoric (which he admits is flattery, 521b) that he thinks will save Socrates from this grim fate.

Although Callicles stresses the possibility of death, Socrates himself comes back to the likelihood of speechlessness, comparing himself to a doctor whose claim to be arguing in the interests of health is shouted down by a jury of children: "don't you think he'd be at a total loss as to what he should say? . . . [T]hat's the sort of thing I know would happen to me, too, if I came into court" (521d–522c). This emphasis on Socrates' speechlessness is noted by both Ober and Yunis, who treat it as a progression of Plato's thought from the *Apology* to the *Gorgias*.[12] The *Apology* celebrates Socrates' "gadfly ethics,"[13] in which the pursuit of virtue and the provocation of the people of Athens are intertwined. Here Socrates is that familiar critical figure (matching Villa's description), pressing uncomfortable and insistent questions on those who think themselves wise. But what Ober sees stressed in the *Gorgias* is the incommunicability between Socrates and the people of Athens, at least as gathered for political purposes. If we see this as a progression of thought from one dialogue to the other, we might ask, with Ober, "what sort of comment on the 'Socratic ethics of criticism' is implied by Socrates' prediction of his own courtroom silence?"[14] But

[11] Cf. Benardete 1991: 38–39.

[12] Ober 1998; Yunis 1996.

[13] Ober 1998: 241.

[14] Ober 1998: 211. For Ober (211 and ch. 4 *passim*), the progression is from the gadfly ethics of the *Apology*, to the *Gorgias*'s exploration of how "Socrates' rhetoric is insufficient to reeducate an individual who has been thoroughly ideologized by the democratic political culture," to the *Republic*'s account of what kind of polity a philosopher could in fact participate in successfully.

we might also read it in dramatic time, from the pre-trial prediction of speechlessness in the *Gorgias* to the speechmaking and question asking of the *Apology*. Here Socrates' daimon does not oppose him speaking, even speaking in his characteristic manner, and although it indeed causes an uproar (*Apology* 21), to his surprise he has some measurable success (*Apology* 36). And far from being reduced to speechlessness, he has something to say even after his condemnation, precisely about how and why he chose to speak.[15] Reading in dramatic time opens up a question, one that is closed down by the progressive account: why, in the *Gorgias*, does Socrates emphasize his inability to speak in conventional political settings? What might Plato's purpose be?

Callicles undoubtedly would regard Socrates' speechlessness (and his conviction) as confirmation of his own position that having the freedom to think and act as he likes requires the power of rhetoric, not the childish play of philosophy. Socrates' perspective, of course, is that the only power that matters is the power that prevents us from doing injustice; thus he insists that the kind of power and powerlessness that concerns Callicles is not particularly important. But what makes Socrates' criticism deeper than it may at first seem is that he also shows that rhetoric does not in fact provide what its proponents want. In other words, Socrates' claim is that the power Callicles desires will not provide what he thinks it will – freedom and control.

Socrates argues that the orator is in fact constrained by the desires of the many, and that attempts to redirect those desires are likely to be met with violent resentment. Let's pause to ask why this violent resentment is such a recurring theme in the *Gorgias* (and indeed in the *Apology*, 31e–32c). For if we imagine current attempts to persuade us away from our desires – anti-smoking campaigns, for example, or efforts to encourage carpooling – people seem most likely to dismiss or ignore them, or perhaps feel mild annoyance and the desire to argue with the implicit conception of the good. But murderous resentment? What is the threat Socrates poses? Recall the witty caricature of democracy in Book 8 of the *Republic*, where the democrat's passion for freedom and equality is a passion for formlessness.[16] Everyone – citizens, noncitizens, animals – gets to do whatever they want, and all doings are seen as having equal value. This latter step is crucial for the moral equality

15 Salkever 1993: 137, argues that Socrates' playful "funeral oration" in the *Menexenus* provides another example of how Socrates could speak to the many collectively and still orient them to "the question of their own virtue."

16 As Saxonhouse 1998: 282, puts it, "true equality" means "freedom from tyrannizing *eidê*." My account here is indebted to her insights.

of this democracy. If doings are not better and worse, then people who want to do some things rather than others aren't better or worse. From this perspective, to suggest that medicinal tonics are healthier than pastries is not simply to criticize the desire for a doughnut, but rather to attack democratic freedom.[17]

Even in a less caricatured context, to claim that bitter remedies are good is to question the judgment of the demos. What *seems* unpleasant in fact *is* good, which means that there is not only a hierarchy of desires, but also of knowledge. No one resents doctors for their superior knowledge of medicine because their exercise of their expertise makes one healthy. On this analogy, no one should resent someone with a superior knowledge of political matters, or resent such people having a superior share of political power, because their exercise of their expertise makes one good. Socrates' democratic credentials might seem shaky here – but only if we suppose, as Bruno Latour does, that Socrates seriously thinks that politics is a techne best left to experts, of which he is one.[18] But this supposition relies on two others: that the many aren't capable of developing this knowledge, and that Socrates himself has it. But Socrates famously and continually hedges his own claims, "I don't know how these things are, but no one I've ever met, as in this case, can say anything else without being ridiculous" (509a). But what of his provocative claim to be the only one to "take up the true political craft" (521d)?

Socrates can say this of himself, he tells us, because he aims at what's best (521d). But this is an aim that he solicits everyone he encounters to "take up." And he does so in part with unfamiliar versions of familiar Athenian democratic practices. As Peter Euben insightfully argues, Socrates' actual practice is a distinctive adaptation of the practices of scrutiny (*dokimasia)* and accountability (*euthunai*) that any Athenian who held political office had to undergo. Socrates' version of accountability is concerned with his fellow citizens' "capacity to render an account of how they came to believe what it is they believe and why they believe it."[19] Socratic practice often renders his interlocutors uncertain of this and unable to render an account. So there is no political techne in this dialogue, despite discussion of it. Yet the idea of a

[17] The analogy here would be the angry smoker who regards any restrictions as an attack on his right to choose. See, for example, the pro-smoking articles at www.forces.org, some of which regard anti-smoking regulations as "violence" and refer to a "cultural war." For discussion, see Cooper 2004: ch. 3.

[18] Latour 1999: Ch. 8.

[19] Euben 1997: 106.

techne plays an important function, which is to provide an aim for the desire to know as a way of cultivating that desire rather than dissolving it into cynicism or relativism.

The *possibility* of a techne can serve to animate the pursuit of knowing. To engage in this pursuit via Socratic practice is to accept (or resist) being shaped in some way. But the same is true for engaging in conventional rhetorical politics. For instance, Socrates insists that political power requires genuinely becoming like those who can give that power – the Athenian people. "You should now be making yourself as much like the Athenian people as possible if you expect to endear yourself to them and have great power in the city," he advises Callicles. "You mustn't be their imitator but be naturally like them in your own person if you expect to produce any genuine result toward winning the friendship of the Athenian people" (513a–b). At first glance, this latter claim doesn't seem intuitively right; surely lots of successful politicians pretend to "be like" their constituents and then act in contrary ways (i.e., they are "imitators"). In Socratic practice, Callicles has to mean what he says for the dialectic to work, to reveal inconsistencies in belief. But why does he have to mean what he says to the people in the political arena? Does he really have to reconcile his scorn for conventional morality and his desire for political power?[20]

For Ober, Callicles is already "thoroughly ideologized by the democratic political culture."[21] But then why is Socrates warning him that a more thorough identification is needed? Or is he? If a democratic political culture is one in which all pleasures are equal, then Callicles has already shown himself not to be thoroughly indoctrinated by acknowledging that of course "some pleasures are better and others worse" (499b–c). But note further that Callicles believes that everyone would agree with this judgment. What seems likely then (since we know that even Athenian democrats didn't regard all pleasures as equal, e.g., the catamite example at 494e) is that both Callicles and the demos hold internally inconsistent beliefs. They do in fact value some ways of living more than others, and for reasons not reducible to power or

[20] Benardete's 1991: 93–94, explanation is that mere imitation is not enough if one is to be truly safe from the people, to avoid the fate that Callicles continually threatens Socrates with. It is only by becoming one of the demos that Callicles can know what in any particular instance will gratify them, for "every regime has its own pleasures and pains, and there is no art by which they can be known." (So much for Aristotle's attempt in the *Rhetoric*.) The rub here is that "by becoming one of the many he will never rule them."

[21] Ober 1998: 211.

pleasure. And this perhaps is what Socrates means ironically to suggest, that Callicles already is like the demos, despite Callicles' assumption that he is superior. On this account, Callicles and the demos are similar in that they want the freedom to do whatever they like and experience any restraints on that as agitating, but at the same time value some ways of life and those who lead them more than others.[22]

A further possibility: Socrates' point may be not that Callicles has to share particular beliefs with the demos, but rather that in gratifying them he becomes a person who takes gratification (in this case, of his desire for power) more seriously than improvement – just like the demos. Thus Callicles' path, rather than providing unrestrained freedom, will end up molding him in certain ways. The ways in which we exercise power (becoming a flatterer, for example) and the ends for which power is exercised, shapes us – even if we are pursuing power precisely in order to avoid limits imposed by others.

By Socrates' argument, then, Callicles can't avoid constraint one way or the other. This is significant because Callicles' concern with power is precisely a concern about being forced or compelled, by the many *or* by Socrates. He has already accused Socrates of maneuvering Gorgias so that he was "forced" to contradict himself, after which Polus was "bound and gagged" by Socrates (482d–e). Wardy argues that Callicles makes the strong claim that Socrates is "dialectically 'violent' (*biaios*)" at 505d, and that renditions like Irwin's "you're so insistent" (or Zeyl's "how unrelenting you are") are "undertranslated."[23] So Callicles at once sees Socrates' method as powerless (he will not be able to defend himself when brought before a jury) and yet forcefully constraining. Socrates' implicit response is that rhetoric too is powerless – with respect to what really matters – and also involves a kind of compulsion of the rhetor himself.

So the life of rhetoric doesn't have that radical freedom and unrestrained power to recommend it after all. From Socrates' perspective, it is philosophy that provides a certain sort of freedom and power – and its own kind of constraint as well. One is never compelled by others, only by the truth; one is free from the desire for worldly goods but possessed by the desire for good. And this does constrain Socrates; he's "held down and bound by arguments of iron and adamant" (508e–509a). So one way to think about what Socrates is doing with Callicles is that

[22] Note the sense in which Callicles admits he's like the many: he thinks Socrates is right and yet he is not really convinced (513c).

[23] Wardy 1996: 172 n. 31; Irwin 1979; Zeyl 1987.

he is trying to get Callicles to rethink what force – what restraints – to embrace and which to fear. Socratic practice can't protect Callicles from what he now most fears, but it's trying to get him to shift what is fearful, and what sort of constraint (or "discipline," 505c) he should be willing to tolerate.

Significantly, Callicles' current practice – political rhetoric – can't protect him from what he now most fears either. When Socrates talks about the "failures" of Pericles and other admired statesmen, he does so by changing the terms of what politicians should be aiming at. But he also draws attention to the fact that rhetoric offered them no protection from the ire of the many. Socrates asserts that Pericles and other commonly admired leaders were not "good at politics" because they did not improve the character of the citizens, which (via analogies with boat making, doctoring, and animal training) Socrates has argued is the goal of politics. These politicians were too willing to gratify current appetites, rather than redirect them (517 b–c); thus the many are made worse rather than better. As evidence of Pericles' failure, Socrates points to the embezzlement charge brought against him toward the end of his career. Pericles' job as politician was to be a "caretaker of men": "a man like that who cared for donkeys or horses or cattle would at least look bad if he showed these animals kicking, butting, and biting him because of their wildness, when they had been doing none of these things when he took them over" (516a–b). Now, this may show that Pericles failed to improve the many, but it also shows that even expert orators are vulnerable. And Cimon was ostracized, Themistocles exiled, Miltiades nearly thrown into the pit. So this way of life doesn't in fact provide the kind of protection and power that Callicles wants.

Socrates insists that he is the only one currently "to take up the true political craft and practice the true politics" – because he aims at "what's best," not at gratifying the people (521d). But even in a dialogue in which he claims to be the true politician, Socrates acknowledges that he will be unable to defend himself if brought before a jury of Athenians. Surely the point could not be more clear: if we apply the same standards to Socrates as he applied to Pericles and others, he is not very good at politics, since he was charged and found guilty by the very people he is supposed to be improving. To be fair, Socrates doesn't seem in this dialogue to think his political practice can work collectively, so maybe the appropriate comparison would be whether the people he engaged in his form of dialogue turned against him. Some obviously didn't, since they were present in support at his trial, offered to pay a fine for him, wanted to help him escape, wept at his death. But others obviously did – hence Meletus brings charges "on behalf of" the poets that Socrates engaged and infuriated, Anytus on behalf of the craftsmen, and so on (*Apology* 23). Indeed, the image that Socrates offers to describe Pericles' failure – an animal wildly kicking and butting – is evocative precisely of an animal bitten by a gadfly.

So whether one gratifies one's interlocutors through rhetoric or provokes them with philosophical dialogue, whether one pursues pleasure or justice, there is still the chance that one will end up "kicked, butted, and bitten." Indeed one crucial point of disagreement between Socrates and Callicles in previous sections of the dialogue is whether it *matters* whether you're kicked, butted, and bitten. Socrates of course has said that it doesn't matter, while Callicles seems to think it matters above all. But now, ironically, if Callicles wants to defend Pericles and others, he ends up having to defend the point that it doesn't matter what people do to you in terms of judging your "success."

Just to drive the point home, Socrates casually mentions as a good politician someone else who cannot meet his criterion. He approvingly cites "Aristides, the son of Lysimachus" as a politician who was just despite the temptations that power brings. Aristides was indeed famous for his justness; Plutarch depicts him as caring more for justice than for personal advantage or even for the advantage of the state (saying in opposition to a plan of Themistocles that "nothing could be more advantageous . . . and nothing more iniquitous" [*Aristides* 22]).[24] We might also recognize Aristides as the one willing to inscribe his own name on the *ostrakon* when asked to by an illiterate who wished to vote to ostracize him (this tale comes from Plutarch as well). Aristides – the one politician Socrates praises by singling him out from the majority of rulers who "prove to be bad" (526a–b), a ruler who cared for justice more than anything else – was also ostracized by the Athenian people. So by Socrates' own criterion he wasn't good at politics.

The fate of both Socrates and Aristides might give us pause. How then are we supposed to take Socrates' criticisms of previous leaders of Athens? If even true practitioners of politics end up being punished somehow by the people, then surely that cannot be a criterion for being good at politics. Perhaps it is not so much a criticism of Pericles and the others, but of rhetorical democratic politics as a way of "making people good." But this ignores that Socrates' own method is not inevitably successful either (besides those who brought charges against him, think of Callicles himself, Euthyphro, and, notoriously, Alcibiades).

[24] Trans. Scott-Kilvert 1960.

I think Plato's text is meant instead to raise questions about whether it's *possible* to make other people good. (And Socrates implicitly does so with his casual aside at 520d, "if it's really true that one can make people good."[25]) What would it mean to "make" people good, what kind of making would this be? Although Callicles is equally dismissive of all Socrates' homely craft analogies, Peter Euben has drawn our attention to the distinct ways in which different crafts "make good."[26] A cobbler, for example, is working on inert materials; a horse trainer on animate but unreasoning creatures. However, "the third analogy, that between a doctor who prevents or cures illness of the body and a political craftsman who prevents or cures political and psychic illness, is of a different order."[27] Although the patient doesn't share the doctor's expertise, there is a certain kind of mutuality; the patient provides certain kinds of information for the doctor to interpret, and the doctor has to explain her diagnosis and why she thinks the proposed treatment would be beneficial. And the patient participates not because it's pleasurable or because it gratifies immediate desires, but for the sake of health.

What this suggests is that a mode of making good has to be appropriate to the "materials" at hand. One cannot treat humans like a piece of wood or leather, nor train them like an animal, but must rather solicit their participation. Their improvement is, in large measure, up to them, to what they are willing to do. Significantly, the collegial and communicative relationship that Euben describes is not how the doctor/patient relationship generally appears in the *Gorgias.* Although Callicles sees Socrates' inability to communicate as a flaw on the philosopher's part, Socrates portrays it as a failure of the recalcitrant patient – a failure to listen without causing an uproar, to care enough about health to go through the pain or restrictions that treatment would involve. And here we come back to Socrates' speechlessness. In defense of his bitter remedies, the doctor can only "tell the truth and say, 'yes, children, I was doing all those things in the interest of health'" (522a). If his audience will not even listen to an argument predicated upon health, then the doctor is indeed "at a total loss" (522b).

What is Plato trying to get us to think about here by emphasizing Socrates' helplessness, his reliance on what his audience will listen to and take seriously? Is the point that neither political rhetoric nor Socratic

[25] Or, in Irwin's (1979) translation, "if he really had the power to make people good."
[26] Euben 1994.
[27] Euben 1994: 219.

philosophy really has the power to make people good unless they already *want* to be good? If this is the case, then we can see Socrates' own activities as aiming not to make people good, but to get them to want to make themselves good, to entice them to the project. How does he do this? Most familiarly, by creating discomfort with their current state (of belief or confusion), by Villa's dissolvent rationality. But this is never enough. He offers Callicles images (493a–494b). He offers motivational myths that he urges us to take seriously (523a). And finally he offers – rhetorically – the *inspiration* of his own practice and discourse:

> For my part, Callicles, I'm convinced by these accounts, and I think about how I'll reveal to the judge a soul that's as healthy as it can be. So I disregard the things held in honor by the majority of people, and by practicing truth I really try, to the best of my ability, to be and to live as a very good man, and when I die, to die like that. And I call on all other people as well, as far as I can – and you especially I call on in response to your call – to this way of life, this contest, that I hold to be worth all the other contests in this life. (527d–e, cf. 482b–c)

It may seem unexceptional to talk about Socrates as inspiring, since he is for us a heroic cultural figure, one we hold to be exemplary in many ways. But recall Socrates' concerns about the sheer intoxication with power and glory that characterized Periclean Athens (which Villa rightly notes[28]) and his commitment to *logos*. These concerns seem to sit uneasily with a notion of inspiration, which implies being *moved*, and moved in some way that is not necessarily rational. This uneasiness should lead us to look more closely at the inspirational and exhortatory aspects of Socrates' practice.

Let me note two characters in Plato's corpus who implicitly urge us to pay attention to Socratic inspiration, one less familiar and the other more so. In the little-discussed dialogue that bears his name,[29] Clitophon's complaint is that Socrates has nothing to offer *but* inspiration. Your marvelous exhortations to pursue virtue and justice are compelling, Clitophon tells Socrates. I'm ready – but neither you nor

[28] See also Salkever 1993.

[29] There has been disagreement among scholars about whether the *Clitophon* is genuine, and whether it is finished, since Socrates never responds to Clitophon's criticisms. See Roochnik 1984 for discussion and for a powerful argument that Socrates' silence in fact makes a crucial philosophical point.

your friends seem to be able to tell me what the next step is. What does it mean to pursue justice, beyond going around exhorting others to be just? Surely that's not all there is? Clitophon relates the very Socratic investigations he has undertaken with Socrates' "companions and fellow enthusiasts" (408c) in an attempt to find out what sort of skill justice is, but not surprisingly no satisfactory answer appears. Socrates himself gives inconclusive or contradictory answers, Clitophon claims, and as such he is not simply useless but actually gets in the way of someone who wants to achieve virtue.

The reader and teacher of Plato's dialogues will see this as an utterly plausible reaction to Socrates. Like some of my students, Clitophon can't decide if Socrates doesn't know or if he just won't tell. But note that what has gotten Clitophon to this state is Socratic exhortation, the powerfully inspiring quality of his public discourse. We might be reminded here of a more familiar Socratic companion, Alcibiades, and his drunken frankness in the *Symposium*:

> You know, people hardly ever take a speaker seriously, even if he's the greatest orator; but let anyone – man, woman, or child – listen to you or even to a poor account of what you say – and we are all transported, completely possessed. . . . I swear to you, the moment he starts to speak, I am beside myself: my heart starts leaping in my chest, the tears come streaming down my face, even the frenzied Corybantes seem sane compared to me – and, let me tell you, I'm not alone. (215d–e)[30]

In the presence of Socrates, Alcibiades is enraptured by the idea that caring for the state of his soul is the most important pursuit. But something in him resists this enchantment, and he works the only countercharm he can: "I refuse to listen."

If Alcibiades and Clitophon are the only examples we have of the workings of Socratic inspiration, we might think that this inspiration necessarily fails. Given Alcibiades' subsequent political career, he can be described in many ways, but "leading a life of virtue" is not one of them; Clitophon has given up on Socrates and become a pupil of Thrasymachus. But I want to argue that, far from being the only examples, Alcibiades and Clitophon alert us to the ongoing presence of

[30] Trans. Nehamas and Woodruff 1989.

Socratic inspiration, and to the need to probe its character, its necessity, and its power.[31]

To investigate this further, let us turn to the *Republic*, where there are at least two levels of soul-craft being exercised. One is the educational and social structuring of the city being built in speech, and one is the interaction between Socrates and his interlocutors (particularly his main interlocutors, Glaucon and Adeimantus). The first seems like a straightforward attempt at "making people good" (but we'll see it's more complicated than that). In the second, Socrates is working with people who already want to be good – but who also want what Mary Nichols has called the "security of absolute knowledge." This security, Plato makes clear, can be provided neither by Socrates nor by philosopher kings. (Just as the life of neither Pericles nor Socrates can provide the security that Callicles aims at in his quest for power.)

THE *REPUBLIC*: EDUCATION AND OTHER DRUGS

The *Republic* is a site for interpretations as numerous as they are incompatible. The most well-known account portrays the dialogue, and Plato himself, as totalitarian or at least anti-democratic.[32] On this view, the *Republic* is a blueprint for a city ruled by philosopher-kings according to knowledge derived from the suprasensible forms, and justice is characterized as a hierarchical division of citizens in terms of the functions to which they are suited. But other theorists draw our attention to contrasting currents in the *Republic*, not least the difference between Socratic philosophical practice and that of the philosopher-kings. The message that these theorists take away from the dialogue is precisely the opposite of its surface meaning: the lesson is that true justice is impossible to achieve, and thus the *Republic* is a caution against radical reform, or at least is designed to moderate the desire for it.[33]

Rather than ask whether Plato means the *Republic* as a blueprint or as a warning against such a plan, I think a better way to read the dialogue is to ask, with Euben and Mara, what does Plato mean to convey by offering both messages?[34] In my experience, working closely

[31] An audience member at the University of Minnesota pointed out that we also might think about Socrates as *inspired* – for example, his daimon, his philosophical trances (*Symposium* 175).

[32] Popper 1966, Nussbaum 1998.

[33] Bloom 1968; Nichols 1984.

[34] Euben 1990; Mara 1997.

with this text affirms Halperin's insight that "Plato has gone out of his way to withhold from his readers the means of sacrificing in good conscience one of the alternatives to the other."[35] In other words, the *Republic* offers both positive content *and* undercutting currents. What are we to learn from holding these in mind together?

Read in this way, the *Republic* is something like what Socrates calls a "summoner," an object that "doesn't declare one thing any more than its opposite" (523b–525). An object that appears to be both itself and its opposite "summons" us to investigate; in such a case, "[t]he soul would then be puzzled, would look for an answer, would stir up its understanding, and would ask what the one itself is" (524e).[36] It's not "the one itself" I pursue here, in the sense of the one "real" meaning of Plato's dialogue, but rather what we can learn from probing the coexisting multiple meanings – by preserving its character as a summoner.

The particular contrast that I want to examine is between two modes of soul-shaping at work in the dialogue. One is, of course, the education given to the guardians, which involves careful attention to stories, music, gymnastics, military training, and later, for some, mathematics and dialectic. The other mode is the Socratic practice of examining the meaning of political concepts like justice. The purpose of both modes is in a sense the same – to create or encourage a deeply rooted commitment to (what is discovered or presented as) the best way of living, the just life.

If one question underlying the *Republic* is "what would it take to make people good," the answer given by the education of the guardians is that neither Periclean nor Socratic politics would be sufficient (i.e., neither of the options presented in the *Gorgias*). Rather, what is required is a thoroughgoing education that makes politics of either sort unnecessary because it ensures that members of the kallipolis already want what they should want. But we are given plenty of reasons to question both the possibility and the desirability of this endeavor.

The focus on the appropriate content of the stories told to young guardians has given rise to protests of censorship, and the kallipolis has

[35] Halperin 1992: 119. In Euben's 1990: 266, words, "To insist that the *Republic* is utopian or anti-utopian, conservative or radical, an epic theory designed to transform belief and action or a repudiation of such transformative aspirations, an idealist blueprint for a good society or a critique of idealism is to posit simplified polarities that beg the questions Plato is trying to raise and cauterize the dialectic he is trying to establish."

[36] Understanding the *Republic* as itself a "summoner" comes from conversations with Liz Markovits.

been justly criticized for its unappealing hierarchy. But let me note some other disturbing features of the soul-craft being exercised in this city. First, what is striking is the violence required for such a city to exist. The meaning of philosophers "wiping the slate clean" (501a) is not particularly ambiguous for a reader of previous decisions to execute those with incurably evil souls (410a) and to get rid of defective children (460c). This meaning is underscored by the move to "send everyone in the city who is over ten years old into the country . . . and take possession of the children" (540e–541a). (One could argue that the latter is merely exile, rather than violence, but it is difficult to imagine citizens peacefully leaving their dwellings and children.) The influence of parents not properly educated is obviously too strong to be allowed to continue, and there will apparently always be some souls too deformed to even provide decent material with which to work. Not only initially, but continuously, the philosopher-kings' soul-craft depends on a violent purging of the city's souls to clear ground for the work at hand.[37]

Second, with respect to this soul-work, we might also be struck by the amount of sheer deceit the rulers must exercise. Think particularly of the myth of the metals in Book 3, or the engineered lottery that governs sex among the guardians in Book 5. It may seem too simple to call this deceit; perhaps we should take seriously the nobility of such falsehoods, as Plato's Socrates urges us to. Falsehoods are legitimate or noble when employed as "useful drugs" against ignorance, and if they are "as much like the truth as possible" (382b–e). So perhaps the myth of the metals is like a medicine for curing the ignorance in the souls of non-philosophers, providing an accessible version of the "truth" that people are naturally suited for different kinds of work or that citizens must act as brothers. But drugs can work as curative tonic or as lulling opiate; note that the rulers are to tell the myth *as if* it were the literal truth and that people are to believe "in fact" that their actual experiences were "a sort of dream" (414c–415e). Socrates is frankly not sure that any drug is powerful enough to accomplish this; he hesitates to tell the myth in the first place, and he and Glaucon cannot think of any "device" to get the first generation of citizens educated under this system to actually believe it (415d).

[37] One can understand this as a metaphor about education, of course, but the terms of the metaphor are still interestingly distasteful, and not just to modern readers. Equally striking is the richly described coercion and violence necessary for reason to succeed in ruling the soul in the *Phaedrus* (253d–256e).

Does Plato's text suggest, then, that there are stubborn aspects of selfhood that escape even the most rigorous education, the most heartless purging, and the most persuasive rulers? I think the case of the rigged lottery supports this view. For with all the care given to the training of the guardians, surely they would have been educated to understand the necessity of appropriate breeding (that the best must mate with the best) and thus wouldn't have to be tricked into it.[38] This hints at a certain recalcitrance of desire to even the most expert soul-craft. The philosophy guiding the rulers, as Mary Nichols has argued, is one "that craves the security of absolute knowledge and control, and attacks whatever threatens that security";[39] thus it doesn't hesitate to use violence and deceit to accomplish its aim. Yet Plato indicates that even so there are forces that will inevitably escape this control. (Even mathematics, their favored tool; see the failure to consistently calculate the nuptial number correctly in Book 8, which brings about the dissolution of the city).

Socrates' own performance in the *Republic* offers an alternative approach to soul-craft. He too uses myth and stories as part of his discourse, and he is well aware of their powers as soul-shapers (this is what prompted the initial restriction of permissible stories in the just city, 377b–379a). But unlike the rulers of kallipolis, Socrates clearly signals his interlocutors what he is doing. The myth of Er is expressly presented as a tale (614b); the parable of the cave, as an imaginary story about "the effect of education and of the lack of it" (514). Socrates doesn't try to convince Glaucon and Adeimantus that the Sun *is* the Good, but rather suggests it explicitly as an image, a way to get at a complicated and difficult concept argument (506e–509).

The distinction between the two modes of soul-craft, then, is not that Socrates uses dialectical argument and the philosopher-kings propagate myths. Kallipolis is an indication that reason too can dominate, and Socrates' activities indicate that the line between reason and storytelling needn't be so sharply drawn.[40] Rather, the difference seems to be whether, in the mix of reasoned argument and storytelling, the hearers

[38] And surely Socratic irony is involved here in likening the "sacred marriages" of guardians of kallipolis to the breeding of dogs (459a). The doglike character of the guardians first appears at 375d.

[39] Nichols 1984: 252.

[40] As has been much discussed in contemporary feminist scholarship. See for example Disch 1993, Abrams 1991. And see the myth at the end of the *Gorgias*, which Socrates thinks is " a very fine account," though he knows Callicles will consider it "a mere tale" (523a).

are told that these *are* stories, ways to approach rather than assert truth. This is simply another way to articulate the well-known character of Socrates' dialogic method, in which listeners are deliberately engaged in the project of coming to understand. What I want to stress is that insofar as listeners are engaged in the very activities that constitute soul-craft, they share in the exercise of power in a way that they do not under the rule of the philosopher-kings. This certainly doesn't mean that Socratic soul-craft is any less crafty or that the exercise of power is somehow equal. But it does mean that the citizens of a Socratic circle of inquiry are not simply passive material to be molded by authority or violence or deceit.[41] (And thus Socrates does not inevitably triumph over his challengers.) To complete the contrast, far from expunging defective souls, Socrates will talk with almost anybody—young and old, native or foreign, sophist, merchant, general, priest, the convention-bound Crito, the excessive Alcibiades. Again, this is perhaps why his method is no more infallible than any other; he doesn't start only with those who already want to be (or have been trained to be) good.

The *Republic* offers a tradeoff, then, that pushes us to think about what we are willing to settle for. A political regime can groom souls according to objective knowledge that need not be understood by all and through methods that do not require mutual engagement. That may seem an appealing strategy to those who question the capacity or desire of the many to aim toward the good and who crave control for that reason. But Plato makes clear the extreme difficulty – and just plain extremes – involved and the mutuality that is being forsaken. The alternative is the deep, difficult engagement and effort that Socrates elicits and models. Socrates' soul-craft aims at the good *and* requires the engagement of others. To have both requires a deep Socratic commitment to "closely examine these same matters often" (*Gorgias* 513c–d) – to lead the examined life. This may seem like its own kind of extreme, given Socrates' singularity. But Socratic practice implies that it is within everyone's power.[42]

Plato also shows us what's involved when Socrates engages those who already want to be good – but who also want "the security of absolute knowledge" as well. Thrasymachus is the main challenger of the aporetic Book 1, but he is relegated to a nearly silent audience member for the rest of the dialogue (although he is invoked several

[41] The moments of aporia in Plato's dialogues – the moments of paralyzing puzzlement, of not knowing whether or what one knows – may be the Socratic version of "wiping the slate clean."

[42] And see *Republic* 518c–d: "the power to learn is present in everyone's soul."

times as shorthand for his earlier argument, e.g., 545a). The primary interlocutors – Glaucon and Adeimantus – are in an odd position. They are not convinced by Thrasymachus that notions of justice are merely screens for interest and power, but they are concerned that they lack a convincing response to those like Thrasymachus. Glaucon has been "deafened" by countless arguments asserting that people practice justice only because of the consequences (legal or reputational) of getting caught. On this view, justice isn't really a good in itself, but rather allows us to attain other goods: political power, business success, social standing. Glaucon is left "perplexed" because he hasn't yet heard an argument sufficient to support what he *already believes*.[43] He can't give an account for how he in fact lives his life (if we are to accept his own and Socrates' assessment of his character and his beliefs), and he has the courage to insist on one (357a; 358c–d, 368a–b). When Adeimantus chimes in, it is to point out that even in poetry and myth about the gods, justice isn't praised for itself; instead, the stories hold out the afterlife as a reward for being just or reassure us that the gods can be placated with sacrifice and prayer if we are unjust. But Adeimantus makes clear – he says it twice from 367 to 368 – that he doesn't want just an "argument" (*logos*), but a showing of the difference it makes in the world and to the person: "Do not merely demonstrate to us by argument that justice is stronger than injustice, but show us what effect each one itself has, because of itself, on the person who has it" (367e). Adeimantus wants better stories, better images, that show justice as its own reward. But more than this, he is urging a deeper sense of what it means truly to show something. As becomes clear later, he wants to avoid the common situation (as he describes it at 487b) of being led by Socrates' argument to a conclusion that he does not in fact think is true of the world.

Plato often alerts us to different ways of holding a belief or asks us to question what it really means to know. Think of Socrates' and Gorgias' account of a rhetorician's audience whose members are convinced without actually gaining knowledge (*Gorgias* 454e–455a); Polus, of whom Socrates insists that his deeper beliefs undermine the beliefs he claims to hold; or Callicles' conflicted remark at 513c that he both thinks Socrates makes sense and yet is not really convinced. And now we have Plato's brothers, who want argument and images to undergird

[43] Desjardins 2002: 118: "a dialogue seeks to understand *why* (under some but not all interpretations) the original opinion is indeed true – and thus might be transformed into real knowledge."

their already existing beliefs. There is a level of conviction already in Glaucon's and Adeimantus' souls that resist both the sophistic arguments for injustice and the conventional stories about justice's rewards.[44] But they want more – they want to be convinced that their conviction is right.

These different situations call for different kinds of shaping or suasion. Part of what is involved is obviously reasoned argument. But as Richard McKim points out in his insightful analysis of the *Gorgias*, what Socrates does in that dialogue is more psychological than logical. Socrates' argument is that everyone already believes deep down that it does harm to oneself to commit injustice (and thus that it is worse than suffering it).[45] Yet there are those like Polus and Callicles who obviously deny it. So Socrates doesn't need to provide logical proofs so much as he needs to do the psychological work that taps into, or gets them to connect with, their deep belief. In the *Gorgias*, McKim argues, Socrates does so through shame.

Socrates is offering something more than logical proof (or, in Adeimantus' words, theoretical argument) in the *Republic* as well. When, at the end of Book 4, Glaucon and Socrates answer the initial question of whether it is more profitable to be just or unjust, the question turns out to be answered by a particular version of what the well-ordered soul is like. Glaucon says that the whole question seems ridiculous now, since who could wish to live with a disordered soul? In other words, justice is a right relationship among parts (of the soul or the city), and who wouldn't rather be rightly ordered than not? This isn't particularly satisfying; one could just as well question whether the soul has a natural order of parts, or argue that Socrates has simply solved the question by definition (it's better to live a just life because we're the kind of creatures for whom it's better to live a just life). My point here is not so much to contest whether Plato's arguments are analytically sound, but rather to examine the character of Glaucon's conviction and desire. Socrates can't give Glaucon the unassailable account that he wants, and in two ways: Socrates can't *give* it to Glaucon, and Socrates doesn't *have* an unassailable account. Socrates' own hesitations throughout the Republic should alert us to this. Socrates is always trying to get Glaucon to question Socrates' authority, to join him in the hunt for justice rather than just following his lead. In addition, Socrates

[44] So, as Mara 1997: ch. 2, says about the *Apology*, Socrates has to argue against both conventional wisdom and sophistic overturning of convention.

[45] McKim 2002.

periodically tries to undermine Glaucon's confidence in the adequacy of the previous argument. What Plato and Socrates know that Glaucon doesn't is that (in David Roochnik's words) "there is no argument which can, without begging the question, establish the goodness of argumentation . . . rational argumentation depends upon a value judgment: that it is good to pursue the argument, to strive to replace opinion with knowledge."[46]

But if the unassailable justification that Glaucon wants is a chimera, what does Socrates have to offer instead? How would we characterize the psychological work that Socrates does with Glaucon and Adeimantus? There is nothing magical here; what Socrates has to offer is simply Socrates, by which I mean the familiar Socratic activities of engaging in argument, telling stories, and offering similes and images, all with the paradoxical insistence that there is no "end of journeying" toward the good and yet that "there is some such thing to be seen" (532e–533b). What Socrates has to offer is a Socratic education, the education that Adeimantus has called for (366d–367b) and that Callicles resists (*Gorgias* 505c, 513c). And "education" is the right concept here, for being educated is different from being shown a proof; it implies an ongoing practice. But what gives us the heart to go on?

I suggest that the psychological glue for sticking with the Socratic education here is in fact something like inspiration. Glaucon clearly wants to feel convinced of his own conviction rather than sheepish about his inability to defend it. And Socrates' interaction with Glaucon suggests that in some cases a necessary accompaniment to a reasoned and storied account is to be inspired to live by it – by images of just souls, by myths that are not simply explanatory but hortatory, like the myth of Er. Indeed, Socrates himself provides an example of why Glaucon should live as he does, for it is Socrates who is the implicit contrast to the unbalanced souls of Book 8, Socrates who shows that it is possible to love wisdom and justice more than honor, or money, or pleasure (or freedom or equality). Socrates' inspirational words and exemplary life can make the choice to live justly appear particularly attractive and provide a kind of psychological appeal even in the absence of absolute knowledge.

Socrates can't provide a logos that is beyond argument, but neither can someone like Callicles or Thrasymachus. How we choose between the two, then, relies not on an unassailable account, but on the strength of our commitment to value dialogic reason. This is not to say that

[46] Roochnik 1984: 141–42.

Plato is a relativist, of course; Socrates' method is distinguished from the sophists by the insistence that there *is* a true account, even if he and his companions are unable to state it adequately. Whether this seems different from sophism to the participants – what the effect on their soul really is – is an open question, given that Socrates won't supply that truth.[47] But if there is a Socratic way of cultivating a commitment to the good that doesn't involve the control possessed by philosopher-kings, then perhaps there is a Socratic way of asking "what is" that doesn't result in the cynicism cultivated by sophists. This Socratic way, I suggest, involves inspiration when reason comes up against its limits.[48]

The psychological work that I am calling "inspiration" is more transparent than the deceit engaged in by philosopher- kings, and more challenging than the gratification offered by rhetoricians. In some sense, however, it does have to speak to people as they are, or at least to identify proto-desires that might be sparked or turned in the right direction (as when Socrates calls living well a "contest" to appeal to the agonistic Callicles [*Gorgias* 526e]). The attentiveness to the individual that is a hallmark of Socratic interaction would seem to indicate that this method of soul-shaping is not institutionalizable.

Or is it?

THE *LAWS*: PRELUDES AND NIGHTLY MEETINGS

In Plato's "second best" regime, the rule of law not only guides citizen action but also aims at shaping citizen desires. This legal method of soul-shaping is no more foolproof than any of the others we've examined, but it takes seriously the possibility of human recalcitrance as well as the possibility of human persuadability. It also takes seriously the indispensability of Socrates.

Although much of the *Laws* is taken up with detailing specific laws and the punishments for those who do not adhere to them, the Athenian Stranger continually emphasizes the additional importance of the *preludes* to the laws. The idea of having these "preambles" is presented as an innovation by the Athenian, who argues that laws need to have this persuasive and informative aspect to supplement their

[47] For a negative answer, we might think of Clitophon, and also the young man who has his traditional convictions shaken by argument and "becomes lawless" (*Republic* 538–39).

[48] In Roochnik's 1984: 142, terms, the project of philosophy "is initiated, not by a demonstration of its value, but by exhortation."

compulsory aspect (718a ff.). The persuasive prelude is intended to "contribute something to making the hearer listen in a more tame and agreeable mood to the advice" of the laws and thus to make the listener "a better learner" (718d). Again, at 723a–b, the purpose of the prelude is to create "a frame of mind more favorably disposed and therefore more apt to learn something." This is a step ostensibly ignored by Socrates in the *Gorgias*, since he seems there to ignore the usefulness of persuasion for the doctor's craft.[49] But the Athenian makes a different use of the doctor analogy. He compares the way a free doctor might treat a free man to the way a slave doctor would treat a slave. The latter "gives his commands just like a headstrong tyrant" while the former "both learns something himself from the invalids and, as much as he can, teaches the one who is sick. He doesn't give orders until he has in some sense persuaded" (720c–e).[50] The need for the "double method" of persuasion and compulsion tells us something interesting about the citizens – that they are to be treated as free and reasonable persons and that persuasion will not always be successful. Thus comes the need for orders and penalties to deal with the recalcitrant, those who refuse to learn from the persuasive teachings of the preambles.

So the preludes are designed as teaching-persuasion (*Gorgias* 455a) as befits free citizens. What characterizes this specific kind of persuasion? It obviously involves offering reasons, as in the arguments intended to persuade skeptics that the gods exist and care about human affairs. But the preludes often seem to involve more than that, and how exactly to characterize them is a subject of disagreement. Christopher Bobonich argues that the initial discussion of the preludes characterizes them as purely rational and that this is confirmed by repeated descriptions of the preludes as involving teaching, learning, or education: "What the person who is to be persuaded is asking for is to be 'taught', that is, to be given good epistemic reasons for thinking that the principles lying behind the legislation are true."[51] Bobonich's explanation of the rhetorical flourishes and mythic stories in later preludes is that such

[49] I say ostensibly because Socrates is equating himself to the doctor, and Socrates uses all kinds of rhetorical means beyond bare *logos* in his own practice.

[50] On this analogy, then, it is the laws that have "in some sense" to persuade in order to claim legitimately that their subjects must obey. This is interesting to think about in terms of the *Crito*, where the laws of Athens tell Socrates that *he* has to persuade or obey. But, as Socrates has the laws argue in their defense, there is a sense in which they have persuaded Socrates, and that is indicated by his remaining in the city and choosing to raise children there.

[51] Bobonich 2002: 104–5.

strategies allow for the needs of a diversity of citizens, some who will be persuaded by reason and others who will need nonrational inducement (and still others who will not be persuaded by any means).[52]

It is not so much the substance of Bobonich's explanation that I take issue with as the assumptions behind it – in particular the assumptions that there is a clear Platonic distinction between reason and other means of persuasion and that teaching and learning involve this kind of purified reason. In many of the passages where the preludes are described as teaching instruments, there is something else added; see for example 888a, where the preludes are "to admonish, and at the same time to teach," or the general prelude to the laws, where the Athenian speaks of "how praise and blame can educate each of them" (730b). There is something going on here that is not the mere processing of reasons separate from praise and blame and admonishment and encouragement. To praise a person, activity, or way of life certainly involves offering reasons why they are admirable, but to praise is to present those reasons in a particular way and tone and for a particular purpose – not just to convey the reasons something is praiseworthy but to kindle the desire to imitate the person or engage in the activity or way of life. Think of the Athenian's own comparison between the simple legal statement "everyone is to marry after he reaches the age of thirty and before the age of thirty-five" and the subsequent "double formula":

> Everyone is to marry after he reaches the age of thirty and before he reaches thirty-five, bearing in mind that there is a sense in which the human species has by a certain nature a share in immortality, and that it is the nature of everyone to desire immortality in every way. For the desire to become famous and not to lie nameless after one has died is a desire for such a thing. Thus the species of human beings has something in its nature that is bound together with all of time, which it accompanies and will always accompany to the end. In this way the species is immortal; by leaving behind the children of children and remaining one and the same for always, it partakes of immortality by means of coming-into-being. (721b–c)

[52] Bobonich 2002: 113–15. This doesn't mean that Plato has rejected "the goal of fostering rational beliefs," Bobonich 2002: 115, argues, since people can come to a "reasoned appreciation" of things they first approved via emotion.

Of course, one distinction between the simple and the double formula is that the first does not give reasons everyone is to marry. But the Athenian could offer reasons in the form of an explanation such as "everyone is to marry after he reaches the age of thirty and before the age of thirty-five, because it sustains the population of the city and continues the human species." To describe the way in which humans are immortal, to invoke fame and time and the children of children, is to animate, to encourage particular actions. This understands reason as intertwined with other human capacities – for feeling, for action.

Morrow's analysis of the *Laws* tries to capture this quality of the preludes. They are designed to set out "the good, individual or social, which the law is intended to secure and the reasons why the citizen should conform to it."[53] They are not imperative, but neither are they narrowly rational; "they are persuasion at the high level of rational insight suffused with emotion."[54] Reason is the flexible golden cord that needs help from other aspects of the soul, and "above all there is the spell exercised by noble words."[55]

Morrow insists that this "enchantment" isn't opposed to reason even if it is nonrational. Indeed, enchantment (like "drugs") has two connotations – we can be enchanted, as under a spell and in someone else's control, or we can be enchanted in the sense of charmed, appealed to, captivated (but not captured) by. The difference between these connotations is something like the difference between an enchanted forest and an enchanting smile. I want to suggest that the "spell exercised by noble words," this engaged enchantment, is also captured by the notion of "inspiration." The laws of this second-best regime thus institutionalize both reason and inspiration.

Here mass instruction is possible via the reading of the preludes and texts of the laws.[56] So the soul-shaping of the *Laws* involves teaching-persuasion and reasoned inspiration, implying a rich conception of human capacity and change. However, from a democratic perspective, there are plenty of unsettling aspects of this dialogue, not least the continued emphasis on "taming" and the creepy authoritarian elements

[53] Morrow 1993: 553.

[54] Morrow 1993: 557–58.

[55] Morrow 1993: 557.

[56] This is a second-best regime in part because it relies on these written texts for instruction – and writing says the same thing to everyone, even though people might need different kinds of inspiration and reasons (although the Athenian does start with the purest possible "stream" of colonists [736a–d], which implies a certain amount of homogeneity).

of specific laws (especially with respect to impiety and the punishment of beliefs). But what is reassuring is that, hidden in the early morning light of this regime, there is Socrates.

What I mean by this, of course, is that although reading the preludes and laws is not like engaging in argument with Socrates, meeting with the nocturnal council might well be. It is in the nocturnal council – the "nightly meetings"[57] – that one actually gets to engage in philosophy. And it is philosophizing of a fairly Socratic sort in that it involves examining what virtue is and engaging with foreigners and travelers and young men. In this sense it is possible to see, in these early dawn meetings, a reflection of those other dialogues in which Socrates stays up all night talking. But I say it is philosophizing of only a "fairly" Socratic sort, because this is a Socrates without Athens. And as Socrates shows us he knows in the *Crito*, this makes a difference. In a regime without Athens' freedom of speech and tolerance for diverse ways, Socratic education is reserved for the few – which makes it not very Socratic and which perhaps explains why Socrates isn't explicitly present as a character in this dialogue. Yet for any reader of Plato's dialogues, he's always present in mind. Is it too outlandish to suggest that Plato had to know this, and thus that Socrates' absence is one of the dramatic elements that we need to engage?[58] To play with this possibility further: to see Socrates in the shadows of the nightly meeting despite his ostensible absence suggests that neither he nor his kind of philosophizing is containable.[59] And this in turn might lead us to question whether, even in a regime that penalizes the holding of heterodox beliefs, those who philosophize really will be able to restrict themselves to the early morning hours and the company of the select few. They might instead find themselves, as Socrates did, asking in the midst of the city what arguments we should accept and what inspirations should move us.

[57] V. B. Lewis 1998: 14–15, points out that the Greek term *sullogos* doesn't have the "formal juridical connotation" that the English term "council" does, and that a more accurate translation would be "something like 'nightly conference' or 'nightly meeting.'"

[58] I appreciate Monoson's 2000: 233, thoughtful suggestion that "[t]he absence of Socrates artfully records Plato's acknowledgment of the limitations of the life of Socrates as a model for understanding the full range of special knowledge that may be politically significant." The further possibility I propose is that Plato is also implicitly acknowledging the limitations of a collective political life that doesn't include Socrates.

[59] Thus we can see the nightly meetings as one of those "institutions that subvert institutionalization," in Sheldon Wolin's words, 1994: 43.

I have argued that to describe Socratic practice only in terms of using critical reason to induce perplexity and hesitancy is to miss much of its complexity. First of all, Socrates' reason is no dry analytic rationality but rather involves weaving a tapestry of images, stories, and analogies that are crucial to the meaning of the engagement. But there is a further dimension to Socrates' practice, one that I've tried to capture with the term "inspiration." It's crucial that what Socrates inspires us to *is* reason.[60] Recall the myth of Er, in which souls choose the next life that they will live. The soul who makes the worst choice – choosing the life of a tyrant who "was fated to eat his own children" – is the soul who in a previous life had "participated in virtue through habit and without philosophy" (619c–d). To be without philosophy is to be without a certain kind of freedom; Glaucon is right to want an account of justice, but the account isn't like an object that can be given, it is rather a practice. The practice to which Socrates urges and entices us is to care for virtue and the state of our soul. That caring practice is the practice of dialogic reason. It is a practice in which Socrates questions our claims to know, and at the same time affirms the pursuit of knowing. To do this paradoxical work requires inspiration and persistence, not only to undermine our certainties, but to offer us answers to examine.

Works Cited

Abrams, K. 1991. "Hearing the Call of Stories." *California Law Review* 79: 971–1052.

Benardete, S. 1991. *The Rhetoric of Morality and Philosophy: Plato's Gorgias and Phaedrus*. Chicago.

Bloom, A., trans. 1968. *The Republic of Plato*. Translated with notes and an interpretive essay. New York.

Bobonich, C. 2002. *Plato's Utopia Recast: His Later Ethics and Politics*. Oxford.

Brann, E. T. H. 1979. *Paradoxes of Education in a Republic*. Chicago.

Cooper, D. 2004. *Challenging Diversity: Rethinking Equality and the Value of Difference*. Cambridge.

Desjardins, R. 2002. "Why Dialogues? Plato's Serious Play." In *Platonic Writings, Platonic Readings*, ed. C. L. Griswold, Jr. University Park, PA.

Disch, L. J. 1993. "More Truth than Fact: Storytelling as Critical Understanding in the Writings of Hannah Arendt." *Political Theory* 21: 665–94.

Euben, J. P. 1990. *The Tragedy of Political Theory: The Road Not Taken*. Princeton, NJ.

[60] This is why, as Peter Euben points out to me, Socrates has to repel as well as inspire, to entice us to the practice and to push us away when we want simply to follow his lead.

1994. "Democracy and Political Theory: A Reading of Plato's Gorgias." In *Athenian Political Thought and the Reconstruction of American Democracy*, ed. J. P. Euben, J. R. Wallach, and J. Ober. Ithaca, NY.

1997. *Corrupting Youth: Political Education, Democratic Culture, and Political Theory*. Princeton, NJ.

Frede, M. 1992. "Plato's Arguments and the Dialogue Form." In *Methods of Interpreting Plato and His Dialogues* ed. J. C. Klagge and N. D. Smith. Oxford Studies in Ancient Philosophy, supplementary vol. Oxford.

Grube, G. M. A., trans. 1975. *Plato*: The Trial and Death of Socrates: *Euthyphro, Apology, Crito, Death Scene from Phaedo*. Indianapolis, IN.

Trans. 1992. *Plato: Republic*, rev. C. D. C. Reeve. Indianapolis, IN.

Halperin, D. M. 1992. "Plato and the Erotics of Narrativity." In *Methods of Interpreting Plato and his Dialogues*, ed. J. C. Klagge and N. D. Smith. Oxford Studies in Ancient Philosophy, supplementary vol. Oxford.

Irwin, T., trans. 1979. *Plato: Gorgias*. Clarendon Plato Series. Oxford.

Latour, B. 1999. *Pandora's Hope: Essays on the Reality of Science Studies*. Cambridge, MA.

Lewis, V. B. 1998. "The Nocturnal Council in Platonic Political Philosophy." *History of Political Thought* 29: 1–20.

Mara, G. M. 1997. *Socrates' Discursive Democracy: Logos and Ergon in Platonic Political Philosophy*. Albany, NY.

McKim, R. 2002. "Shame and Truth in Plato's Gorgias." In *Platonic Writings, Platonic Readings*, ed. C. L. Griswold, Jr. University Park, PA.

Monoson, S. S. 2000. *Plato's Democratic Entanglements: Athenian Politics and the Practice of Philosophy*. Princeton, NJ.

Morrow, G. R. 1993. *Plato's Cretan City: A Historical Interpretation of the Laws*. Princeton, NJ.

Nehamas, A., trans. 1995. *Plato: Phaedrus*. Indianapolis, IN.

Nehamas, A., and P. Woodruff, trans. 1989. *Plato: Symposium*. Indianapolis, IN.

Nichols, M. P. 1984. "The Republic's Two Alternatives: Philosopher-Kings and Socrates." *Political Theory* 12: 252–74.

Nussbaum, M. C. 1998. *Plato's Republic: The Good Society and the Deformation of Desire*. Washington, DC.

Ober, J. 1998. *Political Dissent in Democratic Athens: Intellectual Critics of Popular Rule*. Martin Classical Lectures. Princeton, NJ.

Pangle, T. L., trans. 1980. *The Laws of Plato*. New York.

Popper, K. R. 1966. *The Open Society and Its Enemies*, 2 vols., 5th ed. Princeton, NJ.

Roochnik, D. L. 1984. "The Riddle of the Cleitophon." *Ancient Philosophy* 4: 132–45.

Salkever, S. G. 1993. "Socrates' Aspasian Oration: The Play of Philosophy and Politics in Plato's Menexenus." *American Political Science Review* 87: 133–43.

Saxonhouse, A. W. 1998. "Democracy, Equality, and Eidê: A Radical View from Book 8 of Plato's Republic." *American Political Science Review* 92: 273–83.

Scott-Kilvert, I., trans. 1960. *Plutarch: The Rise and Fall of Athens: Nine Greek Lives*. New York.

Villa, D. 2001. *Socratic Citizenship*. Princeton, NJ.

Vlastos, G. 1991. *Socrates: Ironist and Moral Philosopher*. Cornell Studies in Classical Philology 50. Ithaca, NY.

Wardy, R. 1996. *The Birth of Rhetoric: Gorgias, Plato, and their Successors*. Issues in Ancient Philosophy. London.

Wolin, S. S. 1994. "Norm and Form: The Constitutionalizing of Democracy." In *Athenian Political Thought and the Reconstitution of American Democracy*, eds. J. P. Euben, J. R. Wallach, and J. Ober. Ithaca, NY.

Yunis, H. 1996. *Taming Democracy: Models of Political Rhetoric in Classical Athens*. Rhetoric and Society. Ithaca, NY.

Zeyl, D. J., trans. 1987. *Plato:* Gorgias. Indianapolis, IN.

6: The Political Drama of Plato's *Republic*

David Roochnik

The Opening Scene

The first scene of Plato's *Republic* foreshadows the political questions that the remainder of the dialogue addresses in enormous detail. Socrates has the opening line (which he delivers to an unnamed character): "I went down to the Piraeus yesterday with Glaucon."[1] The Piraeus was the seaport of Athens, a few miles southwest and lower in elevation than the city proper. Most important, it was the setting of the resistance movement that fought against the Tyranny of the Thirty, the brutal group of Spartan sympathizers who in 404 B.C.E., at the end of the Peloponnesian War, had overthrown the Athenian democracy, which had been proudly in place for a century.[2] The democracy was soon restored (in 403), but the trauma suffered by the Athenians was profound. Plato was twenty-five years old at the time, and at least two of his close relatives (Charmides and Critias) were among the Thirty and their henchmen. (The dialogue, which was probably written around 380, is set in approximately 410.)[3]

On its own, then, the setting provokes a political question: how valuable is democracy? Is it worth fighting, and perhaps dying, for? Is

1 The entire dialogue is narrated by Socrates. Citations are from Allan Bloom's 1991 [1968] translation. Many of the themes discussed in this chapter are treated at greater length in Roochnik 2004.

2 In his *Hellenica* (2.3.61–2.4.1), Xenophon describes the brutalities of the Thirty. So too does Aristotle in his *Athenian Constitution* (35–37). Aristotle also recounts (in 33) how the Athenian democracy was briefly overthrown in 411.

3 Howland 2004 [1993] contains a good sketch of the historical context of the dialogue. See 3–10.

tyranny such an evil that it is worth fighting against? These questions are also raised in Plato's *Apology of Socrates*, which is set in 399, for here Socrates acknowledges that during the reign of the Thirty he had not joined the democratic resistance. As he explains, when the tyrants had tried to force him to participate in the killing of Leon of Salamis, he refused. He did not, however, actively oppose the tyrants, nor did he try to stop them from killing Leon. Instead, in describing his own response to the tyrants' edict with a chilling lack of elaboration, he simply says, "I went home" (32d).[4]

The setting of the *Republic* raises another question. Like many seaports, the Piraeus was filled with foreigners. In fact, the home in which the conversation reported in the *Republic* takes place belongs to a "metic," a resident alien, named Cephalus. He was a wealthy arms merchant and the father of Polemarchus, a character who figures prominently in Book 1 (and who was himself killed by the Thirty). By setting the dialogue here, Plato thus encourages his reader to ask, what is the political value of what today we would call "diversity?" Is it good for a political community (a *polis*, as the Greeks would say) to have a wide variety of people in its midst? If so, why?

It is possible that Socrates and Glaucon are attracted to the Piraeus precisely for the diversity it offers, for they travelled there in order to see a festival being held in honor of a new goddess. (Apparently, Socrates enjoys seeing novel spectacles.) The procession of the native Athenians was beautiful, Socrates says, but no less so was that of the Thracians. These remarks suggest that the philosopher is not prejudiced in favor of the contributions of his fellow citizens. Perhaps he is more a cosmopolitan than a nationalist.

Back to the opening scene: Polemarchus bumps into Socrates and forcefully urges him to stay in the Piraeus and come to his home. Their exchange is worth citing in full:

> Polemarchus said, "Socrates, I guess you two are hurrying to get back to town."
> "That's not a bad guess," I said.
> "Well," he said, "do you see how many of us there are?"
> "Of course."

[4] Please note: the "Socrates" named in this chapter refers *only* to the character who appears in Plato's dialogue. No comments will be offered about his relationship to the historical figure who lived from 469–399.

"Well, then," he said, "either prove stronger than these men or stay here."
"Isn't there still one other possibility . . . ," I said, "our persuading you that you must let us go?"
"Could you really persuade [us]," he said, "if we don't listen?" (327c)

This is more than a bit of playful banter, for it mimics the altogether serious issue of political authority and its legitimacy. In a political community, the ruling body, whatever form it takes, must have the authority to compel citizens to perform some actions they do not wish to do (such as paying taxes or serving in the military). The question is, what is the source of such authority, and are some sources legitimate and just, while others not? In the passage cited above, Socrates says that his acquiescence to the demand that he stay in the Piraeus can be secured in one of two ways. Either he will be forced to by the superior numbers of Polemarchus and his companions, or he will be persuaded. There are at least two ways to conceive of the latter. Some persuasion takes place through the giving of good reasons. Socrates could be given a compelling argument why he should stay with Polemarchus, and could then be forced, by the power of reason itself, to accept its conclusion. On the other hand, someone can be convinced by bad reasons, or by some other form of rhetoric, to do something they are disinclined to do. For example, someone can be convinced by an effective emotional appeal or be seduced by means of alluring but false promises.

The passage thus suggests that there are at least three ways in which citizens can be compelled to do something they do not wish to do, and these prefigure three forms of political authority that subsequently are discussed in the *Republic*. In a tyranny, the ruler obtains the compliance of his subjects by means of the threat of violence. A democratic regime, by contrast, employs the wide-open forum of political debate, such as that which took place in the Athenian Assembly.[5] Here speakers attempt to persuade their fellow citizens and use all sorts of rhetorical devices – arguments, appeals to nationalist pride, exaggerated promises – in order to win their debates and elections and to enact authoritative decrees. Finally, one can imagine a regime that would operate on the basis of reason. Its authority would be invested in rulers who know the

[5] An excellent description of the Athenian democracy can be found in Samons 2004. See esp. 3–41.

right thing to do and can give rational arguments to justify their actions. The compliance of citizens would be obtained by the force of reason itself.

Polemarchus alludes to the limits, perhaps the lunacy, of this third option by asking, "could you really persuade [us] if we don't listen?" Most people are not good listeners, and they are especially inept when it comes to listening to carefully constructed arguments. Most people are more likely to be attracted to flowery, fiery, or fulsome appeals to emotion and fantasy than to dry reason. Listening in general, and to reasons in particular, is hard work, for it requires the ability to concentrate on what is being said, to remember it, organize the various elements into a coherent whole, and then to evaluate it rationally. Such work requires discipline and training; in other words, education.

Socrates will discuss these three regimes at length throughout the *Republic.* He will come down terribly hard against tyranny and argue (in Books 8 and 9) that it is altogether illegitimate and unjust. He will come down nearly as hard against the democracy (in Book 8) in which all forms of persuasion, rational or otherwise, are given free play. And (in Books 2–7) he will seem to champion that sort of regime in which reason rules and education is paramount. Indeed, the principal task of the *Republic* seems to be to devise a hypothetical version of precisely such a regime.

To return again to the opening scene: Adeimantus, one of the group of young men accompanying Polemarchus (and, like Glaucon, Plato's brother), lures Socrates to stay in the Piraeus by promising him a treat: later that evening, he says, there will be a horseback race in which the riders will pass torches from one to the other. Socrates seems impressed. "On horseback? That *is* novel!" (328a). Polemarchus augments the invitation by indicating that after dinner Socrates will be able not only to behold this spectacle, but also to converse with many young people. We will never know how Socrates would have responded on his own, for Glaucon interrupts by saying, "It seems we must stay" (328b).

To sum up: important questions are raised by the brief scene that opens the *Republic.* What is the value of democracy and of diversity? And, what form of authority ought to hold sway in a political community? These questions represent only a small fraction of the extraordinarily rich and complex teachings of the dialogue, teachings that are as much concerned with metaphysical, epistemological, psychological, and aesthetic questions as they are with political ones. Nonetheless, they will be used to guide this chapter, for through them we will be able to glimpse the political theory of Plato's *Republic.* We begin with Socrates' treatment of democracy.

Socrates' Critique of Democracy

Socrates explicitly criticizes democracy in Book 8, but much of what he says there is implicit in earlier books. As such, before beginning our analysis of this passage we must first briefly establish the context of his remarks.

After the opening scene described above, Socrates goes to the home of Polemarchus, where he is greeted warmly by the patriarch, Cephalus. Socrates responds to the old man's cordial invitation to stay in the Piraeus by asking a rather rude question. "For my part, Cephalus, I am really delighted to discuss with the very old. Since they are like men who have proceeded on a certain road that perhaps we too will have to take, one ought, in my opinion, learn from them what sort of road it is – whether it is rough and hard or easy and smooth" (328e). In other words, Socrates is asking, what's it like to be really old and close to death?

Cephalus, a master of parlor talk, is not flustered by this intrusive question, and answers readily. Unlike his fellow seniors, who complain about the debilitating effects of their age, he does not mind growing old. His physical desires have quieted, and he is glad to be liberated from their maddening sting. Furthermore, the way he has lived his life has left him unperturbed at the prospect of his impending death.

Again, Socrates is rude, and he reminds Cephalus that many people would say that he bears his old age so easily, not because of his character or the proper living of his life but because he's rich. Cephalus brushes off this objection and is adamant that it is the quality of his life, not the quantity of his wealth, that has rendered him so cheerful. But Socrates is relentless. He asks him what the greatest benefit is that he has received from his money. Cephalus answers that it is the fact that he has not had to lie to people or to perform any unjust act and that he has been able to pay back all his debts. As a result he fears no punishment in the next life.

The word "unjust" triggers Socrates, and he pounces. "What you say is very fine indeed, Cephalus. But as to this very thing, justice, shall we so simply assert that it is the truth and giving back what a man has taken from another?" (331c).

We can imagine Cephalus stunned. From his rather casual remarks, Socrates has extracted what seems to be a rigorous definition of justice.

Socrates treats the conversation as if he had just asked the old man, "what is justice itself?"; the sort of question for which he is famous. The "what is X?" question seeks the "essence" of X. It looks for a definition that would articulate what X is in a manner that is sufficiently universal to apply to or cover all particular instances of X.

We can imagine the old man even more stunned when immediately after foisting upon him an answer to the question, "what is justice itself?" – an answer Cephalus surely had no intention of providing – Socrates refutes it with the following counterexample. What if you borrowed a knife from a friend, and then the friend became insane? Would it be just to return the weapon to someone who now might wield it dangerously? Probably not. And it might be best, and more just, to lie to your now psychotic friend when he asks you where his knife is. Therefore, Socrates concludes, Cephalus' definition has to be wrong. Justice is not simply telling "the truth and paying back what a man has taken from another" (331c).

This exchange establishes a basic task of the *Republic*: to find out what justice itself really is. Book 1 is devoted to examining, and rejecting, the various candidates proposed by Cephalus, then by his son Polemarchus, and finally by his third and most vocal opponent, a man named Thrasymachus.

Thrasymachus is a Sophist, one of those fifth-century teachers who wandered from Greek city to city hawking their instructional wares. The main item in their repertoire was rhetoric, often defined as the art either of speaking well or of persuasion.[6] Not surprisingly, Sophists flocked to Athens, which was famous for its tradition of democratic debate, its protection of free speech, and its generally favorable reception of foreign intellectuals. In such a climate, those who were adept at persuasion could go far, and the Sophists promised to supply their students, usually wealthy and ambitious young Athenians (such as Glaucon and Adeimantus), with tools to further their own political aspirations.

Thrasymachus defines justice as "the advantage of the stronger" (338c). He later explains that by "stronger" he means the ruling body (338e). This implies that justice varies from regime to regime. In a tyranny, for example, the ruling body is the tyrant, and what is advantageous to him would be, according to the definition, just. In a democracy, where power is invested in the people (*dēmos*), what is advantageous to the people would be counted as just. Thrasymachus, then, is a relativist.

[6] A good overview of the Sophistic movement can be found in Guthrie 1988 [1969].

He denies that there is an universal form of justice that would hold sway over all particular instances. Justice is not "absolute" (which comes from the Latin *ab*, "from," and *solvere,* "to loosen"). It does not exist independently of the various political contexts in which it is formulated. Because it varies from regime to regime it is dependent upon, rather than absolved from, the particular regime in which it takes shape.

Socrates is clearly opposed to such relativism. (Indeed, his very question, "what is justice itself?" suggests that there must be some sort of absolute conception of justice.) As a result, he attacks his Sophistic opponent with a barrage of arguments, only one of which (339a–340a) we will sample. Thrasymachus states that justice is what is advantageous to the ruler. Socrates then gets his opponent to agree that because the laws are directives put in place in order to further the advantage of the ruling body, and because there is no higher court of appeal (i.e., because there is no universal or absolute form of justice), it is just for citizens to obey all the laws. Next, he asks Thrasymachus whether the rulers ever make mistakes. Do they ever make laws that are ultimately to their own disadvantage? Thrasymachus answers yes. But because he has already asserted that it is just to obey all laws, only some of which are genuinely advantageous to the ruler, the Sophist is now in the uncomfortable position of having to admit that sometimes it is just for citizens to obey laws, and thus to act in such a way that is disadvantageous to the ruler. He has contradicted himself.

Like many of Socrates' arguments, the merits of this one are debatable, and so it should be carefully scrutinized. But one point emerges clearly: Socrates believes there is a difference between being right and making a mistake. If a ruler, for example, believes it to be to his advantage to levy heavy and oppressive taxes on his subjects, but this proposal so thoroughly infuriates the people that they rebel and overthrow him, then he was wrong in judging what was truly to his advantage. Right and wrong, true and false, are the basic ingredients that go to the heart of the Socratic enterprise.

Thrasymachus is stymied by Socrates, and so he changes tactics. Rather than attempt to refine his definition of justice, he offers an extended praise of injustice, which he describes as "more powerful and more free and more dominating than justice" (344c). Justice, on this view, is for suckers, injustice for those with the wherewithal to take advantage of others. With this tirade the Sophist puts forth a challenge of the highest order: why prefer a life of justice to one of injustice? The remainder of Book 1 is devoted to Socrates' rebuttal of Thrasymachus' position, but it ends with Socrates himself confessing disappointment.

While he has been successful in silencing Thrasymachus, and in this limited sense achieving victory over his Sophistic opponent, he acknowledges that he has failed to answer the very question that sparked the dialogue in the first place: what is justice itself (354b–c)? And without an answer to this question, any debate about the respective merits of the just and the unjust life is premature.

Nonetheless, at the beginning of Book 2 Socrates seems ready to wash his hands of the conversation and to go back home. Once again, Glaucon forces him to stay in the Piraeus. He is eager to pursue the question and to know why he should prefer a life of justice to one of injustice. To press Socrates to go further in his analysis, Glaucon asks him to explain what sort of good justice actually is. Good things, he says, fall into three categories. Some, like harmless pleasures, are desirable for their own sake. Others, like taking an unpleasant medicine, are desirable for their consequences. Finally, some are desirable both for their own sake and for their consequences. Socrates gives the examples of "thinking and seeing and being healthy" (357c). Into which of these three categories does justice fit? Socrates wants to put it in the third, but Glaucon objects. Most people, he says, would count it as a good desirable only for its consequences. In explaining what he means, he offers a simple version of what has come to be known as the social contract theory. On this view, human beings naturally would prefer to do unjust things, like steal their neighbor's property, without being caught or punished. But in advocating this preference, they will have to acknowledge that other people will be authorized to act with similar injustice against them. The condition of mutual injustice would be intolerable, so people opt for a middle path. They make a contract such that citizens bind themselves to laws and thus are no longer free to commit acts of injustice. This requires them to sacrifice the unrestricted ability to do what they wish. But the gain is that they no longer have to fear being acted upon unjustly by others. Political authority will protect them. Justice, on this account, is obeying the law and being protected by it. If such is the way of human life, then the Socratic praise of justice as a supreme good, as one good both for itself and for its consequences, has been blunted.

Glaucon amplifies his challenge by telling Socrates a story. Once upon a time, there was a shepherd named Gyges who stumbled upon a corpse wearing a ring. He stole the ring and discovered that it gave him the power to become invisible. So equipped, he was able to perform with impunity acts of injustice, such as seducing the queen and killing the king. Glaucon's question is this: why should any of us behave justly if we had such a ring and so could perform any unjust action we wished without being caught? In other words, what intrinsic value does a life of justice have?

To meet this radical challenge to the goodness of justice – a challenge Socrates seems to enjoy (see 367e) – Socrates must come to a full understanding of what justice is. To accomplish this task, he proposes what scholars have come to call the "city-soul analogy" (368c–369a). The city, says Socrates, is like the soul "written large." It has the same structure as the individual, but because it is bigger it is easier to see. If an ideal, a perfectly just, city could be "constructed," then what justice itself is, and what a just individual is, would be easier to see. If justice can be seen, then Thrasymachus' challenge, that it is better to live an unjust life, could be adequately confronted.

Thus begins the massive "construction project" that occupies Socrates from Book 2 through Book 7. At 527c he call his construct "the beautiful city," and this, rather than the more familiar "ideal city," is the phrase we shall use throughout the remainder of this chapter.

Finally, we can commence our discussion of Socrates' critique of democracy, for, as we shall see, the beautiful city is radically undemocratic. Consider some of its most prominent features.

1. *The beautiful city deploys a comprehensive censorship program.*

Socrates insists that in order to mold a citizenry capable of obeying the dictates of its leaders – dictates that, as we shall discuss shortly, are designed to be entirely rational – all cultural activity must be tightly regulated. Such strictures apply most directly to the myth-makers, the storytellers who supply the city with its basic stock of narrative models. For example, the rulers of the beautiful city will ban the famous story told in Hesiod's *Theogony* in which the god Cronus overthrows his father Ouranos and usurps his authority (see 378a.). Because this story could be interpreted as justifying an act of rebellion, it is construed as politically dangerous. Compliant and patriotic citizens, who are willing to subordinate the pursuit of their individual interests to the common good of the entire city must, Socrates seems to argue, be shielded from such potentially subversive literary material.

Another example: familiar stories about the afterworld, such as those found in Homer's *Odyssey*, depict death in horrifying terms. These too will be banned. After all, if citizens believe that death is terrible and thus to be avoided at all costs, they may well be less willing to risk their lives in the defense of their city. (See 386a–388b.)

Because, according to Socrates, music plays a significant role in the psychological formation of the young, it is imperative for the beautiful city to monitor carefully what its citizens are listening to. Only those "modes" (or musical scales) that have a positive effect on listeners will be allowed. The Lydian mode will be forbidden, but the Dorian allowed (399a). Another example: the flute, the instrument traditionally associated with Dionysus, will be outlawed (399d).

To state the obvious: freedom of expression, a basic feature of democratic regimes, is eliminated in the beautiful city.[7]

2. *The educational curriculum of future rulers is tightly circumscribed.*

Just as the citizens of the beautiful city are allowed to sample only the most politically correct forms of literature, so too is their education severely restricted. As he describes in Book 7, in their youth future rulers are largely confined to the study of mathematics.

3. *The beautiful city will permit only a governmentally sanctioned form of religion.*

Citizens will be exposed only to certain politically acceptable conceptions of the gods. A myth that depicts a god in an unfavorable light, such as the treatment the tyrannical Ouranos and the rebellious Cronus receive in the *Theogony*, will be banned. Even more extreme, a depiction of the gods as anything but completely stable and unchangingly good will be censored. Clearly, this stricture implies a wholesale rejection of traditional Greek polytheism. (See 380a–383a.)

4. *The city will allocate medical care unequally.*

In the beautiful city only a small category of infirmities, namely wounds and simple, curable illnesses suffered by the otherwise healthy, will be treated. The chronically ill, the weak, and the very old, will be allowed to die (see 406c–8a.). The purpose of this sort of "Asclepian" (406a) medicine is to return citizens to their civic duties as quickly as possible. Socrates is here brutally hard on the practice of medicine as it occurs

[7] S. Sara Monoson 2000 has explored at length the central role that "free speech" (*parrhēsia*), which is precisely what Socrates bans in his beautiful city, played in Athenian democracy. See esp. 51–63.

in his own city of Athens. It is, he says, no more than "an education in disease" (406a). (One can only wonder how strong his language would be in evaluating the practice of contemporary medicine.)

5. *A "noble lie" will be told to the citizens.*

It has two parts. The first states that all citizens were born, not from a mother and father, but from the earth itself. Their filial obligations, therefore, should be directed at the city, not at the individual human beings they identify as blood relations. According to the logic of the lie, all citizens are siblings, and therefore in the beautiful city not only interests, but pains and pleasures, are experienced communally. Socrates seems to justify this extremely non-democratic measure on the basis of its positive political consequences. Solidarity among citizens will be fostered, rebellion and factionalism curtailed, and in general the individuals will come to understand their own interests as identical to those of the city.

The second part of the lie is that all citizens were born with a certain metal in their souls. Some are gold, others silver, and the worst are bronze (or iron). In other words, the noble lie promulgates the view that the city has an unalterable, tripartite class structure. Once again, political stability is the justification for telling such a lie. If all citizens believe that their place in the city is fixed, with no hope of change, there would be no motivation to press for a radical alteration in the power structure.

Again to state the obvious: egalitarianism is not a value in the beautiful city. It is a top-down authoritarian regime in which rulers impose a severe hierarchy and all sorts of restrictions upon the freedom of the citizens.

6. *Private property will be abolished.*

In the beautiful city the rulers will "have common houses and mess, with no one privately possessing anything of the kind" (458c; See also 419a).

7. *The family will be abolished.*

Not only property, but all sexual relationships will also be rendered communal. As Socrates puts it, "the possession of women, marriage, and procreation of children must as far as possible be arranged according to the proverb that friends have all things in common" (423e).

8. *The rulers will practice eugenics.*

Included in Socrates' telling of the "noble lie" is this admonition:

> Hence the god commands the rulers first and foremost to be of nothing such good guardians and to keep over nothing so careful a watch as the children, seeing which of these metals is mixed in their souls. And, if a child of theirs should be born with an admixture of bronze or iron, by no manner of means are they to take pity on it, but shall assign the proper value to its nature and thrust it out among the craftsmen. . . . (415c)

As the dialogue unfolds, this rather chilling proposal gradually evolves into a full-blown program of eugenics. First, individuals are deprived of the right to choose their own sexual partners, and as mentioned previously the family itself is abolished (see 457d). Then we discover that gold-souled people are allowed to breed only with those whose metallic souls are equally golden.

> [T]here is a need for the best men to have intercourse as often as possible with the best women, and the reverse for the most ordinary men with the most ordinary women; and the offspring of the former must be reared but not that of the others, if the flock is going to be of the most eminent quality. (459d)

At the beginning of Book 8 we learn that the rulers of the city have attempted to develop a mathematical science whose province is "better and worse begettings" (546c); in other words, a mathematically based science of eugenics. Although this program fails (and this failure, to be discussed in the third section of this chapter, Monkey Wrenches, is of utmost importance for an understanding of the *Republic*), it signals a fundamental objective of the beautiful city – to sublimate or redirect all private desire, especially sexual desire, toward the well-being of the city.

To sum up: in the putatively beautiful city the good of the community reigns supreme and all individual interests and desires are subordinated to it. A rigidly unequal class structure is in place, and a technical apparatus is designed to preserve it. The city is authoritarian rather than democratic. It must be added, however, that the putative source of the rulers' authority is not in their power or their ability to threaten violence, but in their superior knowledge. The best way to elaborate this dimension of the *Republic* is to turn to a parable Socrates offers in Book 6, the ship of state.

Imagine that the city is a ship. The ship-owner is big and strong, but also deaf, myopic, and ignorant of seamanship. As a result, control of the rudder – in other words, who actually pilots the ship – is up for grabs. (The Greek for "pilot" is *kubernētēs*, the origin of our "governor.") Even though they are as ignorant as the owner, the sailors of the ship compete with one another for this power. Eventually, by using any means necessary, from persuasion to throwing their competitors overboard, a victor emerges. He becomes pilot, but his abilities have nothing to do with sailing the ship well. Instead, he is good only at winning the competition for power.

In direct contrast to the actual pilot, there is the "true pilot," the one who has studied astronomy, meteorology, navigational techniques, and so forth. Such a man could in fact expertly sail the ship toward its destination, but he will never have the opportunity to do so, for his knowledge of seamanship is useless in the competition for the rudder. The true pilot must tilt his head upward to study the stars in order to learn how to navigate well. He is thus singularly ill-suited to engage in the competition taking place on board the ship between his fellow human beings. The sailor who does eventually win the rudder keeps his gaze level, and so knows how to navigate through, and then triumph in, the fracas taking place on board the ship.

This parable paints a dismal picture of "real world" politics – the ship of state is doomed to be piloted badly – and highlights an essential feature of the teaching of the *Republic*. The beautiful city must invert the standard relationship that typically obtains between political power and knowledge, for it must be guided not by someone capable only of gaining power, but by a "true pilot" who knows where the city should go and how it can get there. The various non-democratic features listed previously are meant to create the conditions from which such a ruler can emerge. Furthermore, the principal task of Books 6 and 7 is to explain what it is that the ruler, the true pilot, actually knows. This is far and away the most conceptually difficult material of the *Republic*, for here we learn that the true pilot must be a philosopher. In these sections Socrates discusses his notoriously obscure teaching of the "idea of the good," the supreme principle of knowledge and being. It is impossible in a short essay even to begin discussing what this is. Suffice it to say here that it is the ultimate content of the true pilot's knowledge. As mentioned before, in Book 7, Socrates sketches the rigidly precise course of study that his rulers must undergo. When they are done, they are ready to take control of the city and rule it by knowledge, not opinion. Such a city is a far cry from a democracy, in which superior rhetoric, rather than superior knowledge, is the essential requirement for ruling.

In Book 8, Socrates begins a second stage of his political analysis, namely, a critique of what he calls the "mistaken regimes." These are the sorts of regimes one might actually find in the real world and include the timocracy, rule by the honorable few (which seems to resemble Sparta); oligarchy, rule by the wealthy few; democracy, rule by the many; and tyranny, rule by the tyrant. Most relevant here, of course, is his discussion of democracy.

The most basic feature of a democracy is the freedom enjoyed by its citizens and protected by the city. "Isn't the city full of freedom and free speech?" Socrates asks. "And isn't there license in it to do whatever one wants" (557b)? Within the limits imposed by laws and strictures forged by the people themselves in their Assembly, citizens can act on their desires. They can choose their professions, sexual partners, and preferred forms of cultural activity. They can accumulate wealth. In direct contrast to the austerity of the beautiful city, in the democracy there is an "unleashing of unnecessary and useless pleasures" (561a).

There are three important corollaries to this affirmation of freedom. First is the protection of privacy. As Socrates puts it, in the democracy, "each man would organize his life in it privately just as it pleases him" (557b). Most important, there is no "compulsion to rule" (557e). Again in direct contrast to the beautiful city, where the best and most competent citizens are forced to rule, democratic citizens are free to ignore and not to participate in political affairs.[8] Second, a democracy dispenses "a certain equality to equals and unequals alike" (558c). In other words, because all citizens are counted as members of the *dēmos* and alike share in the freedoms the city protects for them, they are counted as equals whether they are superior, mediocre, or inferior human beings. Third, there is a flowering of diversity. Enjoying the freedom and egalitarianism protected by their city, citizens can live

[8] I refer to the "parable of the cave" that Socrates recounts in Book 7. Here he explains that the philosopher will be "forced" (519c) to return to the cave to rule the citizens trapped therein.

according to their own conception of a good life and pursue an endless variety of projects, from the arts, to commerce, to science, to athletics. They are free to travel and thus to bring home with them what they have learned abroad. As a result, Socrates describes the democracy as being "like a many-colored cloak decorated in all hues . . . with all dispositions" (557c).

Socrates encapsulates his criticism of the democracy by describing what he takes to be its typical citizen. He is "reared . . . without education" (559d), and thus is vulnerable to the lures of an unlimited number of "unnecessary desires" (558d). He

> lives along day by day, gratifying the desire that occurs to him, at one time drinking and listening to the flute, at another downing water and reducing; now practicing gymnastic, and again idling and neglecting everything; and sometimes spending his time as though he were occupied with philosophy. Often he engages in politics and, jumping up, says and does whatever chances to come to him; and if he ever admires any soldiers, he turns in that direction; and if it's money-makers, in that one. And there is neither order nor necessity in his life, but calling this life sweet, free, and blessed he follows it throughout. (561c–d)

The picture Socrates sketches is of a whimsical and impressionable man bereft of any firm convictions. (Although do note that he does participate in philosophy, however inauthentically.) Such a citizen is instinctively hostile to any form of authority. In a democracy, children resist their parents' admonitions, students intimidate their teachers, slaves and women run free, and the exuberantly free citizen "spatters with mud those who are obedient" (562d). The result is chaos.

To summarize again: Plato's *Republic*, in which Socrates constructs and seems to champion a "beautiful city" that is authoritarian (even if its authority is well grounded in reason), contains a brutal attack on democracy. Little wonder then that a famous twentieth-century scholar, Karl Popper, who lived through the horrors of the totalitarian threats of his own age, passionately condemned what he took to be the teaching of the *Republic*. Speaking about a Plato scholar named James Adam, he said the following: "we see that Plato has succeeded at least in turning this thinker against democracy, and we may wonder how much damage his poisonous writing has done when presented, unopposed, to lesser minds." For Popper, "Plato's political programme . . . is fundamentally identical with [totalitarianism]," and as such he was the great opponent of individualism. He was a reactionary who rejected "the emancipation of the individual" that resulted from "the great spiritual revolution which had led to the breakdown of tribalism and to the rise of democracy" in the fifth century B.C.E. "Never," says Popper, "was a man more in earnest in his hostility toward the individual," and toward democracy.[9]

MONKEY WRENCHES

Karl Popper's enormous distaste for Plato's *Republic* may appear well founded, but in fact it entirely neglects an essential feature of the dialogue. Plato is a genius at throwing a monkey wrench into what initially seems to be a smoothly functioning piece of conceptual machinery, thereby transforming it into something far more puzzling and provocative. This section will explain how he does this when it comes to his apparently straightforward criticisms of democracy and diversity, for there are at least five ways in which Plato qualifies, seems to revise, or at least complicate, his views.

(1) *The beautiful city fails.*

And for one specific reason: its putatively wise rulers turn out not to be so wise after all. They fail to determine what scholars call "the marriage number," a phrase that refers to an obscure passage at the beginning of Book 8. Here Socrates tells us that despite their best efforts, the rulers are unable to calculate the "geometrical number" that is "sovereign of better and worse begettings" (546c). In other words, they fail to determine the mathematically precise science of eugenics mentioned previously. As a result, there is a "chaotic mixing of iron with silver and of bronze with gold" (547a), and the dream of a stable and perfectly stratified city, all of whose citizens do the job assigned to them without complaint and who thus live together in peace and harmony, will be shattered.[10]

[9] Popper 1971. The citations come from 42, 87, 101, and 103.

[10] The rulers' inability to calculate the marriage number is a major theme of Roochnik 2004. See esp. 68–69.

It is impossible here to decipher the mathematics of this passage, but what the number symbolizes is clear: the human effort to manage human reproduction through mathematical science. The inability of the rulers to achieve this power over the citizenry implies that, smart as they supposedly are, they cannot comprehend the complexities of sexuality. This passage thus acknowledges that there is something buried deep within human nature that simply cannot be controlled. In turn, this implies that Socrates himself realizes that the dream of a beautifully rational city, one thoroughly harmonious and free from internal strife and senseless war, cannot be realized.

(2) *The conditions required for the beautiful city to come into being are unacceptable.*

One example will suffice. As a culminating requirement for the city to come into being Socrates proposes that the rulers "send out to the country all those in the city who happen to be older than ten" (541a). It is possible that Socrates is being euphemistic here and what he really means is that everyone over the age of ten will be killed. Regardless, the logic of this proposal is painfully apparent. The beautiful city is completely revolutionary, for it requires a comprehensive alteration of conventional politics. Eliminating all citizens over the age of ten gives the rulers the clean slate they need in order to construct a new, thoroughly rational city.

Whether the phrase "send out to the country" means "kill" or not, this proposal is both absurd and monstrous. Therefore, in having Socrates offer it, Plato is either seriously advocating an absurd monstrosity, or is suggesting precisely the opposite; namely, that the requirements for a beautiful city to come into being are unacceptable. If the latter is true, then the purpose of the *Republic* is not to offer a blueprint of a perfectly just city, but instead to criticize political extremism and the ambition to create a rationalized heaven on earth.

(3) *Socrates' goal in the dialogue may be to educate individuals.*

Socrates says that rather than being a political program, the true intention of the beautiful city may be to educate individuals. He says this in response to Glaucon's epiphany that the city he has just helped to construct may in fact be impossible to realize. As Glaucon puts it, "it has its place only in speeches, since I don't suppose it exists anywhere on earth" (592a–b). Socrates agrees:

> But in heaven, I said, perhaps, a pattern is laid up for the man who wants to see and found a city within himself on the basis of what he sees. It doesn't make any difference whether it is or will be somewhere. For he would mind the things of this city alone, and of no other. (592b)

As in (2) above, this passage undermines the notion that the *Republic* presents a blueprint for the sort of totalitarian regime that Popper took it to be. In fact, the dialogue may be engaged in an entirely different sort of project, one whose goal is to help an individual "found a city within himself." To explicate exactly what this means is impossible in this chapter. Suffice it to say here that the true goal of Plato's dialogue may be to provide a philosophical education designed for individuals, rather than a political program suitable for cities.[11]

(4) *What Socrates explicitly says about democracy is actually somewhat ambiguous.*

The most important example occurs in the midst of Socrates' apparent denunciation of the diversity that springs to life in a democracy: "Thanks to its license, [the democracy] contains all species of regimes, and it is probably necessary for the man who wishes to organize a city, *as we were just doing*, to go to a city under democracy" (557d; emphasis added).

The very activity that has just taken place in the *Republic* itself – namely, philosophizing about politics – could probably only occur in a regime that permits and protects freedom of speech and allows its citizens unrestricted access to a diversity of human types. And this is the democracy. So, while Socrates is surely serious in his critique of democracy, he nonetheless acknowledges that this regime has a unique virtue. Because of its commitment to equality and freedom, all sorts of human beings are allowed to flourish. Because the streets are alive and the theaters packed and citizens disagree with one another in public, philosophers in a democratic city have in front of them an enormous

[11] Again, I have tried to explain what this means at length in my book, Roochnik 2004.

resource. From the city they can learn much about human nature, in all its polymorphous perversity, and wonder what, in fact, would be the most just of all possible regimes for such creatures.[12]

The political teaching of the *Republic* thus resembles that found in another Platonic dialogue, the *Statesman*. Here a Stranger from Elea argues that while in principle there is only one legitimate form of political authority, that founded upon knowledge and reason, in the "real world" there are a variety of "second-best" regimes. Among these is the democracy. While it is pilloried as rule by ignorance (292e) and therefore "absurd," "difficult to conceive," and "ruinous" (298e–299e), it is nonetheless not unequivocally condemned. Because a democracy splinters into competing factions, it is a weak and inefficient form of government (303a). But this precisely tokens its unique virtue: it is least burdensome on the citizens and so, especially in the chaotic conditions that so often obtain in political life, it is least offensive and damaging. It is, in short, the best of the worst regimes precisely because it lets people, including (perhaps especially) the philosopher, alone.

(5) *The "Myth of Er" seems to offer a defense of diversity.*

Despite his repeated attacks on poetry, the *Republic* ends with Socrates telling an eschatological myth.[13] Twelve days after he was killed in battle, a man named Er returns to life to report "what he saw in the other world" (614b). It's a complicated place, but the features relevant for our purpose can be briefly summarized. After death, good people are rewarded with a thousand years of pleasure and bad people a thousand years of misery. When their millennium of divinely sanctioned retribution has been completed, the souls are required to choose their lives for their next go-around on earth. "The whole risk for a human being" lies in being able to make this choice correctly, for its consequences will last another millennium. Socrates admonishes his listeners: "[E]ach of us must, to the neglect of our other studies, above all see to it that he is a seeker and student of that study by which he might be able to learn and find out who will give him the capacity and the knowledge to distinguish the good and the bad life" (618c).

The order in which the souls select their next life is based on a lottery, but Er reports that even if one chooses last – as Odysseus does in

[12] Monoson makes much of this passage as well. See, for example, Monoson 2000: 167. Also see Saxonhouse 1996: 102, for expression of a similar sentiment.

[13] There are similar myths at the end of the *Phaedo* and the *Gorgias*.

this story – it is still possible to make a good decision. The reason for this is that "there were all sorts" of lives to choose from and their number are "far more than the souls present" (618a). As such, the greatest asset in making this choice well is a wide familiarity with a large number of different sorts of lives. Little wonder, then, that despite his bad luck in the lottery, Odysseus, the most widely traveled man of all, and so the one most familiar with the variety of forms that human being can take, chooses well. And notice what choice he made: "the life of a private man who minds his own business" (620c).

To reformulate this point: because the number of possible lives exceeds the number of actual ones, the Myth of Er suggests that human beings are always in a position to be surprised, and perhaps even instructed, by the way someone else lives. As a result, we can never be completely certain that the way we live is the best available to us. If we couple this aspect of the Myth with the opening scene of the *Republic*, which finds Socrates traveling to the Piraeus to see a new religious festival and admiring the show put on by the foreign Thracians, we see that the dialogue both begins and ends with an implicit affirmation of diversity. In order to choose our lives well and to engage in political philosophy, we must be exposed to a variety of human types. For only doing so will afford us access to the sort of knowledge that Odysseus has. Only doing so will allow us to engage in the philosophical activity that is the *Republic* itself.

One last point about the Myth of Er: as Socrates tells the story, the man who had won the lottery and so was first in line to choose his next life was someone who had "lived in an orderly regime in his former life, participating in virtue by habit, *without philosophy*" (619c–d, my emphasis). As a result, and despite being first, his choice was catastrophic. Seduced by the apparent power and glory he thought it would bring him, he selected the life of a tyrant. Unfortunately, in doing so "it escaped his notice that eating his own children and other evils were fated to be a part of that life" (619c). In other words, without philosophy, we are doomed.

Conclusion

Only now can the title of this chapter be explained. Rather than containing a political theory, the *Republic* is a political drama, for within its pages lies a conflict. On the one hand, Socrates seems to champion an authoritarian and radically anti-democratic regime. He constructs a city that denies the citizens individual rights and basic freedoms, puts into place a rigid class system, and attempts to control all aspects of literary and musical culture, religion, and education. It is crucial, however, to remember, and easy to forget, that the *Republic* contains more than Books 2–7, more than the construction of the putatively beautiful city. It also includes Books 1 and 8–10, sections that are typically assigned far less weight by scholars.[14] A careful reading of these books, which include the opening scene, the failure of the rulers to find the marriage number, Socrates' ambiguous characterization of democracy, and several passages that can be read as affirmations of the goodness of diversity, significantly complicates the teaching of the dialogue.

The city Socrates constructs is indeed beautiful in some respects. Most of all, it is at peace with itself. It is a city in which the smartest people rule, and they do so for the good of the city rather to further their own political ambitions. Unlike the Athens of 404 B.C.E., it does not tear itself apart into bloody shreds. Compared to such a regime, democracy looks pitifully inefficient and chaotic. Like the individual described at 561c, it is subject to the whims of those leaders whose only talent is in persuading the citizens to follow their lead. Decisions are made recklessly, the voters are fickle and selfish, and the city is run by opinion rather than knowledge. Nevertheless, Socrates is far from unequivocal in condemning the democracy or in championing the beautiful city. The cost of constructing the latter, most notably the requirement that all over the age of ten must be killed, may be far too high, and the technical devices needed for maintaining control, such as the "marriage number," are in fact impossible to attain.

In sum, then, the *Republic* expresses a tension. It acknowledges the benefits of the beautiful city, but questions its costs. It denounces the excesses of the democracy, but tacitly points to its advantages, especially for the philosopher. It is precisely this tension, this internal dialogue with itself, that renders the *Republic* a work of enduring value. It forces its readers to wonder about justice, the city, and the question of political authority, and it sets into motion a series of responses, both positive and negative, that becomes the history of political philosophy itself.

[14] For example, Gregory Vlastos 1991: 248–51, argues that Book 1 is out of character with the rest of the *Republic* because it was written earlier. Julia Annas 1982: 294, dismisses Books 8 and 9 by saying that they "have been admired for their literary power, but they leave a reader who is intent on the main argument unsatisfied and irritated. Plato's procedure is both confusing and confused."

WORKS CITED

Annas, J. 1982. *An Introduction to Plato's Republic.* Oxford.

Bloom, A., trans. 1991 [1968]. *The Republic of Plato*, 2nd ed. New York.

Guthrie, W. K. C. 1988 [1969]. *A History of Greek Philosophy*, vol. 3, part 1: *The Sophists.* Cambridge.

Howland, J. 2004 [1993]. *The Republic: The Odyssey of Philosophy*. Philadelphia.

Monoson, S. S. 2000. *Plato's Democratic Entanglements*. Princeton, NJ.

Popper, K. 1971. *The Open Society And Its Enemies*, vol. 1: *The Spell Of Plato.* Princeton, NJ.

Roochnik, D. 2004. *Beautiful City: The Dialectical Character of Plato's Republic.* Ithaca, NY.

Samons, L. J. 2004. *What's Wrong with Democracy? From Athenian Practice to American Worship*. Berkeley, CA.

Saxonhouse, A. W. 1996. *Athenian Democracy: Modern Mythmakers and Ancient Theorists.* Notre Dame, IN.

Vlastos, G. 1991. *Socrates: Ironist and Moral Philosopher.* Ithaca, NY.

7: Practical Plato

Catherine H. Zuckert

Plato's *Statesman* is a strange dialogue, possibly the strangest he wrote. In it an anonymous Eleatic Stranger not merely argues that a statesman is defined by his knowledge alone, and that it does not matter whether this "statesman" ever puts that knowledge into practice, even simply as an advisor to a ruler.[1] The Eleatic goes so far as to suggest that human beings ought to be understood not in terms of our distinctive ability to reason or speak, but as featherless bipeds or two-legged pigs. He even asks his auditors to suppose that there was a time long in the past when the cosmos reversed the direction of its movements so that the cycle of the generation of animals was also reversed. Human beings sprouted from the earth full grown with gray beards and gradually became younger and younger until their seeds wasted away and the direction of the movement of the cosmos again changed.

Readers might be tempted to conclude that the dialogue is one big, if rather weird, joke.[2] Such a conclusion would be rash, however, because Plato says more in the *Statesman* about the actual possibilities and limitations of political practice than in either of his other two dialogues explicitly devoted to politics: the *Republic* and the *Laws.*

In the *Republic*, Socrates famously argues that evils in cities will not cease until philosophers become kings. But he just as famously shows that philosophers will never want to rule and that it is highly unlikely

[1] Both Rowe 1999 and Waterfield 1995 translate *xenos* as "visitor." They do not preserve the opposition between *xenos* (foreigner, if not barbarian or enemy) and citizen that occurs elsewhere in Plato's works that Joly 1992 points out.

[2] In her "Introduction" to Waterfield 1995, Julia Annas observes: "It is not surprising that the dialogue has been neglected by comparison with the *Republic* or even the *Laws.* To get to the political theory we have to go through lengthy passages which on first reading can strike us as a mixture of the boring and the weird" (x).

that non-philosophers will ever compel them to do so. He concludes, moreover, by stating that the purpose of the description of the just "city in speech" (592b) is to serve as a paradigm for individuals attempting to order their own souls. It does not matter, therefore, whether this city ever actually exists.

In the *Laws* the Athenian Stranger also describes a "city in speech" in proposing a set of laws for some Dorian legislators to adopt in a new colony they are founding. Because the Athenian suggests a set of relatively specific institutions and policies to men with the power to put them into operation, the *Laws* has often been read, particularly in contrast to the *Republic*, as containing Plato's more practical political proposals.[3] The problem with this reading of the *Laws* is that at the end of the dialogue the Athenian admits that the city he has described can be neither founded nor maintained unless they establish a kind of school for legislators called the Nocturnal Council. As several commentators have pointed out, the institution of this council reintroduces the problems associated with the rule of philosophers.[4]

In the *Statesman* the Eleatic also argues that a true statesman will be knowledgeable. Unlike Socrates and the Athenian Stranger, however, the Eleatic does not think a statesman needs to know about the unity of the virtues or the ideas. In other words, the Eleatic does not think that a statesman has to be a philosopher.[5] The knowledge that distinguishes a statesman is more specialized. Rather than treat moderation and courage as two specific kinds of one more general virtue, the Eleatic maintains, a statesman must understand them to be opposed characteristics that he knows how to mix in his citizen body if the polity is to survive.[6]

Few, if any, human beings will actually possess the requisite knowledge. But, the Eleatic explains, even if an individual were to acquire it, the many people who lack the requisite knowledge would never be able to discern it. They will, therefore, never allow a person who has such knowledge to rule without supervision by law. Political associations will never be ruled or governed on the basis of complete knowledge. A people may allow changes in the law, if they are persuaded; they may

[3] E.g., Saunders 1992; Stalley 1983; and Morrow 1960.

[4] E.g., Barker 1918; Brunt 1993; Klosko 1988.

[5] At the beginning of the *Sophist*, the conversation that precedes the *Statesman*, the Eleatic declares (217b) that people from Elea like the "stranger" himself, i.e., members of the Eleatic school of philosophy founded by Parmenides, think that sophist, statesman, and philosopher are three different kinds of things (men or knowledge), although it is difficult to discern and spell out the differences.

[6] Cf. Mara 1981.

even allow magistrates to go beyond the law in special circumstances if those magistrates are then subject to an audit or held responsible for malfeasance in court. But, having learned through bitter experience that rulers completely unrestrained by law kill, maim, and expropriate the property of their subjects, people will not allow a ruler who claims to be prudent to do whatever he thinks best under the circumstances without remaining answerable to them in one way or another. Because the man who knows sees that he will be subject to the judgment of those who do not know, no one who truly understands politics will agree to govern under these conditions. As a result, all actual governments are headed by people who claim to know what is best, but do not.

It is not surprising that bad things happen in politics, the Eleatic concludes, since actual governments are not based on knowledge. What is more surprising is that some polities nevertheless last a long time. The Eleatic does not explain why polities are "strong by nature" (302a) despite the radical lack of knowledge on the part of both rulers and ruled. He indicates the reasons, however, in his earlier, apparently fanciful descriptions of human beings as "featherless bipeds" and the myth of the reversed cosmos. Comical as it is, the Eleatic's description of human beings as featherless bipeds points to the fact that we are not very well provided by nature with protection against the elements (e.g., fur or feathers) or means of defending ourselves from attacks by wild animals (e.g., horns or claws) or fleeing (e.g., fins, wings, or four legs on which to run rather than two). The Eleatic thus concludes his myth by observing that when human beings are not directly ruled and provided with their necessities by higher, divine beings, they have to develop arts – especially the art of politics – in order to preserve themselves. In other words, political communities come into existence because they are needed to preserve both individuals and peoples. Those that are law abiding tend to last longer because laws reflect a certain amount of learning on the basis of experience that becomes encapsulated and expressed in popular opinion and custom.

In this chapter I will first show the way in which the Eleatic somewhat fancifully disputes and disparages other, nobler and more traditional images of political leadership in the first three sections of the dialogue. Second, I will look at the reasons he proposes a new, more modest paradigm of the politician as weaver. Finally, I will examine the implications of the Eleatic's showing that political life always takes place on the level of opinion and is never guided, completely or directly, by knowledge per se. In the process, I will show that the dialogue has a much clearer order and organization than is generally recognized.[7]

The Eleatic's Critique of Traditional Understandings of Statesmanship

The Statesman as Cognitive Commander

The Eleatic begins his attempt to determine what a statesman is by using the bifurcating method of division (*diairesis*) he introduced in the *Sophist.*[8] As a student of Parmenides, the Eleatic proceeds to investigate being or the beings in terms of what "is" or "is not." In contrast to his teacher, however, in the *Sophist* the Eleatic shows that an assertion of "is not" does not necessarily represent a self-contradictory affirmation of what "is." To say that something – for example, statesmanship – is not, for example, generalship – is to say that it is different.

It is not immediately evident that the Eleatic is challenging traditional views of statesmen – as generals, shepherds, or founding legislators instructed by the gods – that were widely held in ancient Greece.[9]

7 Waterfield 1995: x.

8 The *Statesman* (*Politikos*) is the third in a "trilogy" of explicitly linked dialogues. The so-called trilogy begins with the *Theaetetus*, in which Socrates asks the brilliant young student of geometry, what is knowledge? Although they are unable to answer the question, Socrates claims to have moderated the apparently modest young Theaetetus. Because Socrates has to leave to go to the porch of the archon to be indicted, Theaetetus, his friend the young Socrates, and his teacher Theodorus agree that they will meet with Socrates again the next morning. When they come "as agreed," they bring an anonymous "stranger" (*xenos*) from Elea with them. In evident contrast to Socrates, who described himself as a "midwife" the day before, in the *Sophist* (216a) Theodorus introduces the Eleatic as a "real" or, literally, "manly" (*anēr*) philosopher. In the two conversations or dialogues that follow, the Eleatic first successfully defines a "sophist" and then a "statesman" in contrast to a philosopher.

9 Virtually all ancient political leaders were generals. In ancient Greece, these would include Agamemnon and Achilles, Miltiades, Cimon, Themistocles, and Pericles (as well as the two Athenian politician-generals with whom Socrates tries to define courage in the *Laches*). Miller 1980: 40, observes that in the *Iliad* and the *Odyssey* Agamemnon, Menelaus, Odysseus, and others "are given the epithet *poimēn laōn* 'shepherd of the people.' That the phrase is formulaic, however, suggests that the notion is an old one, received from earlier times and no longer necessarily vital." In the *Laws*, the Athenian Stranger refers to the stories according to which Minos received the laws of Crete from his father Zeus and the founder of Sparta, Lycurgus, was instructed by Apollo, when he begins by asking what the source of the laws in Crete is – man or god?

When the Eleatic suggests that statesmen will be found among those who possess a science (*epistēmē*), however, he begins his investigation by challenging the widespread view – then and now – that political rule is based on control of a preponderance of coercive force. He goes even further in a counterintuitive direction when he suggests that statesmanship is not an essentially practical kind of knowledge. Using "arithmetic" (more precisely, number theory) as an example, he draws a distinction between arts (*technai*) that simply produce knowledge (*gnōnai*) and those like carpentry or the handicrafts in general that have practical effects (*praxeis*), and states that the "kingly art" (*basilikē*) is one of the former. The Eleatic observes that "a king can do much less by means of his hands and his body to maintain his rule than with the strength and intelligence of his soul" (259c).[10] Those who identify rule with power confuse the essentially mental ability to coordinate and direct the force of others with physical strength or coercion per se.

Having challenged the widespread belief that rule is based fundamentally on force, the Eleatic goes on to argue that it is not a matter of scale – overseeing a large rather than a small realm – or holding public office. If a statesman is defined by the knowledge he possesses rather than the effects or products of his actions, it does not matter whether he ever puts that knowledge into practice. In other words, it does not matter whether the "statesman" (*politikos*) ever occupies a position of power or not! And if the knowledge required to rule a slave, household, small city, or vast empire is the same – the difference being merely one of size or number in the ruled – then master, householder, statesman (*politikos*), and king are merely different names for people who have basically the same art.[11]

[10] In quoting, I have generally relied on the Benardete 1984 translation; but on some occasions, I have modified the translation on the basis of the Greek text of Duke et al. 1995.

[11] The Stranger obviously disagrees with Aristotle, who begins his *Politics* (1252a7–23) by maintaining that kings, statesmen, household managers, and slave masters do not differ merely in the number of people they rule. According to Aristotle, these four kinds of rule constitute different kinds of relations, "partnerships," or associations (*koinōniai*). They differ not only in the characteristics of the people who form the various partnerships (masters and slaves, husbands and wives, parents and children, ruler and ruled), but also in the ends or purposes of the partnerships. Whereas the family is organized in order to provide for the preservation of both individuals and species, the polity is organized in order to live well by developing the distinctive human faculty to rule ourselves by means of deliberations about what is good and bad, just and unjust, useful or not.

The Eleatic's emphasis on the purely cognitive character of the statesman's knowledge appears to be a bit less strange when he goes on to observe that instead of merely knowing how to distinguish one kind of thing from another, like a student of numbers, a statesman knows what orders to give others to bring something into being. He does not merely communicate the commands of others, as a priest or seer does the command of a god. The statesman himself knows what and how to command. At the end of the first set of diairetic disjunctions between the purely cognitive and practical, injunctive or merely critical, self-originating as opposed to merely communicative arts, the statesman looks more like an architect than a carpenter. His knowledge is purely intellectual rather than practical or productive because he himself does not make anything. He knows how to order and coordinate the efforts and expertise of other human beings to produce a greater, more comprehensive result.

The Statesman as Shepherd of a Herd

Having shocked not only his interlocutor but also Plato's readers into reconsidering the widespread and persistent notion that the statesman is a public figure who possesses the kind of practical knowledge necessary to rule others on the basis of superior force, the Eleatic proceeds to question other common opinions about the nature of the human beings a statesman rules and the reasons such rule is necessary. Having drawn a comparison between the knowledge of the statesman and an architect, he asks what kind of thing, analogous to a house, the statesman brings into being with his commands. Is it living (*empsuchon*) or not?

Because a statesman rules human beings, the Eleatic observes that "supervising soulless things like an architect is never characteristic of the royal science" (261c–d), and that the science of a ruler concerns the generation and nurture of living beings, not singly, but in a group or "herd." In contrast to the Eleatic's emphasis on the primarily cognitive character of the statesman's knowledge, his contention that statesmen deal with groups rather than with individuals in private seems commonsensical; it accords with the experience most people have of politics. The question the Eleatic poses about whether the product of the political art is living nevertheless conceals a fundamental distinction or difficulty. Recognizing that the statesman does not literally bring the human beings he rules into being (by giving birth to them), he suggests that the statesman is somehow responsible for "nurturing," perhaps breeding, and certainly preserving a human "herd." The question to which he turns later in the dialogue is, how? How does a statesman form or maintain a group of individual human beings or their families into a people or polity? And how does the polity, once formed, nurture and protect its citizens? The statesman may be responsible for the coming-into-being of a polity, but the product of his cognitive commands, the constitution or regime, is not so clearly or unambiguously "living" as the people so ordered.

Emphasizing the living or ensouled character of the beings a statesman rules enables the Eleatic to ask, what kind of living being? His interlocutor suggests, again quite sensibly, that the art of nurturing human beings can be distinguished from the nurture of other kinds of animals. At first, the Eleatic's objections to this division appear to be principled, if not technical: Socrates did not distinguish between a part (*meros*) and a species (*eidos*); all species are parts, but not all parts are species. The distinction Socrates drew between humans and other animals is analogous to that Greeks commonly draw between themselves and "barbarians." The Eleatic might appear to be suggesting that, like the political differences among various peoples, the difference between humans and animals is merely conventional, not natural. He indicates that is not his point when he complains that the division between humans and other animals is lopsided and arbitrary, like a distinction drawn between the numbers between one and ten thousand, on the one hand, and all the other numbers, on the other. Distinctions, according to species, should be drawn down the middle, like that between male and female or odd and even. The principle of division by "halves" is not merely quantitative, however. Kinds or species are not defined simply by separating one part off from all the rest (the "not x"). To show that some differ from others does not suffice; it is also necessary to show the respect in which each of the "kinds" is the same as itself. "Barbarians" are defined merely as non-Greeks, not according to any characteristic they themselves share.

When the Eleatic tells the "manliest of all" young Socrates that other reputedly intelligent creatures like cranes might divide themselves off the same way, the Eleatic's objection appears to be more moral or pedagogical than technical. Human beings should not base their understanding of politics or statesmanship on the pride they tend to take in their intelligence (especially when they are brilliant mathematicians like Theaetetus and young Socrates).[12] The Eleatic thus challenges the

[12] In the *Sophist* the Eleatic questions Theaetetus; because Theaetetus is probably tired, in the *Statesman*, the conversation that occurs immediately after that related

views Aristotle would later make famous both of human beings as the rational animals and of political communities as expressions and realizations of that rationality. He defines human beings in contrast to other species on the basis of externally observable characteristics we share in an admittedly comical way to show that we form political societies not because we are particularly well endowed by nature with reason, but because we are much less well equipped than other animals with means of defense.[13]

Attempting to identify the distinguishing characteristics of the herd the statesman tends, the Eleatic begins with the distinction he first drew in the *Sophist* between tame animals, which can be domesticated, and wild animals, which cannot.[14] Civilization (or "citification") would appear to constitute a kind of "taming." He then divides animals that can be domesticated according to whether they live in the water or on land, fly or walk, on two feet or four, with or without cloven hooves, have horns or don't, and interbreed or do not. All but the last of these characteristics are directly related to the animals' ability to fight or flee from those who might attack.[15]

The Eleatic is not propounding a logical technique of definition, we begin to see, so much as he is gradually leading his interlocutors (and Plato's readers) toward an understanding of politics as arising not

in the *Sophist*, Theaetetus is replaced by his fellow gymnast and geometer, "young Socrates."

13 In the myth he tells in the *Protagoras* (320c–22d) the sophist also suggests that human beings are forced to develop arts and form political communities in order to preserve ourselves because we are so ill-equipped by nature. In contrast to the Eleatic, however, Protagoras follows traditional stories in suggesting that the gods gave human beings the capacity to develop the arts and political communities. The Eleatic suggests that human beings had to develop arts for themselves.

14 Although the Eleatic appears to characterize human beings as tame animals here, in the *Sophist* (222b–c) he refused to decide whether human beings were naturally tame or wild and insisted that his interlocutor, Theaetetus, choose which pleased him. Reflecting his own character, the apparently modest, docile young geometer chose tame. At the conclusion of the *Statesman* we nevertheless discover the reason the Eleatic himself was not willing to choose. By nature, human beings tend to divide between the moderate (tame) and courageous (wild). Human beings are, in other words, potentially both tame and wild. How tame or wild humans become depends upon their breeding and education. That is what the statesman supervises.

15 The ability to interbreed is also related, negatively, to the preservation of the species. Horses and donkeys, for example, can interbreed, but their progeny, mules, are sterile. If members of the two species did not breed with their like, but only with others, all three species would come to an end.

from human nobility but from human need. Coming to the end of his definition of the kind of animals the statesman nurtures, the Eleatic admits not only that there are two different ways of identifying the distinctive features of a human being, one longer and one shorter, but also that the two ways produce somewhat different definitions. There are two ways because the bifurcations do not follow neatly one from another in the case of numbers of legs, hooves, and interbreeding. The Eleatic acknowledges (266c), moreover, that the definitions to which they come are comical. Like his initial insistence on the purely cognitive character of the art of ruling, his debunking description of what is distinctively human serves to correct a common misperception about the character and basis of politics.

The Statesman Is Not a God or Instructed by a God

The problem the Eleatic explicitly points out in the definition of the statesman to which they have come is that there are many different kinds of artisans who claim to know what to do (or command) to nourish and nurture the human herd. He does not explain why he needs to use a "large part of a myth" that he calls "childish" (268d–e) to distinguish the statesman from these other artisans. Only after he has retold and reinterpreted three old stories do readers realize that his initial definitions of the statesman as a wise commander (or legislator) and caring shepherd reflected, if obliquely, traditional views. The Eleatic recognizes that mathematically educated young Athenians like Socrates and Theaetetus are not apt to believe such old stories are literally true. He thus acknowledges that there is something playful about his use of the myth. He knows that he will not be able to free the young from the misconceptions of the statesman they have inherited by confronting and trying to refute these views directly; if he did, the young men would simply tell him that they don't believe such old wives' tales. But, having shown that young Socrates retains something of the traditional view of a statesman as an all-wise commander and caring shepherd by arguing very untraditionally that the statesman's knowledge is more cognitive than practical and that the human herd he tends is a bunch of comically defenseless two-legged animals, the Eleatic then reinterprets three old stories to show that the traditional view is childish. In defining the statesman as a wise and caring shepherd, he suggests, they had been looking up to him the way young children look up to their parents. In adopting the image of the shepherd, the Eleatic points out at the end of his myth, they had even implied that the statesman belongs to a higher species – that he is, in a word, a god.

As originally told, all three of the old stories the Eleatic reinterprets – Zeus' changing the direction of the movement of the heavens to signal his preference for Atreus over Thyestes, the rule of Cronus in the golden age, and the autochthonous birth of the original inhabitants of cities like Athens and Thebes – represent accounts of the origins of political regimes. According to the Eleatic, however, all three of these stories refer to one cosmic event. In explicating the reasons for and effects of the reverse in the motion of the cosmos, which all three of these ancient stories reflect in different ways, the Eleatic also gives an account of the origins of political rule. But the account he gives differs significantly from the tradition. Whereas the old stories suggest that political rule arises from the concern gods have for human beings, the Eleatic reinterprets the stories to show that human beings have had to develop arts, particularly the political art, in order to protect themselves from hostile natural forces. The gods may have cared for human beings in the past, but the Eleatic concludes his myth by pointing out that the gods no longer rule us directly. Human beings have to take care of themselves.

The Eleatic begins his account of the reverse in the motion of the cosmos by reminding his interlocutors that only the divine is eternal and unchanging. Because the heavens or cosmos is visible and thus bodily, neither it nor its motion can be maintained without change. The motion of the cosmos first changed, according to the Eleatic, when the god ceased directing it. The god had to stop directing it because the cosmos is not, like a god, eternal; it cannot, therefore, move or be directed always and forever in the same way.[16] When the god let it go, the cosmos tried to retain as much of its original motion as possible, rotating in the same place in the same way, although not in the same direction, by twisting back like a spinning top toward the direction from which it had initially been propelled. When it had finally exhausted its

[16] For something like the motion of the cosmos to begin, it is necessary to posit a divine (preexisting, because eternal) cause. Because nothing bodily remains entirely the same, however, the motion of the cosmos once begun could not persist without change. The gods themselves do not change, so a god cannot be thought to be responsible for the reverse in the motion of the cosmos. Nor, because that which is eternally unchanging is intelligible as such, can the gods be thought to work in opposed or contradictory directions. The traditional story about Zeus' changing the direction of the movement of the heavens is not true.

initial momentum, however, a god had to take control and reverse the motion once more lest the cosmos, having used up its own resources, dissolve into an "infinite sea of dissimilarity."[17] Rather than direct its motion himself, he gave the cosmos an order of its own (thus making it truly a "cosmos"), deathless and ageless.[18]

The Eleatic associates the first period, or the era when the god directly guided the motion of the cosmos, with the traditional stories about the rule of Cronus. During that period, the Eleatic says, Cronus appointed lesser divinities (*daimones*) to rule different parts of the cosmos and kinds of animals. Like shepherds, these divinities saw that all the needs of their respective flocks were met. As a result, there was no conflict or savagery. Among human beings "there were no regimes or possession of women and children either, for everyone came alive from the earth without any memory of those before" (271e–72a). According to the Eleatic, the age of the rule of Cronus thus coincided with the age of autochthonous births. Because food was ready at hand, people did not need to farm. Nor did they need to find shelter or clothe themselves.[19]

[17] There has been a great deal of debate about whether there are two or three periods. Cf. McCabe 1997.

[18] Although the picture of the cosmos the Eleatic presents has some things in common with the cosmic views presented by other Platonic philosophical spokesmen, it also differs from them in significant respects. Like Socrates and Timaeus, the Eleatic begins by emphasizing that only the divine is eternal and unchanging. Because the heavens and the cosmos are visible and thus bodily, they are neither eternal nor perfectly intelligible. No human being could be present or know their origin. Like Socrates (or Er) in the *Republic* and Timaeus, the Eleatic thus presents his account of the cosmos and its motion explicitly as a "myth." Socrates and Timaeus also observe that heavenly bodies move in opposite directions, but they depict these contrary movements occurring simultaneously as part of a beautiful, intelligible order they call good. Like the Athenian Stranger, the Eleatic Stranger suggests that the two kinds of motion remain in opposition. But, in dramatic contrast to the Athenian, who associates the orderly intelligible motion of the heavens with the gods and urges human beings to ally themselves with them in opposing the disorderly motion of the bad soul, the Eleatic sketches a two- or three-part development that culminates in a godforsaken universe.

[19] In the *Laws* (713b–14a) the Athenian urges people to imitate the way of life instituted by Cronus to the greatest extent possible. The Eleatic says, however, that this age was happier than ours, only if people used the opportunity to philosophize provided by their leisure as well as their ability at that time to converse with other animals, "inquiring from every nature, whether with its kind of private capacity it was aware of something different from all the rest, to gather intelligence" (*phronēsis*, 272c). But it does not seem likely that these peaceful, prosperous people philosophized, since the Eleatic later states that human beings developed the arts (and thus their practical intelligence) only when forced to do so by necessity. Because they were

The question arises whether this was a golden age, as poets like Hesiod had suggested. The Eleatic responds that human life would have been happy and satisfying only if people had used the opportunity to converse not only among themselves but also with the other animals, that is, if they had philosophized. Since human beings had no need at that time to develop even the most rudimentary arts, it seems unlikely that they occupied themselves with rigorous intellectual investigations.

Because nothing bodily can remain entirely the same, the god and his subordinates had to stop guiding the movement of the cosmos and caring for the animals living in it. Bereft of divine direction, during this second period the cosmos stopped turning as it had and swung back, revolving on its own momentum in the opposite direction. Great climatic changes and other natural disasters like floods resulted from the change in the motions of the heavens. Most human beings and animals died as a result. Because the generation of plants and animals is observably associated with the movement of the heavens (e.g., in the timing of menstrual cycles or mating seasons), the order of generation changed with the movements of the heavens. People and animals were still spontaneously born from the earth, but now they emerged old, with gray hair, and gradually became younger and younger until they faded back into the earth to become the seeds of another rebirth.

With the passage of time, both the reverse movement of the cosmos in reaction to the cessation of its original impulsion and the generations of living beings living upon the earth became weaker and weaker. Having used up its own resources, the cosmos was in danger of dissolving into a "sea" of infinite dissimilarities. To prevent the degeneration of the cosmos into complete disorder and unintelligibility, the god once again took charge and reversed the motion of the cosmos. Rather than perpetuate a cycle of divine rule followed by threatened chaos when the gods had to depart, the god made the motions of the cosmos self-regulating.[20]

continually growing younger, Scodel 1987: 81 n. 9, points out, people at that time were continually forgetting rather than acquiring knowledge. McCabe 1997: 107, and Rosen 1988: 71, also emphasize the importance of the lack of memory. But if people in this earlier age did not philosophize, the Eleatic suggests, life at that time was neither happier nor better than it is now.

[20] The Eleatic describes the cosmos as a "living animal" (*zōion*) presumably because it is self-moving and thus appears to have a soul. Perhaps because the god applies his divine mind to the ordering of the sensible world, the Eleatic also says that the cosmos has *phronēsis*.

Because the god had made the cosmos self-regulating, the animals also now had to generate, nurse, and grow by themselves – rather than simply receiving what they needed from the earth or the gods. As a result, human beings now find ourselves living in an era of conflict. The cosmos we inhabit is a mixture of the previous two eras. Because the cosmos still contains some beautiful elements left by its divine maker (*dēmiourgos*) and father, it is not entirely unintelligible; but it is not entirely intelligible, either, since everything is in flux. Because of its bodily nature, moreover, many aspects of the existing order are harsh. No longer provided for by deities, animals have to struggle to get and keep what they need to survive. Weak and unguarded by nature, human beings are forced to develop arts to protect and provide for themselves, or they will be torn apart by wild beasts.

According to the older, more traditional tales the Eleatic reinterprets, the gods cared for human beings by ruling them or appointing other suitable rulers and giving human beings the knowledge they needed in order to survive. Although he observes in passing that other old stories attributed the arts to gifts from gods like Hephaestus or Athena, the Eleatic maintains that the kinds of knowledge or "arts" human beings need to protect and preserve themselves were developed and acquired by the humans themselves without "divine" assistance or support.

The Eleatic had initially said that he would need to use "a large part of a big myth" (268d) to distinguish the statesman from other human caretakers, but at the conclusion of his tale he blames himself and young Socrates for having "raised up an amazing bulk of the myth" and then having been "compelled to use a greater part than they should have" (277b). It is easy to see why the Eleatic emphasizes how big his myth is: it concerns the origins, development, and final character of the cosmos. He had to use such a big, cosmic myth to show young Socrates (and the assembled auditors) that human beings do not acquire political knowledge as a result of their god-given or natural advantages.

But why did the Eleatic complain that they had been "compelled to use" more than they should? As the Eleatic's use of the myth indicates, our understanding of the function or work (*ergon*) of the statesman is connected to our understanding of nature as a whole. The first reason the Stranger criticizes himself for using a myth would thus appear to be that his account of the cosmos is and remains essentially mythical. Unlike the explicitly mythical descriptions of the motions of the heavenly bodies given by Socrates, Timaeus, and the Athenian Stranger, the Eleatic's account of the effects of the reversed motion of the cosmos is not based on observations of the mathematically calculable orbits of the heavenly bodies.[21] His reinterpretation and rationalization of the three old tales does not appear to be very scientific. The cosmological basis of his argument about the kind of political knowledge human beings need to develop consequently seems weak.[22]

The second and more fundamental reason the Eleatic objects to their use of so much myth seems to be that human beings do not, in fact, know their origins – or the gods. That is why accounts of both are "mythical." Rather than relying on high-minded speculations or inferences, he suggests, we should begin from what we do know – our own immediate, present experience. And when we reflect on our own experience, without the mythological or cosmological dressing up we have inherited, we are confronted with our own natural weakness. Whatever

[21] Skemp 1952: 89, points out that "the *Timaeus* tries to give us a fully consistent cosmology in which astronomical facts have a supreme significance, whereas the *Politicus* uses for didactic purposes the notion of a periodic cosmic reversal which no astronomer could accept and which would be inconsistent even with the earlier half-mythical astronomy of the myth of Er in *Republic* X. Yet once the impossible 'reversal of rotation' is tolerated, the *Politicus* account seems to do less violence to observed facts than the *Timaeus* does – for the basic principle that reason causes circular physical movement leads in the *Timaeus* to extraordinary psychological and physiological conclusions."

[22] If the Eleatic had begun not with old stories but with astronomical observations of the mathematically calculable orbits of the heavenly bodies, however, he would have been led, as Socrates, Timaeus, and the Athenian Stranger are, to emphasize the intelligible and thus beneficent order of the world. All three of these philosophers suggest that studying the intelligible motions of the heavenly bodies will help human beings learn not merely how the cosmos is ordered, but, even more important, how to order their own souls. Political societies are established and maintained, according to all three of these philosophers, to enable human beings not merely to preserve themselves, but to live the best life possible by acquiring as much virtue as possible. Political societies should encourage at least some of their members to study the orderly movements of the heavens because such studies help people learn how to become more virtuous by bringing order to their own souls. Cf. Griswold 1989: 150, who notes "a fundamental difference between the ES's cosmology and that of Socrates . . . as well as a striking difference between their respective notions of political science and of dialectic." Nightingale 1996 also draws out the many differences, indeed incompatibilities, between the cosmological myth in the *Statesman* and those to be found in the *Timaeus* and the *Laws*. Convinced that "Plato" must somehow be made consistent (and that he apparently was unable to imagine different characters putting forth different understandings), she nevertheless tries in the end to merge them.

may have been the case in the past, we have no direct experience of divine care or rule.

The Eleatic's reinterpretation of the old stories may appear to represent a sketch of the view of nature as a whole upon which his view of politics is based; but, in fact, he has merely reinterpreted three old stories in order to free young Socrates (and their audience) from the remnants of the old, mythological views of statesmen or kings as god-like shepherds and all-knowing commanders. The Eleatic knows that he has not presented an empirically based or scientific account of the character of the cosmos.[23] That is not, as he sees it, the place to begin trying to understand politics or the art of the statesman. We should, instead, acknowledge our lack of natural equipment and then investigate the means, the arts human beings have gradually developed to protect and preserve ourselves, beginning with the smallest and most menial. If the art of the statesman is a discrete form of knowledge, distinguishable from both sophistry and philosophy, it should not and does not require knowledge of nature as a whole to determine what that art is.

If human beings cannot know the origins or first principles, human knowledge will always be incomplete. And if human knowledge is incomplete, human beings will disagree not only about the character of the natural order but also, and more stridently, about the ends of politics. At the end of his myth, the Eleatic thus points out that they had erred not only in treating the statesman as a shepherd and thus implicitly as a member of a higher species, but by neglecting to differentiate between caring (*therapeuein*) and nourishing (*trophē* or *agelaiotrophikē*), they had also failed to distinguish care for the entire community from concern for a part. Finally and perhaps most importantly, they had not paid attention to the difference between rule based on force and rule based on consent. If human knowledge is both rare and tenuous, the few who actually learn what is needed to establish and maintain a polity will have difficulty persuading the many who lack such knowledge. That is the reason, we subsequently see, that the rule of law becomes a problem – perhaps the central problem – when the Stranger begins, again, to define the art of politics as it really exists rather than as it has been traditionally and more nobly portrayed, using the menial, even feminine, art of weaving as a paradigm.

[23] I thus agree in part, but only in part, with the warning in Rowe 1996: 160 n. 17, against taking the myth as "serious history or cosmology."

The True Understanding of the Art of Politics

Weaving as the Paradigm

Young Socrates thinks they have come to an adequate definition of the statesman as a human ruler who knowledgeably cares for the entire community on the basis of consent rather than force. But, the Eleatic insists, they have just begun. Having brought out the defects of the old model or paradigm of divine rule, he suggests, they need a new example or paradigm.

The Eleatic indicated earlier that the political art involves the coordination of other, lesser arts when he compared the statesman to an architect (259e). He thus proposes another paradigm of a simpler kind of coordination or interweaving of arts that enables human beings to protect themselves from natural afflictions.[24] Because defense is not a good in itself, the Eleatic does not talk about the "end" of politics; instead, he describes its function (*ergon*) or concerns (*pragmata*). By choosing an art practiced primarily by women in ancient Greece as a paradigm of politics, the Eleatic emphasizes the source of its defensive character and thrust in physical weakness.[25] According to the Eleatic, politics is not essentially acquisitive or aggressive.[26]

The Eleatic quickly defines the character of the product of weaving (279c–d) by contrasting it in a series of bifurcations to arts that make or achieve some effect (*poiein*) as opposed to repelling or preventing (*mē paschein amuntēria*). Then he points out that weavers need to employ two other kinds of artisans – those who know how to make the instruments they use and those who produce the materials they weave together with those instruments – in order to exercise their own art. To define the art of weaving, it does not suffice to determine what no other artisan but a weaver does (plaiting the warp and the woof); one also has to show how the weaver uses the products of other arts.

24 As forms of knowledge, the arts are, of course, intelligible. Their intelligibility may be a product simply of the intelligence of the human artisan. The materials with which the artisans work – or the "elements" – may not be intelligible in themselves.

25 I disagree, therefore, with Rosen 1995: 153, when he declares that "weaving is also defective as a paradigm . . . because it is a peaceful, feminine art of the household." Lane 1998: 164–71, notes that Aristophanes had used weaving as a metaphor for politics in his *Lysistrata*.

26 In contrast, for example, to the Cretan elder Clinias at the beginning of the *Laws* (625e–26b).

The Necessity of Recognizing Two Kinds of Measure

Having indicated more fully than he had in his first diairesis how the statesman, like an architect or a weaver, has to bring together the work of a variety of different artisans in order to bring something into being, the Eleatic clarifies the difference between the kind of knowledge involved in this kind of coordination and that represented by other, primarily cognitive arts like mathematics. Like other clever men who want to appear wise, the Eleatic worries, the young geometers may later observe that everything that becomes can be measured mathematically and thus recognize one and only one kind of measurement. Such people deny that the "arts" (*technai*) which bring beautiful and good things into existence are, strictly speaking, forms of knowledge. They do not understand that such arts use not merely one, but two different kinds of measurement.

The first kind of measurement is that characteristic of mathematical arts – like arithmetic, geometry, and astronomy – which measure things relative to each other in terms of a common standard, for example, units, inches, pounds, motion. The arts that produce good and beautiful things or people – like architecture, weaving, and politics – also use this kind of measure. As Stanley Rosen points out, one has to know how big a man is to make an effective cloak.[27] But this kind of measurement does not enable a cloak maker to know how soft the woof should be to provide the requisite amount of warmth to repel the cold under particular climatic conditions or how tough the warp should be to make the cloak fit to repel rain.[28]

The second kind of measurement involves a determination of how much of each of a variety of essentially different and so incommensurable activities and constituent materials are necessary in order to achieve a desired result, function, or "effect." The amount of each component varies according to the circumstances and the interaction of the parts. It is extremely difficult, therefore, to determine what is "fitting," "opportune," or "needful." One needs to possess an extraordinary kind of precision in judging how much of a variety of components is needed to achieve the desired "mean" (*metrion*). Unlike the external, independent standards of measurement used in mathematics, this measure or "mean" is "internal," at the center or core of the product.

27 Rosen 1995: 123.

28 The discussion of the two kinds of measure in Rosen 1995: 123–25, is extremely useful.

Because the softness or toughness of the fiber used to make a cloak would appear to depend on its purpose, protecting people from the natural elements, commentators like Rosen have identified the mean with the purpose of the art in question. As we have already seen, however, the Stranger does not define arts in terms of their ends (*telē*); he speaks instead about their work or function (*ergon*). Although ends and functions may appear to be very similar so long as we are talking about things, human purposes have to be intentional whereas functions do not. It is possible to determine how something functions simply by observing it; to determine what a person's purpose is, however, it is necessary to talk to him. Most of the Eleatic's arguments rest upon externally observable characteristics and acts of human beings.

The Eleatic's description of the mean as the measure of what is fitting, opportune, or needful sounds a great deal like Aristotle's definition of practical wisdom, as knowing the right thing to do, in the right way, at the right time, by the right person.[29] That seems to be what knowledge of "the precise in itself" would involve. As Charles Griswold points out, however, the Eleatic does not associate such knowledge with "the Good in itself" or "virtue."[30] Although he says that good and bad people differ primarily in exceeding or falling short of the mean (283e), he does not propose the mean as a measure of human character or virtue. The Eleatic is not trying to show his interlocutors that political leadership requires an extraordinarily good character or moral virtue. He is attempting to show some young mathematicians that political leadership requires a kind of knowledge that involves more rather than less precision than mathematics and that is even more difficult, therefore, to acquire.

To identify what sort of knowledge the statesman has, moreover, the Eleatic shows that they need to use and master another art – the art of dialectics. People who fail to distinguish between the two kinds of measure show that they are not in the habit of dividing things into classes (*eidē*). These people include the mathematicians who deny that there is any other kind of measure or knowledge as well as, perhaps, the Pythagoreans who claimed that everything is constituted, and so measurable, by number. These people show that they have not mastered the art of "dialectics" (which the Eleatic identified with philosophy in the *Sophist* [253c–d]) because they group similar things together as the same without inquiring about the differences among them.

[29] Rosen 1995: 125–26, admits that the Eleatic does not mention *phronēsis* in this passage any more than he does *telos*.

[30] Griswold 1989: 152–53.

Mathematicians recognize the difference between the intelligible measures and the observable or sensible things measured, but they do not recognize the differences among the kinds of intelligible measures or the resulting need to use different kinds of "images," examples, or paradigms in learning about the different kinds of intelligibility or beings. A weaver is not an image or imitation of a political leader the way a circle drawn in the sand is a visible image of the intelligible definition and concept. (Both commanders and shepherds are images of statesmen more like the visible circle.) Although there are certain similarities in the basic function and the coordinating structure of the two kinds of essentially defensive arts, there are also obvious and very important differences. "No one with any wit would investigate the character of the weaving art for its own sake" (285d), the Eleatic observes. He has analyzed the art of weaving as a paradigm of the political art because it is necessary to use examples that are "naturally there for easy understanding . . . which are not difficult to make plain . . . apart from speech," since "no image has been devised as plain as day for human beings in the case of the biggest and most honorable things" (285e–86a). The Eleatic does not say whether the science of the statesman (*epistēmē politikē*) or the kingly art (*basilikē*) is one of the biggest and most honorable things. It appears, in fact, to be somewhere in between the easily perceptible and the entirely bodiless. The Eleatic later states that the "science of the rule of human beings [is] pretty nearly the greatest and most difficult to acquire" (292d). Although it is easy to see and thus point out leaders and cities, both the intelligence it requires to maintain a city and the regime or order the statesman establishes in it are invisible and difficult to discern, acquire, or make effective.

The Statesman and His Art

Using weaving as an example, the Eleatic now admits that it is difficult to separate the art of the statesman from the products and services that other artisans contribute to the final product by cutting down the middle. They will proceed, therefore, as Socrates does in the *Phaedrus*, by dividing it as if it were a "sacrificial animal," limb from limb. It is tempting to conclude that the Eleatic's insistence on cutting things down the middle in his diaireses earlier had been a rhetorical ploy, designed particularly to appeal to two young geometers. We should resist that temptation, however, by remembering that the Eleatic's method of division arises from his contention that beings can and should be sorted into classes, not only according to the respects in which they are the same but also according to the several ways in which they may differ. Politics has been shown to require a different kind of knowledge than mathematics. The Eleatic thus has to use a somewhat different method of sorting, proceeding in stages or parts, rather than simply by means of bifurcations, to distinguish political science not only from the arts that contribute to it, but also from its competitors and imitators.

The Eleatic first cuts off all the arts that provide useful tools and services. The "tools" include instruments, vessels, supports, defenses, ornaments, raw materials, and all forms or sources of nourishment. The services begin with the labor of slaves, who obviously do not claim to be kings, and include merchants as well as free laborers, heralds, scribes, and priests. The most important public servants from which the statesman must be distinguished are, however, those who pretend to be statesmen by actually governing. These are "the greatest enchanter[s] of all the sophists" (291c). All actual rulers are "sophists," according to the Eleatic, because they lack the knowledge of a true statesman.

THE TENSION BETWEEN KNOWLEDGE AND LAW. Why are no actual governments conducted on the basis of knowledge? Why are there no true statesmen ever actually in office? The Eleatic proceeds to explain.

Governments are usually characterized by the number of people in power – one, few, or many. They are further differentiated by whether the rule is voluntary or compulsory, whether rulers are rich or poor, and whether their rule is by law or lawless. People thus generally distinguish between the rule of a legal, often hereditary monarch and the force-based, lawless rule of a tyrant as well as between the rule of a few law-abiding aristocrats and rapacious oligarchs. But there is usually no distinction drawn in name between the lawful and lawless rule of the many, who are always poor. If the statesman or true king is distinguished from all others by his knowledge, however, none of these characteristics suffices to define him.

In contrast to Aristotle – who distinguishes six basic types of regime on the basis of the number of rulers and whether they serve the common good or their own self-interest, and then, recognizing that the few are rich and the many poor, modifies his classification to include the economic or other characteristics of the rulers – the Eleatic draws one hard and fast line between knowledgeable and ignorant rule. He does not distinguish rulers on the basis of their just intentions or moral virtue. The reason, although he does not state it, seems to be that a ruler could not serve the common good without knowing what it is. There are, therefore, no virtuous rulers who are not knowledgeable.

Instead the Eleatic emphasizes the distance and resulting tension between the few knowledgeable rulers and the many people they govern. If the only true and best form of government requires knowledge, he observes, democracy never represents the best form of government. Only a few people are able to possess even lesser forms of knowledge. One person – or at most a few – can attain the complex kind of knowledge called statesmanship that enables them to rule justly, to improve the city as much as they can while still keeping it safe, whether they use force or persuade others.[31]

His interlocutor is shocked to hear that the only right regime does not involve the rule of law or consent, so the Eleatic elaborates. Because no one or small number of rulers can supervise each and every citizen individually and at all times, even scientific rulers would have to lay down laws to guide people in general. But these laws would never represent more than general rules of thumb – stating what is best most of the time, in most places, for most people. Because "the dissimilarities of human beings and their actions are so great, and the human beings themselves are constantly changing" (294b), no general rules like laws ever fit the circumstances or the individuals exactly. No scientific or true ruler would, therefore, feel completely and unalterably obliged to follow the law in opposition to his own judgment.

If the defects of laws as general rules are so clear, we might wonder why people generally think that the rule of law is desirable. The Eleatic thus proceeds to explain why, although the rule of law is decidedly second best to the rule of knowledge, people virtually have no choice but the second best.

[31] Because the Eleatic speaks about just rule and improving the city, commentators like Dorter 1994 have argued that, in the end, the Eleatic's understanding of politics is no different from that Socrates presents in the *Republic*. It is important, therefore, to stress the Eleatic's explicit qualifications on the ruler's "employing science and the just and, *in keeping it safe*, make it better from worse, *to the best of their ability*" (293e) and later his distributing "to those in the city that which with mind and art is most just, and *can keep them safe* and make them better from worse *as far as possible*" (297b; emphasis added). Although Socrates introduces guardians as needed for defense, in legislating for *kallipolis* later he does not pay much attention, if any, to the requirements of defense. His concern becomes, first, the justice, and then the preservation or decay, of the regime. In the *Laws* the Athenian Stranger more explicitly disagrees with the Eleatic when he insists that nothing – not even the preservation of the regime or the city itself – should take precedence over the attempt to enable "every member of the community, male or female, young or old, . . . to acquire the virtue of soul that befits a human beings" (770d–e).

Possessed at most by a few, the Eleatic had observed, all kinds of knowledge are rare. Knowledge of the art of rule or government is, however, especially difficult to obtain and, once obtained, to exercise.

In most arts experimentation with new methods of production or preservation is allowed – with or even without the consent of those the artisan treats – and incremental additions to knowledge result from the ongoing experimentation. Recognizing that patients are sometimes unwilling to undergo painful treatments and circumstances differ, people understand that expert physicians or pilots may not merely have to contravene the rules and go against accepted practice; they may even have to force their patients or passengers to follow their recommendations to do what is good for them. The "proof" is in the proverbial pudding – whether the people who claim to have knowledge can save lives or, in cases when they fail, show that they made a good faith effort. Even when particular treatments or courses of navigation fail, doctors and pilots learn from the failures.

Things are different in politics. Not merely does a statesman have to acquire knowledge of a vast array of other productive activities if he is to coordinate them in preserving the city. The rare person who acquires such knowledge has to exercise it according to rules laid down by people who lack that knowledge. If he breaks the rules (i.e., the law), he is subject to a public audit and possible punishment by those who know less than he. No one who truly understands politics, the Eleatic concludes, would agree to rule under these conditions.

The requirement that rulers should be subject to laws as are their subjects or citizens arises from bitter experience. Recognizing that they do not know what to do in order to save themselves, their families, and cities, people are willing to follow more knowledgeable leaders. They thus initially trust individuals who claim that they know what to do, especially after these individuals demonstrate the requisite knowledge and ability to lead in emergencies. People grant such leaders unrestricted power only to find that unrestrained rulers use their power to enrich themselves by oppressively taxing their people and exiling or killing those who do not obey their commands.

Insofar as it reflects lessons drawn from experience, the demand that rulers, too, obey the law constitutes a kind of approximation or "imitation" of knowledge. The particular form or wording of the laws also reflects the advice of leaders who know how to persuade a multitude. The Eleatic thus calls the rule of law "a second sailing" or "second best." It is clearly inferior to the scientific rule of an expert who knows precisely what to do for each and every individual under changing circumstances, but it is better than the self-serving, lawless rule of a tyrant.

There are two enduring problems with the rule of law or "second best." The first is that the rule of law, once established, threatens to cut off any possibility of gaining further knowledge and so of improving government. Every attempt to innovate involves a critique of the existing law and hence a challenge to its wisdom. Every question concerning the wisdom or justice of the law undermines popular support for the law and the willingness of the people to obey it. Because the rule of law is justified by the need to secure the people as a whole from tyranny, the Eleatic points out, anyone who questions it will be regarded as a potentially tyrannical pretender seeking wealth and power for himself. He will be called a "sophist" (rather than a philosopher). He can, moreover, be accused, indicted, and dragged into court by anyone who wishes on the grounds that he is "corrupting the young" by encouraging them to question and hence to disrespect and even disobey the laws, if only by his own example.

Many commentators have noted the similarity between the Eleatic's description of the fate of a person who, contrary to the writings, seeks knowledge of politics and the plight of the elder Socrates, silently listening to the conversation, who had been indicted by the city of Athens for impiety and corrupting the young the day before.[32] There are, however, at least two significant differences between Socrates and the seeker of knowledge the Eleatic describes. First, Plato's Socrates never questioned the law per se for the sake of learning the political art. On the contrary, as Socrates emphasizes in both the *Apology* and the *Republic*, he stayed out of the public assembly (or "sphere") and questioned individuals about their opinions in private, precisely because he recognized the danger of speaking in public.[33] Like other philosophers, Socrates explains in the *Republic*, he did not want to rule or to learn how to rule. He wanted to discover the best form of human existence, and he thought he had found it in the conversations he held every day about

[32] Rosen 1995: 6–7; Howland 1998: 276; Miller 1980: 98–99. Rowe 2001 attempts to forestall an application of the prohibition of questioning to Socrates by offering a new translation of 300a1–7, but he admits that the Greek does not settle the issue.

[33] *Apology* 31c–e; *Republic* 496c–e. In the *Apology* 29c–d Socrates explicitly states that the only law he *would* disobey would be a law that forbade him to philosophize. Such a law had not been passed or "written" in Athens until his trial. Famous for the freedom of speech it allowed, the city of Athens (and its laws) had allowed him to interrogate the opinions of others for over thirty years.

what constitutes human virtue.[34] Second, Socrates was indicted under the democratic laws of Athens, which allowed extraordinary freedom of speech, including the freedom to challenge and change the laws in public assemblies. He was accused and convicted, not generally for challenging the wisdom of the laws, but more specifically, like other philosophers, for raising questions about the character and existence of the gods and teaching other young people to do so as well. Having suggested that, like other arts, the art of politics becomes necessary precisely because the gods do not take care of human beings, the Eleatic is not concerned about belief in the gods or piety. Nor is he suggesting that there is a tension between philosophy per se and the rule of law. The Eleatic's point is more general. Law qua law cannot allow its wisdom or imperative force to be questioned and remain effective as law, that is, as a command that must be obeyed or the disobedient will be punished. He thus concludes (300e–1a) that the best imitations of the regime based on knowledge will stick to the laws that have been written down and not allow any exceptions or changes.

In endorsing the rule of law as the "second best" the Eleatic seems to be endorsing an absolutely rigid regime with no possibility of improvement. His interlocutor underlines the difficulty by observing that if the practitioners of other arts were subjected to the kinds of restraints placed upon the statesman, all the arts would perish.[35] Having been reminded by the myth that human beings need to develop arts in order to survive, he adds that life, which is hard enough now, would become unbearable in the absence of art.

The Eleatic assures his interlocutor that the rule of law is not as rigid and unreasonable as he has made it seem. "The laws have been laid down on the basis of much experience" (300b). Certain advisors have, moreover, examined these experiences in detail and persuaded the multitude to set down the laws that embody them. As in democratic Athens, the law itself can specify the process by which it can be changed. Someone who disobeys the law is challenging accumulated wisdom. That means, however, that wisdom does accumulate with experience, and people can be persuaded to change the laws.

[34] *Apology* 37e–38a.

[35] Like politicians subject to audit, both doctors and pilots (the Eleatic's examples) could then as now be hauled into court and charged with malpractice. If many physicians or pilots were convicted, however, fewer would be willing to practice these arts or experiment with new techniques. In the United States today we are all too familiar with the problems caused by medical malpractice suits and insurance costs.

The problem with the rule of law is not simply or fundamentally that changing the law is difficult. Practical wisdom or knowledge itself is accumulated gradually and slowly on the basis of much experience. The problem is, more fundamentally, that recognizing their own ignorance and need for knowledgeable leadership, people cannot identify the right leaders. If someone able to rule with virtue and knowledge were to arise, the Eleatic claims (301d), he would be welcomed warmly and in piloting with precision would steer the right regime in happiness. It is never evident to others who has the requisite ability, however, because "a king does not come to be in cities as a king bee is born in a hive, one individual clearly superior in body and mind" (301e). Practical wisdom, or precise knowledge of what is best to do under specific circumstances, can only be displayed in action. It cannot be seen or identified in advance.[36] People have learned from bitter experience, moreover, that they cannot trust the individuals who seem to have displayed such wisdom and virtue on one occasion to retain it once in power. People have no choice, it seems, but to rely on the "second-best" laws.

If the best possible regimes are those based on law, which itself represents, at best, partial knowledge, the Eleatic observes, we should not be surprised that bad things occur in them. We should be surprised, rather, by the fact that cities survive despite the sorry state of their captains and crews. We see, therefore, that "a city is something strong by nature" (302a). It can be improved by art, but it does not require much art on the part of its leaders to survive for a time. The three regimes ruled by one, a few, or many on the basis of law are better than the three of the lawless variety. Although the lawful rule of many is the least good imitation, because a great many people do not and cannot possess a great deal of wisdom, democracy is the least bad lawless regime, because power in it is so diffused. For that reason, some commentators have concluded, the Eleatic recommends democracy as the best possible practical option.[37] It is, as the elder Socrates' life would seem to prove, the least dangerous to philosophy. In fact, however, the Eleatic says "monarchy, if it's confined by good . . . laws, is the best of all the six" (302e). It bears the same name and looks the most like the rule of the

[36] One thinks of the example of Abraham Lincoln, arguably the greatest American president, who was nominated as the second-best choice of a bare majority after many, many ballots at the Republican party convention. The legality or constitutionality as well as the wisdom of his acts as president have, moreover, been subject to constant criticism ever since.

[37] E.g., Griswold 1989: 161–62; Roochnik 2005.

one virtuous and knowledgeable statesman, whose right regime should be separated from the others "as a god from human beings" (303b).

The rule of monarchs or founding legislators characterizes peoples at relatively early stages in their existence. Their rule often represents public recognition of and tribute to the excellence of character and demonstrated practical judgment of the individual leader. So understood, the rule of founding kings or legislators would "imitate" or look like the rule of a statesman who knows what the right thing to do under all specific circumstances is. If laws represent the fruit of experience or trial and error, however, such often mythical kings or founders are not apt, in fact, to have had the knowledge of the statesman, strictly speaking. Nor would they have been able to codify it in law. As the Eleatic has pointed out, such knowledge cannot be codified. It takes account of particular circumstances in a way laws as general rules cannot. Since the rule of law never can or will equal the rule of knowledge, the Eleatic does not equate the statesman and his knowledge with the achievement of a founding legislator like Lycurgus (who was said to have copied or imitated the laws of Crete) or Solon (who reformed the laws of Athens). He certainly does not credit stories like those that attribute the laws Minos gave Crete to his instruction, if not inspiration by his divine father, Zeus.

The Eleatic does not explicitly state the most remarkable conclusion that flows from his argument: The reason it is so difficult to find the true statesman is that no true statesman will ever actually be found in office or exercising political power. The statesman is defined by his knowledge. As the Eleatic pointed out at the beginning of the dialogue, that means that his art is not practical or productive so much as it is cognitive. He certainly does not need to hold a powerful position in the city in order to possess it. On the contrary, the Eleatic concluded, no one who truly understands politics would accept a position of responsibility under the conditions those who lack the knowledge themselves would impose.

THE STATESMAN'S KNOWLEDGE. The fact that a true statesman will never seek or accept office does not mean that it is impossible to isolate and define the particular kind of knowledge he has. Having successfully distinguished the statesman, who would necessarily lay down laws as part of his rule but not feel himself bound by them, from the law-abiding regimes that resemble his precisely because they rule according to laws based upon a certain kind and degree of knowledge, the Eleatic is finally able to isolate and describe the distinctive kind of knowledge the statesman possesses. A statesman will use the three kinds of knowledge or art that are closest to his in ruling – the arts of the rhetorician, the general, and the judge – but his art is not the same as any of theirs. There is a difference between knowing how to persuade a large crowd and knowing what to persuade them of as well as knowing when to use persuasion and when to use force. The first kind of knowledge belongs to the art of rhetoric; the second is part of the royal art (*basilikē*) or statesmanship (*politikē*). Likewise, it requires one kind of knowledge to fight wars; another kind to determine when and why wars should be fought. Rulers also need to know how to apply their own laws and uphold contracts between particular people under specific circumstances; such judgments are, however, obviously subordinate to the laws rulers make. The true king or statesman knows how to care for everything in the city by weaving together these arts with the laws. On the basis of his comprehensive knowledge, like an architect, the statesman commands and supervises other artisans to produce and preserve the polity and its people.

To do that, the Eleatic emphasizes, a statesman needs to know, above all, how to weave together two different kinds of people – the moderate and the courageous. Like the elder Socrates, most people think that courage and moderation are two parts or kinds of virtue. But the Eleatic boldly suggests that, instead of being friendly or "of a kind," these two "virtues" actually represent opposed inclinations and characteristics. Whereas moderate people are gentle, slow, and orderly, courageous people tend to be quick, speedy, and intense. A predominance of either of these opposed inclinations in his people creates a problem for the statesman. Because moderate people tend to be "exceptionally well ordered," they live a "quiet life, minding their own business" (Socrates' definition of political justice in the *Republic*). As a result, moderate people are unprepared for war and become the prey of aggressors. The courageous, on the other hand, are always tensing up for wars, which they wage until they are defeated and enslaved by their enemies. If a city is to remain free and well ordered but able to defend itself, its population has to combine both these virtues. Since like is naturally attracted to like, however, it requires art to produce the necessary composite. Like a weaver, a knowledgeable statesman must get others to test and purify the materials with which he will work by purging – punishing, exiling, killing, or enslaving – people who prove themselves "incapable of sharing in a manly and moderate character and everything else that pertains to virtue, but are prone to godlessness, insolence and injustice by a bad nature" (308e). Then he must bind together the moderate and courageous both with divine ties, by seeing that they acquire true opinions about the noble, just, and good things in the part of their soul that is eternal, and with human ties, by arranging suitable marriages and exchanging children, with other cities as well as within the city itself. He holds the community together by making sure that in allocating offices and honors they go to individuals who are both moderate and courageous themselves or to groups that have members with each of the contrary tendencies to balance each other.

Several things should be noted about the "art" or "knowledge" the Eleatic finally attributes to a statesman. First and foremost, the most important part of this knowledge consists in the ability to bind citizens together by seeing that they acquire true opinions about what is noble, good, and just. The Eleatic agrees with Aristotle about what holds a regime together; it is not merely economic need or the requirements of an effective defense. It is what the people believe is noble, good, and right. Political association is nevertheless shown to be a matter of opinion – not knowledge. In dramatic contrast to the *Republic*, at the end of the *Statesman* nothing is said about the education of future statesmen or the acquisition of true knowledge. This is not part of the statesman's work. (If we take a cursory look at individuals who have traditionally been regarded as great statesmen – Pericles, Caesar, Napoleon, Washington, Lincoln, Churchill, for example – we see that they can all be characterized as saviors, if not builders or architects of their polities; but none of them instituted a system of educating his successors.) Second, in explicit contrast to what the Athenian Stranger says in the *Laws*, the goal of the statesman, according to the Eleatic, is not to make his people as virtuous as possible. It is rather to see that they are unified, both in opinion and in natural inclination, so that they will be able to preserve and defend themselves. All citizens do not have to have (or be molded so that they will have) exactly the same natural inclinations or characteristics. The Eleatic concludes by suggesting that a statesman will know how to "mix" the requisite characteristics by allocating offices, honoring and so encouraging the development of different inclinations and arts by different citizens. Third, it is nevertheless remarkable that the Eleatic says so little about the way in which a statesman binds his citizens together by means of the allocation of offices, by instituting an educational regime or regimen, and by arranging marriages. In both the *Republic* and the *Laws* readers learn that attempts to regulate marriage and the breeding of the next generation will falter. The Eleatic speaks as if the statesman will have no trouble overcoming individual inclinations. He does not deal with the practical difficulties a statesman would face in trying to bind his people by molding their opinions (or the limits of rhetorical persuasion), or constitutional design, or breeding and selecting members of his polity, we suspect, because he thinks no one will ever truly and completely seek what is "pretty nearly the greatest and most difficult science to acquire," much less have an opportunity to put it into practice. No one will seek to acquire "the science of ruling human beings" because anyone who comes close to understanding the requirements of politics will have learned that polities will never be ruled or ordered on the basis of knowledge alone. Those who seek to rule do not seek knowledge. They seek to rule for other reasons. That is why their rule turns out, so often, to be unjust and in need of legal restraint.

CONCLUSION

The *Statesman* is a strange dialogue because the view of political knowledge it presents is extremely paradoxical. On the one hand, the Eleatic shows, the kind of knowledge a statesman would need to possess in order to rule "scientifically" is "pretty nearly the greatest and the most difficult to acquire." It has an extremely broad scope, encompassing studies both high and low, and it requires extraordinarily precise judgments about what is necessary and right to do in an almost infinite variety of particular circumstances. Politicians, properly speaking, are not contemptible. On the contrary, individuals who possess the requisite learning and judgment are extremely rare and admirable, not simply or even primarily because of the power they exercise or the wealth and fame they acquire, but because of their intellectual acumen and achievement. The problem, on the other hand, is that individuals capable of acquiring the "science of the rule of human beings" will learn that they will not be able to exercise that knowledge without endangering their own survival. There is little if any incentive for such individuals to perfect their knowledge, especially if they see that they will never be able to put it into practice for long, if at all. Those who claim to rule in the interest of others are not apt to know how or what to do, even if they have the best of intentions, which is not usually the case.

The rule of law is a second-best "imitation" or very rough approximation of the rule of wisdom, the Eleatic shows, but it is the best most peoples are going to be able to do most of the time. Like his interlocutor, young Socrates, those of us who live in liberal democracies are prepared to believe that the power of people in positions of power ought to be limited by law, that progress in government as in most forms of knowledge is incremental, and that laws should be made and changed only with the consent of the governed. Plato's *Statesman* serves to remind us, however, that limited government under the rule of law is only second best. Most, if not all, politicians actually in government may legitimately be regarded as mere "sophists" who seek to establish justice and provide for the common defense, but don't really know how. The true politician or "statesman" does not deserve to be suspected or contemned. Rather than a vulgar self-seeking search for power, political leadership properly understood requires extraordinary intelligence and learning. Precisely for that reason, it is also extremely rare, if it exists at all.

WORKS CITED

Barker, E. 1918. *Greek Political Theory: Plato and His Predecessors*. London.

Benardete, S., trans. 1984. *Plato's Statesman* (part III of *The Being of the Beautiful*). Chicago.

Brunt, P. A. 1993. *Studies in Greek History and Thought*. Oxford.

Dorter, K. 1994. *Form and Good in Plato's Eleatic Dialogues: The Parmenides, Theaetetus, Sophist, and Statesman*. Berkeley, CA.

Duke, E. A., W. F. Hicken, W. S. M. Nicoll, D. B. Robinson, and J. C. G. Strachan, eds. 1995. *Platonis Opera*, vol. 1. Oxford Classical Texts. Oxford.

Griswold, C. L., Jr. 1989. "Politikē Epistemē in Plato's Statesman." In *Essays in Ancient Greek Philosophy*, ed. J. Anton and A. Preus. Albany, NY.

Howland, J. 1998. *The Paradox of Political Philosophy: Socrates' Philosophic Trial*. Lanham, MD.

Joly, H. 1992. *Études platoniciennes: La question des étrangers*. Bibliothèque d'histoire de la philosophie. Paris.

Klosko, G. 1988. "The Nocturnal Council in Plato's Laws." *Political Studies* 36: 74–88.

Lane, M. S. 1998. *Method and Politics in Plato's Statesman*. Cambridge.

Mara, G. 1981. "Constitutions, Virtue and Philosophy in Plato's *Statesman* and *Republic*." *Polity* 13: 355–82.

McCabe, M. M. 1997. "Chaos and Control: Reading Plato's Politicus." *Phronesis* 42: 94–117.

Miller, M. H., Jr. 1980. *The Philosopher in Plato's* Statesman. The Hague.

Morrow, G. R. 1960. *Plato's Cretan City: A Historical Interpretation of the Laws*. Princeton, NJ.

Nightingale, A. W. 1996. "Plato on the Origins of Evil: The Statesman Myth Reconsidered." *Ancient Philosophy* 16: 65–83.

Roochnik, D. 2005. "Residual Ambiguity in Plato's *Statesman*." *Plato: The Internet Journal of the International Plato Society* 5: 1–13. http://www.nd.edu/~plato/plato5issue/Roochnik.pdf.

Rosen, S. 1988. "Plato's Myth of the Reversed Cosmos." In *The Quarrel between Philosophy and Poetry: Studies in Ancient Thought*. New York.

1995. *Plato's* Statesman*: The Web of Politics*. New Haven, CT.

Rowe, C. J. 1996. "The Politicus: Structure and Form." In *Form and Argument in Late Plato*, ed. C. Gill and M. M. McCabe. Oxford.

Trans. 1999. *Plato:* Statesman. Indianapolis, IN.

2001. "Killing Socrates." *Journal of Hellenic Studies* 121: 63–76.

Saunders, T. J. 1992. "Plato's Later Political Thought." In *The Cambridge Companion to Plato*, ed. R. Kraut. Cambridge.

Scodel, H. R. 1987. *Diaeresis and Myth in Plato's* Statesman. Göttingen.

Skemp, J. B. 1952. *Plato's* Statesman, 2nd ed. Bristol.

Stalley, R. F. 1983. *An Introduction to Plato's Laws*. Oxford.

Waterfield, R., trans. 1995. *Plato:* Statesman, ed. J. Annas and R. Waterfield. Cambridge.

8: Reading Aristotle's *Nicomachean Ethics* and *Politics* as a Single Course of Lectures: Rhetoric, Politics, and Philosophy

Stephen Salkever

The *Nicomachean Ethics* and the *Politics* present themselves to us as a single course of lectures, the former anticipating the latter, the latter expanding on and referring back to the former. But it is still too often the case that the two texts are taught and studied as if they were utterly separate treatises, concerned with two different subject matters. Aristotle tells us in the first book of the *Ethics* (1.2, 1094a–b) that his subject matter in that book as well as in the *Politics* can be classified as an especially comprehensive kind of political science (*politikē*), and yet, in spite of this clear statement of Aristotle's pedagogical intention, for many years it was a commonplace to assign the two works to separate academic departments. The *NE* was there to be taught and argued over by members of philosophy departments, while the *Politics* required the attention of political theorists. For a variety of reasons, this is now, fortunately, not always the case; while it is not quite yet the norm, one frequently finds interpretations of one text drawing on the other.[1] But pedagogy has lagged behind scholarship on this point, and my aim here is to help correct that gap by proposing a way of reading the *NE* and the *Politics* that ties the two together in terms that are accessible to students, and readers in general, who approach the works from different backgrounds and levels of theoretical sophistication. What follows, then,

[1] See Kraut 2002, Frank 2005, Collins 2006, Smith 2001, and Tessitore 1996, among others.

is an overview that I hope will help other teachers and students put the two books together in their own terms and thus become better able to bring Aristotle into conversation with other philosophical voices both old and new.

My reading of the *NE* and the *Politics* rests on two assumptions about the texts, ones that are fairly widely accepted.[2] First, I take the texts as we have them to be Aristotle's notes or summaries of his lectures to students in the Lyceum. This means that our texts are inevitably marked by shorthand expressions that Aristotle presumably developed in the classroom and that there is something not only "in outline," as he himself says (*NE* 2.2, 1104a), but also provisional about the words on the pages before us. They are provisional not only because of the lecture format, but also because Aristotle believed, as he often explains, that one necessarily distorts *human* affairs, in particular, by trying to speak of them with too much precision. My second assumption is that these lectures are intended, in the first instance, for a particular audience – young Athenian men with political ambitions, an admiration for great leaders like Pericles, and a certain ambivalence about the value of philosophizing as a way of life. We can imagine them as not unlike some of Socrates' young Athenian interlocutors in the Platonic dialogues; it helps to think of Aristotle, in the *NE* and the *Politics*, as if he were speaking to Glaucon and Adeimantus. This does not mean that Aristotle, any more than Socrates, can be reduced to a typical man of his time. Quite the contrary: he shares with Plato's Socrates an intention to alter the horizon of beliefs and values within which his audience lives, not to articulate or systematize them. His rhetorical and pedagogical goal is to shift the perspective of those who hear and read him, and to shift it in the direction of a more universal and less parochial horizon. Thus, understanding Aristotle's political philosophy well requires us to pay careful attention to the reader or auditor Aristotle seems to have in mind as the primary audience for his discourse. When we do, it will not surprise us to discover that Aristotle's goal is to persuade his audience to ask an unfamiliar set of political *questions*, rather than to adopt a novel set of moral and political *principles*. His approach to politics, like Plato's, is both less direct and more radical than most subsequent political philosophy: less direct, in that he refuses to supply his audience, now as well as then, with a set of concrete rules for organizing political life; more radical, in that he asks us to see political activity as something

[2] I discuss these assumptions in Salkever 2000 and 2007.

quite different from the vision we carry with us prior to the theoretical reflections his discourse tempts us to follow.[3]

The Strategy of Aristotle's Discourse in the *NE*[4]

In the first book of the *NE*, Aristotle says that the primary aim of his course of lectures is to improve action (*praxis*) rather than to increase knowledge (*NE* 1.3, 1095a4–6). His inquiry is undertaken not to acquire theoretical knowledge, but in order to become good (*NE* 2.2, 1103b26–30). But Aristotle's message about the value of theoretical knowledge is as charged with ambiguity as is his rhetorical intent. From Book 1 of the *NE* through the rest of the *NE* and the whole of the *Politics*, he asserts what appear to be two distinct views of the human good, one supporting a life of action and politics, the other supporting a life of philosophical inquiry that keeps the concerns of a political life at a certain distance. At the same time, however, Aristotle repeats in various contexts the idea that there *is* a unified way of answering the question of the good life, since by understanding the specific human work or activity (*ergon*) we can understand the human good. His initial definition of the best life, in Book 1 of the *NE*, fully endorses the political life: "We posit that the ergon of a human being (*anthrōpos*) is a certain way of life (*bios*), and this *bios* is an activity (*energeia*) of the soul and activities (*praxeis*) that are with articulate speech (*logos*), and that it is the work of a serious male (*spoudaios anēr*) to do these things nobly and well" (1098a13–15).[5] This emphatic reference to maleness and to praxis as components of the best life, reminiscent of Pericles' funeral oration in Thucydides, looks like a clear resolution to the problem. The human good is not the life Aristotle says the many prefer, based on the quest for sensual gratification (1095b15–17), but the life chosen by "refined and active (*praktikoi*) people" who see the good as honor (*timē*), "the *telos* of the political life" (1095b22–23). But Aristotle does not allow this

[3] In this respect, Plato and Aristotle are unusual but not unique. More modern examples of similarly indirect yet radical approaches to political philosophy might include Machiavelli, Rousseau, Nietzsche, and Foucault.

[4] This section draws heavily on my more extended treatment of this subject in Salkever 2007.

[5] Translations from Aristotle are my own, informed by those of Lord 1984, Simpson 1997, and Irwin 1999.

initial formulation to stand unchallenged. Immediately after stating that "we posit" the human good to be the life of the serious male *politikos*, he appends a lengthy series (1098a20–b8) of cautions, saying that this is only an inexact "sketch" to be "filled in" later.

He has already suggested, a few pages earlier (1095b–96a), a third way of life that might claim to be definitively human: the *bios theōrētikos*, the life of study, which will be examined later. Aristotle alludes to this third life and its preeminence once more in the discussion of the intellectual virtues in *NE* 6 and of super-human virtue in *NE* 7, but does not discuss it thematically until *NE* 10.7–8, where he argues that such a life surpasses the political life in embodying the human *ergon*.[6] Praxis and maleness recede together as normative features of humanity, but this recession is not announced until the very last book of the *NE*.[7]

And thus from Book 1 until Book 10, the *Ethics* unfolds with the theoretical life as a sort of subliminal presence, a cloud in the bright sky of honor, maleness, and political virtue. This will not be apparent to the listener or reader encountering Aristotle for the first time. Aristotle will introduce the theoretical alternative as a candidate for the title of the serious human life only after he has shown a variety of ways in which the way of life of the serious male devoted to politics and honor, a life so immensely and unproblematically attractive to his Greek audience, is internally inconsistent. Before praxis can be rehabilitated in the light of a new theoretical understanding, it must (rhetorically) be allowed to fall of its own weight. My interpretive claim is that unless we understand this, the design of the *NE* and the *Politics* as a course in political science makes no sense at all.[8] The question of the identity of the shared "we," of who we are and what we assume, is one of the central unstated but

[6] He says there that the happiness of the political life, the life of the serious male devoted to honor, is *not* the happiest or best life for a human being (he uses "human being," *anthrōpos*, in Book 10, not "male" or "real man," *anēr*); the happiest is the life of inquiry and the study of the unchanging things, the theoretical life (1177b).

[7] Strikingly, the very same depreciation of maleness and praxis occurs in the next to last book of the *Politics*, though now with more elaborate explanation as well as a new account of ways in which the two lives might coexist.

[8] Even earlier in *NE* 1, Aristotle has suggested a possible incoherence within the political life itself (1095a18–26). He says there that both the many and the cultivated (*charientes*) agree that happiness or flourishing (*eudaimonia*) is the highest good, and that "happiness follows living well (*eu zēn*) and acting well (*eu prattein*)." Good *praxis* and good living lead to happiness. But the many and the wise (whom Aristotle now substitutes, without comment, for the political *charientes* as the alternative to

unavoidable perplexities or *aporiai* that constitute the "beginning" of Aristotle's *politikē*. In raising it, he invites his audience to reconsider who they are, or who they want to be – though without explicitly thematizing this invitation.

Is a virtuous life always happy? No, since bad fortune can destroy not only contentment but real happiness as well, as in the case of Priam (1100a, asserted again in 10.6, 1176a33–35). Can we ever know with certainty whether a particular life is happy? No, because the quality of one's life is affected by how one's descendants and friends live (1101a). The impact of fortune and the indefiniteness of the boundaries of a human life exclude the possibility of any certainty about matters of virtue and happiness. But Aristotle neither removes the *aporiai* about happiness and virtue nor treats them as the end of the story. He pushes the logos on with perplexities still in place, saying that such *aporiai* are evidence for the view that any stability in human happiness is due to virtue rather than fortune (1100b) and that we should therefore want to know better what virtue is. He further indicates that whatever this virtue is, it may have less to do with praxis and with political honors than with intelligence or *phronēsis* (1095b26–30), whatever that may turn out to be. As we will see, the question of the happiest or most choiceworthy way of life is a question opened anew at a number of places throughout the *NE* and the *Politics*, as late as the beginning of *Politics* 7. It is, for Aristotle, a permanent question to which there is no permanent universal solution. And it is this question that he wants to teach his audience to ask.

In the first book of the *Ethics*, Aristotle places widely held views about virtue and the political life in such a new light that he may well have puzzled his original auditors in two respects: his ambivalence

the many) disagree about what happiness is. The many, he says, see *eudaimonia* this way, as

> one of the things that are visible and apparent, such as pleasure or wealth or honor (*timē*), and others think other things – and often the very same person will have different opinions: when sick thinking it health, when poor wealth; and when they are aware of their own ignorance, they wonder at those who speak of something great (*mega*) or something beyond them.

The many are not presented here as slavering gratification seekers, but include those who identify living well with honor and greatness – which in the next Bekker column will be attributed not to the many but to the refined and active (compare 1095a23 and 1095b22–23).

about the value of the political life, and his reliance on terms whose meanings are evidently technical, not drawn from ordinary language or the *endoxa*.[9] *NE* 1 concludes with a discussion of the human soul as a preliminary to considering human virtue in the light of the question of the best way of life yet again. In this account, the central place is occupied by logos rather than by any distinctly political faculty, such as spiritedness (*thumos*). The soul is composite, with several "parts," although these may be separable in analysis only. One part has logos; a second does not, though there is no clear specification of what logos means as yet. The part without logos is further divided into one part, including growth, decay, and digestive activity, that works without logos, and another, involving a variety of desires, that may or may not "listen to" logos. This latter part Aristotle calls character (*ēthos*) and he says that specifically human virtues can be of two kinds: "ethical" or moral virtues – those involving *ēthos*, such as liberality, manliness, and moderation – and virtues of thought, "dianoetic" virtues, such as wisdom and *phronēsis*. The moral virtues are those that arise from habit (as *ēthos*, character, arises from *ethos*, habit), and will be considered first. It will soon turn out that these "moral" virtues are impossible without the "intellectual" virtue of *phronēsis*; this weakening of the distinction between moral and intellectual virtue will not surprise the careful listener or reader who recalls Aristotle's remark in Book 1 that political people should realize that what matters is *phronēsis* rather than honor and greatness.

Acknowledging that the indefiniteness of human happiness in the abstract limits the power of theory to clarify human life, Aristotle proceeds to outline his own biological account of human life and human virtue, which runs from the beginning of Book 2 to the middle of Book 3, culminating in three linked propositions:

(1) Excluding those forces we cannot control, such as fortune and inborn aptitude, virtue is the key element of happiness.

9 "Endoxic" answers are those that are prominent in the Greek culture he and his students share: "The *endoxa* are opinions about how things seem that are held by all or by the many or by the wise – that is, by all the wise, or by the many among them, or by the most notable (*gnōrimoi*) and endoxic (*endoxoi*, most famous) of them" (*Topics* 100b21 ff.). The fact that Aristotle identifies a belief as respected does not imply that he finds it respectable. His distance from the *endoxa*, like Plato's, is signaled by the fact that each avoids using words like *gnōrimos* (notable) and *kalos k'agathos* (gentleman) as terms of genuine praise, referring instead to the less familiar *spoudaios* (serious) and *epieikēs* (equitable, decent).

(2) Character (*ēthos*), developed by habit and by growing up under a particular set of laws and practices, is the key element of virtue.
(3) "Thoughtful choice," or *prohairesis*, is the key element of character: "The virtues are prohairesis, or not without prohairesis" (1106a3–4). Without *phronēsis*, all the well-intentioned habituation in the world cannot guarantee the development of virtue of character.

We must not confuse this last proposition with the Kantian identification of virtue and reason. For Aristotle, desire for the human good intertwining with thought about that good mutually transform each other into a "prohairetic hexis," a firm inclination to thoughtful choice that is the indispensable foundation for human virtue. Such a psychic condition is our natural destination, though it cannot be achieved without appropriate habituation (not to mention good luck).

From the middle of *NE* 3 on, Aristotle gives his readers or auditors a series of exemplary figures who exhibit and embody human virtue in different ways. His task, as he sees it, is not to provide systematic theory, but to bring abstractly theoretical eudaimonia to imaginary life by showing us individuals or types that in different ways and to different degrees embody his idea of human happiness. This is Aristotle's "virtue ethics": as in Plato's dialogues, the human good is realized in particular individual ways of life rather than in action-guiding rules. These exemplary types are arranged in a particular order: *from* images of virtue that are most familiar and accessible to Aristotle's students, *to* images of virtues and ways of life farther from the conventional Periclean Greek wisdom and closer to Aristotle's own notion of the human good.[10] As he suggests he will do, he begins with the virtues and lives most accessible to his audience and ends with the vision of the human good that seems truest to him. Aristotle does not, in other words, write as a "public philosopher" whose task is to articulate and clarify the deepest insights of his tradition, but instead criticizes that tradition in terms of a standard that is not a familiar part of the culture's

[10] My reading differs from the more common view that the order of the virtues is an ascent from the most material to the most "spiritual." On the latter, stemming from Aquinas, see Sparshott 1994: 147–49. I would say instead that the movement is from the virtues that make least use of practical wisdom or *phronēsis* (like manliness and moderation), through those (like justice and decency) that make most use of *phronēsis*, and finally to a virtue and way of life that seems, but only seems, to be beyond *phronēsis* altogether.

vocabulary. At the heart of his rhetorical task is a dilemma similar to the one Plato faces in the dialogues, the problem of introducing such a vocabulary without calling excessive attention to its strangeness. Leo Strauss puts it this way:

> Such a philosophic critique of the generally accepted views is at the bottom of the fact that Aristotle, for example, omitted piety and sense of shame from his list of virtues, and that his list starts with courage and moderation (the least intellectual virtues) and, proceeding via liberality, magnanimity and the virtues of private relations, to justice, culminates in the dianoetic virtues.[11]

Aristotle's arrangement of the moral virtues is part of his rhetorical attempt, one that is consistent throughout both *NE* and *Politics*, to move the philosophical life closer to the center of the world of thought of his audience and to push the manly life closer to the margins.

While each exemplary figure portrayed in the *NE* represents a mature and coherent way of life that goes beyond immature pleasure seeking regulated only by an unsteady sense of shame, they do so in quite different ways. The differences between them stem from the different horizon-like visions of the human good that animate them. The first two figures to be considered here, the manly man (*andreios*) and the great-souled man (*megalopsuchos*), take the Periclean goods of freedom, honor, and greatness as their limiting horizon. The third and fourth, the just man (*dikaios*) and the decent man (*epieikēs*) discussed in *NE* 5, go beyond Periclean freedom and greatness to embody nomos and the public good as a limit. The fifth and sixth ways of life, the phronimos (defined in Book 6) and the friend (discussed in Books 8 and 9), go beyond nomos and politics to treat the human good itself as the ultimate goal. The last way of life presented in the *Ethics*, the theoretical human being (sketched in *NE* 10.7–8), goes beyond humanity to adopt the divine or the good of Aristotle's (though not the conventional Greeks') *theos* as the central aspiration of a well-lived human life.

[11] Strauss 1959: 94. Sparshott makes a similar point, citing both the rejection of shame as a virtue and Aristotle's assertion that several key virtues and vices have no Greek names. Like Strauss, he claims that we must pay close attention also to what Aristotle omits: "More strikingly, the virtues of 'piety' (*eusebeia*) and 'holiness' (*hosiotēs*) are not on his list. Actual Greek life was saturated in religion; Aristotle's failure to countenance it shows clearly enough that, whatever he is doing, he is not simply describing the folkways or the prevailing value system" (Sparshott 1994: 142).

From the middle of Book 3 (1115a) through the end of Book 4, Aristotle takes up ten particular virtues of character, ones he had already mentioned briefly in the form of a diagram in Book 2 (1107a–8b).[12] Aristotle says nothing about why he has chosen these particular virtues rather than others, nor does he give reasons for the order of their presentation. But thinking through these questions suggests a great difference between Aristotle's list and one his audience of young Greek males might be expected to bring to the lectures. The first two virtues he discusses, manliness and moderation, would no doubt appear on any endoxic Greek list of the virtues, and it would be common to list manliness first. But Aristotle, without comment, drastically narrows the scope of both of these virtues relative to the endoxa. Manliness strictly speaking refers, according to Aristotle, only to our response to the fear of death and wounds in battle, and not, for example, to our willingness to risk the security of private life in order to achieve preeminence in the polis: "In the decisive sense, one is said to be *andreios* when he fearlessly faces a noble death and those things that lead to it – such things especially concern military affairs" (*NE* 3, 1115a32–35). For Aristotle, war is unavoidable if one is to escape slavery in a world of warring *poleis*, and thus manliness is a genuine virtue because it is needed to protect the prohairetic life, which cannot flourish without a polis and its laws and practices. But Aristotle's account of the occasion and activity of manliness in the *NE* is like Plato's in the *Republic*[13] in that it leaves out all of the vitality and daring that characterize Pericles' funeral oration, in which the Athenian war dead are congratulated for trading in their fleeting mortal existence for an earthly immortality as part of the shining narrative of Athenian imperial adventure. Aristotle treats manliness, in both the *NE* and the *Politics*, as a necessary virtue, but not of the highest order; to seek occasions for the display of the

[12] They are, in order, manliness (*andreia*) and moderation, both concerned with "feelings"; four virtues concerning the external goods of money and honor: liberality (*eleutheriotēs*) in matters of small sums of money, magnificence (*megaloprepeia*) regarding great sums, a nameless virtue that is a mean between lack of ambition and love of honor in matters of small honors and dishonors, and greatness of soul (*megalopsuchia*) where large-scale honors and dishonors are concerned; one virtue again concerned with a feeling, this time anger (*orgē*), a "nearly nameless" mean between irascibility and slavishness that Aristotle proposes to call "gentleness" (*praotēs*); and finally, three virtues having to do with "logoi and actions in communities": truthfulness (as opposed to self-deprecating irony and boastfulness), wittiness (as opposed to boorishness and buffoonery), and affability (as opposed to grouchiness and obsequiousness).

[13] Speaking to Glaucon in *Republic* 3, Plato's Socrates says that the guardians will be *andreios* if "they choose death in battles over both defeat and slavery" (386b5–6).

manly virtues makes no Aristotelian sense. War, he notes, is the occasion for the greatest of honors, but this proves only that honor is a seriously imperfect guide to virtue when virtue is defined, as Aristotle wants it to be, in terms of prohairesis.

The figure of the great-souled man brings the horizon of freedom, honor, and manliness into sharper critical focus. That the pursuit of honor and greatness may actually threaten the pursuit of the human good comes into focus in Aristotle's discussion of the great-souled man.[14] The *megalopsuchos* is concerned with greatness to the exclusion of every other good and virtue, and greatness requires being seen as great by others. The quest for greatness leads the *megalopsuchos* into a life without the wonder that opens the way to philosophy and without the friendship within which (Aristotle will argue in *NE* 8 and 9) human virtue and happiness can flourish.[15]

Book 5 is a new beginning: Aristotle here introduces a new and more comprehensive virtue (justice and decency) and a new and more comprehensive horizon (the nomoi). This is a very different way of being political than we have seen to this point (though it is still exclusively male, and thus not simply human). The indication of this comes in Aristotle's statement that it is not necessary to discuss universal justice at length, since that is the same as complete virtue. Invoking universal justice, he says, is simply a way of reminding ourselves that the laws instruct us to practice every virtue and lay down an education to promote the common good. Aristotle then adds the following: "It is necessary to set aside until later the decision whether the education through which an individual becomes an unconditionally good man (*anēr*) is in *politikē* or something else; for, presumably, being a good man (*anēr*) is not the same as being every good citizen" (1130b26–29). Aristotle's gender-specific language here is significant, and is frequently obscured in translation into English. Whenever he speaks of human virtue or the human ergon in the *NE* and the *Politics*, as in Book 1 of the *NE*, he uses the expression *anthrōpos*, human being, without specifying gender. When he speaks of the political life, by contrast, he consistently uses the word *anēr*,

[14] "In truth, only the good person (*ho agathos*) is worthy of honor" (1124a25) – not the great man, unless he also happens to be good, which is especially hard, according to *Politics* 4.11, 1295b, for those who possess extremely large quantities of the goods of fortune, such as wealth and high birth.

[15] Sparshott 1994: 151–53, ingeniously proposes that Aristotle must imagine the *megalopsuchos* as the sort of god-like ruler called the absolute or all-powerful monarch (*pambasileus*) in *Politics* 3 1284a3–b34. But nothing in Aristotle's text supports the view that the *megalopsuchos* holds or desires to hold any public office at all.

male.[16] Aristotle consistently treats politics as a male world, and so when he raises again in *Politics* 3 the question of the virtue of the good citizen, he asks whether the good citizen is a good male, *anēr*, and *not* whether the good citizen is a good human being, *anthrōpos* (1276b). But since Aristotle, like Plato, is consistently in control of whether to say *anēr* or *anthrōpos*, the question of whether the good citizen is also the good man raises a more comprehensive question, whether the good man is a good human being.[17]

The laws open greater scope for *phronēsis* – this horizon is much more demanding, intellectually, than the horizon of honor and greatness. It is hard to know what the just thing to do is (1137a9–12) because the just itself is not the same as the legal. Thus the reflection on justice and the laws leads to a sense of the inadequate or at least provisional quality of the horizon they supply. But the inadequacy of these perspectives doesn't require Aristotle to discard them or absorb them into a more comprehensive perspective. Instead, he retains honor and the nomos as plausible orientations toward the question of the good life, along with his criticisms of them, as he goes on to consider a more directly theoretical orientation in the rest of the *NE* and the *Politics*.[18] Perhaps the strongest evidence for Aristotle's retention of the political orientation as a plausible answer to the question of the human good is that, in his ultimate discussion of the best life in *Politics* 7 (1324a–25a), he says that the primary contenders in the permanent debate about the best life are those who defend the political life and those who defend the philosophic life (1324a29–32). His position there is summarized in this carefully worded sentence: "It is clear that there are just about two ways of life that are thoughtfully chosen (*proairoumenoi*) by those human beings who are most ambitious about virtue (*tōn anthrōpōn hoi*

[16] The reason why politics is necessarily a male affair according to Aristotle becomes clearer in Book 1 of the *Politics*: politics involves ruling as well as being ruled, and women cannot rule men because their deliberative ability is not sufficiently "authoritative" – although it is not clear whether the cause of this lack of authority is that women are by biological inheritance incapable of decisive practical reasoning, or that males are generally unwilling to listen to women, however reasonable. For discussion of this passage at 1260a13, see Salkever 1990: ch. 4.

[17] Stated otherwise, this is the question of whether the two male orientations so far elaborated in the *NE*, the perspective of honor and the manly or great-souled man, and the perspective of nomos and the decent man, are an adequate background for the prohairetic life. The movement beyond justice and the nomos in the next book of the *NE* suggests a negative answer.

[18] Moreover, Aristotle consistently uses the word *epieikēs*, along with *spoudaios* and *phronimos*, as his principal names for the best sort of human being.

philotimotatoi pros aretēn), both now and in the past. The two I mean are the political and the philosophic lives." The political life thus remains a plausible answer to the question of the human good, but now we see that it must be considered from the horizon of the *anthrōpos*, not from that of the *andres* alone.

Books 6 and 7 are the most analytic books of the *NE*, concerned to make distinctions generated by Aristotle's theory itself, rather than by the substantive and rhetorical problems of moral education the work addresses. Book 6 presents relatively precise distinctions[19] among ways of thinking or intellectual excellences or virtues, situating *phronēsis* in relation to scientific inquiry (*epistēmē* and *sophia*), to craft (*technē*), to political science, to amoral instrumental shrewdness (*deinotēs*), to a general grasp of human affairs that doesn't lead to action (*sunesis*), to good guessing (*eustochia*), and to a non-deductive grasping of either the first principles of the unchanging things or the nature of a particular situation calling for action (*nous*). Aristotle opens Book 7 by announcing a new beginning, one that recognizes that vice is not the only kind of character to be avoided. Vice must now be distinguished from incontinence (*akrasia*) and bestiality; as a result, virtue itself must be distinguished from two other admirable states of character (*hexeis*): continence and divinity. But the distinctions so carefully drawn in Books 6 and 7 are not classifications for their own or for theory's sake; instead, they serve Aristotle's delineation of a *third* kind of moral horizon, the human good, and a way of life that centers around the activities of practical reason and *prohairesis*. This horizon is more comprehensive and theoretically coherent than the horizons of greatness/honor and justice/nomos set out in the first five books. But like the earlier horizons, Aristotle's depiction of the prohairetic life devoted to the human good includes the recognition of a limit that serves to temper our enthusiasm, a limit supplied by his indication of a yet more comprehensive and coherent horizon, the one supplied by Aristotle's own idea of divinity, or of the best kind of being, or the most complete good. This is not simply added on to the picture of the human good; as Books 6 and 7 make clear, it is impossible to understand what the human good is without understanding in some detail the ways in which it is less than perfect. In particular, while we hear early in Book 6 that a life of thoughtful choice, a prohairetic life, is emphatically and normatively a human life (Book 7, 1139b4–5), we also hear by the middle of Book 7 that such a life can be devoted to

[19] Irwin's (1999) glossary provides a helpful guide to Aristotle's usage of terms in Books 6 and 7.

vice (*kakia*) as well as to virtue (Book 7, 1151a5–7). As with greatness and justice, in order to understand clearly the life guided by the human good it is necessary to see beyond it.

Aristotle's discussions of pleasure and of friendship in Books 7–10 respond to this perplexity. His two separate discussions of pleasure, at the end of *NE* 7 and the beginning of *NE* 10, which serve as brackets to the lengthy discussion of friendship in 8–9, are dialectical throughout. His intention is not to propose a systematic theory of pleasures and pains but to persuade his auditors that in this matter at least they are better off listening to the many than to a more distinguished few who either demonize (in *NE* 7) or deify (in *NE* 10) pleasure. His contempt for simplifying moralists is more colorful and acerbic than the general tone of his prose: "Those who assert that we are happy when we are broken on the wheel or when we fall into great misfortunes, so long as we are good, are willingly or unwillingly saying nothing" (1153b19–21). Aristotle also rebuts the sophisticated hedonist position set forth by Eudoxus, especially in Book 10, but seems to see hedonism as closer to the truth than antihedonist moralism: "The fact that all pursue pleasure, beasts as well as human beings, is some kind of sign that pleasure is somehow the best thing in itself. . . for everything that is by nature has something of the divine" (1153b25–32). But his central teaching is that both sides fail to see that pleasure and pain are not independent entities, but feelings an animal agent has subsequent to its performance or non-performance of some activity, *energeia* – eating or fighting or crafting a law, for example, or listening to music or gazing at the heavens or at the parts of an animal, or simply being alive. What matters, so far as happiness is concerned, is which *activities* we choose to pursue; pleasure and pain can't themselves be chosen as ends to be pursued or avoided, since they are only signs of the way a particular agent feels about a particular activity.[20]

If "the pleasure question" proves to be a blind alley for those puzzled by the problem of how to counter the uncertainty of the prohairetic life, the discussion of friendship (*philia*) – which is utterly novel, not a standard Greek philosophical topos like the relationship of the pleasant and the good – is much more positive. The friend is concerned with the

[20] "It is necessary to treat the pleasure or pain that follows upon an activity (*ergon*) as a sign of the *hexis*" (*NE* 2.2, 1104a3–5). Aristotle does say that pleasures and pains are also "activities," since they are neither potentialities to do something nor movements from one condition to another, but activities of a special dependent sort, ones that are consequences of and somehow complete the primary activities for each actor (*NE* 10.4, 1175a10–21).

good fully actualized human life. *Philia* absorbs justice (1155a). The peak of living together (*suzēn*) for human beings is sharing discourse, articulate speech (*logos*), and thought (*dianoia*) (*NE* 9, 1170b12–15). Friends seem to be the greatest external good (1169b9–10), directly contradicting a judgment made in the context of the *megalopsuchos* that honor is the greatest external good (1123b20–21). This is because "friendship furnishes the primary context within which human beings may grow in self-knowledge and virtue." This is not to say that other contexts are replaceable by virtue-friendships; families and polities are still necessary. But friendship matters most and will be noted least, thus requiring two full books of the *NE*. Nevertheless, he suggests (*NE* 8.7–8, 1159a) that some incoherence, some degree of aporia still remains: Friends don't really wish their friend the greatest good, to become a god, because we need the friend as another self, as our equal (*NE* 9.4, 1166a); moreover, we are friends to ourselves most of all (1168b). Yet we need friends to actualize our excellence – in one sense, we need such friends even more than we need good nomoi and the freedom that depends upon manliness.[21]

The rhetorical strategy of the *Nicomachean Ethics* is such that the horizons or focal points presented later rank above earlier ones – being as such over human being, human being over human law, human law over human freedom. Similarly, later exemplary ways of life are in some sense superior to earlier ones – the philosopher over the friend, the friend over the practically wise man without friends, the practically wise man over the decent man, the decent man over the just man, the just man over the great-souled man, and the great-souled man over the manly man – but they are all unstable in various ways, both theoretical *and* practical. As a result, later exemplars and horizons do not erase or "supersede" earlier ones in a Hegelian manner. Given the unique and immense variety and contingency of human life, and given that we do not and cannot know or choose in advance the challenges our lives will set for us, each way of life (as well as their relative rank order) must be kept in mind as a theoretical guide to the prohairetic life.[22] One way of putting this relationship among the different horizons would be to say that Aristotle wants to caution his audience against treating some good things as if they were the only good things. He does not say that

[21] I discuss Aristotle's position on the ways in which the activity of friendship, of "friending" (*philein*), contribute to human virtue and flourishing, in Salkever 2008.

[22] My discussion here is greatly indebted to Tessitore 1996.

the *phronimos* should stop caring about honor or about justice or about the human good or about the divine good. His intention, instead, is threefold: first, to rank these goods or horizons relative to the standard implicit in the activity of being; second, to warn us against being too serious (or not serious enough) about any one of them;[23] finally, to indicate that theory cannot go beyond the first two points, and that decisions of each individual or community about the mix among these plural goods that is appropriate for them is not a task for philosophy, but for *phronēsis* informed by a serious engagement with philosophy.

In chapters 7 and 8, the two penultimate chapters of *NE* 10, Aristotle makes a case for the superiority of the theoretical life to the practical; he presents it as more secure and less vulnerable to contingency than any practical life. It is continuously *active* – something that we sublunary beings cannot possibly be. The reason that the political life is ranked lower than the philosophic life is not that it is dependent on other people and external goods, but that the excellent citizen is dependent on other people and institutions in a particular way: the political life is limited by the connection between politics and war and by the dependence of the political life on nomos.[24] Human happiness is "unimpeded activity" (*energeia anempodistos*).[25] The word *anempodistos* appears to be an Aristotelian coinage; the image it conveys is a freedom from anything under your feet to trip you up. What impedes us all is death; we are creatures of conflicting pleasures because we are mortal (1154b20–25), vulnerable to mortality as well as to vice. What trips up good citizens is not other people – since nothing prevents the people we live with from being philosophic friends who help remove obstacles to *energeia* – but rather the exigencies of war and of the nomoi. Is it possible to imagine a political life that transcends war on the one hand and law on the other, one that is thus as free from "trouble" within the defining limits of inherited human potential as the philosophic life? If not, why not? In a sense, these are the central questions the last book of the *NE* bequeaths to the *Politics*.

[23] He is most worried that his Greek audience will take honor too seriously and the nature of the whole not seriously enough. Even so, he never denies that honor is indeed a genuine human good by nature: "Some people are mastered by or pursue against logos naturally noble and good things by being more serious than they ought to be about honor or about children and parents" (*NE* 7.4, 1148a28–31).

[24] Cf. Tessitore 1996: 108.

[25] *NE* 7.13, 1153b9–12. See also *Politics* 4, 1295a36–37: "As was said in the *Ethics*, the being (*to einai*) of the happy way of life (*bios*) is according to unimpeded virtue."

THE QUESTIONS THE *POLITICS* TEACHES

The *NE* takes for granted a "decent upbringing" and goes on to ask how theorizing about actions and ways of life can improve the character of already well-raised people. The answers that it gives to this question are varied and complex, and cannot be reduced to a system. But they all presuppose that "we," the community of well-raised souls the lectures seek to establish in speech, are already present. There are, to be sure, indications throughout the text that the prejudices of well-raised Athenians about the best life cannot so easily be sustained – in particular, the views about honor held by the typical Athenian gentleman – but the overriding message is almost always one of a harmony between Aristotle's theory and existing practice. Dissonance is kept in the background, even in places, such as the discussion in Book 10 of the inferiority of the political life to the theoretical life, where we expect it to be strong and clear. But the *Politics* continually brings such dissonance into view; its central purpose may be to address directly the question bracketed by the *NE*, the question of just what it means to have a "decent" upbringing, how such upbringing may be achieved, and the conditions both within and beyond our control that support and/or obstruct the practice of moral education or character formation.

The whole of the *Politics* encompasses a more careful tour of the possibilities covered by the horizon of the laws – possibilities that are criticized, such as the life of the master and of the merchant in Book 1 and the utopian solutions to the political problem proposed in Book 2; possibilities that seem promising though flawed, such as the lives of the citizens of Sparta, Crete, and Carthage in Book 2, of the just and manly citizen in Book 3, and of the semi-political farmer of middling means in Books 4–6. Once more, as in the *NE*, the culmination of this political discourse, in Book 7, is a glimpse at a trans-political horizon. Once more, the end of the *Politics*, just like the end of the *NE*, leaves us with the question of the extent to which political life, necessary as it is, can be brought into some sort of harmony with the highest human aspirations. That question is posed in at least two ways, first by Aristotle's exposition of "the polis according to prayer" in Book 7, and second by his discussion of liberal education in Book 8. I will argue in a moment that we are meant to see the first as deeply flawed; the second gives us the beginnings of an account of what Aristotle hopes we have been doing all this time (using leisure well) and leaves it to us to continue.

Politics 1.1 begins by affirming the standard endoxic view that the polis is the most authoritative human community, but goes on immediately to reject the standard view that politics is entirely about ruling or power over others. What matters, Aristotle goes on to argue in 1.2, is not only who rules, but also and especially the purpose or purposes served by such rule. He makes the central claim in chapter 2 that human beings are by nature political. But his assertion of our political nature is not based on a belief that politics is an intrinsic good, or that the political life is a natural ideal.[26] The argument developed here (1253a) is that political activity, a uniquely human activity that is essentially connected to acquired respect for nomoi, for humanly made laws and customs, can, if properly organized, channel our inherited potentiality for living according to logoi in the direction of justice and practical reason rather than injustice and despotism.

Another way of saying this is to note the two related meanings of the famous phrase that *anthrōpoi* are by nature political animals (1253a2–3). The first is that we have an inborn tendency[27] to live politically, reflected in our strong, though by no means unopposed, preference for *suzēn* rather than a solitary life and our relatively strong inclination to accept the authority of laws and conventions (see also *NE* 9.9, 1169b16–19). This tendency is opposed by the difficulty we seem constantly to have in getting along with others (*Politics* 2.5, 1263a15–16). Moreover, this unreflective tendency seems to carry within it the seeds of its own destruction, since polities have a strong and understandable tendency to turn into armies (*Politics* 7.14, 1333b5–21) – what we seem to care most about is not the joys of sociality or community but mastery over others.[28] The second, and I believe the primary, sense of saying here

[26] Because of this, it is essential to avoid reading Aristotle as a proto-republican or communitarian theorist. As he makes plain in Book 3, good citizens are not necessarily good men, and, as he makes clear in Book 7, good men (*andres*) are not necessarily good human beings (*anthrōpoi*).

[27] I use "tendency" here to translate Aristotle's *hormē* at 1253a29; his point is that our inborn inclination to political association is not a deterministic instinct, but an element of our biological potentiality that is not self-actualizing but must be shaped by experience and habituation and, to some degree, by our own choices.

[28] Thus, we might say that part of our natural longing for political life can easily turn into what Erik Erikson called "pseudo-speciation" – the characteristically human mistake of treating other humans as if they were members of entirely different species. What explains our inclination to adopt this false belief? Perhaps it is an evolutionarily adaptive error – pseudo-speciation gives an advantage in the struggle for survival to groups who practice it most strongly. For discussion of a terrifying modern version

at the start of the *Politics* that we are political animals is to make the non-obvious point that we have a *need* for political life when politics is defined more narrowly – not simply as *suzēn*, but as the practice of ruling and being ruled in turn with an eye to the nomoi in matters concerning the public interest – that is, political life supplies a discipline, a habit of public deliberation, within which we can become more prohairetic animals. The chances for genuinely human political life seem then to depend on our capacity to distinguish politics from various forms of mastery that resemble political life but threaten to distort and corrupt it. To say this is not to ignore Aristotle's claim at 1253a18–19 that the political association is by nature prior both to the family or household and to the individual. But it is also true, as Susan Collins says, that "the regime is prior to both city and citizen."[29] The reason for this is that the regime, the particular aspirations and institutions that define the actuality of any polis, as Aristotle understands it, embodies an answer to the question apparently inseparable from human life, What is the best life for a human being? Thus Aristotle's claim about the priority of politics to individual life is not an assertion of the superiority of the collective to the individual interest, and it certainly does not mean that we should take our identity from our role as citizen of a particular regime. Instead, it is an assertion of the priority of living well to living, of the form of a human life to its matter, and of the centrality of the question of the best life.

In 1.2, then, Aristotle sketches his own answer to the question of the meaning of political life, his alternative to the endoxic view that politics is a struggle for power. As in his discussion of the most flourishing life in Book 1 of the *NE*, his response to the endoxic conception of politics in the *Politics* begins by shifting the question toward a biological inquiry, in this case by asking about the role politics can play in the actualizing of the human potentiality for living well: what does the political process, the process of participating along with our fellow citizens in authorized discourse about how best to apply shared (and humanly made and revisable) nomoi to particular questions facing us, contribute to a choiceworthy human life? His brief answer, in a nutshell, is twofold: politics is motivated by our need to secure the instrumental goods associated with living, but our continuing commitment to political life is justified by the extent to which participating in

of this tendency, see Arjun Appadurai's reflections on the prevalence of what he calls "predatory identities" in Appadurai 2006: ch. 4.

[29] Collins 2006: 119–20 n. 1.

political life disciplines and educates our capacity for acting according to logos. Thus politics, properly understood, is always directed at two sets of human goods: the instrumental goods directed toward security and self-preservation, and the intrinsic goods associated with human virtue and flourishing.

The remainder of Books 1 and 2 elaborate this view, but indirectly: they attempt to show why a series of plausible endoxic answers to the question of political life should be rejected as adequate guides to politics, but at the same time retaining aspects of these endoxic views as partially true. Thus in 1.3–7, mastery over productive slaves is presented as a necessary (until such time as we might discover machines that could take the place of slaves) means to securing leisure for politics and philosophy, but at the same time as involving the risk of acting unjustly by enslaving those who do not merit slavery (1.6), and of tempting masters to treat mastery as an end in itself, rather than the merely instrumental good that it is (1.7). In its carefully restricted place (only enslave those who are slaves by nature, do not regard mastery as something important and something to be proud of), slavery can be useful; misused and misunderstood, it can lead to serious vice. The main point of this discussion is neither to defend nor to condemn slavery, but rather to show that it is a serious and common mistake to identify freedom and political activity with mastery, a critique that is picked up again later in the *Politics*.[30] The key distinction between just and unjust regimes outlined in Book 3 is labeled as that between political regimes aiming at the common good and masterly regimes aiming at the good of the rulers only.

The discussion of commerce (1.8–11) that follows is similarly an argument against the endoxic view that wealth gathering through trade is an end in itself, an intrinsic good. Just as Aristotle refuses to call for

[30] In 6.2, Aristotle says that democracy tends to misunderstand freedom as not being a slave. The misunderstanding here arises from the all too common failure to recognize that it is perfectly possible to be both a master and not free, because truly human freedom means ruling and being ruled in turn, not simply living as you please. In 7.14, he argues that ruling over free men is different from and nobler than ruling in the spirit of a master. In a fragment surviving from around the year 1858, Abraham Lincoln states, in effect, a conception of democracy very much in the spirit of Aristotelian political philosophy: "As I would not be a *slave*, so I would not be a *master*. This expresses my idea of democracy. Whatever differs from this, to the extent of the difference, is no democracy" (Lincoln 1989: 484, italics in text). For Aristotle, all genuinely political life requires a substantial degree of both juridical and material equality. This is the core of his frequently overlooked – but, for the *Politics*, vividly expressed – argument in favor of the "middling" regime, or polity, in *Politics* 4.11.

abolition as a reasonable response to the risks slavery poses for the souls of the masters, so here he refuses to condemn commerce altogether in favor of a non-commercial economy, saying that successful politics requires commerce (end of 1.11), and what is called for instead is a better understanding of the risks and limits of commerce as a way of securing the instrumental goods associated with "living." As in the case of slavery, Aristotle's call for a careful consideration of commerce suggests that the pursuit of genuinely instrumental human goods is at least sometimes and in some ways incompatible with the achievement of the intrinsic goods that constitute human living well. The concluding chapters of *Politics* 1 provide a similarly critical treatment of endoxic views concerning yet a third role within the *oikos*, that of the male head of the household. Although rejecting the radical view of gender equality he attributes to Socrates, Aristotle in effect warns his young male audience against adopting the view that women should be treated as natural slaves or as lacking the capacity for deliberation about common affairs. Women should be regarded as equals even while the paterfamilias exercises authority over them (1.12), and as half of the free population of the polis (1.13). Though not stated explicitly, I think it is clearly implied by the examples and direct quotations Aristotle imports from Herodotus and Sophocles in these two chapters that, in his view, men who fail to take women seriously as free and rational beings run the risk of becoming like the upstart tyrant Amasis or the mad Ajax. As with commerce and slavery, the role of the male as head of household is confirmed but chastened and restricted as a necessary but limited aspect of a good human life.

Book 2 leaves the question of whether the *oikos* should be viewed as an end in itself behind, turning instead to six well-known and highly regarded answers to the question of how and toward what end the regime itself should be organized, three proposed by theorists (2.1–8: Plato, Phaleas, and Hippodamus), and three implicit in the structure and functioning of actually existing *poleis* (2.9–11: Sparta, Crete, and, strikingly, the non-Greek city of Carthage). As in the case of Book 1, Aristotle's procedure here is to show that each of the six answers contains a valuable truth about what politics requires, but that in every case that truth is exaggerated into a seriously misguided understanding of what sort of a regime might best undertake the work of actualizing the human capacity for living well. His goal is to show that all six illustrate by their shortcomings the complexity of the problem of politics and the need for care and nuance in political analysis. They do this by exaggerating the importance of one element of good politics: Plato exaggerates the importance of unity among citizens; Phaleas exaggerates the value of equality; Hippodamus exaggerates the value of abstract rationality as a guide to political action. Unity, equality, and theoretical rationality are all important aspects of a justifiable polis, goods that aim at enabling good human lives. Any praiseworthy political actor must attempt to incorporate them as much as possible into the life of the polis. But if we treat each of these desiderata in isolation from the others and from the acquisition of sufficient instrumental goods, we are on the road to failure. Plato's obsession with unity obscures the conditions necessary for good human development; Phaleas's focus on equality obscures the variety of, and some possible cures for, human vices; Hippodamus's devotion to the cause of rationality obscures the extent to which a degree of stable custom and habit are needed to hold citizen bodies together. We need to see both the variety of political goods and the extent to which the pursuit of each good is sometimes incompatible with the achievement of others. The point of Aristotle's critique is not to promote disunity, inequality, and the unexamined acceptance of customary forms of public life. His purpose, I suggest, is to alert his audience to the difficulty and importance of striving to find a balance among the goods promoted with too little qualification by Plato, Phaleas, and Hippodamus.

Aristotle's critique of the three regimes in the second part of Book 2 has a similar complicating quality. All three, he says, deserve praise because of the remarkable degree to which "the people voluntarily acquiesce in the arrangement of the regime," joined with the facts that in each "there has never been factional conflict worth mentioning, or a tyrant" (2.11, 1272b). But by looking closely at the details of political life in the three regimes, he brings out the extent to which each regime contains institutions and practices that fail to accord with its overall end, as well as notes the shortcomings of the apparent purpose of each regime – manliness and success in war in Spartan and Crete, wealth in Carthage – when measured against the standard of "living well" Aristotle presented in outline in 1.2. Both the ability to engage in war and the production of wealth are important aspects of public life, and no serious citizen can neglect them. But promoting these goods to the highest rank is not the way to proceed. Again, balance is required – but what sort of balance? The work of Book 3 is apparently to answer that question by resuming the discussion of the sketch of the best regime opened and provisionally closed in 1.2. It should come as no surprise that, in fact, the presentation of Aristotle's own conception of good politics in Book 3 ends not with a doctrinal answer telling us how to strike the appropriate political balance, but with a further clarification and refinement of that question.

Book 3 is, in a way, the theoretical core of the *Politics*, although that core is presented as a set of questions rather than a set of doctrines; or, better, the doctrines Aristotle arrives at here take the form of questions that cannot be answered theoretically or universally but are in permanent need of context-sensitive practical resolution. Book 3 is another of Aristotle's new beginnings, and at first it may appear that what is novel here is a switch from the dialectical style pursued throughout Book 1 and 2 to something more straightforwardly doctrinal and independent – having cleared the ground of the theories, explicit and implicit, of other thinkers and regimes, Aristotle is at last going to give us his own views about politics. But we soon see that his own views emerge only in the context of dialogue with the views of others, and that the forms his theory takes, as in the earlier books of both *Politics* and *NE*, is the articulation of a series of problems that serious human beings will inevitably confront and that theory cannot resolve for them. These problems or *aporiai* concern how citizenship should be defined (chapters 1–3); the circumstances under which a good citizen is also a good man[31] (4–5); and how to distinguish between a true polis and various forms of mastery concealed by the name *polis* (6–8). Chapter 9 stands back from these "inside politics" questions to raise the most fundamental issue of all: What is the role that political activity can play in a well-lived human life? Aristotle's answer here is that politics must serve three partly incommensurable goals at once: to promote the prohairetic life, to promote friendship and civic harmony, and to promote human life itself. Chapters 10–12 argue that these plural goals or goods cannot be reduced to a single measurable good and conclude from this that no certain theoretical answer can be given to the question of what group or what principle should be authoritative in any given polis. Book 3 concludes (13–17) in a notably aporetic way, by staging a long debate

[31] We must note that in discussing the question of the circumstances under which a good citizen can be a good "man" in Book 3, Aristotle consistently uses *anēr*, thus identifying political activity with a certain kind of maleness. But when he returns to the question of the best life at the beginning of Book 7, he switches back to the gender-neutral *anthrōpos*. In other words, Aristotle defers the question of the circumstances under which a good *anēr* can be a good *anthrōpos* until he explicitly introduces, for the first time in the *Politics* (and hence for the first time since *NE* 10 in our course of lectures), a horizon more universal than the political one at the beginning of Book 7.

over whether the rule of law is better or worse than the absolute rule of a single, vastly superior monarch. This unresolved disputation between the conflicting claims of dispassionate laws and excellent personal leadership serves primarily to sharpen our appreciation of the merits and drawbacks of each theoretical solution to the question of who or what should rule.

By the end of *Politics* 3, Aristotle has established the three major ideas that define his unique approach to understanding politics. The first of these is that the theoretical basis for understanding politics is biological or psychological.[32] In other words, the basis for Aristotle's political philosophy is human nature in his sense. The work of genuine politics, the activity of equal citizens ruling and being ruled in turn with an eye to laws and customs that aim at promoting living well, as he says in 1.2, is to propose a solution to the problem set for us but not solved by the potentialities that constitute our inherited human nature, the problem of human flourishing. But we have to be very careful not to confuse Aristotle's position with various forms of modern biological reductionism. His naturalism is not reductive: it is very clear from both the *NE* and the *Politics* that he does not believe that biology equals destiny. His rejection of biological reductionism turns on his empirical thesis that the person we turn out to be is decisively shaped by the habits we acquire, habits that define a large part of the business of both polis and *oikos*. The *NE* (2.1, 1103a–b) asserts that habituation, and not natural potential, is the major cause of different outcomes in human development: "The virtues come to be in us neither by nature nor against nature. Rather, we are by nature able to acquire them, and we are completed [or 'perfected' – the verb contains *telos*] by means of habit." The defining work or telos of politics is to guide this process: "What goes on in cities is a witness for this. For lawmakers make citizens good by habituating them, and this is the wish of every legislator; if he fails to do it well, he misses his goal, and this is what separates a good regime (*politeia*) from a worthless one." The way we develop as individuals is more strongly shaped by nurture than by inherited nature: "It makes no small difference, then, whether we are habituated in one way or another right from our youth – it makes a very

32 Strictly speaking, psychology is an aspect of biology for Aristotle, since the soul (*psuchē*) is not a separate entity but one aspect of the life of each living thing – the other being body. The soul is what the living being characteristically *does*: "if the eye were an animal, sight would be its soul" (*De Anima* 2.1, 412b18–19).

large difference, or rather all the difference." The *Politics* confirms this judgment of the unique plasticity of human nature: the lives of other animals are determined primarily by their inherited nature, though habit plays a certain role in some of their lives. For humans, habit is necessary to resolve the ambiguity of our conflicting drives, potential inclinations that can lead us to become either the best or the worst of animals, in the language of 1.2. Not only does habit count for so much in human development; in the end we are capable of overcoming habit by the use of our logos capacity (7.13, 1332a–b). Our inherited potentialities are not accompanied by a solution to the difficulties they pose. Political activity, like all art and education, aims implicitly, though not usually self-consciously, at supplying this natural lack (7.17, 1337a).

But while nature does not solve the problem of living well, reflection on our nature does indeed suggest a goal to strive for, a way of life that seems, to Aristotle, naturally best for human beings. That life is the one he identifies in the *NE* (6 1139a) as the characteristically human way, the prohairetic life.[33] So the best human lives are prohairetic; they may also be political, but only insofar as the political activity involved promotes the development of something very close to what Plato's Socrates calls the examined life in the *Apology*. There is considerable agreement with Aristotle here: an unexamined life, for both Aristotle and the Socrates of Plato's *Apology*, is not worth living for a human being. Nonetheless, just as he did in the *NE*, Aristotle reminds us that education and prohairesis can go badly astray: "even if everyone receives the same education, it may lead them to thoughtfully choose *pleonexia*, of either money or honor, or both" (*Politics* 2.7, 1266b35–38). In the same chapter of *Politics* 2, he concludes that political life has no answer for the strongest criminal ambition, the longing for complete mastery that leads to tyranny. Against that desire, he says, moderation and the other moral virtues are of no use, and "there is no remedy to be sought except from philosophy" (1267a11–12). The *NE* has given us some idea

[33] Now the beginning – in the sense of the source of the action, rather than the goal or end toward which it moves – of an action is *prohairesis* – and the source of *prohairesis* is mixed logos and desire for something. So *prohairesis* cannot be without either thought or a good character, since doing well or badly in action requires both thought and character. Thought by itself moves nothing – what moves us is thought aiming at some goal and concerned with action. . . . Now desire is for a goal. Hence *prohairesis* is either mind combined with desire or desire combined with mind. And an *anthrōpos* [human being] is such a beginning of action (*NE* 6.2, 1139a).

of the kind of activity "philosophy" might be; the *Politics* will pick up the question once again in Books 7–8.[34]

The second major thesis of *Politics* 3 is that political activity (where politics is defined as equal citizens, sharing rule, voluntarily limited by laws/customs that are stable but revisable, and aiming at living well) can enable citizens to live a prohairetic life in three distinct ways: by educating in the virtues and combating our all too natural tendency to *pleonexia*, or limitless desire for wealth, honor, or independence; by promoting civic friendship and combating our pervasive inclination to factional conflict (*stasis*); by securing the goods necessary for human life and preventing poverty and enslavement. Aristotle ranks these three tasks in descending order in terms of their contribution to the human, or prohairetic, life, but they seem to be ranked in ascending order as contributions to staying alive and free: security first, then integration, then education in virtues. He rules out the possibility of discovering a precise universal rule for deciding which of the three goals should predominate at any given moment – that judgment can only be made by active citizens in particular circumstances.

Aristotle's third major thesis of Book 3 is less evident, but powerful nonetheless: political activity is necessary for living well, but even the best politics requires a degree of compromise with the project of living the best human life. As Book 7 makes explicit, even the best political order has a certain tendency toward the anti-politics of despotic control. Why should that be so? The first reason Aristotle gives is that there is, empirically, a deep connection between political activity and military activity, both historically and psychologically – and military activity develops only a few, and not the highest or most prohairetic, of the human virtues. He calls attention, both in 2.6[35] and 3.7

[34] Getting a clear idea of what Aristotle means by "philosophy" is never easy, and we need some such idea if we are to get a sense of how this activity might lead an ambitious soul away from *pleonexia*. He clearly does not mean to limit the term to the reflections on the unchanging things he talks about in *NE* 6 and 10, or to the "first philosophy" described in the *Metaphysics* 12. Music, as described in *Politics* 8, is one possible example of a more accessible variety of philosophizing. I think, though, that the most striking expression of this kind of philosophizing in Aristotle's work comes in his picture of doing biology in *Parts of Animals* 1.5, 644b–645a. Every modern student of Aristotle's ethics and politics must read and keep firmly in mind the account of the transcendent philosophical joys of the decidedly non-reductive approach to scientific inquiry celebrated there.

[35] He says at 1265b28–29 that the word *politeia*, "polity" or "regime," is derived historically from "*hopliteia*," an organization of hoplites, citizens who became heavy-armed soldiers in time of war.

to a historical link between the emergence of hoplite warfare and of the polis in Greece. That link, he says, is no accident; it is reasonable (*eulogos*) because the entire range of human virtues can only be achieved by a few, but a multitude is capable of achieving one sort of human virtue, military virtue, the virtue connected with war (1279a38–b4). Manliness (*andreia*) and politics inevitably run together, the preeminence of manliness in politics indicating the essential limits of political activity as a serious way of life. The deep connection of politics and war is restated in the account of the best practicable regime, the polity, in 4.13 (1297b), and manliness is defined as the least human (that is, least prohairetic) of the human virtues when Aristotle raises the question of the best life for a final time in 7.15 (1334a).

This important limit on politics as a solution to the human problem augments the difficulty Aristotle foregrounds in Book 3 by staging the dispute between the rule of law and the rule of the supremely best leader. All political activity has to involve the rule of law (nomos), yet even the best and most just laws are too universal and abstract to be the wisest possible guides to action or practice (*praxis*) in context. This could be remedied if we could be ruled by a god-like king or by a set of perfectly adequate natural laws. But the first case is highly unlikely (and if it were to occur would spell the end of political life as Aristotle defines it), while the second is impossible given the irreducible plasticity of human nature and the complexity of the structure of human goods. Moreover, in addition to its connection to the rule of law and to the practice of warfare, political life depends, to a certain and hard to specify extent, upon the maintenance of traditions, including religious traditions, that cannot be defended by arguments and reasons that transcend the traditions of the polis. Aristotle brings this out in his critique of Hippodamus in Book 2 and returns to it in his mention of the necessity of civic religious observance in 7.8.

Therefore, by the end of Book 3 we are in a position to see that the major lesson the *Politics* wants to teach its listeners or readers is the awareness of a difficulty – though not at all an impossible or tragic paradox – that is natural to human beings. The difficulty can and should be addressed and contained, though never resolved. We can formulate that Aristotelian difficulty as an assertion of the following two propositions: Political activity is an essential component of the prohairetic life; political activity always and necessarily compromises and limits the prohairetic life. Bearing both these propositions in mind, we can concentrate on finding ways to establish regimes that stress the first and minimize the second; or, we can think about activities that transcend the limits of politics by means of activities indicated by the capacious term "philosophy," but without seeking to damage or destroy decent political orders. Or we can do both. I think this combined approach is what Aristotle suggests to the students of his political science in the remainder of the *Politics*: he focuses on the possibilities of improving actually existing politics in Books 4–6, while indicating ways of appropriately distancing ourselves to a degree from political life in Books 7 and 8.

At this point in our overview of the *Politics* we have to confront the controversy surrounding the question of whether the traditional order of the books of the *Politics* should be replaced by one in which Books 7 and 8 come after Book 3 and before Book 6. The latter position has been suggested by Carnes Lord and argued for strenuously by Peter Simpson.[36] I do not think the question of the proper order of the books can be settled on the basis of clear evidence independent of how you interpret the text: there are signs that point both ways, and so our choice here is necessarily an interpretive one rather than one that can be settled by reference to unquestionable matters of fact. Where you place the traditional Books 7 and 8 depends on whether you think Aristotle would be willing to defer the question of the best life and his "regime according to prayer" until after his discussion, in Books 4–6 as traditionally numbered, of practicable regimes – ones that are possible, for better and worse, under the practical circumstances Aristotle sees around him. I think it makes good sense for him to do just that; Simpson disagrees. I would frame the issue thus: If you believe that Aristotle wants to use his discussion of the best life as a ground from which to deduce binding political principles, then what have been called Books 7 and 8 should indeed be repositioned as Books 4 and 5; but if you think, as I have been arguing, that Aristotle's intention is to teach his students to ask seriously the questions surrounding the problem of the best human life rather than to present them with a doctrine specifying just what that life is in concrete ready-to-apply terms, then it makes better sense to leave the books as they are. The reordering proposed by Simpson and others carries with it a very different message about the meaning of the text: for them, Books 7–8 contain Aristotle's answer to the question of the best regime, whereas Books 4–6 tell us how that ideal can be applied in less than ideal particular circumstances. My reading, on the

[36] Lord 1984; Simpson 1997.

other hand, is that Books 4–6 deepen and complicate our understanding of the goals and problems of political life as sketched in Book 3, while *Politics* 7 and 8, like *NE* 10, quite explicitly return us the heart of the human problem itself, and ask us again to reflect on the extent to which that theoretical and practical problem can be solved once and for all by the institution of a polis that we might pray for in ideal circumstances. This reading, to which I will return briefly in a moment, holds that Aristotle in Book 7 gives us a sharply negative response to the dream of a perfect political order and begins in Book 8 to set out what he sees as a more promising path for us to follow, the path of music education rather than utopian political speculation.[37]

Once this overview of the *Politics* as a whole is in place, I can sketch my sense of the general direction of Aristotle's discussions in Books 4–6 and 7–8. My reading of these books differs from the standard interpretation, and I will present it here briefly, as a suggestion to the reader, bearing in mind that one of Aristotle's enduring charms is that his texts are open to a variety of plausible interpretations.

Books 4–6 contain a great deal of historical material, reminding the reader of a great variety of political events and structures as they elaborate and modify extensively the simple classification scheme of types of regimes set out in Book 3. But the goal is never simply descriptive or explanatory in a value-free sense: Aristotle's project in these books is to persuade the reader that a certain type of political regime has the best chance of securing the education in virtue that is the justification of political life itself. He names that regime in several ways, first referring to it as a *politeia* (regime), but later suggesting that the same regime might also be called a farming democracy[38] (the decisive chapters here are 4.6, 4.11, and 6.4), a regime in which citizens of middling wealth concentrate most on their families and their work, but respect the laws and actively participate in public life to the extent of electing leaders for a certain term *and* auditing the conduct of these same leaders when their terms are expired, as well as serving as jurors. Such a regime requires

[37] Much depends on whether you think that the regime "according to prayer" is meant to serve as a model for practical reform (with Simpson) or a warning against treating politics as the final and perfect human horizon. I think it is such a warning, and not a simple one. Instead, Aristotle uses the regime according to prayer as a point of departure for his final discussion of human virtue and human nature, and for his discussion of education in Book 8 – an education Simpson misleadingly refers to as "education in the best regime." I develop this argument at length in Salkever 2007a.

[38] "The regimes we now call polities were formerly called democracies" (4.13, 1297b24–25).

neither extraordinary material and human resources,[39] nor an elaborate system of public education. It is no utopia, but it has the advantage of avoiding the disastrous – to security as well as to human development – tyrannical and oligarchic injustices that are likely to follow monarchical or aristocratic revolutions.[40] But such "middling" democratic regimes are not machines that will sustain themselves indefinitely. They need philosophical support largely to defend against the all too typically democratic notion that freedom is the most desirable thing of all, and that freedom means living as you please. This belief lends itself to demagoguery and democratic tyranny (4.4). The central political problem for the best practicable regime, according to Aristotle's teaching in the *Politics*, is thus the problem of persuading the people that freedom and lawfulness go hand in hand (5.9, 1310a27–36; 6.2, 1317a40–b17).

That lesson concluded, Book 7 returns us to the horizon of the best human life, reminding us that the ultimate standard for evaluating a political order is the quality of lives it enables, and that the best of all human lives may not be one that is devoted to active political life. Chapters 1–3 return us to the quarrel between politics and philosophy visited in *NE* 10, and again, as in *NE* 10, conclude that the life of fully actualized theorizing ("the god") should be treated as the standard of human happiness, not the life of political praxis. Chapter 3 concludes with a brief gesture toward a polis that is most like this theorizing life – an autotelic and peaceful polis (7.3, 1325b16–32).

There is a clear break in the argument between chapters 3 and 4 of Book 7. What follows in chapters 4–12 is not an elaboration of the argument about the best life in 1–3, but a description of the sort of polis political *men* (the gendered term is used throughout this section, though not throughout the rest of Book 7) might pray for, those whose moral horizon is supplied by a dream of the perfect polis (one in which citizens use their leisure in military pursuits, conventional religious observance, and in sharing rule according to laws for the sake of developing human virtue), rather than an image of a life of focused study like that sketched in 7.3. Are we meant to conclude that this political model sets a better agenda than the middling regime of Books 4–6? I doubt this, for several reasons: 1) Leisure for the citizens is provided by the agricultural labor of a class of slaves or serfs, who are not

[39] As for human resources, such a "middling" regime would be unnecessary if an individual or a group might emerge who were *both* greatly superior in virtue to all the rest, *and* whose superiority were visible to the great majority.

[40] "But many of those who want to create an aristocratic regime thoroughly err not only by distributing more to the rich, but also by deceiving the *dēmos*" (4.12, 1297a7–10).

described as natural slaves (7.10, 1330a). Aristotle says nothing about the quality of their logos capacity, only that they must be deficient in spirit (*thumos*); 2) All the citizens serve as soldiers when they are young men, and all of them become politically active deliberators as they mature. But Aristotle never says that soldiering prepares the young citizens for just, moderate, and prudent political activity; instead, he says only that no polis can dare to risk arming the young without promising them political power later on (7.9, 1329a2–17); 3) Finally, when the citizens become old men they do not turn to philosophy, but become priests in service to the conventional gods (1329a27–34). It requires no interpretive legerdemain to see that Aristotle could not have lived his life in such a polis, nor does such a regime reflect any prayer that someone serious about philosophy would utter. Finally, it must be noted that while Aristotle does refer to the prayer polis of Book 7 as the best polis, he never calls it an "aristocracy," a polis ruled by the best human beings.

This lesson is driven home in the remainder of Book 7. In chapters 13–15, Aristotle's final return to the questions of the best life and the human psyche opened at the beginning of the *NE*, he stresses again, as in *NE* 10, the deep and dangerous links between political activity, as such, and war (7.14, 1333b). He prefaces this judgment by asking us yet again to step back from the political world and to consider the content of human *eudaimonia* as a question (7.13, 1332a2–7). As in the *NE*, his move is, in effect, to answer that question with another question, saying that *eudaimonia* is the complete practice of human virtues. Since the virtues are plural, we must ask whether they are equal in rank, and Aristotle answers this question explicitly in the negative in 7.15, 1334a. Philosophy and the theoretical life, unmentioned in the description of the polis according to prayer,[41] are now named as the most human of the virtues while manliness (*andreia*) is the lowest, more akin to *karteria* (1334a22–23) – that admirable and necessary but non-virtuous capacity to endure hard times when we must – than to justice and moderation. Book 7 thus does not alter the basic political question implied by Books 4–6, the problem of how to combine freedom and lawfulness in a democratic polity; just before returning to the problem of *eudaimonia* in 7.13, Aristotle is quite explicit in dismissing the usefulness of any discussion of how to realize the prayer regime in deed (7.12, 1331b18–23). What we gain from Book 7 is not a utopian vision to be

[41] Except, interestingly, as a source of defensive military technology at 7.11, 1331a14.

applied in practice, but a sense of the need to reflect on two questions simultaneously in situations involving action, the political question and the question of human happiness. Neither question can be subsumed under the other.

The final book of the *Politics*, incomplete as we have it, is an argument for the importance of music education, quite broadly understood as something close to our notion of liberal education, for the development of the human potential for virtue and happiness. In the Greek context, there is nothing surprising in this. But Aristotle's unusual treatment of music in Book 8 reinforces the need to consider the differing requirements of politics and philosophy in thinking about matters of action. Many commentators note that music, for Aristotle, should develop moral virtues in the young, but it is less frequently noted that he argues that music is also a path to the "extraordinary things" (*ta peritta*; 8.1, 1337a42). Music has several jobs to do, and one of them is linked to a kind of theorizing: "At present most people participate in music for the sake of pleasure, but those who arranged to have it in education at the beginning did so because nature itself seeks, as has often been said, not only to act rightly (*orthōs*) when not at leisure but to be able to act beautifully (*kalōs*) when at leisure. For this is the one principle (*archē*) of all things, if we may speak of it once again" (8.3, 1337b28–33).[42] This one principle is in fact a problem: What is, and what is not, a beautiful or noble use of leisure?

Conclusion: How Political Philosophy (*Politikē*) Makes Us Better

Toward the beginning of the *NE*, Aristotle says that the purpose of studying *politikē* – the science he leads us through in our two texts – is not to do theory as an end in itself, but to become good human beings (2.2, 1103b26–29). But what can that mean, if 1) the best human beings are those who theorize as an end in itself, and 2) the way we become good is primarily by habit and moral education rather than by theory of any kind? I suggest that our tour of the texts puts us in a particularly good position to answer that question. The problems that Aristotle teaches

[42] In *Republic* 8, 549a–b, Plato's Socrates describes the timocratic person, the lover of honor, as left behind by virtue's best guardian, "logos mixed with music." This is a very Aristotelian moment, as well as a Platonic one.

that we human beings must face have a sort of solution in the texts: the best life is the prohairetic life, and true political activity is almost a necessary and constitutive condition for leading a prohairetic life. But this is a highly tentative solution only, since Aristotle goes out of his way to indicate that even genuine political activity can incline us to choose the life of war and manliness above all else, a way of life that limits our exercise of our prohairetic potential; moreover, he makes it plain that living an examined or prohairetic life does not guarantee that we will be flourishing or happy human beings. Aristotle himself endorses the claim that the prohairetic life is the humanly flourishing life for human beings as such, men and women; but he also forces us to see how bad luck can undo us in all sorts of ways beyond our control, and even more significantly, he asserts in no uncertain terms that true vice is as much a prohairetic human condition as true virtue. The unexamined life may not be worth living for a human being, but there is no guarantee that the examined life will be a good one. Injustice and *pleonexia* may be chosen prohairetically: there is no psychological or conceptual principle that rules this out, no Kantian categorical imperative, no utilitarian felicific calculus. I suggest that the central task of the *NE* and the *Politics* is to get us to the point of wondering about how we can cope with this difficulty and suggesting some means of doing so.

Aristotle's two basic answers involve the practices of virtue friendship and just politics. But these practices by themselves are clearly not fully adequate because, without further qualification, they raise the question of the substantive meaning of human virtues in general and of justice in particular. Aristotle's answer to this dilemma is that there are certain kinds of studies that can lead souls in the right direction by giving us a clearer and richer sense of reality. *Politikē* is one of those studies, especially if we insist that it include an awareness of the limits of precision that necessarily attend the kind of inquiry we make when we think along with the *NE* and the *Politics*. Another study that can perform this office is the kind of music presented in *Politics* 8 that opens insights into beauties more worthy of wonder than the achievements of political man. Still another is natural science, valuable not only because it forms an essential element of Aristotle's naturalistic *politikē*, but because, as *Parts of Animals* 1.5 beautifully proclaims, biological inquiry can provide access to the most universal truths about our world, the world of living animals that is our home. Both *NE* 10 and *Politics* 7–8 lead us to the conclusion that these studies have value as preparation for more transcendent metaphysical flights, but that is by no means their only value. The more important conclusion this suggests is that these sublunary studies – music, natural science, *politikē* – lead us, in ways that civil religion and parochial mythology, for example, do not, to understand the possibilities of our lives with a clarity that is the best possible guard we possess against the ever-present danger of deliberately choosing an unsatisfactory way of life.[43]

If my understanding of Aristotle is plausible, the last word on his intention can come from Plato's Socrates. This passage from *Republic* 10, 618b6–c6, in the myth of Er, describes the point at which souls must choose what they will become in their next life. Souls must choose from among the lives of all sorts of animals and from all sorts of human beings – women as well as men. Although no way of life is here identified as uniquely or divinely philosophic, the implication, made explicit a few lines later (619c6–d1), is that any choiceworthy human life must be in some degree philosophic:

> Now here, my dear Glaucon, is the whole risk for a human being, it seems. And on this account each of us must above all take care, to the neglect of other studies, to be an inquirer and a student of that study by which one might be able to learn and discover what will give one the capacity and the knowledge to distinguish a worthwhile life from a worthless one, and so everywhere and always to choose the life that's better from among those that are possible.

Depending on circumstances, the life so chosen may or may not be a deeply political one, as Socrates' was and Aristotle's was not. Either way, the reflection on the possibilities of human development that political philosophy inspires is a necessary condition for choosing wisely. Only necessary? Yes: there are no guarantees. But very necessary: *politikē* is an essential component of any truly liberal education, then as now.

[43] Several recent works of contemporary political theory and empirical social science explicitly articulate Aristotelian standards for evaluating political life: Scott 1999, Elkin 2006, Sen 1999, Flyvbjerg 2001. Similarly, for critical Aristotelian reflections concerning modern democratic theory, see both Frank 2005 and Collins 2006. For a much-discussed argument for the superiority of Aristotle's non-reductive naturalism to modern versions of either Hobbesian reduction or Kantian transcendence, see McDowell 1996. I discuss the importance of McDowell's Aristotelianism for contemporary political philosophy and social science in Salkever 2007b.

Works Cited

Appadurai, A. 2006. *Fear of Small Numbers: An Essay on the Geography of Anger*. Public Planet Books. Durham, NC.

Collins, S. D. 2006. *Aristotle and the Rediscovery of Citizenship*. Cambridge.

Elkin, S. L. 2006. *Reconstructing the Commercial Republic: Constitutional Design after Madison*. Chicago.

Flyvbjerg, B. 2001. *Making Social Science Matter: Why Social Inquiry Fails and How It Can Succeed Again*, trans. S. Sampson. Cambridge.

Frank, J. 2005. *A Democracy of Distinction: Aristotle and the Work of Politics*. Chicago.

Howland, J. 2002 "Aristotle's Great-Souled Man." *Review of Politics* 64: 27–56.

Irwin, T., trans. 1999. *Aristotle: Nicomachean Ethics*, 2nd ed. Indianapolis, IN.

Kraut, R. 2002. *Aristotle: Political Philosophy*. Founders of Modern Political and Social Thought. Oxford.

Lord, C. 1984. *Aristotle: The Politics*. Chicago.

Lincoln, A. 1989. *Speeches and Writings 1832–1858: Speeches, Letters, and Miscellaneous Writings: The Lincoln-Douglas Debates*. New York.

McDowell, J. 1996. *Mind and World*, paperback edition. Cambridge, MA.

Salkever, S. G. 1990. *Finding the Mean: Theory and Practice in Aristotelian Political Philosophy*. Studies in Moral, Political and Legal Philosophy. Princeton, NJ.

2000. "Aristotle and the Ethics of Natural Questions." In *Instilling Ethics*, ed. N. Thompson. Lanham, MD.

2007. "Teaching the Questions: Aristotle's Philosophical Pedagogy in the *Nicomachean Ethics* and the *Politics*." *Review of Politics* 69: 192–214.

2007a. "Whose Prayer?: The Best Regime of Book 7 and the Lessons of Aristotle's *Politics*." *Political Theory* 35: 29–46.

2007b. "Neo-Aristotelianism in Contemporary Political Studies: Breaking the Spell of Modernity and Post-Modernity." *Journal of Korean Politics* 16: 229–46.

2008. "Taking Friendship Seriously: Aristotle on the Place(s) of Philia in Human Life." In *Friendship and Politics: Essays in Political Thought*, ed. J. von Heyking and R. Avramenko. Notre Dame, IN.

Scott, J. C. 1999. *Seeing Like a State: How Certain Schemes to Improve the Human Condition Have Failed*. Yale Agrarian Studies. New Haven, CT.

Sen, A. 1999. *Development As Freedom*. New York.

Simpson, P. L. P. 1997. *The Politics of Aristotle*. Translated, with introduction, analysis, and notes. Chapel Hill, NC.

Smith, T. W. 2001. *Revaluing Ethics: Aristotle's Dialectical Pedagogy*. SUNY series in Ancient Greek Philosophy. Albany, NY.

Sparshott, F. 1994. *Taking Life Seriously: A Study of the Argument of the* Nicomachean Ethics. Toronto.

Strauss, L. 1959. "On Classical Political Philosophy." In *What Is Political Philosophy? And Other Studies*. Glencoe, IL.

Tessitore, A. 1996. *Reading Aristotle's Ethics: Virtue, Rhetoric, and Political Philosophy*. Albany, NY.

9: Lived Excellence in Aristotle's *Constitution of Athens*: Why the Encomium of Theramenes Matters

Jill Frank and S. Sara Monoson

An important and well-established trend in classical Greek political theory reads texts in their historical and political context as fully as the sources allow, believing that what we know about these texts' roles in the vigorous controversies of their own time helpfully informs efforts to use this material to reflect on our own time.[1] In this chapter we bring this interpretative approach to bear on Aristotle's *Constitution of Athens* (hereafter *AthPol*), a text that tells the story of Athenian constitutional history over several centuries and presents a detailed account of the laws and institutions of the Athenian democracy of Aristotle's time. This text, recovered only in 1891, is often assumed to be of interest to historians and constitutional scholars but not to political theorists because, beyond occasional philosophical observations and/or expressions of political bias, it is said to neglect matters

[1] A great deal of work on Greek thinkers and political theoretical issues concerning Greek antiquity by scholars in departments of philosophy, political science, classics, and literature in the United States and United Kingdom (including the flood of work on "democracy ancient and modern") stands in this emerging tradition of interpretation. For discussion of this trend, see Frank 2006:175–92; Monoson 2000: 9–12.

This paper is a revised and expanded treatment of material we first explored in an earlier jointly authored article, "Aristotle's Theramenes at Athens: A Poetic History" (*parallax* 2003, vol. 9, no. 4, 290–40). We thank Peter Euben for inviting our contribution to that journal, the Taylor & Francis Group for permission to reprint material from that article, and Marianne Hopman, Gerry Mara, and Kurt Raaflaub for helpful comments on this chapter.

of normative concern.[2] We disagree. In our view, complex normative concerns shape the *AthPol*, and history and theory inform each other in that text, as they do in Aristotle's ethical and political writings, more generally. For these reasons we support an integrated and continuous reading of Aristotle's practical works, including the *Politics, Nicomachean Ethics, Rhetoric, Poetics*, and *AthPol*. Although we do not address the issue of authorship directly, our argument contributes reasons for favoring Aristotle's authorship.[3]

In a recent essay on the tradition of "writing on the constitutions," Stephen Menn points out that although the written *politeiai* Aristotle considers in the *Politics* fall into what *we* may consider to be two distinct categories – "normative" (i.e., accounts of the ideal polity, writing on "constitutions" in general, and writing on a specific form of constitution like aristocracy or monarchy) and "historical" (the various "constitutions of the so-and-so's," for example, of the Spartans or Athenians) – "Aristotle often does not bother to distinguish the two types, and they would have covered heavily overlapping ranges of topics."[4] Menn concludes that Aristotle treats both idealizing "*Politeiai*-of-the-so-and-so's" and purely ideal *politeiai* like Plato's *Republic* as proposals for how a city might best be governed.[5] An essential step in this dual project, as Aristotle explains toward the end of the *Nicomachean Ethics*, is "to consider, out of the *politeiai* that have been collected what kinds of thing [i.e., what laws and customs] preserve and destroy cities and what kinds [preserve and destroy] each of the *politeiai*, and by what causes some [cities] are governed [*politeuontai*] rightly or wrongly" (*NE* 1181b17–20, tr. Menn). For Aristotle, then (as for others who took up this form of writing), "texts on the *politeiai* of the so-and-so's

[2] One important exception is Mara 2002: 307–42. For an example of an historian attending to "philosophical reflections" in the *AthPol*, see Chambers 1993: 51–52.

[3] There is no consensus in the scholarship about Aristotle's authorship of this text. For arguments in favor of Aristotle's authorship, see Keaney 1992: 12–14, 39–40. *Contra* Rhodes 1981: 63. For discussion, see Mara 2002: 310–11; Whitehead 1993: 25–38; and Lévy 1993: 65–90. The *AthPol* is, however, widely regarded as the work of Aristotle's school during his lifetime. Such an assumption informs all the contributions to *Aristote et Athènes* (Piérart 1993), an edited volume based on a 1991 conference in Fribourg (Sw.) on the occasion of the 100th anniversary of the recovery of the *AthPol*.

[4] See Menn 2006: 3.

[5] Aristotle refers to Plato's *Republic* this way at *Politics* 2.1, 1261a6, 6, 1264b28; 4.4, 1291a12; 5.12, 1316a1 and 8.7, 1342a33 and *Rhetoric* 3.4, 1406b32, cited by Menn 2006.

are instruments of the normative study of how a city should best be governed."[6]

Menn maintains that investigations "*peri politeias*" "feel freer to take liberties with the truth of the details than 'history' does."[7] This is certainly true of the *AthPol* and perhaps, most especially, of Aristotle's account in the *AthPol* of Theramenes, an Athenian politician active for an extended period in the late fifth century and a major player during periods of political turmoil in the later years of the Peloponnesian War.[8] Remembered by most of his countrymen as a scandalous opportunist who betrayed both oligarchs and democrats, Aristotle, by contrast, proposes that, "if one tries not to judge lightly" (*AthPol* 28.5, cf. *NE* 1181b12) it can become clear that Theramenes was actually a good citizen (*agathos politēs*) and among the best Athenian statesmen of the post-Periclean period (*dokousi beltistoi gegonenai tōn Athēnēsi politeusamenōn meta tous archaious Nikias kai Thoukudidēs kai Theramenēs, AthPol* 28.5).[9] Aristotle's account of Theramenes, rather glaringly from the point of view of Aristotle's contemporaries, omits mention of this politician's well-known involvement in activities that cast him in an unfavorable light. Moreover, although Aristotle reports that Theramenes disobeyed the laws of the regimes under which he lived, Aristotle also presents Theramenes as a *preserver* of Athens' lawfulness. These features of Aristotle's portrayal of Theramenes have troubled commentators, leading some to conclude that Aristotle simply is a poor historian.[10] But if we reject the premise that the text aims only to present a comprehensive factual account and insist also on its normativity, how might

[6] Menn 2006: 4. See *NE* 1181b15–25. On the evidence for Aristotle's school having composed accounts of 158 constitutions, see Rhodes 1981: 1–2.

[7] Menn 2006: 10.

[8] The main sources for Theramenes are: Xenophon, *Hellenica* 2.3.2–5; Lysias, *Against Eratosthenes* 50, 62–79, *Against Agorastus* 9–19; Aristophanes, *Frogs* 541, 967; Thucydides, *History* 8.68, 89.2; Diodorus 13.38.1–2, 98.3, 101.1–7. Thucydides' assessment of Theramenes is ambiguous (see below for discussion). Lysias and Aristophanes are negative. Diodorus, writing after Aristotle, is apologetic. The ancient debate is mimicked in recent scholarship. *Anti-Theramenes*: Buck 1995; Ehrhardt 1995; Adeleye 1973; Adeleye 1976; Grote 1890: viii, 60ff.; Hignett 1952: 276, 290. *Pro-Theramenes*: McCoy 1997: 171–92; Perrin 1904; Ehrenberg 1968: 344; Kagan 1987: 155; Krentz 1982: 36; Merkelbach 1977: 111–17. Keaney 1992: 133–52, makes no attempt to assess Theramenes' politics, focusing instead on the stylistic features of Aristotle's account of him.

[9] Translations from the *AthPol* are from von Fritz and Kapp 1974 [1950], unless otherwise noted.

[10] Harding 1974: 111; Buck 1995: 16; Day and Chambers 1962: 58, 147–48; Wilamowitz 1893, I: 308, 373. *Contra* de Ste. Croix 1992: 23–32, and n. 43.

we understand the construction of Theramenes? And what follows for our understanding of Athens's constitution? Do the demands of theory constrain these *bios* and *politeia* portraits so that Aristotle's omissions do not undermine the credibility of his argument?

Our answers to these questions pivot on Aristotle's discussion, in the *Poetics*, of the relation between "usual history" and "poetry." Aristotle describes history in its usual sense as providing a "narrative of random events" to recount "all that happened during [a] period concerning one or more persons, however disconnected the several events may have been" (*Poetics* 1459a21–24, also 1451a36–b11).[11] Usual histories, in other words, attend to events and persons in their singularity. Aristotle contrasts usual history to poetry which, he says, deals in universals and addresses "what is possible according to probability and necessity." As such, he maintains, poetry is "more philosophical and more worthwhile than history" (*Poetics* 1451a36–b11, 1451a36–b11). Aristotle's contrast between poetry and history in its usual sense opens the possibility of a different kind of history, one oriented to not only particulars but universals.[12] A precedent for this practice of history, available to Aristotle and arguably referenced in these *Poetics* passages, may be Thucydides' *History of the Peloponnesian War*. As the scholarship on the shape of that text has stressed in recent decades, Thucydides' narrative is not only an account of the "facts" of a particular war, but also a theoretical and normative study of these singular events.[13] Because its crafted narrative grounds compelling arguments about what can happen in the future by way of an historical account of what has happened in the past (1.21.1), it will be judged "useful" and treated as a "possession for all time" (1.22.4). Bringing past, present, and future into meaningful conversation, it opens opportunities for readers to think in new ways about the choices they face in their lived lives and to act accordingly.[14]

[11] Translations of the *Poetics* in this paragraph are by de Ste. Croix 1992, who identifies the description of the "usual histories" at *Poetics* 1459a21–22 with the reference to "history" disparaged at *Poetics* 1451a36–b11, and assumes that Aristotle leaves room for a different kind of history writing that might be more poetic. Davis 1999: 60, argues that Aristotle intentionally undermines the distinction between history and poetry with a view to rendering histories poetic. See also Halliwell 1987, regarding chapters 9 and 23; and Halliwell 2001: 87–107.

[12] We do not here assess Aristotle's discussion of universals and particulars in *Poetics* chapter 9 or the attendant scholarship.

[13] Connor 1977 calls attention to this development in the scholarship.

[14] See Raaflaub forthcoming, who argues that to the ancients "objectivity was not a goal in itself." Rather, seeking "historical truth" was more a matter of finding

The *AthPol*, in our view, does the same. It is not history in its usual sense. Neither is Aristotle's story of Theramenes or his account of the development of the Athenian constitution. Concerned not just with preserving the memory of singular "events which have occurred" but also with illuminating "the kind of events which could occur" in the future, Aristotle's commentaries on Theramenes and on Athenian constitutionalism are better understood poetically. As what we call "poetic history," they exhibit a remembering of exemplary actions and a forgetting of missteps in patterns of lived experiences to create a well-structured plot. This is not to say they are fictional.[15] Nor are they, strictly speaking, philosophical. In line, rather, with the genres of *politeia* and *bios* writings, Aristotle's poetic history of ethical and political excellence in the *AthPol* looks to the past to identify possible and plausible and, from his point of view, *better* futures for Athens's constitutional development with and through Theramenes. Theramenes is to Aristotle much like Socrates was to Plato, namely, a figure of lived excellence, even if he does not readily appear as such to his contemporaries.[16] Like Socrates, Theramenes offers a model of lived excellence that a people can emulate. Indeed, as we discuss below, Aristotle describes the collective action of the Athenian demos during the amnesty that followed the defeat of the Thirty in 403 in terms that reprise the political excellence he models by Theramenes. Unlike Socrates, however, Theramenes sought positions of leadership and, in that capacity, more visibly navigated the moral ambiguities of the politics of his time. Examining Aristotle's account of Theramenes not with a view to rehabilitating the reputation of Theramenes but in order to elaborate Aristotle's understanding of lived excellence as it pertains to an individual life (*bios*) and to a constitution (*politeia*), we find the analogy between *bios* and *politeia* from Aristotle's *Politics* (1323a–24a4, 1295a40–b1) to prevail in the *AthPol* as well. We explore the force and content of this analogy through an analysis of Aristotle's figuration of Theramenes and of the constitutions with which he associates Theramenes, namely, the Constitution of the Five Thousand and the ancestral constitution. Before doing so, however, we set out the portrait of Theramenes gleaned from a full range of classical sources.

a "true reality" that could "open a flow of information" and generate "more free discussion." See also Finley 1965.

15 *Contra* Bassi 2000: 13–34, esp. 18–21.

16 For a similar analogy between Theramenes and Socrates that also insists on both the similarities and differences between the two, see Mara 2002: 330–31. See also Keaney 1992: 147–48.

THERAMENES' CAREER AT ATHENS

Sources agree that Theramenes was most notable for his participation in three periods of civil turmoil at Athens: the oligarchic revolution of 411/10 including the "rule of the Five Thousand," the aftermath of the battle of Arginousae in 406, and the rule of the Thirty in 404/03.[17] In particular, Theramenes advocated the dissolution of the democracy and the establishment of the rule of the Four Hundred after the disastrous defeat of the Athenian fleet in Sicily during the Peloponnesian War in 411. Months later, however, Theramenes opposed the new oligarchic regime, charging that the fortifications the hoplites were ordered to build at Eetionia aimed not to keep the (democratic) fleet amassed at Samos out but to let the Spartans in. Soon Theramenes joined with a hoplite commander, Aristocrates, to depose the Four Hundred, and to empower instead a larger pool of citizens, the period known as the Constitution of the Five Thousand. The rule of the Five Thousand was short lived, and efforts to restore a full democracy, led by Cleophon, succeeded within the year.

Five years later, during a period of restored democracy in 406, Theramenes served as a trierarch in the infamous battle of Arginousae, when the Athenian fleet defeated the Spartans but failed to recover their dead and rescue the crews of their disabled ships. In Athens, some charged that insufficient effort had been made to save the men, and the assembly collectively and, thus, illegally tried the generals present at the battle.[18] The generals blamed the trierarchs, one of whom was Theramenes, for not executing orders. After the trierarchs countered that a terrible storm had rendered the mission impossible, the generals were condemned and executed.

Two years later in 404, the Athenian assembly chose Theramenes to conduct peace negotiations with the Spartan commander Lysander after the decisive defeat of the Athenian fleet at Aegospotami. Theramenes remained in Lysander's camp for three months during a

[17] For Theramenes' involvement in the upheavals of 411 see: Thucydides, *History* 8.68, 89.2, 91.1; Xenophon, *Hellenica* 2.3.30; Lysias, *Against Eratosthenes* 65; Aristotle, *AthPol* 28.3, 28.5, 29.1–33.2; Diodorus 13.38.1–2. For his involvement in the Arginousae affair see: Xenophon, *Hellenica* 1.6.35, 7.4–31; 2.3.32, 35; Diodorus 13.98.3, 101.1–7. For his involvement in the Thirty see: Xenophon, *Hellenica*, 2.2.16–22, 3.2–56; Lysias, *Against Eratosthenes* 73–79, *Against Agorastus* 9–19; Aristotle, *AthPol* 34.2–37.2; Diodorus 14.3.6–7, 4.1, 4.5–5.4, 32.5.

[18] Socrates, a member of the presiding council on that date, opposed the procedure: Plato, *Apology* 32b; Xenophon, *Hellenica* 1.7.15, *Memorabilia* 1.1.18.

period of food shortages in Athens, returning to Athens in Lysander's company. Worn down by famine and intimidated by the presence of the Spartan general, the people voted to dissolve the democracy and set up an oligarchic order. Theramenes became a member of the new ruling elite, the Thirty, but soon opposed this regime from within. When, under the influence of Critias, the Thirty became systematically brutal, killing for revenge and confiscating property, Theramenes spoke out. Critias denounced him in the assembly and, possibly fearing both Theramenes' growing popularity and his connections with the exiled democrats led by Thrasybulus (with whom Theramenes had served at Arginousae), he orchestrated Theramenes' swift condemnation and execution.

Classical sources, exhibiting both oligarchic and democratic sympathies, for the most part portray Theramenes as a conniving opportunist who was concerned first and foremost to advance his own personal standing.[19] This is how they explain, for example, Theramenes' selective obedience to the laws of Athens when Athens veered between oligarchy and democracy. Aristophanes counts on this being a common view when the chorus in the *Frogs* sings:

> The mark of a man
> With brains and sense,
> One who has voyaged far and wide,
> Is ever to shift
> To the comfy side of the ship
> And not just stand fast
> In one position, like a painted
> Picture; to roll over
> To the softer side
> Is the mark of a smart man,
> A born Theramenes. (533–41)[20]

Xenophon reports that Critias gave Theramenes the nickname *kothornos* (buskin), the stage boot, which could be worn on either foot. But Xenophon also portrays Theramenes responding to that allegation, casting himself as resisting Critias' power. Lysias argues, on the other hand, that Theramenes was in collusion with Lysander during the peace negotiations at the end of the war and remained away for so long so that the famine would worsen and the Athenians would have no choice but to

[19] See note 8 above.

[20] Trans. Henderson 2002.

yield. Theramenes, he maintains, died a "victim of his own baseness" and not as a champion of the victims of the Thirty.[21]

Thucydides' judgment of Theramenes, in the *History*, is more difficult to assess. He includes a detailed account of Theramenes' considerable influence during the constitutional upheavals of 411/10, explicitly praising the rule of the Five Thousand (though without mentioning Theramenes by name), but his narrative breaks off before the other events in which Theramenes figured so memorably (the Arginousae affair and the period of the Thirty). Thucydides gives some reason to view Theramenes in a negative light. He reports Theramenes' part in the establishment of the Four Hundred and in its dissolution (8.68.4, 89.2–4) and notes that most oligarchs favoring the Five Thousand at this political moment (though, again, he does not mention Theramenes by name) did so to curry favor with the people, for they believed that the oligarchy was weakening (8.89.2–4). Thucydides also, however, praises the rule of the Five Thousand as "the best government [enjoyed by the Athenians] . . . at least in my time" (8.97.2). Given Theramenes' prominent role in the establishment of that constitution, Thucydides' historical view of Theramenes appears ambiguous. We return to a more poetic view of Thucydides' normative interest in Theramenes below.

A Poetic History of Theramenes

Aristotle attributes the disunity of opinion about Theramenes to the difficulties of interpreting events "when public affairs were in a turmoil" (*AthPol* 28.5). Casting Theramenes as a model citizen (*agathos politēs*), Aristotle maintains that Theramenes did not "overthrow all constitutions" to advance his personal ambitions as his critics allege, but "worked for the good of any established government as long as it did not transgress the laws, and in this way showed that he was able to participate in governing under any kind of political setup, which is what a good citizen should do" (28.5, trans. modified).

Aristotle's assessment stands out among the classical sources for its unambiguous praise of Theramenes' actions and motives. So too does his account of the events of 411–3 as they pertain to Theramenes. Discussing the circumstances of the oligarchic revolution that empowered the Four Hundred in the year 411, Aristotle alone includes a lengthy

[21] Xenophon, *Hellenica* 2.3.31, 47; Aristophanes, *Frogs* 533–41; Lysias, *Against Eratosthenes*.

description of a draft constitution favoring a more inclusive (but not fully democratic) government drawn up "for the future" and never fully realized (31.1) and he identifies Theramenes as a key promoter of this more inclusive constitution.[22] Moreover, Aristotle links efforts to bring about civil peace in the aftermath of the defeat at Aegospotami with calls for a return to "the ancestral constitution." Reporting that advocates of both democracy and oligarchy celebrated this tradition in their rhetoric, Aristotle, alone again among the extant sources, isolates an additional group, led by Theramenes, whose members "did not belong to the clubs, *hetaireiai*" (34.3). Finally, Aristotle omits aspects of Theramenes' career, failing to address three damaging charges found in other sources: that Theramenes favored the illegal execution of the generals who served at Arginousae; that he colluded with the Spartan leader Lysander in 403; and that Theramenes was himself a member of the Thirty.

Aristotle's treatment raises three puzzles: first, what is it about Theramenes that Aristotle finds so praiseworthy? Why does he use Theramenes as a model *tropos tou biou*? Second, why does Aristotle associate Theramenes with the ancestral constitution and the Constitution of the Five Thousand? How does understanding Theramenes' *bios* inform our understanding of what Aristotle believes preserves (and destroys) *politeiai*, specifically the *politeia* of the Athenians? Third, why does Aristotle fail to answer specific charges and to address Theramenes' part in episodes that reflect poorly on him? And why does he associate Theramenes with constitutions whose past and future are so contested? Is the *AthPol* simply a poor record of events or might there be a theoretical point to its shape? As we argue next, Aristotle's account of Theramenes suggests the normative aspirations of the *AthPol* as a work of poetic history.

Scholars generally agree that Aristotle omits aspects of Theramenes' career so as to avoid diminishing the persuasiveness of his praise of Theramenes. They also agree that Aristotle's commendation rests on his own portrait of Theramenes as a moderate.[23] Some argue that in associating Theramenes with the Constitution of the Five Thousand, Aristotle portrays Theramenes as promoting the constitutional polity, *politeia*, that Aristotle himself appears to recommend in the

[22] For discussion of how far other sources assume or suggest that such a draft document was produced at the period of the establishment of the Four Hundred, see Ostwald 1989: 375 ff.

[23] Wolpert 2002: 12–13; Buck 1995: 20; Harding 1974: 111.

Politics.[24] Others maintain that he uses Theramenes to exemplify the *mesos politēs* of the *Politics*.[25] These views assume that, in the *AthPol*, Aristotle applies his theory from the *Politics* to the facts he collects in his historical-cum-empirical investigations and judges, on the basis of his theory, that Theramenes is to be lauded and not excoriated. Aristotle, in other words, doctors "the historical record" to promote his philosophical convictions, considering historical particulars only so that they can be put in the service of his political theory.[26]

To level this charge is, in our view, mistaken in its own terms. It also misunderstands the overall project of the *AthPol*. As we establish next, there are substantial differences, on the one hand, between the Constitution of the Five Thousand and the constitutional polity of the *Politics*, and, on the other, between the lawfulness and moderation Aristotle attributes to the *mesos politēs* and these virtues as they are associated with Theramenes. If Aristotle's aim is to distort evidence to prove his theory, then, in light of these differences, he is not only a poor historian but a poor theorist as well. We think he is neither. Instead, Aristotle uses his commentary on Theramenes and on the constitutions with which he associates Theramenes to open a course both for citizen virtue and for Athenian constitutional development, a course of lawfulness and moderation absent from the regimes under which Theramenes lived, but available for the future through an understanding of Athens's past and present.

The overarching story in the *AthPol* is that of a long struggle between oligarchs and democrats to shape the Athenian constitution so that it might structurally favor one faction over the other. The text plots the shifting fortunes of each faction and the constitutional alterations that Athens experiences – now in the direction of oligarchy, now of democracy, now of tyranny, and back and forth – the long-range results being changes in the direction of "more democracy" (9, 10, 22.1, 23.1, 41.2). One episode stands out as an interruption of this pattern: the

24 Newman 1887; Sandys 1912 [1893]; Bury and Meiggs 1975; Perrin 1904. Newman 1887: 470–71 n.1, writing before the recovery of the *AthPol* in 1890, makes this identification by connecting Plutarch's quotation from the *AthPol* in his *Life of Nicias*, which names Theramenes along with Nicias and Thucydides as fine statesmen, with Thucydides' implication of Theramenes in the Constitution of the Five Thousand. This view has colored the approach of later scholars even if they do not explicitly tie the Constitution of the Five Thousand to any constitution Aristotle discusses in the *Politics*. See Vlastos 1952; Ferguson 1926.

25 Harding 1974: 111.

26 Harding 1974: 111; Buck 1995: 16. See also Day and Chambers 1962: 58, 147–48. *Contra* Mara 2002.

brief period of the Constitution of the Five Thousand that followed the collapse of the rule of the Four Hundred in the year 411. Aristotle affirms its status as an outlier by omitting this episode from his summary of changes the Athenian constitution undergoes over the years (41.2). In 411, an oligarchic regime, severely weakened by military defeat, is abolished (33.1), but Athens does not immediately swing back to a democratic constitutional order. Instead, Theramenes and the hoplite commander, Aristocrates, lead an effort to transfer the administration of the affairs of the city from "the Four Hundred" to "the Five Thousand," the larger number being men with whom the Four Hundred had been legally obligated to consult and share power, but did not (31.1–2, 32.3, 33.2). Strikingly, Aristotle applauds the actions of these reformers for ushering in a period of good government (33.2, cf. Thucydides 8.97.2), albeit a brief one.[27]

Usual accounts of Aristotle's interest in Theramenes identify him as the chief architect of the lauded Constitution of the Five Thousand and link this lived regime to the idea of a mixed oligarchic-democratic constitution, named simply *politeia* in the *Politics* (1293a40). This line of interpretation may stem from the fact that Thucydides uses the terminology of "mixture" to describe the regime of the Five Thousand (*metria gar hē te es tous oligous kai tous pollous sungkrasis egeneto*, "a judicious mixture of the few and the many," 8.97.2). But a linkage between Aristotle's conception of the mixed polity of the *Politics* and his account of the rule of the Five Thousand in the *AthPol* does not stand scrutiny. Aristotle explicitly mentions only two features of the Constitution of the Five Thousand in the *AthPol*. The Five Thousand were all to be capable of military service "with full equipment" (as hoplites) and "there was to be no pay for any public office" (33.1–2). The *Politics*, likewise, suggests that restricting (at least full) political participation to citizens who "possess heavy armor" (1297b2) is characteristic of *politeia*.[28] Discussing how *politeia* might be brought into being, however, Aristotle recommends incorporating into the structure of the courts and assembly the democratic practice of payment for public office and the oligarchic practice of imposing fines for non-attendance (*Pol.* 1294a40–b5, 1297a40–b1). Whereas at the time of the Five Thousand Athens had not yet started

[27] For discussions of the Five Thousand in Aristotle and Thucydides, see Harris 1990; Ostwald 1989: 395–411; and Gomme 1981: 323–40.

[28] The only proviso, impossible to assess here, is that the property qualification needs to allow for "those who have a share in the constitution [to be] more numerous than those who have not" (*Pol.* 1297b1–5). Translations from the *Politics* are from Rackham 1977 [1932].

paying stipends for assembly work and so it is unclear whether Aristotle would have expected a mixed constitution at this historical juncture to initiate such a payment, pay for jury service and for certain magistrates was already well established. Abolishing this form of pay is, therefore, at odds with Aristotle's account of *politeia*. Moreover, Aristotle acknowledges that the Constitution of the Five Thousand was short lived, reporting that the Five Thousand "were quickly deprived of their political power by the people" (*AthPol* 34.1). In the *Politics*, by contrast, he maintains that "the better the constitution is mixed, the more permanent it is" (1297a7–8). Assuming that achieving such a mixture was indeed the aim of the reformers, the swiftness of the fall of the Five Thousand suggests that it represented a very poor approximation of Aristotle's *politeia* indeed.

In our view, Aristotle does not praise the Constitution of the Five Thousand because it blends oligarchy with democracy and so is similar to the constitution called *politeia* in the *Politics*. Aristotle may claim that "the mark of a good mixture of democracy and oligarchy is when it is possible to speak of the same constitution as a democracy and as an oligarchy" (*Pol.* 1294b14–16). But the Constitution of the Five Thousand, unlike the mixed polity of the *Politics* with which it is often identified, had the virtue Aristotle praises *elsewhere* in the *Politics* of being both oligarchic and democratic and neither (1294b35–37). What does it mean for a constitution to be democratic and oligarchic and neither, in contrast to a mixture of both? It is for it to have virtues cultivated by neither democracy nor oligarchy, alone or together, virtues that conduce to lawfulness.[29] Aristotle's account in the *AthPol* of the constitutional crisis at Athens after the catastrophe in Sicily lingers on the Athenians' striving for these virtues. He gives the impression that the Athenians conducted remarkably orderly and thoughtful deliberations about what to do, describing in detail the legal procedures they followed to dissolve the democracy and empower the Four Hundred and to appoint *anagrapheis* to draft two documents stipulating a governing body of no fewer than Five Thousand citizens for the "salvation" of the city (29–33).[30] He specifically commends the leading advocates of these changes – Theramenes, Pisander, and Antiphon – for their attempts to sustain norms of lawfulness in highly volatile times (32.2). What did these norms amount to? These politicians guided legislation and publicized their plans, submitting their proposals to scrutiny and

[29] For discussion, see Frank 2005: 163–69.

[30] For discussion of the *anagrapheis*, see Ostwald 1989: 379.

ratification (29.1–2, 30.1–2, 32.1). Initially at least, it appears that they promoted a concentration of authority not to give power to the wealthy, but as a means of curbing the tendency to slip into factional strife in times of war.[31]

Unlike Pisander and Antiphon, Theramenes goes on to play a similarly important part in the next and less savory stage of the oligarchic revolution of 411. When Aristotle turns to describe the actual behavior of the Four Hundred, he is curt, reporting only that although the Five Thousand had been chosen, the Four Hundred, together with ten possessing absolute power, entered the Council house, ruled the city, and sent an embassy to Sparta to negotiate an end to the war (which failed) (32.3). Aristotle's tone and his compression of events suggest disapproval of the oligarchic cabal acting in a preemptory fashion. He reports that the rule of the Four Hundred lasted only about four months and attributes its downfall to more military misfortunes that embittered the people. At this time, the Athenians did not simply reprise democracy. Instead, Theramenes, this time joined by Aristocrates, and suspicious both of the ill-considered and unaccountable exercises of power by the Four Hundred and of the prospect of similar exercises of power by triumphant democrats, successfully reinvigorated the principle of rule by the Five Thousand. In that context, and given the war's effect on the city's population, that principle, in Mark Munn's judgment, "would hardly exclude any able-bodied citizen in Athens."[32] The changes in the direction of oligarchy underwritten by the Constitution of the Five Thousand thus had decidedly democratizing effects. This unusual outcome confirms once again its status as an outlier in Athens's constitutional history. It also provides another explanation for why, later in the *AthPol*, when Aristotle recounts the series of constitutional changes endured by the Athenians, he moves directly from the period of the Four Hundred to the restored democracy, leaving out the Constitution of the Five Thousand (41.2).

All of this suggests that Aristotle does not praise Theramenes for adhering to one particular regime over another or for his design of a new regime, but for his actions, and specifically for acting in ways conducive to lawfulness. Rhodes finds Aristotle's identification of Theramenes with lawfulness unconvincing. Accepting that, in the name of fidelity to the law, Theramenes may have opposed the Four Hundred,

[31] The more common oligarchic view informs Ps.-Xenophon, *The Constitution of Athens*. For commentary, see Ober 1998: 14–26.

[32] Munn 2000: 150.

the Thirty, and also, perhaps, the democracy after Aegospotami, Rhodes says, "it is hard to apply a charge of illegality to the democracy overthrown in 411," thus implying that Aristotle's praise of Theramenes rests on ideological grounds.[33] Aristotle's commentary in the *AthPol* suggests otherwise. Calling the post-Periclean democratic leaders "demagogues and deceivers" who "induced" the people to do something improper and whose main aim was to cater to the wishes of the masses, having nothing in mind but their most immediate interests, Aristotle describes their actions as contrary to *nomos* (here signifying both law and custom, though neither in a purely positivist sense), "corrupting" and "violent" (28.3–4). Aristotle's remarks, along with his pejorative use of the word "demagogue," do not simply reflect an ideological bias against democracy. As Rhodes notes, Aristotle generally uses the word "demagogue" to signify "the extreme democracy in which the demos considers itself above the laws" (*Pol.* 1292a5–33).[34] To Aristotle, then, the democracy of 411 was no more lawful than the other regimes Theramenes worked to overthrow. Whether oligarchy or democracy, Athens, on all four occasions on which Theramenes acted, was ruled not by a stable set of laws but by individuals who considered "their own advantage" (*Pol.* 1279b6–10). Owing to the subordination of law in these regimes to the interests of the rulers, those regimes, in Aristotle's taxonomy, did not deserve to be called constitutions at all (*Pol.* 1293b28–31).

Aristotle reiterates his commendation of Theramenes' lawfulness in his commentary on the period of the Thirty. In 404, the Athenians are again struggling with military defeat (the destruction of the Athenian navy at Aegospotami) and fear a foreign power interfering in domestic affairs (the Spartan general Lysander). In this case, unlike in 411, Theramenes' efforts to restrain both oligarchs and democrats in guiding the city's response to these trials are unsuccessful (34.3). Aristotle reports that the people were "intimidated by Lysander" and "felt compelled" to side with the advocates of oligarchy, namely, the returning exiles and some members of the wealthier classes. The ensuing regime "paid no attention to the other regulations concerning the constitution which had been passed" (35.1). If, at first, the Thirty appeared to behave moderately (35.2), once they secured their hold on the city by suppressing or killing dissenters, their rule turned brutal. At this point and fully aware of the risks involved, Theramenes publicly rebukes the leaders of the Thirty, notably Critias (36.1–2). Fearing that Theramenes may lead

[33] Rhodes 1981: 361, 323–24, 358.

[34] Rhodes 1981: 323.

a popular uprising, they try to appease him, but Theramenes continues to challenge the regime and, finally, they contrive a legal pretext to execute him (37.1).[35] Subsequently, the Thirty become even crueler. In Aristotle's account, as Theramenes was crushed so were the principles of lawfulness that guided his political efforts. Aristotle's commentary on the Constitution of the Five Thousand thus associates Theramenes with a practice of internal critique and with a kind of lawfulness that, insofar as it is neither beholden to nor controlled by any faction, is democratic and oligarchic and neither.

Aristotle's commentary on the ancestral constitution elaborates this understanding of lawfulness and its realization in a *politeia*. Calls to return to governance by the "ancestral constitution" appear twice in the *AthPol* in the course of Aristotle's report on the period 411–402: in Cleitophon's rider to a proposal resolving to change Athens's democracy into the regime of the Four Hundred (29.3)[36] and in Athens's peace treaty with Sparta that ultimately led to the Thirty (34.3). Scholars maintain that these references reflect a widespread movement at the time calling for a return to the ways of the past, but that there is not much to be learned from them since all the political factions in Athens during that period defended the "ancestral constitution." Radical democrats invoked it to claim traditional support for their ideas and oligarchs invoked it so as to appear to be defending a democratic platform when, in truth, their aims were to secure power for a few. Scholars, therefore, tend to treat invocations of the ancestral constitution as a rhetorical tool deployed by these parties to suit their political purposes.[37]

Aristotle's account, especially in the context of the peace treaty negotiations, is different. He reports that, unlike those who invoked the ancestral constitution in the name of democracy and those who did so with the aim of establishing oligarchy, there was a group of citizens, led by Theramenes, who advocated the ancestral constitution for something other than factional reasons (34.3). Aristotle refers to the members of this group as *gnōrimoi*, notables, but distinguishes them from oligarchs, whom he also calls *gnōrimoi*, by maintaining that the *gnōrimoi* of Theramenes' group did not belong to any political clubs (*hetaireiai*).[38] Aristotle's intention to disassociate this group from any classist, factional

[35] On Critias, see Xenophon, *Hellenica* 2.3.24–49.

[36] See Fuks 1975, ch. 1.

[37] Finley 1975, ch. 2; Rhodes 1981: 376–77.

[38] For discussion of *gnōrimoi* in contrast to the *dēmos*, see Rhodes 1981: 88, 345, 427, who describes the uses to which Aristotle puts these terms, sometimes using them to denote a distinction between the wealthy and the poor and sometimes without class

political platform may be gleaned from the fact that he specifically names its members: Archinus, Anytus, Cleitophon, and Phormisius. One might expect these men to have oligarchic sympathies since, just after their call for the ancestral constitution, the Thirty was established with Theramenes as one of its members. But none was a member of the Thirty. On the contrary, Archinus and Anytus, who served with Thrasybulus, and Phormisius, who did not, were all prominent democrats.[39]

Comprised of democrats and oligarchs, this group might be understood as bipartisan, advocating a mix of democratic and oligarchic arrangements, acceptable, through negotiation and compromise, to members of either party. As we have just seen, however, mixing oligarchy and democracy does not produce constitutional virtue in Aristotle's commentary. Nor is such mixing what distinguishes Theramenes or his supporters. They are, rather, moderate in the mode of nonpartisanship, which is to say, they are resistant to factionalisms that blind to what is best for the polity and to its attendant vindictiveness.[40] Aristotle reports, for example, that Theramenes rejected both oligarchic and democratic policies when they were unlawful and "guided them all forward into a fully law-abiding course" (*pasas proagein heōs mēden paranomoien, AthPol* 28.5).[41] If Theramenes appears to most sources and commentators to shift identities with Athens's changing constitutional forms, to Aristotle he is, instead, consistently lawful in his opposition to excessive and arbitrary power.[42] On this point Aristotle and Xenophon are in agreement. In his recreation of Theramenes' speech answering Critias' call for his execution, Xenophon has Theramenes express a

connotations. For Aristotle's "threefold division" of the supporters of the "ancient constitution," see Rhodes 1981: 428.

39 About Cleitophon less is known. See Rhodes 1981: 431–32. Anytus was one of Socrates' accusers: Plato, *Apology* 18b.

40 See Rhodes 1981: 432–33.

41 Trans. Rackham 1996 [1935]: 85, who brings out the point we are stressing more clearly. Von Fritz and Kapp 1974 [1950] render the passage: "He worked for the good of any established government as long as it did not transgress the [fundamental] laws."

42 Aristotle notes that opinion in his time about the figure Theramenes is divided but, in the course of the *AthPol*'s account of the man's actions, we encounter only the consistently good reputation Theramenes enjoyed among his own contemporaries among the people of Athens. Aristotle does not report contemporaneous controversy over his reputation. See 32.2 where Theramenes is said to be "renowned" for "outstanding political insight and well-balanced judgment" (this comes at the start of the account of the Constitution of the Five Thousand) and 36.1 where Aristotle reports that "the masses took the side of Theramenes" in his dispute with the Thirty.

principled opposition to the concentration of power and the excesses it spawns as well as a desire to protect his city from its consequences:

> He [Critias] dubs me a *kothornos*, because, as he says, I try to fit both parties. But for the man who pleases neither party – what in the name of the gods should we call him. . . . I am forever at war with the men who do not think there could be a good democracy until the slaves and those who would sell the state for lack of a shilling should share in the government, and on the other hand I am forever an enemy to those who do not think that a good oligarchy could be established until they should bring the state to the point of being ruled absolutely by a few. (*Hellenica* 2.3.47–48)[43]

Opposition to excessive and arbitrary power does not mean being unwilling or unable to use considerable force when necessary. And consistent lawfulness does not preclude disobedience.

What exactly does Theramenes' consistent lawfulness amount to? Some scholars argue that Aristotle praises Theramenes because he embodies the lawfulness characteristic of the *mesos politēs* celebrated in the *Politics*. The *mesos*, however, preserves his constitution by obeying its laws, which Aristotle calls "a worthwhile goal whenever the constitution is not entirely bad."[44] By contrast, Theramenes, living under regimes that veered between oligarchic and democratic extremes, preserves Athens's constitution not by following the laws of those regimes but by disobeying them. Knowing how and when to disobey also requires lawfulness, but a lawfulness guided by something other than the laws currently in force. Guiding lawfulness so understood is good judgment, which Aristotle calls the greatest thing in determining good laws (*NE* 1181a19). And preserving the good judgment necessary to knowing how and when to disobey laws is moderation (*NE* 1140b14).[45]

[43] Xenophon here attributes to Theramenes a view that is directly opposed to a far more common understanding of how to strengthen a favored constitution. This common view is evident in the orientation of Ps.-Xenophon's *Constitution of the Athenians*. This author recounts the success of the democrats at Athens in pursuing precisely the strategy that Theramenes here denounces and admits that while he disagrees with their democratic principles, he nevertheless admires the brilliant way in which the democrats pursue their goals. On the theoretical sophistication of this text, see Ober 1998: 27–48.

[44] Kraut 2002: 382, 379–84.

[45] Compare Socrates' determination to continue practicing his questioning in Plato's *Apology* and his discussion of lawful resistance and punishment in *Crito*.

Aristotle thus portrays Theramenes as a moderate, to be sure. But Theramenes is moderate not because he led a political group called "the moderates," or because he combined oligarchic and democratic policies to promote a mixed outcome, or because he reflected the *mesos politēs*. He is moderate insofar as he practiced the virtue of moderation and thereby preserved not only his own good judgment and lawfulness but also that of the constitutions he advanced as well. Like the *mesos*, Theramenes is a good citizen centrally concerned with maintaining lawfulness rather than wealth or freedom or honor but, unlike the *mesos*, he is also a "maker and adjudicator of the law," a model citizen and exemplary statesman, orienting Athens toward both democracy and oligarchy and neither, which is to say, toward the well-being of all.[46]

A Poetic History of Athens

The *AthPol* has two main parts. The first part offers a history of Athenian constitutional identity (chs. 1–41). In the words of Rhodes, "What is distinctive about the first half of *AthPol* is its purpose: to supply not a universal history or a history of a great war or even a general history of Athens, but a history of the *politeia* showing the stages by which it has developed to its present . . . form."[47] In this widely shared view, the first part of the *AthPol* is a story about the growing power of the demos in relation to the elite few, from Solon's time through to the radical democracy of the present day, in which, Aristotle says, "the people have made themselves masters of everything and administer everything through decrees of the Assembly and decisions of the law courts in which they hold the power" (41.2; also see 9, 10, 22.1, 23.1). By contrast, the second part of the *AthPol* sets out the condition of "the present constitutional order" (42.1, 42–69). To Rhodes, it "is the second part of the work which is more original," showing Aristotle to be not "a mediocre historian" but "a first class describer of constitutional practice."[48]

The usual view of the relation between the *AthPol*'s parts is that the text as a whole draws a "kind of graph of the progression, with

[46] Kraut 2002: 107, 383. Theramenes thus provides an example not of the best a human being can be but of the best sort of citizen.

[47] Rhodes 1981: 59.

[48] Rhodes 1981: 60. See also Keaney 1992: 4 (the second half is "Aristotle's innovation"); Whitehead 1993.

occasional regressions, of the Athenian constitution toward its culmination in the radical democracy of the late fifth and fourth centuries."[49] The text thus records a movement toward a particular *telos*, the end described in the second part, which becomes the driving interpretative tool for making sense of the constitutional history of the first part. That way of reading the *AthPol*, with its focus on the occurrence of particular events to explain changes in the structure and organization of power at Athens, offers, in the terminology of the *Poetics*, a "usual history" of Athenian constitutional development.

In our view, reading the *AthPol* as teleology so understood, in which the past is read in light of the present and the present is viewed as the culmination in a *telos*, does not capture the scope of Aristotle's normative theorizing in the *AthPol*. Aristotelian teleology is future oriented, to be sure. But insofar as the future depends on what is possible in the present, and insofar as what is currently possible depends on what has been, Aristotelian teleology is backward looking as well. The past must not only be read in the light of the present. The present and, indeed, the future must be read in the light of the past.[50] For this reason, the first part of the *AthPol* is, in our view, no less important an interpretative tool than is the second part. This is not to say that there is a specific future toward which the first part points. Rather, as we have argued, Aristotle's examination of Athens's past identifies possible pathways that might have led to a future for Athens quite different from the radical democracy it came to be. By recalling individual ways of living and actions exemplary of moderation and lawfulness in tumultuous settings, Aristotle's poetic history of Athens models ethical and political virtues that could have shaped and still can shape a better possible future.

Against this normative backdrop, Aristotle's neglect of Theramenes' missteps, attested to in other sources, becomes comprehensible.[51] If Aristotle's objective in the *AthPol* is to tell the story of Athens's

[49] Keaney 1992: 117.

[50] For discussion, see Frank 2005: 138–42.

[51] We might think of Aristotle's notion of poetic history as an effort to theorize the role of what Wolpert 2002: 87, has called "mindful forgetfulness" in the process of political change. But we must also be alert to the fact that the project of poetic history may involve the recovery of poorly remembered details. Aristotle's account in the *AthPol* of the end of the Peisistratid tyranny and his insistence on highlighting the forgotten role of Spartan military intervention and on downplaying that of the celebrated "tyrant slayers" Harmodius and Aristogeiton in the liberation of Athens from tyranny and founding of democracy are cases in point (17.1–19.6). See

constitution with a view to opening opportunities for actors to gain critical understanding coupled with an appreciation of the resources available for articulating new ideas and directing action (e.g., opportunities for "refounding" practices), he must achieve a "unity of plot," which, as he argues in the *Poetics*, is critically important when a work is to "describe, not the thing that has happened, but a kind of thing that might happen, i.e. what is possible" (1451a35–39). To produce this poetic history, Aristotle mines the record of "historic occurrences," eschewing some details and highlighting others (*Poetics* 1451b30).[52] Since figures are included only to advance an account of the significant action (1450a15–40), thorough character assessment is not appropriate here (1451a15–20). Rather, it is by focusing on actions and, specifically, on actions conducive to moderation and lawfulness as Aristotle understands them that Aristotle's history can point to opportunities for actors to accomplish Athens's refounding.[53] Aristotle's foregrounding of Theramenes' consistent commitments to lawfulness and moderation as key practices in the preservation and refounding of Athens's constitution is a paradigmatic example of this project.[54]

In addition to Theramenes, the ancestral constitution, and the Constitution of the Five Thousand, other key figures in this poetic history include Solon and Archinus, Nicias and Thucydides (the general, not the historian), and, most jarring and significant, the Athenian demos itself. Textual parallels between Theramenes, on the one hand, and Solon, Archinus, and the demos, on the other, bear out this claim. As he does with Theramenes, Aristotle describes all of these figures, including the Athenian demos, as "statesmanlike."[55] And, again as with

Monoson 2000: 49–50; and Mara 2002: 324–27, for discussions of the normative import of Aristotle's account of the tyrant slayers in the *AthPol.*

52 Translations from the *Poetics* are from McKeon 1941. See also discussion of these passages in Halliwell 1987: 105–7.

53 For an example of the kind of refounding based on a critical understanding of a polity's history and internal resources we have in mind, see Wills 1992 who argues that in the Gettysburg Address Lincoln sought to re-ground American self-identity firmly in the language of the Declaration of Independence ("We hold these truths to be self-evident . . .") instead of the Constitution (which permitted slavery) and thus give the nation, in the words of Lincoln's Address, "a new birth of freedom."

54 Cf. Raaflaub 2000: 31–34, who notes that Homer's Agamemnon, despite his earlier horrendous mistakes, is ultimately praised as "more just," having achieved a higher level of justice, because he has succeeded in overcoming the rift and uniting the community.

55 On the "statesmanship" of Solon see 7.1 and 11.2; of Nicias, Thucydides, and Theramenes see 28.5; of Archinus and the demos see 40.2.

Theramenes, he parses their political virtue in terms of their lawfulness and moderation, practiced to preserve not one particular Athenian regime or another but Athens's constitution itself. In the cases of Solon, Archinus, and the Athenian demos, as in the case of Theramenes, lawfulness and moderation do not mean obedience to the policies of one particular regime or another, nor do they mean molding Athens's policies so that they will appeal as much as possible to oligarchs and democrats alike. Instead, again as in the case of Theramenes, these virtues as practiced by Solon, Archinus, and the demos may involve acting against all extant policies and parties and "preferring to antagonize (or incur hatred from) both factions while saving the country and giving it the laws that were best for it, under the circumstances" (11.2 on Solon; 28.5 on Theramenes).

Quoting extensively from Solon's well-known poetry, Aristotle shows that Solon understood and self-consciously practiced lawfulness and moderation in precisely these ways:

> Firmly, I stood, holding out my strong shield over both of them and I did not allow either party to triumph over the other in violation of justice. (12.1)
>
> If I had been willing to do what pleased the enemies of the people at that time, or again what their opponents planned for them, this city would have been deprived of many of her sons. For this reason I had to set up a strong defense on all sides, turning around like a wolf at bay in the midst of a pack of hounds. (12.4)
>
> I set myself up as a barrier between the battleline of the opposing parties. (12.5)

It is notable that Aristotle quotes lines of poetry to celebrate the difficult practices of lawfulness and moderation central to the normatively rich poetic history presented in the *AthPol*.

Aristotle's brief but dramatic discussion of Archinus' actions during the amnesty that followed the restoration of democracy after the ouster of the Thirty (40.1–4) echoes his accounts of Solon and Theramenes. Aristotle explicitly states that Archinus "appears to have acted as a true statesman" (40.2) on three specific occasions, all of which concern advancing the cause of the reconciliation. First, he prevented oligarchs from emigrating to Eleusis by aborting the registration period, thus ensuring that they would remain members of the demos.

Second, he suspended a measure brought by Thrasybulus to grant citizenship to all foreigners in the democratic army, including slaves, which would have strengthened the power of the democratic exiles. Third, he was chiefly responsible for the summary arrest and execution of someone accused of violating the terms of the amnesty (40.1–3). In the words of one commentator, Archinus' actions show that "he was not prepared to let [technical] legality stand in the way of what he considered a wise decision."[56] While technically illegal, Archinus' actions demonstrate the lawfulness and moderation Aristotle takes to be necessary to preserve Athens's (at that time) fragile constitution.

Bearing consistent, though not consistently partisan, political identities, Solon and Archinus, like Theramenes, refuse to act out of set political predispositions: a prominent democrat, Archinus acted against not only oligarchic policies but democratic ones as well. A prominent oligarch, Theramenes acted against both democratic and oligarchic policies. Both, like Solon, rejected policies that they deemed unjust and that might further entrench constitutional factionalism. In so doing they moderated their regimes, preserved the lawfulness of Athens's constitution, and in these ways modeled the "education *pros tēn politeian*" Aristotle describes in the *Politics* (1310a20–25). In Mara's words, "A healthy political education does not overbreed the citizens in the regime's specific character, but instead fosters moderation, nourishing both civility and a decent way of living."[57] It is for thus negotiating the complexities of their immediate circumstances to admirable purpose, that Solon, Theramenes, and Archinus earn Aristotle's high praise.

Another key figure in Aristotle's poetic history of Athens merits mention, the Athenian demos itself. In the midst of his account of Archinus' (successful) efforts to support the amnesty, and using language anticipated in his treatments of Solon and Theramenes, Aristotle says, "It appears that their [the Athenians'] attitude both in private and in public in regard to the past disturbances was the most admirable and the most statesmanlike [*kallista dē kai politikōtata*] that any people have ever shown in such circumstances" (40.2). He goes on to explain what they did to deserve such praise, citing specifically the generous way in which

[56] Rhodes 1981: 477.

[57] Mara 2002: 311.

democrats treated what had only recently been an opposing domestic faction:

> For, apart from having wiped out all considerations of guilt in regard to past events, they [the demos] even refunded at common expense the money which the Thirty had borrowed from the Lacedaemonians for the war, though the agreement said that the two parties, namely, that of the city and that of the Piraeus, should pay their own debts separately. For they thought that this was the way to start the restoration of concord and harmony. (40.3–4)

During the extraordinary period of the amnesty, the Athenian demos acted so as to preserve Athens's constitution by endorsing only laws that effectively blocked the production of arbitrary power in one part of the citizenry over another.

Like Theramenes, Archinus, and Solon, the Athenian demos acted lawfully and moderately by acting against constitutional factionalism. The actions of the Athenian demos, amounting, in a sense, to their collective *bioi*, along with the actions of Solon, Theramenes, and Archinus making up their individual *bioi*, together form the plot of Aristotle's poetic history of *politikos* action, and thereby, in the tradition of writings *peri politeias*, track the development of the best *politeia*. These actors, alone and together, model the best way to act in accordance with a famous Solonian law requiring that in times of "violent political dissensions" citizens not withdraw but rather take part or suffer *atimia* (being stripped of political rights, *AthPol* 8.5).

Aristotle's use of Theramenes as an anchor in his examination of good statesmanship and citizenship in the *AthPol* echoes that of Thucydides in the *History*.[58] Describing Theramenes as someone "able in council as well as in debate" (*anēr oute eipein oute gnōnai adunatos*, 8.68.4) and detailing the matters about which Theramenes counseled and debated, Thucydides attributes to Theramenes at least three times a consistent and laudable commitment to meliorating conflict among domestic factions with a view to preserving Athens's constitution. Thucydides describes Theramenes as acting, in 411, to secure reconciliation and cooperation among determined oligarchs, disaffected

[58] Cicero, *Tusculan Disputations* 1.100, also speaks of Theramenes as someone "preeminently famous for virtue and wisdom" (trans. King 1945).

oligarchs, hoplites, and the people to safeguard Athens against Spartan occupation. In his account of Theramenes' initial support of the Four Hundred, Thucydides says that Theramenes, along with the Athenian demos, endorsed this constitutional change in the direction of oligarchy at that moment in the war because it was the best way to protect their sovereignty for the time being (8.54.1, with 8.68.4, cf. *AthPol* 29.1). And in his analysis of Theramenes' resistance to the corrupt and extreme elements of the Four Hundred and of his part in the establishment of the Five Thousand, Thucydides focuses on Theramenes' efforts to urge people to demolish the fortifications that the Four Hundred had ordered built because, in Thucydides' view, this wall "was not so much to keep out the army of Samos in case of its trying to force its way into the Piraeus as to let in, at pleasure, the fleet and army of the enemy" (8.90.3). This last episode gets considerable attention in the *History*. Thucydides discusses how the demos, hoplites, and disaffected oligarchs all responded to Theramenes' vigorous efforts to get them to act in concert to demolish the walls (8.92.10–93.2). Hewing to any partisan program in this context, Thucydides suggests, would have been to "ruin the polis and drive it into the arms of the enemy" (8.93). In sum, Thucydides' portrayal of Theramenes in Book 8 refuses to identify Theramenes with any particular constitutional form (whether oligarchic or democratic or mixed) and shows him instead to be, depending on the circumstances, a supporter of both and neither. Thucydides thus directs his readers to an appreciation of the unconventional ways, appropriate to periods of turmoil and panic (8.96.1), by which Theramenes reliably acted to preserve the Athenian *politeia* and to moderate civil discord.

Aristotle, similarly, focuses on Theramenes to consider what acting politically in an ethical manner under conditions of upheaval might mean both theoretically and practically. Exemplifying lawfulness and moderation that, by eschewing partisanship in times of factional turmoil, work to preserve Athenian constitutionalism, Theramenes, for Aristotle and for Thucydides too it seems, models individual and constitutional lived excellence.

Conclusion

When he introduces Theramenes in the *AthPol*, Aristotle underscores that his evaluation is contested (*AthPol* 28.5). He does the same when he discusses Solon and Archinus. Aristotle's candor is important. It flags the normativity of his history of Athens, reminds his readers that they are themselves judges, and prompts those readers familiar with the well-known details of Athens's past and its figures to ask why he nurtures certain memories to the exclusion of others. The answer to this question lies in understanding the project of the *AthPol* as a poetic history, one that both reports singular events and illuminates the universal significance of those events.

As we have argued, Aristotle's commitment to poetic history is evident in the substance of his story about Theramenes, specifically, in his characterizations of Theramenes' practice of citizenship, of the constitutions he claims Theramenes advocates, and in his association of Theramenes with constitutions past and future. It is evident as well in his treatments of Solon, Archinus, and the Athenian demos as a collectivity. The way in which these figures practiced citizenship is, in Aristotle's story, the way good citizens should, namely, moderately. The constitutions these figures advocated are, in Aristotle's story, what good constitutions should be, namely, lawful. By associating these figures with past and future constitutions, Aristotle shows that the practices that make these constitutions possible and the lawful procedures that inform them have been part of Athens's past and can be part of Athens's present and future as well.

Aristotle chooses to discuss Theramenes not because Theramenes' whole life is consonant with these exemplary acts but because he did indeed perform them. It might even be that Aristotle chose Theramenes in part because his missteps were so well known. Given this setting of cultural knowledge and in the context of Aristotle's candor regarding the contested character of his own treatment of Theramenes, Aristotle's neglect of Theramenes' misdeeds may be read as a reminder to his (imperfect) readers that it is possible, despite past and present missteps, to act well in relation to one's constitution. Indeed, Theramenes and the Athenian demos are particularly good examples for Aristotle's audience of the possibilities for ethical and political excellence during difficult times to some degree because other aspects of Theramenes' life along with Athens's alternating constitutions are markedly less savory. When Aristotle wrote the *AthPol*, neither Theramenes' actions nor the constitutions with which Aristotle associates these actions had been recognized for their possibility or realized. Challenging the memory of Athenian readers, Aristotle's commentary reveals to them the ways in which they could have and, more importantly, still can actualize their human and political possibilities. To thus recover practical ideals in the mode of poetic history requires remembering and, on occasion, a good measure of forgetfulness as well.

Seeing this normative recovery project as the main purpose of the *AthPol* clarifies the importance Aristotle attaches to the collection of constitutions he refers to at the end of the *Nicomachean Ethics* in the schematization of his political theory.[59] The *NE* concludes with the following question: "from whom or how [is] the science of legislation [to] be learnt?" (1180b30). Aristotle proposes that "those who aspire to a political science require practical experience as well as study" (*dio tois ephiemenois peri politikēs eidenai prosdein eoiken empeirias*, 1181a12–13). Study involves becoming familiar with collected laws and constitutions not as raw facts in a data set but as products of the art of politics (1181b1). Collections of laws and constitutions, this means, are only useful to students capable of "studying them critically" (*tois dunamenois theōrēsai kai krinai*, 1181b8–9). Using these materials of politics well and judging them correctly, Aristotle continues, requires a "practiced faculty" (*tois d'aneu hexeōs ta toiauta diexiousi to men krinein kalōs ouk an huparchoi*, 1181b10–11), the same faculty that, as we have seen, is required for the practice of politics itself. That faculty, possessed in Aristotle's *AthPol* by the most *politikos* statesmen and, on occasion, by the Athenian demos, is also, on our reading, the faculty Aristotle aims to train by his poetic history of the constitution of the Athenians, which is to say, by the *AthPol* itself.

Works Cited

Adeleye, G. 1973. "Theramenes and the Overthrow of the Four Hundred." *Museum Africum* 2: 77–80.

1976. "Theramenes: The End of a Controversial Career." *Museum Africum* 5: 9–19.

Bassi, K. 2000. "The Somatics of the Past: Helen and the Body of Tragedy." In *Acting on the Past: Historical Performance Across Disciplines*, ed. M. Franco and A. Richards. Hanover, NH.

Buck, R. J. 1995. "The Character of Theramenes." *Ancient History Bulletin* 9: 14–24.

Bury J. B., and R. Meiggs. 1975. *A History of Greece to the Death of Alexander the Great.* London.

Chambers, M. 1993. "Aristotle and his Use of Sources." In *Aristote et Athènes*, ed. M. Piérart. Fribourg.

Connor, W. R. 1977. "A Post Modernist Thucydides?" *Classical Journal* 72: 1289–98.

Davis, M. 1999. *The Poetry of Philosophy: On Aristotle's Poetics*. South Bend, IN. Originally published as *Aristotle's* Poetics: *The Poetry of Philosophy* (Lanham, MD, 1992).

Day J., and M. Chambers. 1962. *Aristotle's History of Athenian Democracy*. Los Angeles.

Ehrenberg, V. 1968. *From Solon to Socrates: Greek History and Civilization during the Sixth and Fifth Centuries* B.C. London.

[59] Translations in this paragraph are adapted from Rackham 1982 [1934].

Ehrhardt, C. 1995. "Lysias on Theramenes."*Ancient History Bulletin* 9: 125–26.

Ferguson, W. 1926. "The Constitution of Theramenes." *Classical Philology* 21: 72–75.

Finley, M. I. 1965. "Myth, Memory, and History." *History and Theory* 4: 281–302.

1975. *The Use and Abuse of History*. London.

Frank, J. 2005. *A Democracy of Distinction: Aristotle and the Work of Politics*. Chicago.

2006. "The Political Theory of Classical Greece." In *The Oxford Handbook of Political Theory*, ed. J. Dryzek, B. Honig, and A. Phillips. Oxford.

Fritz, K. von, and E. Kapp, trans. 1974 [1950]. *Aristotle: Constitution of Athens*. In *Aristotle's Constitution of Athens and Related Texts*. New York.

Fuks, A. 1975. *The Ancestral Constitution: Four Studies in Athenian Party Politics at the End of the Fifth Century* B.C. Westport, CT.

Gomme, A. W., A. Andrewes, and K. J. Dover. 1981. *A Historical Commentary on Thucydides*, vol. V, book VIII. Oxford.

Grote, G. 1890. *History of Greece*. New York.

Halliwell, S. 1987. *The Poetics of Aristotle: Translation and Commentary*. London.

2001. "Aristotelian Mimesis and Human Understanding." In *Making Sense of Aristotle: Essays in Poetics*, ed. O. Anderson and J. Haarberg. London.

Harding, P. 1974. "The Theramenes Myth." *Phoenix* 28: 100–11.

Harris, E. 1990. "The Constitution of the Five Thousand." *Harvard Studies in Classical Philology* 93: 243–80.

Henderson, J., trans. 2002. *Aristophanes: Frogs*. In *Aristophanes IV: Frogs; Assemblywomen; Wealth*. Loeb Classical Library. Cambridge, MA.

Hignett, C. 1952. *A History of the Athenian Constitution to the End of the Fifth Century* B.C. Oxford.

Kagan, D. 1987. *The Fall of the Athenian Empire*. Ithaca, NY.

Keaney, J. J. 1992. *The Composition of Aristotle's* Athenaion Politeia: *Observation and Explanation*. New York.

King, J. E., trans. 1945. *Cicero: Tusculan Disputations*. Loeb Classical Library. Cambridge, MA.

Kraut, R. 2002. *Aristotle: Political Philosophy*. Oxford.

Krentz, P. 1982. *The Thirty at Athens*. Ithaca, NY.

Lévy, E. 1993. "Politeia et politeuma chez Aristote." In *Aristote et Athèn*, ed. M. Piérart. Fribourg.

Mara, G. 2002. "The Culture of Democracy: Aristotle's *Athēnaiōn Politeia* as Political Theory." In *Aristotle and Modern Politics: The Persistence of Political Philosophy*, ed. A. Tessitore. Notre Dame, IN.

McCoy, W. J. 1997. "The Political Debut of Theramenes." In *Polis and Polemos: Essays on Politics, War and History in Ancient Greece in Honor of Donald Kagan*, ed. C. D. Hamilton and P. Krentz. Claremont, CA.

McKeon, R., ed. and trans. 1941. *The Basic Works of Aristotle*. New York.

Menn, S. 2006. "On Plato's *Politeia*." In *Proceedings of the Boston Area Colloquium in Ancient Philosophy*, vol. 21, ed. J. J. Cleary and G. M. Curtler. Boston.

Merkelbach, R. 1977. "Egoistic and Altruistic Motivation in Historiography: An Excursus to the Papyrus of Theramenes." *In Ancient and Modern: Essays in Honor of Gerald Else*, ed. J. H. D'Arms and J. W. Eadie. Ann Arbor, MI.

Monoson, S. S. 2000. *Plato's Democratic Entanglements: Athenian Politics and the Practice of Philosophy*. Princeton, NJ.

Munn, M. 2000. *The School of History: Athens in the Age of Socrates*. Berkeley, CA.

Newman, W. L. 1887. *The Politics of Aristotle with an Introduction, Two Prefatory Essays and Notes Critical and Explanatory*, vol. I. Oxford.

Ober, J. 1998. *Political Dissent in Democratic Athens: Intellectual Critics of Popular Rule.* Princeton, NJ.

Ostwald, M. 1989. *From Popular Sovereignty to the Sovereignty of Law: Law, Society, and Politics in Fifth-Century Athens.* Berkeley, CA.

Perrin, B. 1904. "The Rehabilitation of Theramenes." *American Historical Review* 9: 649–69.

Piérart, M., ed. 1993. *Aristote et Athènes.* Fribourg.

Raaflaub, K. 2000. "Poets, Lawgivers, and the Beginnings of Political Reflection in Archaic Greece." In *Cambridge History of Greek and Roman Political Thought*, ed. C. Rowe and M. Schofield. Cambridge.

Forthcoming. "Ulterior Motives in Ancient Historiography: What Exactly and Why."

Rackham, H., trans. 1982 [1934]. *Aristotle XIX: Nicomachean Ethics*, rev. ed. Loeb Classical Library. Cambridge, MA.

1977 [1932]. *Aristotle XXI: Politics.* Loeb Classical Library. Cambridge, MA.

1996 [1935]. *Athenian Constitution.* In *Aristotle XX: Athenian Constitution; Eudemian Ethics; Virtues and Vices.* Loeb Classical Library. Cambridge, MA.

Rhodes, P. J. 1981. *A Commentary on the Aristotelian* Athēnaiōn Politeia. Oxford.

Ste. Croix, G. E. M. de. 1992. "Aristotle on History and Poetry." In *Essays on Aristotle's Poetics*, ed. A. O. Rorty. Princeton, NJ.

Sandys, J. E. 1912 [1893]. *Aristotle's Constitution of Athens: A Revised Text with an Introduction, Critical and Explanatory Notes, Testimonia and Indices.* London.

Vlastos, G. 1952. "The Constitution of the Five Thousand." *American Journal of Philology* 73: 189–98.

Whitehead, D. 1993. "1–41, 42–69: A Tale of Two Politeiai." In *Aristote et Athènes*, ed. M. Piérart. Fribourg.

Wilamowitz, U. von. 1893. *Aristoteles und Athen.* Berlin.

Wills, G. 1992. *Lincoln at Gettysburg: The Words that Remade America.* New York.

Wolpert, A. 2002. *Remembering Defeat: Civil War and Civic Memory in Ancient Athens.* Baltimore, MD.

10: The Virtue Politics of Democratic Athens[1]

Ryan K. Balot

In the past three decades, contemporary Aristotelians have posed effective challenges to liberal theory by stressing the importance of citizenship, political virtue, civic prudence, and the political passions. Without denying the manifest goods made possible by the liberal political order, neo-Aristotelian theorists have argued that we can improve our understanding of political life by directing attention to the resource-rich tradition of Aristotelian political science. Dissatisfied with the apathy of liberal citizens, for example, Susan Collins has revived a specifically Aristotelian model of citizenship that is the product of authoritative civic education focused on seeking the human good.[2] Gerald Mara argues that the Rawlsian and Habermasian vision of "public reason" and the autonomy of political agents can be helpfully supplemented by the Aristotelian exploration of the passions that shape public rhetoric and communication.[3] Ronald Beiner has redeployed the Aristotelian concepts of *eudaimonia*, *phronēsis*, and virtue in order to criticize the subjectivism of liberal "values" and the emptiness of liberal neutrality.[4] Beiner's view is that active, Aristotelian citizenship focused on working out a shared human destiny is the best way to realize, in practice, our higher and distinctively human capacities for

[1] For their helpful comments and suggestions, I thank Edward Andrew, Matt Christ, Matt Edge, Alex Livingston, Clifford Orwin, Stephen Salkever, John Wallach, and an audience of students and colleagues in the Stanford Workshop in Political Theory, especially Chris Bobonich, Josh Cohen, and Josh Ober. All translations are my own unless otherwise indicated.

[2] Collins 2006.

[3] Mara 1985.

[4] Beiner 1992.

judgment.[5] Stephen Salkever theorizes an Aristotelian "ethics of natural questions" as a deliberative model superior to that offered by the typically Kantian exponents of deliberative democracy, such as Habermas.[6]

As a complement to such efforts, I propose to explore a prior, and in some sense rival, ancient tradition of "virtue politics," namely, that of democratic Athens. In addition to complementing the neo-Aristotelian "turn," democratic Athenians provide us with theoretical and imaginative resources that are largely unavailable within Aristotelian political science. These resources are two-fold. First, classical Athenian democrats espoused an unusual blend of virtue and individual freedom; democratic ideology promoted civic virtues while also self-consciously cultivating the public and private freedoms of Athens's citizens. Amidst his searing criticisms of "ancient freedom," even Benjamin Constant praised the democratic Athenians for respecting both the freedom of active political participation and the freedom from intrusion by the political authorities into what would now be called "private" life.[7] It is of particular interest for modern liberal democrats, as heirs to the great liberal tradition of freedom, to understand how the Athenians' language of political virtue could be balanced against and combined with an ideal of political and personal freedom. Instead of meditating, like their modern counterparts (Hobbes, Locke, etc.), on the relationship between freedom and political obligation, the Athenian democrats sought to work out a coherent synthesis of freedom and political virtue.[8] The Athenians' synthesis of freedom and virtue should recommend their case to us over the potentially competing claims to our attention made by either the Aristotelian or the republican traditions of virtue.

Second, by comparison with the Aristotelian alternative, analysis of Athenian political ideology brings us into closer contact with the concrete realities and contingent relationships of everyday political life.

[5] Cf. MacIntyre 1984, 1988.

[6] Salkever 2002; cf. Salkever 1974. I leave out of account here the equally compelling Aristotelianism of Martha Nussbaum (see Nussbaum 1988, 1993, and 2002), because Nussbaum is engaged in what might be called a "legislative," rather than a critical, effort. Like Rawls, Dworkin, and many other liberal theorists, Nussbaum approaches political theory as a means to guide political practice. By contrast, the Aristotelians mentioned here are engaged in a chiefly critical project. They do not aspire to reconcile Aristotelian theory with liberal theory or politics.

[7] Constant 1988 [1819].

[8] This is why a recent historical work on the relationship between freedom and obligation in classical Athens, studied through the prism of Rawlsian political theory, strikes me as anachronistic; see Liddel 2007.

Democratic Athenians debated questions of war and peace; they fought against specific internal threats such as corruption and apathy; they adjudicated particular legal cases between named individuals; and they deliberated with their fellow citizens about civic education, public expenditure, social welfare, and the conferral of public honors. Most interestingly for us, they grappled with ever-present tensions between leaders and ordinary citizens, which, on the face of it, was the manifestation of a deeper tension within the democratic ideal of equality. Could leaders have distinctive virtues in a democracy without compromising political equality? How could the Athenians both regulate disruptive political rivalries and promote desirable elite competition oriented toward the common good? For their questions as well as their answers, the Athenians' public conversations should be of great interest to theorists of virtue ethics and politics, who have paid perhaps insufficient attention to practical realities, legal cases, and political deliberations in which the virtues and vices were invoked in philosophically important ways.

When I speak of the Athenians' specifically democratic virtue politics, I mean the conceptions of political virtue that can be recovered from Athenian democratic ideology. The major source for this ideology is the corpus of Attic oratory. This corpus of roughly 150 speeches is widely acknowledged to be the most direct point of access to the democratic ideology and mentality of ancient Athens. These deliberative, forensic, and epideictic speeches were written and delivered by members of the Athenian elite to popular audiences consisting of ordinary Athenian citizens. As Ober has argued, these speeches were not instruments of elite rhetorical power over the Athenian demos.[9] Instead, they show members of the elite competing with one another for the favor of ordinary citizens. These speeches express a democratic ideology that promoted freedom, equality, and other characteristically popular ideals. They provide evidence of how popular ideals were publicly expressed within an institutional and cultural framework that truly expressed and promoted "people-power."

Before turning to Athenian democratic virtue (see The Democratic Model), I begin with a synthetic account of ancient and modern virtue theory. Because of the Athenians' own contact with the philosophical tradition, I find it most helpful to present "virtue theory" as it has been reconstructed by "virtue ethicists" working within the Aristotelian tradition, broadly construed (see Virtue Theory: A Sketch).

[9] Ober 1989.

The Athenians were not philosophers, to be sure, but their understandings of virtue and vice can be meaningfully illuminated by the virtue ethical tradition. As we shall see, the Athenians' own conversations about virtue provided the critical vocabulary and ethical landscape in which the Platonic and Aristotelian traditions could grow. In order to bring out what is distinctive about the democratic virtue tradition, I then offer several criticisms of Aristotelian and republican traditions of "virtue politics" (see Virtue Politics: Prospects and Criticisms) before turning to my own analysis of classical Athens. Ultimately, my goal is to show that democratic Athenians provide an attractive critical language with which to approach the many problems, as well as hopeful prospects, of contemporary political theory and political life.

Virtue Theory: A Sketch

"Virtue ethics" has recently recommended itself to a variety of normative ethical theorists who argue that virtue (as opposed to duties or consequences) provides the clearest and most plausible standard for evaluating moral behavior as well as the best way of accounting for and explaining our basic moral intuitions. Virtue (*aretē* in Greek) is a praiseworthy, enduring character trait (*hexis*) that disposes a person to make good moral choices for the right reasons.[10] Virtue requires habit formation and emotional education but is identical with neither habit nor emotion. To be sure, virtuous agents must act well with a full heart and with pleasure, rather than against their emotions or desires. Yet, in addition to possessing good habits and a healthy emotional life, the virtuous agent also rationally appreciates the grounds of his moral choices. He can rationally explain the intrinsic nobility of his behavior. Thus, virtue ethics presents a complex and realistic view of our moral psychology – the ways in which our emotions, desires, lasting states of character, and practical reason function together to produce correct moral behavior. In focusing on individual psychology and prudence, virtue ethical approaches give priority to moral agents over individual acts or specific rules of behavior.

[10] This section is based on my own readings in virtue ethical theory in the ancient and medieval traditions, supplemented by the helpful accounts of Annas 1993, 1998; Hursthouse 1999, 2003; Crisp 1996, as well as the studies cited in the next section. Unless otherwise indicated, all translations of Greek texts are my own, though I have consulted published translations, especially the volumes of the Loeb Classical Library, in preparing my own translations.

Building on their robust accounts of moral psychology, virtue ethicists locate virtue within a theory of the agent's overall good. Indeed, the central question of virtue ethics is, How should one live? Typically, the response that one should live virtuously is grounded in the belief that acting upon virtuous dispositions is an intrinsic part of the agent's own happiness or flourishing (*eudaimonia*). To substantiate the connection between character and *eudaimonia*, virtue theorists have recourse to a normative conception of nature: human flourishing consists in the activities of our properly developed, distinctively human, and natural capacities for moral and intellectual virtue. These natural capacities are social in orientation. We are naturally inclined, as human beings, to participate in group projects, to care about the well-being of others, and to deliberate with members of our community about justice.

Because they emphasize our natural sociability, virtue theories are not, as some have claimed, committed to egoism.[11] To use the ancient Greek idiom, the virtuous person behaves morally for the sake of the noble or fine (*to kalon*). Intrinsic concern for nobility was expressed in acting justly, generously, and thoughtfully out of care for others per se. The virtuous agent could live with self-respect only if he were the type of person who cared deeply about others for their own sake. He acts, on particular occasions, with the thought that he wants to benefit others, as (for example) Aristotle made abundantly clear in his discussion of friendship.[12] In reflecting on his behavior, the virtuous agent is proud to be the kind of person who characteristically behaves justly, generously, honestly, and moderately in the right way and for the right reasons.

Virtue Politics: Prospects and Criticisms

Is it possible to extend the foregoing characterization of virtue theory to politics? The example of democratic Athens suggests that the answer is yes. Classical Athenian democrats looked to the virtues to provide normative standards of moral appraisal. They emphasized practical judgment, the proper ordering of emotion, and the intrinsic value of the virtues as constituents of an overall desirable, flourishing condition of both individuals and the city. Accordingly, my own presentation of the Athenians' "virtue politics" will focus on the democratic understandings

[11] Hurka 2001: 219–55.

[12] Cf. *Eth. Nic.* 1155b31, 1166a2–4, with Kraut 1989: 78–86.

of character, education, emotion, practical reason, and human flourishing as they were represented in popular oratory of the fourth century B.C.E.

Despite the evident attractions of virtue theory for political philosophy, however, specialists in virtue ethics have not extended the theory to politics. Politics plays almost no role in the flurry of recent studies of ancient[13] and modern[14] virtue theory, despite the nearly universal ancient acknowledgment of the interconnectedness of ethics and politics. Aristotle's political theory, for example, was self-consciously informed by his ethical theory of the virtues (*Eth. Nic.* 10.9). Aristotle's "best polis" enables citizens to live flourishing human lives, through helping them develop their natural capacities for theoretical reflection, practical reasoning, and proper, or "healthy," moral decision making and praxis. It is arguably possible, indeed, to read Aristotle as sympathetically envisioning democracy as "a set of possibilities" in which the development of individual virtue could play a critical role in politics.[15]

Yet, despite their attraction to Aristotle's ethics, virtue theorists have hesitated to resuscitate Aristotelian political theory, because, even if Aristotle is the forefather of virtue ethics, his politics may be elitist and therefore unacceptable.[16] Despite ambitious recent attempts to democratize Aristotle,[17] and despite Aristotle's own optimism that democracies might be improved through inculcating virtue in citizens,[18] I, too, find Aristotle elitist in three ways. First, Aristotle's politics of virtue demanded an extremely high level of virtue among all citizens of his best polis. Aristotle's "best polis" (*Politics* 7–8) is a special aristocracy, a community of those who have cultivated their moral and intellectual powers to a highly advanced degree. It is unclear whether, in Aristotle's view, most people have the requisite moral talents. Second, along the same lines, some of Aristotle's particular virtues, such as "greatness of soul" (*megalopsuchia*), are quintessentially inappropriate to democratic politics because the great-souled man (*ho megalopsuchos*), for example, regards himself as superior to others and rightly (according to Aristotle) takes no serious account of his inferiors. As the Athenian democrats would have recognized instantly, the "superiority complex" of the great-souled man is an affront to democratic equality. Third, Aristotle's politics of

13 Gardiner 2005; Gill 2005; Casey 1990; White 2002; Prior 1991.

14 Darwell 2003; Statman 1997.

15 Salkever 1990: 219–26, 237–44.

16 Crisp and Slote 1997.

17 Ober 2005; Frank 2005.

18 Salkever 1990: 219–26; Frank 2005.

virtue requires extended leisure, which would rule out the participation of ordinary citizens – and possibly, in a pre-mechanized world, rule out all but the most exploitative classes. In these respects, Aristotle offers an aristocratic model of "virtue politics" that directly conflicts with our, and the Athenians', democratic aspirations. As John Wallach has argued, it may be difficult to detach Aristotelian theory from the elitist and anti-democratic philosophical thought-world in which it was initially created.[19]

This evaluation of Aristotle might also cast negative light on the republican traditions of civic virtue, since Aristotle has long, and with some legitimacy, been considered the father of the republican tradition.[20] However, the developed republican theories of Polybius, Cicero, Livy, Sallust, and their early modern followers arguably provide a different, non-Aristotelian, and more plausible theory of civic virtue. The chief attraction of their theories is their egalitarianism. Modern "civic humanists" such as Hannah Arendt,[21] as well as contemporary "civic republicans,"[22] have, indeed, turned to this tradition in order to understand how the civic virtues might contribute to an attractive picture of republican freedom.

By comparison with the Athenian politics of virtue, however, the republican tradition faces distinctive problems of its own. The ancient republican virtues have rightly been criticized for furthering the causes of sexism and bellicosity.[23] Perhaps cooperating with traditional republican militarism, the republican tradition – even in its most "updated" forms – tends to reflect the conservative Roman virtues, such as obedience, respect for authority, deference, and traditionalism. These qualities have often been counted as virtues because they support representative institutions. As Benjamin Barber has said, however, "The trouble with representative institutions is that they often turn the act of sovereign authorization into an act of civic deauthorization. . . . Under the representative system, leaders turn electors into followers; and the correct posture for followers is deference."[24]

[19] Wallach 1992.

[20] Pocock 1975.

[21] Arendt 1958.

[22] Pettit 1997; Skinner 1978, 1998.

[23] Salkever 1990: 165–204. It is worth noting that certain contemporary republicans still lay claim to heroic self-overcoming, obedience, manliness, reverence for tradition, and respect for the authority of leaders (see Pangle 1998, and, on manliness, Mansfield 2006).

[24] Barber 1998: 98.

It takes substantial work for republican theorists to think their way out of such quandaries. Rejecting deference and docility, for example, Barber himself urges that the appropriate republican remedy for citizen passivity is to develop civic competence and to promote democratic participation.[25] Such a move would be true to the traditional republican view that freedom consists in self-government. At the same time, though, Barber also endorses analogies for leadership that would have been understandably repugnant to ancient Athenians. The "facilitating leader," he declares, is "more the teacher than the administrator, the judge than the legislator, the therapist than the surgeon."[26] However, Athenian citizens, like their modern liberal counterparts, would bristle at the thought of being "improved" by a civic therapist. Despite its claims to egalitarianism, the republican tradition has always promoted hierarchies of political participation based on a belief in unequal political talent. This is perhaps why civic republicans[27] place little emphasis on cultivating the individual judgment of citizens.

The Democratic Model

The democratic Athenians provide a strong challenge to all the previously canvassed accounts of civic virtue. By contrast with Aristotle's aristocratic model, the Athenians cultivated excellence of character and practical reasoning in all citizens, including the very poor, and they could rationally explain why their egalitarian extension of virtue was possible. The Athenians' "virtue politics" makes clear, moreover, that civic republicans do not sufficiently emphasize individual judgment, autonomy, flexibility, the willingness to take initiative, and an openness to innovation – in other words, the virtues of a more radical, more truly egalitarian, more individualistic, and – in a word – more *democratic* conception of the virtues. By contrast with liberal theorists of virtue,[28] finally, the Athenians illustrate that substantive judgments about human goodness can be presented in public life without compromising freedom. And by contrast with both republican and liberal theorists, but in agreement with Aristotle, the Athenians could plausibly explain why

[25] Barber 1984, 1998: 109–10; cf. Sandel 1996.
[26] Barber 1998: 103.
[27] E.g., Pettit 1997.
[28] E.g., Galston 1991; Macedo 1990, 2000.

the exercise of virtue was intrinsically valuable for the moral agent, as well as useful for his community.

If we as modern democrats value the autonomous exercise of the virtues but also aspire to temper individualism and innovation with moderation and respect for others, then our best bet for finding the resources for a meaningfully democratic "virtue politics" comes neither from Aristotle nor from the republican theorists, but rather from the radical, individualistic Athenian democracy. Like the republicans, the Athenians valued patriotism, loyalty to the city, and democratic leadership. Yet, through cultivating the good judgment of citizens as individuals, the Athenians were able to unite their traditional patriotic virtues with the virtues of autonomy and innovation, so as to produce an attractive and distinctively democratic model of virtue politics. Democratic virtue politics provided both for public-spirited motives for action and for the private choices and friendships of individuals aspiring to lead a well-conceived, flourishing life. The proper balance could be attained only through the citizens' individual judgments of complex particulars. As virtue theorists rightly emphasize, a central component of the exercise of virtue is rational judgment in particular situations of moral complexity. The Athenian democracy strove to develop the rational faculties of each individual citizen and called forth each citizen's practical judgment in complex deliberations. In its emphasis on individual judgment, the Athenian democracy promoted radically egalitarian forms of intellectual autonomy, self-reliance, and individuality.

In traveling backward in time to ancient Athens, however, one must ever keep in mind the differences between the classical Athenian democracy and our own, so as to avoid any naïve faith that Athenian ideology or praxis could easily be brought to bear on our own political life.[29] Classical Athens was a slave-holding polis with a citizen body of roughly 60,000 adult men at its height; it practiced no separation of "church" and "state"; it was pre-Christian and polytheistic and had no knowledge of the seventeenth-century religious and political controversies in which liberal ideology was initially forged; it excluded women from political life; it was a direct democracy; and it placed a very high, some would say excessively high, value on political participation.

Yet, for all these differences, classical Athens can be educational for us because, as a democracy, its chief values were freedom and equality; it took justice to be not only the "first virtue of social institutions," as

[29] Constant 1988 [1819]; Holmes 1979.

Rawls would have it,[30] but also the chief social virtue of individuals; it valued the rule of impartial law; it envisioned citizen participation, public deliberation, and reflective patriotism as democratic ideals; and it respected the distinction between public and private. The Athenian political community had thick moral and educational commitments that were, nonetheless, not parts of a thoroughly "monistic" conception of the good. And the Athenians had standards that were flexible, capacious, and dependent upon individual judgment in particular circumstances. None of this is to say that we should take over the Athenians' values for ourselves without revision. We cannot do so. But we can find in the Athenian virtue politics a practical, and largely successful, example of the attempt to square virtue politics with freedom. This alone should make the Athenian case good to "think with."

Negative Evaluations of Democracy

Why have previous students of political life shied away from the virtue politics of democratic Athens?[31] In order to clear the ground of certain common misconceptions, it is worth considering the following "error theory." Theorists have refused to regard the Athenian case as exemplary because of the ancient philosophers' and ancient republicans' suspicion of democratic freedom. More precisely, ancient philosophers and ancient republicans wondered how the Athenians could ever have aspired to provide an education to virtue, given their democratic inclination to locate freedom at the top of their table of social ideals. Critics of democracy accused democrats of fostering an overly tolerant, indulgent lifestyle that shunned any rigorous cultivation of virtue.[32] Ancient democracy was truly "people-power." As positive as this characterization may sound, many ancient thinkers identified excessive and arbitrary people-power as democracy's biggest problem. As a Herodotean character explains, "The masses are a feckless lot – nowhere will you find more ignorance or irresponsibility or violence" (3.81, tr. De Selincourt, rev. Marincola).

[30] Rawls 1971.

[31] To my knowledge, only one other recent theorist has taken this approach to ancient virtue: see Wallach 1994, which discusses Athenian democratic virtue and its relation to America's democratic possibilities, specifically with reference to Pericles' Funeral Oration from Thucydides' *History* and Protagoras' Great Speech from Plato's *Protagoras*.

[32] Ober 1998; Roberts 1994.

It was in the writings of Plato, above all, that such criticisms were elevated to a systematic critique of the democrats' neglect of virtue. In the *Republic*, for example, Plato criticized democracy for its tolerance toward criminals (558a), for its lack of attention to moral education (558b), and for its development of an excessively appetitive and disorderly citizenry (561b–d). To the extent that the Athenian Empire was a projection of specifically democratic power, these problems were amplified to an extraordinary degree by the Athenians' successful fifth-century imperialism. In the Platonic *Gorgias*, Socrates criticized Athens' leaders for indulging the citizens' self-destructive desires for "harbors and dockyards and walls and tribute and other such nonsense without justice and temperance." Although the Athenians viewed these possessions as a sign of their greatness, they had in fact acquired something more like a "tumor, scabbed over and festering," which would lead inevitably to a "fit of weakness" (518e–519a, tr. Allen). Examples from Platonism and other ancient philosophical traditions could readily be multiplied. The central point is that the democrats' inattention to virtue, and their overemphasis on freedom, established a self-defeating, and even self-destructive, politics that eventually led Athens to ruin. The narrative of Athenian moral degeneration had its origins in the centuries when democratic Athenians were self-consciously striving to assert their own vision of the politics of virtue.

Through Polybius, Cicero, and others, the Platonic criticisms of democracy became firmly established within traditional republican theory. Republican theorists (even to the present day) have always set up an opposition between the republican cultivation of civic virtue – particularly the Spartan and Roman virtues of austerity, discipline, order, and respect for tradition – and the disorder and rashness of (direct) democracy. As an admirer of Rome, for example, the second-century B.C.E. historian Polybius advanced his case by criticizing Athenian democracy on the grounds that its "national character" was unstable, its populace was "headstrong and spiteful," and its decisions were made on the basis of the "random impulses" of the "masses" (*Histories* 6.44, tr. Scott-Kilvert). For Polybius, the democratic character contrasts sharply with the republican courage and self-discipline of the Spartans (6.48) and the still more impressive bravery, patriotism, honesty, and self-control of the Romans (6.53–56). The American Founders, picking up on Polybian and Ciceronian *topoi*, often praised the "manly spirit" and nobility of the new American republic, anxiously distinguishing its brand of politics from that of the turbulent, factious, and oppressive ancient democracies (e.g., *Federalist* 10, *Federalist* 14).

Honoring the Virtues of Leaders in Democratic Athens

Democratic Athenians had a straightforward response to all of these charges – no contest. For the Athenians legitimately saw themselves as fostering both individual autonomy and initiative, on the one hand, and self-control, orderliness, and respect for law on the other. They viewed democratic practice as the school of civic virtue.

Our best sources for unearthing the democratic virtues are the popular genres of classical Athenian literature, including comedy, tragedy, and oratory, along with publicly funded inscriptions carved into stone. Perhaps the most "demotic" conceptions can be elicited from such inscriptions, since they provided the most unmediated access we have to the multifarious voices of the Athenian people. These inscriptions enable us to identify the "cardinal virtues" of the classical Athenian democracy.[33] Chief among these were the virtues of piety, moderation, good order, patriotism, and, in general, "manly virtue" (*andragathia*). This latter was a catch-all democratic coinage that captured the essential qualities held up for admiration by the Athenian community.[34] Its sexist implications are undeniable. Yet, to the extent that its core concept was the virtue of courage, it implied less the hotheaded bellicosity of the republican tradition than a thoughtful, rationally informed exercise of inner fortitude.[35] This emphasis on thoughtfulness and judgment gave the Athenians' virtues altogether a distinctive cast.

To dig more deeply into the Athenians' ways of locating these virtues within political life, we must turn to the narratives and analyses found in literary sources, particularly fourth-century Attic oratory. Like the inscriptions, the Attic orators often focused on the Athenian aristocracy, and they ascribed virtue chiefly to those of high social and political standing. Yet they still offered a specifically democratic conception of the virtues because, as we shall see, even the highest-level Athenian leaders presented themselves as "middling" (*metrios*) citizens whose outlook and even lifestyle corresponded fully to those of their ordinary fellow citizens.[36] They represented their virtues as exemplary rather than different in kind from those of other citizens. Their self-presentation along these lines was an outgrowth of the Athenians' emphasis on legal and political equality. Aristocrats did not enjoy any formal legal privileges, and they were held strictly accountable to the ordinary citizens. Thus,

[33] Whitehead 1993.

[34] Pritchett 1974: 280–83.

[35] Balot 2001, 2004, 2004a, forthcoming.

[36] Ober 1989; Morris 2000.

despite necessarily cultivating good leaders, Athens was far less hierarchical than Sparta or Rome, antiquity's two most famous republics. It was also less hierarchical than most modern democratic nation-states, including the Republic theorized by the American Founders.

In order to illustrate the democratic ideology of virtue in practice, I propose to examine two speeches in which Aeschines and Demosthenes, toward the end of their careers, debated their respective services to the city. The occasion was perfect for such a retrospective. In 336 B.C.E., an Athenian citizen, Ctesiphon, had moved that Demosthenes be awarded a golden crown for his leadership after the Athenians' defeat at the Battle of Chaeronea (338 B.C.E.). Aeschines attacked this motion as illegal, but, for reasons that remain unclear, the case came to trial only six years later. Despite the technical nature of Aeschines' charges, Aeschines' main purpose was to discredit the honorific presentation of Demosthenes as singularly virtuous and useful to the city (Aeschin. 3.49–50). In scrutinizing Demosthenes' character, Aeschines was not interested in specific actions, but rather in criticizing Demosthenes' career and life as a whole, including his private life (3.51–53, 77–78). The real object of the trial was to figure out what kind of man Demosthenes was (cf. Dem. 18.297–323) and by extension what kind of city Athens aspired to be when it honored such men (3.247). In response, Demosthenes delivered his *On the Crown*, an extended analysis of his virtues and Aeschines' vices. A cross section of ordinary democratic citizens, including the very poor, was called upon to analyze the arguments of these leaders, to reflect on their conceptions of virtue and vice, and to render judgment as political equals.

In his criticisms of the original motion, Aeschines exhorted the ordinary citizens to exercise their rational judgment regarding the standards of virtue and vice. He criticized contemporary Athenians for awarding crowns too easily, on the basis of habit rather than careful thought and deliberation (3.178), and out of deference to self-aggrandizing leaders rather than out of appropriate self-respect (3.183–87). Virtue was a social practice of character penetrated by the rational judgments of Athenian citizen-equals. The citizens' judgments were particularly important because awards for virtue had to satisfy objective, non-relative standards that the community as a whole discovered through collective practical reasoning. As Aeschines declared, "[F]or those who claim a crown, the standard is virtue itself (*autēn tēn aretēn*)" (Aeschin. 3.189, tr. Adams). However, making judgments had political and ethical significance that went beyond the particular verdict in question. In its honorific practices, the democratic community played a critical role in stimulating virtue (3.180) and in maintaining the civic loyalty of Athens' best citizens (3.47), or, if it judged badly, in corrupting decent people (3.180). Democratic honorific practices both depended on, and helped to educate, the citizens' capacities to make rational judgments within, and in support of, their own deliberately chosen ethical frameworks.

To explain his conception of the cardinal democratic virtues, Aeschines enumerated the characteristics of the demotic (*tōi dēmotikōi*) and moderate (*sōphroni*) man (not "leader"), by contrast with those of the typically worthless oligarchic man (*ton oligarchikon anthrōpon kai phaulon*) (Aeschin. 3.168–70). He took himself to be outlining the distinctively democratic features of such virtues; the virtues of democratic Athenians were generically similar to those of other Greeks, but the Athenian orators argued strenuously that democracy produced distinctive versions of these virtues because of its public practices of rational deliberation.[37] The praiseworthy democratic citizen, he argued, must be a man of good judgment (*eugnōmona*). He must also possess durable states of character that enable him to serve the demos wholeheartedly, without being emotionally distracted by the competing claims of his family, his own excessive desires for money or luxury, or fear for his own safety (3.169–70). The truly virtuous democrat should not face internal conflict tending to make him disloyal; therefore, perfect virtue was rare and laudable (3.179–80) and was not equivalent to self-mastery (*enkrateia*).

This demanding criterion – wholeheartedness based on internal psychological order – depended both upon a correctly ordered set of emotions and upon a cluster of allied virtues that shored up the citizen's self-conscious dedication to the political community. The democratic man should, Aeschines said, have the courage to act and speak on behalf of the people so as to avoid preferring his own narrowly construed good to the city's welfare (e.g., 3.160, 163, 167, 170, 175–76, 214). All the Attic orators emphasized the citizens' appropriate emotional responses, such as feeling a proper degree of anger toward the hostile behavior of other states (Dem. 8.57) and toward non-virtuous fellow citizens (Lys. 10.28–29, 18.19), feeling a sense of shame that motivates honorable behavior (Dem. 8.51, 17.23), and feeling appropriate levels of fear (Dem. 11.15–16, 15.23). In this trial particularly, Demosthenes reproached Aeschines for not having the same normatively appropriate feelings as

[37] I have argued this case with reference to the Athenians' democratic "courage" (*andreia*) in Balot 2001, 2004, 2004a, and forthcoming.

the ordinary citizens (18.292); Aeschines rejoiced, for example, when others grieved over the Athenians' defeat at Chaeronea (18.286–87). By contrast, the Athenian demos chose Demosthenes to deliver the funeral oration over those who had died at Chaeronea because they recognized that Demosthenes would not feign grief like an actor, but rather "feel pain together with them in his soul" (*tēi psuchēi sunalgein*) (18.287).

Throughout his speech, Demosthenes recalled the honorific terminology of Ctesiphon's original motion in order to pinpoint the wholeheartedness of his democratic virtue. He had always acted with *eunoia* (loyalty, patriotism) and *prothumia* (eagerness, zeal) on behalf of the city (18.57, 110; 18.286; cf. 18.312). *Prothumia* consisted in a willingness to take initiative, to accept personal responsibility, and to stand up and pursue the city's welfare actively, in the right way, and for the right reasons (cf. Dem. 38.26). *Prothumia* might initially appear to be an odd virtue, but it captures, in a way characteristic of virtue ethical frameworks, the combination of properly ordered emotions, states of character, and well-informed practical reasoning.

To prove his point, Demosthenes told the story of his own courage (18.72, 136, 173), integrity (18.62–65), intelligence (18.69–71), and nobility (18.69–70) in encouraging the Athenians to live up to the city's highest ideals of noble self-sacrifice, generosity toward others, and protection of the Greek community as a whole (18.53–109, 18.160–251).[38] In all his political actions, moreover, Demosthenes was supported by the noble character and rational deliberations of the Athenian citizens themselves (18.86). Thus, in response to Aeschines' criticisms of his character, Demosthenes accepted the demanding standard of showing that his entire life conformed to the Athenians' standards of loyalty, zeal, courage, and nobility, because he, too, accepted that noble character traits must be deep and abiding features of character, which are exhibited over the course of one's life as a whole (e.g., Dem. 18.10, 297–323).

If the Athenian account is to hold any promise for us, however, then the ancient democrats must explain why the virtues, as such, not only benefited the city, but also contributed to the virtuous agent's *own* flourishing. In the rhetorical context, of course, Demosthenes could not appeal to his own self-interest in explaining the importance of virtue. Yet, in the course of his narrative, Demosthenes shows that he clearly regarded virtue as an intrinsic part of his own and the city's flourishing. Specifically, Demosthenes showed that his and the city's

[38] Cf. Yunis 2001.

self-respect depended on behaving nobly because nobility was central to their self-image, all the way down and without remainder (18.95–101). In reviewing the decision to fight Philip at Chaeronea, Demosthenes argued that, despite the eventual Athenian defeat, the decision to go to war was correct in light of the city's self-image and thus its own properly understood self-interests (18.174–80, 199–210). Even if defeat had been certain at the outset, the city nonetheless *had* to go to war for its own freedom as a matter of pride, nobility, and self-respect. This thought explains why virtue was *intrinsically* a part of living well: the Athenians could not live with self-respect unless they did things "worthy of the city," as they often put it, *whatever the consequences* (18.178).

This idea was obviously important for Demosthenes' present argument against Aeschines, since his advice had led to the Athenians' devastating defeat at Chaeronea. Yet such sentiments were common in Attic oratory and were typically fleshed out in a speaker's emphasis on protecting "our fatherland, our life, our customs, our liberty, and all things of that sort," as well as ancestral traditions and graves (Dem. 14.32), even if this meant death in combat. Living with self-respect was a necessity for free Athenian democrats because without it life would be slavish and thus worthless, a disgrace in the sight of the Athenians' ancestors (Dem. 8.51, 11.22, 13.35, 17.3).[39]

In order further to explain the intrinsic goodness of virtue, Demosthenes declared that his loyalty to the city was so deeply entrenched and valuable as to be natural (18.321).[40] He did not mean that virtue came easily or without benefit of civic education, or that he viewed himself as part of an organic whole, like a limb moved by the body politic. Rather, Demosthenes' self-conception, all the way down, was that of a rationally ordered individual who voluntarily conferred benefits on his city out of a rational appreciation that his own flourishing condition depended on his exercise of the civic virtues.[41] He summed up his own naturalistic understanding of virtue by admiringly evoking the natural sociability of the outstandingly virtuous Athenians of the past:

> They [our forefathers] did not think life worth living, unless they could live freely. For each one of them thought that he had been born not only to his father and mother, but also

39 Cf. Williams 1993.

40 Cf. Aeschin. 3.275 and Loraux 1986: 150–55, 172–74.

41 Cf. Balot 2001.

> to his fatherland. What is the difference? That the one who thinks he has been born only to his parents waits around for death when it comes, all on its own, on the appointed day, whereas the one born to his fatherland will die willingly in order to avoid seeing his native land enslaved, and he will consider the violence and dishonor which an enslaved polis must suffer to be more fearful than death. (Dem. 18.205)

Two points militate against the idea that Demosthenes' admiration for the ancestors' patriotism had either totalitarian or chauvinistic implications. First, as he says, every one of the ancestors was born *both* to his parents *and* to the city, and so the duty of each one was to achieve a proportionate balance between private and public concerns; this balance would be an outgrowth of his nature, perfected by civic education, and it would come to sight as an intrinsic feature of the sort of man he was. According to Demosthenes, every one of the ancestors maintained the proper balance between public and private through his own reasoned judgments about what self-respect required of him. Second, as Alasdair MacIntyre has argued, we should distinguish between those dedicated to their fatherland for the sake of its noble ideals and those dedicated to their fatherland simply or chiefly because it is *theirs*.[42] Demosthenes was certainly no cosmopolitan idealist recommending a way of life for all and sundry to follow, whatever their cultural background, yet his idealistic account of Athens's justice and nobility (e.g., 18.203–5)[43] also reduces the potentially chauvinistic implications of his dedication to the city. Like Demosthenes, the Athenians' ancestors were not blind supporters of the city, come what may. Instead, they furthered the cause of the city because they self-consciously believed that Athens was committed to justice, security, and benevolence throughout the Greek world.

One might also criticize the Athenians' self-image, as expressed in these speeches, as self-serving or ideological, or as simply phony and unrealistic in practice. Yet, even if the Athenians failed to live up to their own ideals, and even if they, like all other political agents, pursued their own interests too selfishly, their normative virtue politics is promising for two reasons. First, their language of the virtues helped them understand and appraise the psychological structure – including emotions, character, and practical reasoning – of political motivations

[42] MacIntyre 1995: 210–11.

[43] Cf. 18.66–68 with Yunis 2001: 150–51, 221–22.

in a more realistic way than conceptions of political morality based on duties, utility, or consequences pure and simple. Second, their virtue politics enabled them to explain how virtuous political behavior was also beneficial to individual political agents through the medium of concepts of self-respect and nobility. Individuals believed, plausibly and reasonably, that they could live with self-respect only if they showed appropriate care for others and for their political community.

Even so, if modern democrats are interested in finding imaginative resources in Athenian political ideology, then they might reasonably wish to soften the Athenians' apparent emphasis on the "primacy of politics."[44] Before this point looms too large, however, we should observe that the preceding discussion has examined the speeches of dedicated career politicians. These men voluntarily chose politics as a vocation and were discussing their lives in a forensic context that led them to emphasize patriotism. There were certainly *other* discussions of Athenian life in which the private goods of friendship, intellectual cultivation, and family life were prominent themes. And, as Josiah Ober has argued, Athenian society was one of "thin coherence" rather than thick identification.[45] Like certain contemporary republican theorists,[46] the Athenians regarded political engagement as one among many essential elements of a flourishing life. In an "updated" form, perhaps, their view would suggest that the relative primacy of politics ought *itself* to be a matter of individual and public deliberation.

Virtues of Athens' Democratic Citizenry

If leaders were supposed to be exemplary moral and political agents, then can we also find ways in which the democratic virtues were visible in the citizenry at large? If the Athenians did not envision ordinary citizens as virtuous, then we will be left either with Aristotle's aristocratic account or with the hierarchical republican models. The Athenians managed this problem through exemplarity: the fourth-century Athenian speeches regarded the leaders' virtues as applicable to ordinary citizens, too. Using the famous ship-of-state image, for example, Demosthenes exhorted his fellow citizens, "So long as the ship is safe, whether it is large or small, then it is necessary for the sailor and the pilot and every man in succession to work zealously, and to see to it that no

44 Cf. Rahe 1992; Constant 1988 [1819].

45 Ober 2005.

46 Sandel 1998: 323–27.

one capsizes the ship either voluntarily or through negligence" (Dem. 9.69). The exemplarity of the leaders' other virtues is also illustrated (for example) by the prominence accorded to the ordinary citizens' courageous acts of patriotism throughout the corpus of Attic oratory (e.g., Lys. 10.24–25, Dem. 4.42–43, 60.25–26; Hyp. 6.24–25).

Even though democratic citizens admired many virtues, including justice (*dikē* or *dikaiosunē*), piety (*eusebeia*), and military courage (*andreia*),[47] it is worth concentrating on apparent cases of conflict among the virtues. Examining the apparently antithetical virtues of order and autonomy will help us uncover the importance of practical reasoning in the democratic conception of virtue. Considering this pair of "virtuous opposites" also offers us an exceptional opportunity to see how the ancient democratic polis both utilized virtue as a mode of social control and recognized in virtue the means to promote voluntary individual effort and the production of new ideas.

As if responding to democracy's "law-and-order"-hungry critics, democratic litigants frequently made reference to the "good order" (*kosmos*) of the normatively decent (*metrios*) democratic citizen. In his well-known defense speech, for example, a certain Euphiletus explained to an Athenian jury that he had rebuked his wife's adulterer for lawlessly indulging his desires rather than choosing "to obey the laws and to be orderly (*kosmios einai*)" (Lys. 1.26). Euphiletus explicitly exhorted the jurors to feel appropriate anger and indignation on his behalf and, contrary to democracy's critics, he remarked on the unlikelihood of their being tolerant in responding to such outrageous criminals (1.1–2). The entire community had a stake in enforcing standards of orderliness in individual souls because only thus could the citizens defend the laws against established wrongdoers (Lys. 1.16–17, 47–50). The jurors' normative anger in rendering severe, yet fair, verdicts would make citizens more disciplined and orderly (*kosmiōterous* or *sōphronesterous*) in the future (Lys. 14.9–14, 15.9–10).

In a parallel argument focused on the consequences of private pleasure seeking, Aeschines charged his rival Timarchus with prostitution and argued that his contempt for the law and for self-control had conditioned his soul to be disorderly and his lifestyle to be correspondingly immoderate.[48] Excessive pleasure seeking tends to destroy democracy; consequently, the ordinary citizens must educate the young to

[47] Cf. Whitehead 1993.

[48] Aeschin. 1.189; Roisman 2005: 192–99; Fisher 2001: 115.

virtue (Aeschin. 1.189–91). These cases show that good order (*kosmos*) and moderation (*sōphrosunē*) were virtues that called forth a sense of shame. If they lacked psychological order but had not been thoroughly corrupted, Athenians would be embarrassed when they failed to live up to rationally informed social ideals of good order. In this way, the democratic virtues were a means for the community to hold individuals accountable for their behavior (cf. Lys. 3.45). Shame-driven accountability was a last resort, to be deployed only after the Athenians had done their best to educate individuals properly with a view to their voluntarily embracing the city's laws and unpublished norms.

Yet, alongside the punitive implications of these latter two evocations of "good order," explicit discussions of psychological order also had a positive, productive dimension. Fortified by the democratic understanding of good order, individuals had the cognitive resources to understand what it meant to live with self-respect. For example, a certain Mantitheus tried to withstand his scrutiny for office by demonstrating his courage and military discipline, which he described with reference to good order: "I never fell short on any other expedition, or when I was assigned to guard-duty; I have always followed my practice of marching out in the front rank and retreating in the last. On the basis of such evidence, you must judge which citizens carry out their civic duties with a proper concern for honor (*philotimōs*) and in an orderly way (*kosmiōs*)" (Lys. 16.18). In this case, Mantitheus overcame his fear of death and fought courageously and energetically as a sign of his well-functioning soul and his psychological commitment to the city. Psychological order, as we saw in Demosthenes' case, was a prerequisite of the internal harmony that enabled individuals to exert themselves wholeheartedly in civic causes with which they had good reasons to identify.

Whether the virtues of good order were held to be a constraint or a catalyst, the examples we have just examined show that, in their political life, democratic Athenians paid due attention to the psychological formation of citizens. The healthy political functioning of the city depended on the civic education of citizens and then the maintenance of their souls in a proper and healthy condition. The intimate connection between healthy politics and rationally ordered souls is illustrated in the frequent argument that the disorderly behavior of a single individual could irrevocably damage the good order embodied in Athenian law and maintained by the citizens' good nature, public-spirited habits, and civic friendship (Dem. 25.20–26; Lyc. 1.147–48). As a result, democratic Athenians had strong motivations to reform disorderly souls and, at the limit, to punish disorderly behavior. No audience member of Demosthenes' speech against Aristogeiton could accept the philosophers' charge that democracy was overly tolerant:

> Consider, by the gods: if everyone in the city acted with the daring and shamelessness of Aristogeiton, and calculated, like this man, that in a democracy everyone can say and do whatever he wishes, bar nothing, if only he neglects his general reputation in doing such things, and that no one will execute him straightaway for any wrongdoing; if, with these ideas in mind, a citizen who failed to obtain an office by lot or to be elected should seek to be on a par with the one chosen or elected, and to share in the same honors, and if, altogether, neither the young nor the old should do their duty, but each one, driving all order from his life, should take up his own wish as law, as first principle, as everything – if we acted this way, could we govern the city? What? Would the laws have any authority? How much violence, arrogance, and lawlessness do you think would arise in the city each and every day? (Dem. 25.25–26)

Athenians saw themselves as cultivating virtue in the souls of all mature citizens and young, prospective citizens through the demos's public activities – the activities, in particular, of rendering verdicts, of honoring and punishing, praising and blaming, and erecting exemplars and bugbears (Lyc. 1.117–19; Dem. 15.35, 19.343, 25.8–10; Aeschin. 3.245; cf. Plato, *Rep.* 492a). Because these activities inculcated the correct emotional responses in citizens, responses which they were supposed to have learned first in the family (Dem. 54.23), democratic Athenians did not portray the virtues of good order (*kosmos*) and moderation (*sōphrosunē*) as burdensome, but rather as dispositions that they exercised voluntarily in the belief that these dispositions were crucial to their and their city's well-being.

For all the public approval they received from the demos, however, the virtues of Eunomia (or Good Order) were traditionally the pillars of conservative social regimes such as Sparta. By contrast with the conservative republican traditions, however, democrats viewed good order not as an expression of deference or obedience, but rather as an expression of a thoughtfully ordered soul, one informed by self-conscious beliefs about what a good life consists in. To see how good order was integrated within a democratic paradigm of the virtues, let us consider the Athenian democracy's cultivation of the virtues of individuality and autonomy. In the case of these virtues, too, democracy's critics argued vociferously that democratic voters were sheep-like followers of their leaders (Hdt. 5.97), that the democratic majority tyrannized over and silenced the wiser minority (Thuc. 6.13, 24; cf. Dem., *Pr.* 50.1), and that democratic citizens could understand political life only as the instrumental means to satisfy pre-existing, and *a fortiori* uneducated, desires (Plato, *Grg.* 518e–519d).

The democratic Athenians responded to these criticisms through locating the virtues of individual citizens within well-functioning institutions that solicited positive contributions from all citizen-equals. The premise of Athenian public deliberation was the potentially equal contribution that all citizens could make to public discussion; hence the traditional question, before all Assemblies of citizens, "Who wishes to speak?" (Dem. 18.170, 191; Aeschin. 1.23–24, 3.4, 3.220–21). This practice made sense only because the community expected individuals, personally, to reflect on matters of public concern and then to bring forward their judgments for public consideration.[49] Far from being zombies controlled by manipulative leaders, the democrats were individually responsible for understanding group problems and articulating possible solutions.

In one striking example, Demosthenes distinguished carefully between, on the one hand, hierarchical relationships among military commanders and rank-and-file soldiers and, on the other hand, the participatory ethos of the Athenian Assembly, where, he said, "each one of you yourselves is a general" (*Pr.* 50.3, tr. DeWitt and DeWitt). Similarly, Aeschines argued that "by law and by his vote the private citizen rules like a king in a democratically governed polis" (3.233; cf. Dem. 10.40–41). Finally, Demosthenes urged that "the many," and especially the oldest among the ordinary citizens, had a special obligation to show good sense in public deliberations, even beyond the practical wisdom expected of career politicians (Dem., *Pr.* 45.2).

Democratic deliberation depended on courage, frankness, honesty, civic trust, and the willingness of each citizen to accept responsibility for the development and execution of political policy. Demosthenes envisioned the brave (*andreios*) and useful (*chrēsimos*) citizen as "whoever often opposes your wishes for the sake of what is best, and never speaks to win favor, but to promote your best interests, and chooses that policy in which chance rather than calculation has more

[49] Balot 2004, Monoson 2000.

power, and yet makes himself accountable to you for both" (8.69, tr. Vince [adapted]; cf. 10.54). When all pistons and cylinders were firing correctly in the hearts of each citizen, Athenian politics was highly successful because each citizen recognized the importance of individual effort and acted accordingly (Dem. 14.15). The democratic polis worked best when individuals acted as "their own agents" and took responsibility for themselves (Dem. 3.14–17), then accepted the corresponding rewards for their own actions (Dem. 13.19–23). Self-reliance was a key democratic virtue (Dem. 13.3–4). It followed that no one was to blame for the Athenians' lack of prudence and political failures other than the citizens themselves (Dem. 10.75–76).

In all of these ways, the democrats effectively answered the critics' charges that voters were sheep-like followers and that they engaged in politics purely in order to satisfy unreconstructed preferences. No: democrats thought for themselves and self-consciously formulated their own plans for leading good lives, not with reference to pre-political desires, as in Hobbes, Locke, Spinoza, and the modern liberal tradition, but rather with reference to the non-relative standards of virtue that they had themselves deliberately arrived at in conversation with fellow citizens.

Good order, then, went "all the way down" in the souls of citizens, but it did not conflict with the democrats' individualism, their openness to revision, and their imaginative, deliberate engagement in politics. Rather, in both state and soul, the Athenian democrats reflectively fashioned a harmonious balance of the virtues of individuality and of moderation and good order. Yet one might object that this account of the democratic virtues collapses, in the end, into the version offered by contemporary republican and liberal theorists in that it regards the virtues as merely instrumentally useful in helping us maintain democratic institutions.[50]

But this was not the Athenian democratic way. In *On the Crown*, Demosthenes proposed that, despite failure at the Battle of Chaeronea, both he and the Athenians collectively *had* to live up to their highest ideals in order to live with self-respect. They appreciated the necessities involved in their political practices, ideology, self-conception, and behavior. The Athenians' way of understanding themselves as self-made constructs of their own history of political practice was often represented in the terminology of doing the things that were "worthy of" (*axia*) oneself, the city, and the ancestors (Dem. 13.32–33, 14.41, 18.96–99,

[50] Pettit 1997; Galston 1991; Macedo 1990.

20.119, 48.2, 60.27; Aeschin. 2.113, 3.247; Hyp. 6.3; Lyc. 1.104, 110; cf. Thuc. 2.41–42, 7.69). As individuals and as a group, the Athenians had to do things that were worthy of themselves – or, in other words, they worked hard to become the actors of ideals that were truly their own.

Cultivating the Citizens' Practical Judgment

Consider, however, that the democratic virtues of individualism and good order oriented citizens in different directions – the one toward innovation and self-reliance, the other toward the reliable exercise of collectively defined functions. It is at this point that we can recognize the importance of practical reasoning in the exercise of virtue. Cultivating good judgment in the citizenry was a pressing political and personal necessity. How were good order and individualism supposed to be aligned appropriately within the souls of individuals? There is obviously no prescription one could offer, in advance of particular situations, to guide individuals in their efforts to balance their proper virtues. Instead, democratic virtue politics, like the virtue theory of the philosophers, relied on the good judgment of virtuous citizens to "thread the needle" between excess and deficiency in the world of rapidly changing "ultimate particulars." In this way the Athenians erected a hierarchy of virtue that placed practical wisdom at the top, as the architectonic virtue that exercised overarching control over the others.

Demosthenes argued such points particularly clearly in his deliberative speeches on the city's foreign policy. He urged his fellow citizens to temper their benevolence (*philanthrōpia*) toward other cities by consideration of their own well-being: while he admires taking risks for the benefit of others, he also assumes that "it is the task of prudent men (*sōphronōn anthrōpōn*) to give equal consideration to their own affairs as to those of others, so that you may show that you are not only benevolent but also sensible (*noun echontes*)" (Dem., *Prooemia*. 16). Such prudence, which is capable of balancing apparently antithetical virtues, was held to be cultivated in all citizens within the family and through "working the machine"[51] of democratic government. Lest we think that democratic leaders were somehow undemocratically "teaching" their fellow citizens, Demosthenes emphasizes that precisely the opposite is the case: leaders must be guided by the noble ambitions, judgments, and sentiments of the ordinary citizens (Dem. 13.31, 36).

[51] Ober 2001.

What held true in the deliberative assembly also held true in the popular law courts of Athens. In the vast majority of legal cases, Athenians expressed "not only a normative belief that a wide variety of contextual information was often relevant to reaching a just decision, but also a political commitment to maximizing the discretion wielded by popular juries."[52] "Working the machine" cultivated the practical judgment of citizens in a variety of institutional forums, but most clearly in the Athenians' popular jury courts.

In these courts, all Athenian citizens, as political equals, were invited to judge complex arguments without benefit of legal experts and without benefit of rigorous legal definitions enshrined in a precise law code. Take, for example, the speech of 347/6 B.C.E. in which Demosthenes brought Meidias to trial for punching him in the nose at the Festival of Dionysos. Throughout the speech, Demosthenes railed against Meidias' *hubris* – an ethical abstraction that means "arrogant overreaching," often with the intent of doing physical harm. Whether or not Demosthenes specifically indicted Meidias under the laws against *hubris* (i.e., in a *graphē hubreōs*), jurors had to judge individually whether Demosthenes was right to apply this condemnatory language to these particular circumstances. To make his case convincing, Demosthenes offered a narrative of his previous victimization at the hands of Meidias (starting at 21.77), as well as detailing Meidias' generally aggressive behavior toward others (21.83–102), in order to show that Meidias' punch constituted culminating evidence of his settled disposition to abuse others.

Demosthenes recognized that the jury would have to consider his case on the merits, in light of the local norms governing ethical and legal concepts such as *hubris*. As a result, he invited the jury to reflect upon the meaning of *hubris* by referring to exemplary cases:

> Many people know that Euaion the brother of Leodamas killed Boiotus at a public banquet and gathering because he had received a single blow. The blow itself did not cause the anger so much as the dishonor. For a free man being hit, though terrible, is not the point – rather, it's being hit with *hubris*. The man who strikes another could do many things, men of Athens, some of which the victim might not be able to communicate to another man, such as his attacker's gesture, the look in his eye, the tone of his voice,

[52] Lanni 2006: 4.

> when he strikes with *hubris* or out of hatred, with the fists or on the cheek. These things stir up a man and make him crazy, when he is unaccustomed to being treated abusively. Men of Athens, no one, in reporting these things, would be able to convey the outrage to his audience, in the strikingly clear way it appeared in truth and in the deed itself to the victim and to onlookers. Men of Athens, consider by Zeus and the other gods, and reckon up amongst yourselves how much greater is the anger that I would rightly feel, having suffered such things at Meidias' hands, than that Euaion felt then, at the time he killed Boiotus. He was struck by someone he knew who was drunk at the time, before six or seven witnesses, whom he also knew, who would have denounced the one man for what he did, and praised the other for controlling and restraining himself after being hit, even though he had gone to a house for dinner voluntarily. I, on the other hand, was outraged by a sober enemy, early in the morning, a man acting arrogantly and not because he was drunk, before many foreigners and citizens, even though I was in a temple and had, as chorus-leader, to be there. Men of Athens, I think that I judged sensibly, or rather blessedly, when I held back then and was not driven to do anything desperate. Yet I can easily understand the behavior of Euaion and all those who come to their own defense when they are dishonored. (Dem. 21.71–74)

This passage illustrates many facets of the workings of virtue politics in democratic Athens. First, Demosthenes called upon the jury of ordinary Athenian citizens to observe the situation carefully, to mull things over, and to reflect upon the distinctiveness of this particular situation. Since there were no consultations with a judge or private deliberations among jury members, it was up to the individual jurors themselves to weigh facts and values judiciously and to render verdicts based on their own individual, albeit socially informed, understandings of the virtues and vices. The Athenian citizens themselves had to judge whether and how virtue terms could be truly and properly used to describe Demosthenes' behavior (cf. 19.57).

Second, the jury had also to form a judgment of Demosthenes' emotional response to being punched: were his level of anger and his intuitive reasoning appropriate, or perhaps deficient in some way, perhaps through being disproportionate, self-pitying, or vengeful? Just as the wise man (*phronimos*) of Aristotelian virtue theory had to make a judgment about courageous, moderate, and just behavior amidst the rapidly evolving world of particulars, so too did the Athenian jury need, finally, to make just such a judgment about the narratives they had heard, and even to act as the final and legitimate authority within the city on questions of virtue and vice. Service on the jury-court was both an exercise of practical reasoning and an excellent way for jurors to educate themselves in political virtue and vice through becoming acquainted with a broad range of moral possibilities as well as forms of ethical reasoning.

In democratic Athens, "virtue politics" was decidedly not reserved for members of the elite. Athens's politics of virtue was truly populist in that the democratic virtues applied to the entire citizen body and were evaluated by the entire citizen body. In no other non-democratic tradition do we find such an emphasis on practical reasoning, egalitarianism, individualism, and freedom as we find in the democratic virtue politics of Athens. And, as a fuller account would indicate, we must imagine these emphases as being even stronger and more radical in the Athenians' local politics, since it was there that Athenian citizens participated, day in and day out, in the exercise and cultivation of virtue and practical reasoning, all with a view, as we have seen, to attaining *eudaimonia*, or flourishing.

CONCLUSION

Even amidst the vibrant and healthy pluralism of modern democratic societies, it is plausible to think that public arguments and judgments based on a belief in the intrinsic and instrumental value of justice, courage, kindness, good judgment, and so forth should be legitimate, because it is hard to imagine denying the goodness of these virtues or quarreling with the self-respecting life that they make possible. This is one of the reasons, in fact, that the language of virtue still has popular currency in the political rhetoric of the world's developed democracies. Political theorists should take the point and ask why this language is still so powerful. If they do pursue this line of reasoning, then their task – or at least one of their tasks – will be to draw out the ethical and political implications of this language. Political theorists can improve political language by helping us become more intelligible to ourselves and more in touch with our own democratic intuitions – or rather with the demands and ramifications of our own democratic commitments.

To be sure, the question of which virtues are worth cultivating should itself be a subject of discussion, as should the question of how much political engagement is adequate or necessary for a good life.[53] As Ronald Beiner has persuasively argued, we would be better off if we, as citizens, accepted the responsibility publicly to express critical judgments about what constitutes human flourishing.[54] It is to our detriment that we exclude such topics from the public forum or, even worse, that we uncritically accept substantive visions of the good (such as market-driven consumerism) presented as simply neutral, procedural standards. The rigorously and radically egalitarian virtues of the Athenian democracy, suitably updated, might provide us with more life-affirming concepts and more appropriate political starting points as we think seriously about the sorts of lives we want to lead and the sorts of people we want to become.

WORKS CITED

Annas, J. 1993. *The Morality of Happiness*. Oxford.

1998. "Virtue and Eudaimonism." *Social Philosophy and Policy* 15: 37–55.

Arendt, H. 1958. *The Human Condition*. Chicago.

Balot, R. K. 2001. "Pericles' Anatomy of Democratic Courage." *American Journal of Philology* 122: 505–25.

2004. "Free Speech, Courage, and Democratic Deliberation." In *Free Speech in Classical Antiquity*, ed. I. Sluiter and R. M. Rosen. *Mnemosyne* Supplementum 254. Leiden.

2004a. "Courage in the Democratic *Polis*." *Classical Quarterly* 54: 406–23.

Forthcoming. "Democratizing Courage in Classical Athens." In *War, Culture, and Democracy in Classical Athens*, ed. D. Pritchard. Cambridge.

Barber, B. R. 1984. *Strong Democracy: Participatory Politics for a New Age*. Berkeley, CA.

1998. "Neither Leaders nor Followers: Citizenship under Strong Democracy." In *A Passion for Democracy: American Essays*. Princeton, NJ.

Beiner, R. 1992. "Moral Vocabularies." In *What's the Matter with Liberalism?* Berkeley, CA.

Casey, J. 1990. *Pagan Virtue: An Essay in Ethics*. Oxford.

Collins, S. D. 2006. *Aristotle and the Rediscovery of Citizenship*. Cambridge.

Constant, B. 1988 [1819]. "The Liberty of the Ancients Compared with That of the Moderns." In *Benjamin Constant: Political Writings*, trans. and ed. B. Fontana. Cambridge Texts in the History of Political Thought. Cambridge.

Crisp, R. 1996. "Modern Moral Philosophy and the Virtues." In *How Should One Live? Essays on the Virtues*, ed. R. Crisp. Oxford.

Crisp, R., and M. Slote, eds. 1997. *Virtue Ethics*. Oxford Readings in Philosophy. Oxford.

53 Cf. Sandel 1998: 323–27.

54 Beiner 1992: 39–79.

Fisher, N., ed. and trans. 2001. *Aeschines: Against Timarchos*. Clarendon Ancient History Series. Oxford.

Frank, J. 2005. *A Democracy of Distinction: Aristotle and the Work of Politics*. Chicago.

Galston, W. A. 1991. *Liberal Purposes: Goods, Virtues, and Diversity in the Liberal State*. Cambridge Studies in Philosophy and Public Policy. Cambridge.

Gardiner, S. M., ed. 2005. *Virtue Ethics, Old and New*. Ithaca, NY.

Gill, C., ed. 2005. *Virtue, Norms, and Objectivity: Issues in Ancient and Modern Ethics*. Oxford.

Holmes, S. T. 1979. "Aristippus in and out of Athens." *American Political Science Review* 73: 113–28.

Hurka, T. 2001. *Virtue, Vice, and Value*. Oxford.

Hursthouse, R. 1999. *On Virtue Ethics*. Oxford.

2003. "Virtue Ethics." In *Stanford Encyclopedia of Philosophy*, fall 2003 ed., ed. E. N. Zalta. http://plato.stanford.edu/archives/fall2003/entries/ethics-virtue/.

Kraut, R. 1989. *Aristotle on the Human Good*. Princeton, NJ.

Lanni, A. 2006. *Law and Justice in the Courts of Classical Athens*. Cambridge.

Liddel, P. 2007. *Civic Obligation and Individual Liberty in Ancient Athens*. Oxford Classical Monographs. Oxford.

Loraux, N. 1986. *The Invention of Athens: The Funeral Oration in the Classical City*, trans. A. Sheridan. Cambridge, MA.

Macedo, S. 1990. *Liberal Virtues: Citizenship, Virtue, and Community in Liberal Constitutionalism*. Oxford.

2000. *Diversity and Distrust: Civic Education in a Multicultural Democracy*. Cambridge, MA.

MacIntyre, A. 1984. *After Virtue: A Study in Moral Theory*, 2nd ed. Notre Dame, IN.

1988. *Whose Justice? Which Rationality?* Notre Dame, IN.

1995. "Is Patriotism a Virtue?" In *Theorizing Citizenship*, ed. R. Beiner. SUNY Series in Political Theory: Contemporary Issues. Albany, NY.

Mansfield, H. C. 2006. *Manliness*. New Haven, CT.

Mara, G. 1985. "After Virtue, Autonomy: Jürgen Habermas and Greek Political Theory." *Journal of Politics* 47: 1036–61.

Monoson, S. S. 2000. *Plato's Democratic Entanglements: Athenian Politics and the Practice of Philosophy*. Princeton, NJ.

Morris, I. 2000. *Archaeology as Cultural History: Words and Things in Iron Age Greece*. Social Archaeology. Oxford.

Nussbaum, M. C. 1988. "Nature, Function, and Capability: Aristotle on Political Distribution." In *Oxford Studies in Ancient Philosophy*, supplementary vol., ed. J. Annas and R. H. Grimm. Oxford.

1993. "Non-Relative Virtues: An Aristotelian Approach." In *The Quality of Life*, ed. M. Nussbaum and A. Sen. Oxford.

2002. "Aristotelian Social Democracy." In *Aristotle and Modern Politics: The Persistence of Political Philosophy*, ed. A. Tessitore. Notre Dame, IN.

Ober, J. 1989. *Mass and Elite in Democratic Athens: Rhetoric, Ideology, and the Power of the People*. Princeton, NJ.

1998. *Political Dissent in Democratic Athens: Intellectual Critics of Popular Rule*. Martin Classical Lectures. Princeton, NJ.

2001. "The Debate Over Civic Education in Classical Athens. In *Education in Greek and Roman Antiquity*, ed. Y. L. Too. Leiden.

2005. "Culture, Thin Coherence, and the Persistence of Politics." In *Athenian Legacies: Essays on the Politics of Going On Together*. Princeton, NJ.
Pangle, T. L. 1998. "The Retrieval of Civic Virtue: A Critical Appreciation of Sandel's *Democracy's Discontent*." In *Debating Democracy's Discontent: Essays on American Politics, Law, and Public Philosophy*, ed. A. L. Allen and M. C. Regan, Jr. Oxford.
Pettit, P. 1997. *Republicanism: A Theory of Freedom and Government*. Oxford Political Theory. Oxford.
Pocock, J. G. A. 1975. *The Machiavellian Moment: Florentine Political Thought and the Atlantic Republican Tradition*. Princeton, NJ.
Prior, W. J. 1991. *Virtue and Knowledge: An Introduction to Ancient Greek Ethics*. London.
Pritchett, W. K. 1974. *The Greek State at War*, part II. Berkeley, CA.
Rahe, P. A. 1992. *Republics Ancient and Modern: Classical Republicanism and the American Revolution*. Chapel Hill, NC.
Rawls, J. 1971. *A Theory of Justice*. Cambridge, MA.
Roberts, J. T. 1994. *Athens on Trial: The Antidemocratic Tradition in Western Thought*. Princeton, NJ.
Roisman, J. 2005. *The Rhetoric of Manhood: Masculinity in the Attic Orators*. Berkeley, CA.
Salkever, S. G. 1974. "Virtue, Obligation and Politics." *American Political Science Review* 68: 78–92.
1990. *Finding the Mean: Theory and Practice in Aristotelian Political Philosophy*. Studies in Moral, Political, and Legal Philosophy. Princeton, NJ.
2002. "The Deliberative Model of Democracy and Aristotle's Ethics of Natural Questions." In *Aristotle and Modern Politics: The Persistence of Political Philosophy*, ed. A. Tessitore. Notre Dame, IN.
Sandel, M. J. 1996. *Democracy's Discontent: America in Search of a Public Philosophy*. Cambridge, MA.
1998. "Reply to Critics." In *Debating Democracy's Discontent: Essays on American Politics, Law, and Public Philosophy*, ed. A. L. Allen and M. C. Regan, Jr. Oxford.
Skinner, Q. 1978. *The Foundations of Modern Political Thought*, vol. I: *The Renaissance*. Cambridge.
1998. *Liberty before Liberalism*. Cambridge.
Statman, D., ed. 1997. *Virtue Ethics: A Critical Reader*. Washington, DC.
Wallach, J. R. 1992. "Contemporary Aristotelianism." *Political Theory* 20: 613–41.
1994. "Two Democracies and Virtue." In *Athenian Political Thought and the Reconstruction of American Democracy*, ed. J. P. Euben, J. R. Wallach and J. Ober. Ithaca, NY.
White, N. 2002. *Individual and Conflict in Greek Ethics*. Oxford.
Whitehead, D. 1993. "Cardinal Virtues: The Language of Public Approbation in Democratic Athens." *Classica et Mediaevalia* 44: 37–75.
Williams, B. 1993. *Shame and Necessity*. Sather Classical Lectures 57. Berkeley, CA.
Yunis, H., ed. 2001. *Demosthenes: On the Crown*. Cambridge Greek and Latin Classics. Cambridge.

11: Origins of Rights in Ancient Political Thought

Fred D. Miller, Jr.

The concept of rights is a prominent feature of modern political thought. The principle that all human beings possess inalienable or imprescriptible rights was endorsed in the American Declaration of Independence (1776), the French Declaration of the Rights of Man and of the Citizen (1789), and the United Nations' Universal Declaration of Human Rights (1948). Previously, natural rights were central to influential political treatises by Hugo Grotius (1583–1645), Thomas Hobbes (1588–1679), Samuel Pufendorf (1632–94), John Locke (1632–1704), and others. There is a growing consensus that the origins of rights theory can be found in the later Middle Ages, with Marsilius of Padua (*c.* 1280–*c.* 1343), William of Ockham (*c.* 1285–1349?), or Jean de Gerson (1363–1429), or still earlier with twelfth and thirteenth century canon lawyers such as Rufinus, Ricardus, Huguccio, and Alanus.[1]

Some scholars view the rights tradition as reaching all the way back to the ancient Greeks and Romans, or even to the ancient Hebrew Bible, while others regard it as a strictly modern phenomenon, for example, Alasdair MacIntyre: "[T]here is no expression in any ancient or medieval language correctly translated by our expression 'a right' until near the close of the middle ages: the concept lacks any means of expression in Hebrew, Greek, Latin or Arabic, classical or medieval, before about 1400, let alone in Old English, or in Japanese even as late as the mid-nineteenth century."[2] This suggests that the issue involves, in part, the meaning of words. Early modern writers treated "right" as equivalent to the Latin *ius*, which was commonly used for legal claims

[1] Gerson is credited with "the first rights theory" by Tuck 1979: ch. 1; Ockham by Villey 1964; and the canon lawyers by Tierney 1997: ch. 2, and Reid 1991.

[2] MacIntyre 1981: 67. For similar views see Villey 1946, Tuck 1979, and Brett 1997.

in ancient Roman law. This is not, however, a mere lexicographical dispute. Whether or not the ancients had even a nascent concept of rights bears on their view of the legal and political standing of individuals. Examination of this question may thus contribute to a clearer comparison between ancient and modern political theory. It may also encourage fruitful speculation about what it means to possess a right and how rights claims are to be justified and applied.

Before embarking on this inquiry, however, it is necessary to confront an oft-noted fact: There is no single expression in ancient Greek corresponding to "a right." (Modern Greek in contrast has the word *dikaiōma*.) Does this show that the ancient Greeks had no concept of a right? Some invoke the lexical principle that speakers cannot recognize a concept unless they have a specific word for it. But this principle seems too strong: Although English has no synonym for the German *Schadenfreude*, English speakers all too readily understand what it means: enjoyment of another's misfortunes. (Curiously, ancient Greek has a synonym: *epichairekakia*.) This shows that speakers of different languages can possess the same concepts even if their vocabularies differ. Can a similar point be made about rights?

A helpful framework for this investigation is provided by Wesley Hohfeld, who demonstrated that the word "right" is used ambiguously in modern legal argument. In an influential analysis, he distinguishes four senses in which one person *X* might have "a right" against another person *Y*:

(1) *X* has a *claim* against *Y* to *Y*'s doing *A*, in which case *Y* has a correlative duty to *X* to do *A* (e.g., the right to repayment of a debt).
(2) *X* has a *privilege* or *liberty* to do *A* against *Y*, in which case *X* has no duty to *Y* to forbear from doing *A* (e.g., the liberty to use one's own property).
(3) *X* has a *power* or *authority* to *A* against *Y*, in which case *Y* is liable to *X*'s doing *A* (e.g., the authority to arrest someone).
(4) *X* has an *immunity* against *Y*'s doing *A*, in which case *X* is not liable to *Y*'s doing *A* (e.g., immunity against being required to testify against oneself).

Sections I and V below will argue that the ancient Greeks and Romans employed locutions that correspond to the four conceptions distinguished by Hohfeld.[3]

[3] Hohfeld 1919.

For the purposes of this chapter, "a right" may be defined as a claim of an individual against other members of the same community, a claim justified on the basis of justice, law, or some comparable norm. Apart from this linguistic issue, however, there is the question whether the ancients had an underlying conceptual network corresponding to the modern idea of a right. Some scholars object that even if the Greek word *dikaion* or the Latin word *ius* can be translated as "right," this does not mean "a right" as understood today. For the ancients meant what is "right" in an *objective* sense, involving a correct assignment or relation of things to persons. According to this interpretation, the Greeks and Romans did not make claims of *subjective* rights, that is, that rights belonged to a claimant as a person.[4] Modern political theorists also frequently invoke *rights of persons* and *human rights*. This chapter will consider whether the ancient Greeks and Romans had a concept of rights in any sense. Section VII will also consider briefly what evidence there might be for the concept of rights in the Hebrew and Christian Scriptures.

I. Rights in Ancient Greek Law

The first question is whether the ancient Greeks had the linguistic resources to make "rights" claims. Evidence from legal inscriptions and speeches indicates that they used distinct legal expressions corresponding to the different conceptions of rights distinguished by Hohfeld.[5]

Table I

Hohfeld	Greek
just claim	*to dikaion*
liberty, privilege	*exousia*
authority, power	*kurios*
immunity	*adeia, ateleia*

Just Claim (to dikaion)

The most important Greek locution is *to dikaion* (plural, *ta dikaia*), literally "the just." Though sometimes equivalent to "justice" (*dikē,*

[4] Villey 1946 is an influential source for this interpretation of Roman *ius*. Strauss 1953 offers a similar interpretation of the Greek notion of "classic natural right."

[5] Section I is drawn from Miller and Biondi 2007: 102–9. Permission granted by Springer Publishing.

dikaiosunē), it often signifies a just claim, or an act claimed from another party on the basis of justice. This expression occurs early, in connection with rights of pasturage in a law recorded on a bronze plaque from a Locrian community settling new territory (*c.* 525–500 B.C.E.): "Pasturage-rights (*epinomia*) shall belong to parents and son; if no son exists, to an unmarried daughter; if no unmarried daughter exists, to a brother; if no brother exists, by degree of family connection let a man pasture according to what is just (*kata to dikaion*)."[6] Although *to dikaion* is used in the objective sense here, the implication is that the colonists have a just claim to pasture in a location and the entitlement is inherited according to the degree of consanguinity prescribed by the law.

A later inscription refers to "rights" in the subjective sense. A decree on a marble stele from the Athenian acropolis (325/4 B.C.E.) complains that the city of Heraclea has illegally seized the sails of Heraclides of Salamis, an ally of Athens, and authorizes an ambassador to go to Heraclea and demand the return of Heraclides' sails and to obtain "the just things (*tōn dikaiōn*) of the people of Athens."

Liberty or Privilege (exousia)

The noun *exousia* or verb *exesti* (infinitive *exeinai* or *exeimen*) is used for an act it is permissible for someone to do, and thus defines a sphere of liberty or privilege within which the agent is free to choose. This locution is used for the civil liberties of colonists in a law inscribed on a bronze plaque by the Hypocnemidian Locrians concerning their colony at Naupactus (*c.* 500–475 B.C.E.?). For example, a colonist shall "be at liberty (*exeimen*) to share in religious privileges and to make sacrifice as a visitor (*xenos*), when he is present, if he wishes. . . . If compulsion drives the Hypocnemidian Locrians out of Naupactus, they have to be at liberty (*exeimen*) to return, each to his place of origin, without entry fees. . . . If anyone leaves behind (in Locris) his father and a portion of his property (which he has consigned to his father), when (his father) dies, the colonist shall be at liberty (*exeimen*) to recover his property."[7]

Authority or Power (kurios)

The term *kurios* signifies that the bearer has the authority to carry out acts in a specific domain. The authority may reside in a private

[6] Fornara 1977: no. 33. Some translations from Fornara have been modified slightly for the sake of consistency.

[7] Fornara 1977: no. 47.

individual, group, official, political body, city-state, treaty, contract, will, or the law itself. What distinguishes an authority is its ability to bestow duties and rights on others. The word *kurios* (in some dialects *karteros*) is often used in connection with property rights. An early example is found in the civil laws of Gortyn in Crete circa 450 B.C.E. (engraved on the inner surface of a circular wall). A section dealing with intestate inheritance begins, "The father has authority (*karteron*) over his children and the division of his property and the mother over her property."[8] This particular code was distinctive in recognizing the legal rights of women over their own property. The wife's property was not merged with her husband's, and women could inherit property in their own right. Neither her husband nor her son could alienate or promise her property.

In a later Athenian decree the assembly granted the council limited discretionary authority over the establishment of a new colony in the Adriatic (325/4 B.C.E.), including the election of a board of representatives: "If this decree needs anything in addition for the representation, the council is decreed to have authority (*kurian*), but not to nullify anything decreed by the people."[9]

Immunity (adeia *and* ateleia)

The term *adeia* denotes legal immunity, for example in an Athenian decree moved by Callias concerning the allocation of funds for work on the acropolis of Athens (434/4 B.C.E.):

> But for no other purpose shall use be made of the monies unless the people pass a vote of immunity (*adeian*) just as when they pass a vote about property taxes. If anyone proposes or puts to a vote, without a decree granting immunity having been passed, that the funds of Athena be utilized, he shall be liable to the same penalty as one proposing to have a property tax or putting this to the vote.

Ordinarily, anyone who attempted to divert the funds to another purpose would be subject to prosecution, but this decree allows for a vote of special immunity from such prosecution.[10]

[8] Meiggs and Lewis 1988: no. 41. Some translations from Meiggs and Lewis have been modified slightly for the sake of consistency.

[9] Tod 1948: no. 200; cf. no. 157.

[10] Fornara 1977: no. 119.

The term *ateleia* refers to exemption from obligations such as taxation or military service. An Eritrean inscription (411 B.C.E.) grants to a foreigner, Hegelechos of Tarentum, "immunity from public burdens (*ateleia*) and seating privileges at the games, since he joined in the liberation of the city from the Athenians."[11] Similarly, the Athenians in 338/7 B.C.E. granted to the Acarnanians exemption (*atelesi*) from the ordinary tax on resident aliens, equality with citizens in court, as well as *enktesis*, the privilege to acquire and own property. The right of a resident alien to pay taxes at the same rate as a citizen is elsewhere called *isoteleia*.[12]

It is evident from the foregoing that the ancient Greeks possessed a panoply of legal terms corresponding to modern "rights" locutions. But did individual rights play a significant role in the political theories of Plato, Aristotle, or Demosthenes, as some have claimed? These theories shall be considered in turn.

II. RIGHTS IN PLATO'S *REPUBLIC*

Although Plato (*c.* 429–347 B.C.E.) has been pilloried as an "enemy of the open society,"[13] Gregory Vlastos argues that he was actually committed to individual rights. The central theme of Plato's *Republic* is justice, which Vlastos defines as "the disposition to govern one's conduct by respect for the rights of those whom that conduct affects."[14] This conception is expressed in what Vlastos calls the Principle of Functional Reciprocity: "All members of the polis have equal right to those and only those benefits which are required for the optimal performance of their function in the polis."[15]

Though never made explicit in the text, Vlastos argues that the principle is tacitly assumed throughout the *Republic* by the leading speaker, Socrates, starting with the first primitive community (called Protopolis by Vlastos). Drawn together by mutual need and lack of self-sufficiency, different individuals perform special jobs for which they have different natural talents: farmers, weavers, shoemakers, carpenters, merchants, and so forth (2.369–371e). Such specialization of labor illustrates a nascent idea of justice: "everyone must practice one

[11] Fornara 1977: no. 152.

[12] Schwenk 1985: nos. 1 and 12.

[13] See Popper 1962.

[14] Vlastos 1977: 5–6; cf. Vlastos 1978. The *Republic* had an alternate title, *On Justice*.

[15] Vlastos 1978: 178.

of the occupations in the city-state for which he is naturally best suited" (4.433a).[16] When it is objected that Protopolis is a mere "city of pigs," Socrates argues that a more advanced city-state will require three specialized classes: guardians (i.e., rulers), auxiliaries (i.e., warriors), and producers (2.374a–e, 3.414b). In the ideal city-state (described as Callipolis at 7.527c) the rulers will be philosophers who must undergo a strict program of education and training. The Principle of Functional Reciprocity implies that the philosophers alone have the right to rule over the city-state and the right to the associated benefits, such as publicly funded housing, meals, and salary. But the rulers' rights are limited: "none of them should possess any private property beyond what is wholly necessary"; hence, they have no right to own private land or houses or to handle gold, silver, or money generally, because this would only distract them from their vocation (3.416d–417b, 5.464b). Nor may they interfere with the rights of the other citizens to pursue their respective nonpolitical vocations (4.433d). Vlastos's claim that "all members of the polis have equal rights" is potentially misleading. It might suggest an egalitarian principle that "distributes a sort of equality to both equals and unequals alike," but Socrates emphatically rejects this principle, which he associates with extreme democracy and anarchy (8.558c). "Equal right" for Vlastos means simply that those who are equally qualified to do a job have an equal right to the wherewithal to perform it properly. This has radical implications, however, including what Vlastos calls "a ringing manifesto of equality between the sexes within the guardian class."[17] For, Socrates argues, "women born with the appropriate natures should share everything equally with men" (7.540c), including equal rights to education and vocational opportunity, marital rights, and legal and political rights. This proposal was remarkable because women in ancient Athens were second-class citizens with inferior legal, political, and social status. Plato might even be called a "feminist," if this is defined as one who denies that equal rights can be denied or abridged on account of sex.[18]

The evidence presented so far establishes at most that Plato's *Republic* allows for *functional rights*, that is, rights that individuals possess based on their proper functions within the city-state. Even if it is conceded that these are rights, they are rights in only a special sense. Moderns think of a right as involving the freedom to decide among

[16] Translations of *Republic* are by Grube 1997 (rev. Reeve), with occasional revisions.

[17] Vlastos 1978: 180.

[18] Vlastos 1989.

alternatives, but this cannot be what Plato has in mind. For the citizens of Callipolis are assigned to jobs and compelled to do them; they are not free to choose their own professions. Each citizen has a duty as well as a right to carry out his function within the city-state. Moreover, the citizens have the rights to benefits only if they can do their jobs. For example, Socrates agrees that a doctor should not treat a man who cannot live a normal life, "since such a person would be of no profit either to himself or to the city" (3.407d–e).

Even if Plato has a theory of functional rights, these are far removed from *rights of persons*, that is, rights that individuals possess as separate persons and not as mere means to a further end. Some scholars argue that it is misleading to speak of "rights" at all in explicating Plato because his arguments have a purely utilitarian foundation.[19] For example, when Socrates argues for female guardians, he is not concerned about whether disenfranchised women are miserable, but about whether the city-state is squandering half its human resources. Again, he proposes that children be raised and educated in common because this will facilitate the production of future guardians, not because the traditional nuclear family impedes the well-being of women.

This objection gains support by Socrates' injunction: "[I]n establishing our city, we aren't aiming to make any one group outstandingly happy but to make the whole city-state so, as far as possible" (4.420b). Just as a sculptor should try to make the statue as a whole as beautiful as possible even if this requires making the parts such as the eyes less beautiful than they could be, the legislator should aim at the happiness of the city-state as a whole. Socrates also prescribes that the guardians merge their self-interest and regard the same things (including parents, children, and property) as "mine" (5.462a–466c). On the basis of such passages, Karl Popper contends that Plato is concerned about the city-state viewed as a "super-individual" or "super-organism," not about individual rights.[20]

Vlastos replies that this objection overlooks the fact that for Plato justice entails *reciprocity*.[21] In the ideal city-state the philosophers have a duty to serve as administrators of the city-state for fifteen years even if they would be less happy during this term. The reason is that the aim of law is "to spread happiness throughout the city-state by bringing the citizens into harmony through persuasion and compulsion and making

[19] See Annas 1976; and Schofield 2006: 227 and 247 n. 97.

[20] Popper 1962: 1.169.

[21] Vlastos 1977: 16.

them share with each other (*allēlois*) the benefits that each of them (*hekastoi*) can confer on the community" (7.519e). This implies that the citizens have duties to each other and not merely to an overarching social organism. Another passage states that the virtue of wisdom involves "the knowledge of what is advantageous for each part and for the whole (*hekastōi te kai holōi*), which is the community of all three parts" (4.442c).[22] This implies that the rational ruler is not concerned solely with the good in a purely collective sense. But hard questions remain: Do the real interests of the individual citizens ultimately merge together (as suggested by 5.462a–466c, cited above)? If individual interests conflict with the good of the whole, must the latter take precedence? If the answer to either question is affirmative, the basis for rights of persons seems tenuous.[23]

On the whole, the thesis that the rights of persons are recognized in the *Republic* has met with skepticism. The dominant view is that Plato's principle of justice is about social duties and natural human abilities and talents, rather than about individual rights.[24]

III. RIGHTS IN ARISTOTLE'S *POLITICS*

In contrast with Plato, Aristotle (384–322 B.C.E.) has often been represented as an early proponent of individual rights. Ernest Barker remarked, "Plato thinks of the individual as bound to do the *duty* to which he is called as an organ of the State: Aristotle thinks of the individual as deserving the right which he *ought* to enjoy in a society based on (proportionate) equality."[25] Similarly, Eduard Zeller observed, "In politics as in metaphysics the central point with Plato is the Universal, with Aristotle the Individual. The former demands that the whole should realise its ends without regard to the interests of individuals: the

[22] Although 4.442c deals with wisdom in an individual's soul, Socrates holds that the same virtues are found in the soul as in the city-state (435a–b).

[23] Compare Plato's *Laws*: although the true political art aims at the common interest rather than individual interests, "it is advantageous for both the common and the private if the common rather than the private is well served" (9.875a–b; cf. 10.903d).

[24] See Santas 2006. Due to limited space it is not possible to discuss Plato's *Laws*, which describes a second-best approximation to the ideal constitution in which the rule of law takes the place of philosopher-rulers. However, the *Laws* seems to agree with the *Republic* in subordinating individual interests to the common good: "I shall legislate entirely with a view to what is best for the whole city-state and family, and will justly assign what belongs to each individual to a lower rank" (*Laws* 9.923b).

[25] Barker 1906: 340 n. 1.

latter that it be reared upon the satisfaction of all individual interests that have a true title to be regarded."[26] Recently I have also argued that rights play a significant role in Aristotle's political theory.[27]

It is noteworthy that Aristotle defines the citizen as "someone who has the liberty (*exousia*) to participate in deliberative or judicial office" (*Politics* 3.1, 1275b18–19).[28] In some city-states citizens take turns holding such offices, and they do not cease to be citizens when they are out of office as long as they remain eligible to hold office.[29]

The rights of citizens are based on distributive justice as follows. In a just distribution, individuals receive shares of a common asset based on their merit or desert. This results in what Aristotle calls a "geometrical proportion," in the simplified case of two individuals:

$$\frac{\text{Merit of } X}{\text{Merit of } Y} = \frac{\text{Value of } X\text{'s Share}}{\text{Value of } Y\text{'s Share}}$$

A just distribution is thus a function assigning to each person a particular share of the common asset.[30] As a result, each person has a *just claim* or *right* to this share. This is so far a purely formal principle of justice. In practice Aristotle indicates that the merit of individuals should be compared on the basis of their contributions. For example, in a business venture, if *X* contributes one mina (i.e., one hundred drachmas) to a business venture while *Y* contributes ninety-nine minas, *X* has a just claim to only one-hundredth of the net earnings, and *Y* could justly complain if *X* took half the earnings. The application of distributive justice to political offices is far more controversial: "Everyone agrees that justice in distributions ought to be according to a sort of merit, yet everyone does not say that merit is the same thing; advocates of democracy say it is freedom, some advocates of oligarchy say it is wealth, and others good birth, and advocates of aristocracy say it is virtue" (*NE* 5.3, 1131a25–9, cf. *Pol.* 3.9, 1280a16–19). Aristotle agrees with aristocrats that virtuous persons make the most important contribution

[26] Zeller 1897: vol. 2, 224–26.

[27] Section III is based on Miller 1995. See also Miller 1996.

[28] Translations of Aristotle's texts are my own.

[29] Aristotle also mentions that citizens (as well as resident aliens in some places) share in *ta dikaia* "in so far as they prosecute others in court or are judged there themselves" (*Politics* 3.1.1275a8–11). Compare 3.9.1280b10–11, which speaks of law as "a guarantor of *ta dikaia* against one another." Finally, he speaks of political rivals as claiming a greater share of *ta politika dikaia* on the basis of their alleged superiority (3.12.). I argue that *ta dikaia* means "just claims" in these contexts.

[30] See Keyt 1991.

to the political community, which is a community devoted to living happily and nobly (*Pol.* 3.9, 1280b40–81a8). Hence, virtuous persons have a just claim or right to citizenship and political office.

Granted that Aristotle recognizes political rights in some sense, are they merely functional rights or are they rights of persons? Clues to solving this problem are Aristotle's claims that in a just constitution the rulers aim at the common advantage rather than their own private advantage (*Pol.* 3.7, 1279a28–31) and that the common advantage is the same as universal justice (*Pol.* 3.12, 1282b16–18; *NE* 5.1, 1129b14–19, 8.9, 1160a13–14). Hence, whether Aristotle recognizes just claims in the sense of the rights of persons depends on what he means by "the common advantage" (*to koinon sumpheron*). This expression may be interpreted in two quite different ways. The first is *holistic*: the common advantage is the good of the whole city-state, as distinct from, and superior to, the ends of its individual members. The other interpretation is *individualistic*: to promote the common advantage is simply to promote the well-being of the individual citizens.

It is significant that Aristotle criticizes Plato's ideal as excessively holistic. Against the "hypothesis that it is best for the entire city-state to be one as far as possible," Aristotle objects that

> as it becomes more one it will no longer be a city-state; for the city-state is with respect to its nature a sort of multitude, and if it becomes more one it will be a household instead of a city-state, and a human being instead of a household; for we would say that a household is more one than a city-state, and one [human being is more one] than a household; so that even if one could do this, it ought not to be done; for it would destroy the city-state. (*Pol.* 2.2, 1261a16–22; cf. *Rep.* 4.422d1–23d, 5.462a9–b2)

Aristotle also criticizes the collectivistic aim of Plato's ideal regime:

> [H]e says that the lawgiver ought to make the city-state as a whole happy. But it is impossible for a whole to be happy unless most or all or some of its parts possess happiness. For being happy is not the same as [being] even; for the latter can belong to the whole, even if neither of its parts does, but being happy cannot. (*Pol.* 2.5, 1264b15–24; cf. *Rep.* 4, 419a1–421c6, 5, 465e4–466a6)

In rejecting Plato's ideal, Aristotle assumes a comparatively weak necessary condition: The city-state is happy only if most or all or some members of the city-state are happy. This disjunctive requirement is satisfied even by deviant constitutions that promote only the advantage of the rulers (see 3.7, 1279b30–31). But the first two disjuncts – "most or all" – suggest two competing standards for the best constitution, which correspond to alternative interpretations of the common advantage: *The overall advantage*: the city-state is happy only if most of the members are happy. *The mutual advantage*: the city-state is happy only if each of the members is happy. The overall advantage permits trade-offs, that is, sacrifices of the basic interests of some individuals in order to promote the advantage of others. The overall advantage could not be deeply committed to the rights of individuals. The *mutual* advantage, on the other hand, reflects the requirement of individualism that the happiness of *each* of the participants must be protected by political institutions. In rejecting Platonic holism, Aristotle does not say which of these standards should be applied in the best constitution. But he is committed to individual rights only if he understands the common advantage as the *mutual* advantage.

There is compelling evidence that Aristotle does understand the common advantage in this way. First, he says that "the best constitution is that order under which anyone whatsoever (*hostisoun*) might act in the best way and live blessedly" (7.2, 1324a23–25). This implies that no citizen will be excluded from a happy life in the ideal regime. Later he distinguishes between citizens and mere adjuncts such as slaves and vulgar workers (7.8, 1328a21–25). Whereas adjuncts merely perform necessary functions, the citizens are genuine members of the city-state who partake of its end (1328a25–33, b4–5; cf. 4.4, 1291a24–28). When he says the city-state is "a community of similar persons for the sake of the best possible life" (1328a35–36), he implies that *all* its genuine members – citizens – partake in this end. This requirement is also asserted in support of universal property rights: "a city-state should be called happy not by viewing a part of it but by viewing *all* of the citizens" (1329a23–24). He also proposes that two lots of land be distributed to each citizen, one near the border and one near the city, to bring about "equality and justice and unanimity regarding border wars" (10, 1330a14–18). This implies that all citizens have equal property rights.[31]

[31] See Miller 2005.

Furthermore, Aristotle lays down a principle to guide the founder of the best regime:

> . . . a city-state is excellent (*spoudaia*) due to the fact that the citizens who partake in the constitution are excellent; but in our case all the citizens partake in the constitution. We must therefore inquire as to how a man becomes excellent; for even if all the citizens could be excellent without each of the citizens [being excellent], the latter would be more choiceworthy; for "all" follows from "each." (13, 1332a32–38)

Aristotle thus distinguishes between two principles that could guide the lawgiver: *All* the citizens (in a collective sense) should be excellent, or each citizen (as an individual) should be excellent. "Each" is logically stronger than "all," because each entails, but is not entailed by, all. For all is compatible with the overall advantage, that is, a state of affairs in which the interests of some citizens are sacrificed in order to advance the happiness of most of the citizens. Each requires the *mutual* advantage, that is, the promotion of the excellence of each and every citizen. It is noteworthy, then, that Aristotle describes the "each" principle as the more choiceworthy. This requirement rules out the holistic view that the city-state is excellent even if some of the citizens only "merge" their lives in the life of the city-state as a whole. Such a condition, in which some citizens bask in the reflected excellence of others, may be consistent with the weaker principle that *all* the citizens be virtuous (in a collective sense of all), but it does not meet Aristotle's more stringent requirement that *each* of the citizens attain excellence. Only a mutual-advantage interpretation of justice will satisfy this requirement. This stronger requirement clearly assumes that the happiness of the citizens is *compossible* – that is, that there are no deep, irremediable conflicts of interests among them – but this is precisely what distinguishes the best constitution from the inferior constitutions.

The thesis that Aristotle was committed to a theory of rights has met with various objections. First, he was unconcerned with rights because his ideal regime contains slaves (7.10, 1330a31–33). Farmers, craftsmen, and vulgar workers are disenfranchised because their occupations are inimical to the virtue and leisure required by citizens (9, 1328b33–29a2). Women are also treated as second-class citizens, excluded from political offices because their rational faculty lacks authority and their natural function is confined to the household (1.13, 1260a13, 2.5, 1264b4–6). Second, Aristotle could not have endorsed a theory of rights because such a theory assumes a kind of radical individualism that Aristotle could not have accepted in the form of "what Hegel calls the 'principle of subjective freedom' – the idea that in possessing this power of arbitrary self-determination we have something of infinite worth in each of us individually."[32] Third, it is objected that Aristotle thinks of citizens as *deserving a share* of political offices rather than as *having a right* to them.[33] For if *X* has a right to *A* this cannot be because *X* has done something to deserve *A*. As Richard Kraut observes, "no modern theorist holds that in order to retain the right to life one must use one's talents to benefit the community."[34]

But granting that Aristotle was no modern theorist, was he some kind of rights theorist? The thesis that someone may be entitled to something even if it is not deserved (e.g., entitled to one's own bodily organs) is a fairly recent development. But even if true, people also have a right (i.e., just claim) to what they deserve, for example, to the fruits of one's labor. The first two objections exclude John Locke as a rights theorist. For Locke held that slavery and the subordination of women are justified "by the right of nature."[35] Further, Locke derived natural rights not from a Hegelian principle of subjective freedom, but from the doctrine that human beings, as the creations and servants of God, "are his property, whose workmanship they are, made to last during his, not one another's pleasure."[36] It is unreasonable to hold Aristotle to a standard that paradigmatic rights theorists could not meet.

IV. Rights in Demosthenes' Orations

Demosthenes (384–322 B.C.E.), a contemporary of Aristotle, left a corpus of legal speeches in which rights locutions occur very frequently.[37] (1) He uses *to dikaion* for a "just claim" against another party, for example for his own just claims (*ta dikaia*) against his guardian Aphorbus to his inheritance (27.1, 3; cf. 13.16). This clearly refers to a subjective right because Demosthenes speaks of litigants as "*having* this just claim

[32] Cooper 1996: 863.
[33] Schofield 1996.
[34] Kraut 1996: 763.
[35] Locke, *Second Treatise of Government*, Ch. 7.85–86.
[36] Locke, *Second Treatise of Government*, Ch. 2.6.
[37] See Cohen 2006 and Miller 2006, which form the basis for this section.

(*to dikaion*)" (44.29) and he contrasts "*our* just claims" with "the just claims *of others*" (3.27; cf. "*your* just claims," 24.3). (2) *Exeinai* is used in the sense of a "liberty" or "privilege"; for example, "Indeed, Callicles, if you have the liberty (*exesti*) to enclose your land, surely we also had the liberty to enclose ours. But if my father did you an injustice by enclosing his land, you also do me an injustice by enclosing yours" (55.29). The implication is that all owners are at liberty to erect walls around their property, provided they do no injustice to their neighbors. Regarding inheritance law, Demosthenes reports that "Solon made a law that one had the liberty (*exeinai*) to give his things [i.e., property] to whomever he wishes, if there were no legitimate children" (20.102). (3) *Kurios* in the sense of "authority" is used to distinguish masters from slaves: masters are *kurios* over slaves but not vice versa; only a free man is *kurios* over himself (37.51, 47.14–15, 59.46). A guardian is the legal authority over an estate for a minor heir or widow (27.55). The adjective *kurios* (fem. *kuria*) also applies to laws (20.8, 34; 24.205), decrees (23.96), wills (36.34), and contracts (47.77, 59.46). (4) *Adeia* means "immunity," for example from punishment of debtors for failure to pay debts on time (24.103) and for safe conduct granted to foreign troops (23.159) or an actor on tour (5.6). *Ateleia* denotes "exemption," for example, exemption from public service granted by the assembly (20.1–2, 25, 127).

Demosthenes' appeal to individual rights was an integral part of his democratic ideology.[38] For example, he contends that the right of individuals to protect their property is based on a higher law common to all human beings, and not merely on a conventional law (holding for example in Athens but not Sparta, or vice versa): "Earth and gods! Is it not monstrous, and manifestly contrary to law – I don't mean only contrary to the written law but also contrary to the common [law] of all human beings – that I should not have the liberty (*exeinai*) to defend myself against a person who comes and takes my possessions with force as though I were an enemy?" (23.61). He also argues that the legal treatment of accused criminals should be according to their guilt or innocence: A voluntary wrongdoer should be punished; an involuntary wrongdoer should be pardoned; an innocent man should not be punished at all. "These things appear not only thus in our laws, but nature herself has laid it down in her unwritten laws and the moral character of humanity" (18.275).

[38] See Hansen 1991: 73–85.

A central principle in Demosthenes' democratic ideology is that the people are sovereign (*ho dēmos kurios*). Athens had various safeguards (including laws, institutions, even curses) against powerful individuals gaining sovereignty, whereas in Sparta, the members of the Senate (Gerousia) were masters over the people (20.107). It is important to note that Demosthenes does not endorse the extreme form of democracy, denounced by Plato and Aristotle, in which the populace does whatever it wishes in a tyrannical fashion. Instead, Demosthenes advocates popular sovereignty limited by the rule of law. In *Against Meidias* he tells the people in the Athenian Assembly: "The laws are strong through you, and you through the laws" (21.224). Although the people are sovereign, they follow the law in carrying out their will, for example, concerning the grant of the right of citizenship (59.88). The Athenians maintained the rule of law by making it difficult to change the laws. This included a legal process called "indictment for illegal acts" (*graphē paranomōn*), whereby a citizen could be prosecuted for proposing an unconstitutional measure (24.154). Demosthenes speaks with approval of the Locrians, who were even more dedicated to legal stability: "If anyone wishes to propose a new law, he legislates with a noose around his neck. If the law is deemed noble and beneficial, the proposer lives and departs, but if not the noose is tightened and he dies" (24.139). In the Athenian system the laws were more permanent and took precedence over decrees, which could be easily passed by the assembly. If a decree was shown to conflict with a law, it was regarded as null and void. As Demosthenes says, "The law annuls decrees" (20.44). This anticipated judicial review in modern legal systems.[39]

A cardinal principle of democracy is that all citizens are equal before the law (23.86). "The law states: 'nor shall it be permitted to enact a law applying to an individual, unless the same law applies to all individuals.' This law demands that we should govern ourselves with the same laws and not different persons with different laws" (46.12–13; cf. 24.59). In addition, all citizens have the right of free speech. Partaking of a public constitution implies that whoever wishes to speak is at liberty (*exon*) to do so (51.19). Demosthenes maintains that justice concerns the good of the entire rather than of a particular class (19.1, 23.18). However, he opposes radical egalitarian proposals to take from

[39] John Marshall, Chief Justice of the United States Supreme Court, in *Marbury v. Madison*, affirmed "the principle, supposed to be essential to all written constitutions, that a law repugnant to the constitution is void" (5 US [1 Cranch] 137, 2 L.Ed. 60 [1803]).

the rich and give to the poor. To protect the advantage of the city-state is to protect the poor against rich, and vice versa (10.36). For justice requires impartiality to all social classes (21.183). In a democracy *everyone* shares in equal and just claims (*ta isa kai ta dikaia*, 21.67).

In conclusion, Demosthenes used "rights" locutions to express the fundamental principles and ideals of the democracy. His statements that all citizens have rights based on a higher unwritten law and that everyone is equal under the law make him sound like a modern liberal. He was a rhetorician rather than a philosopher, however, and his claims lack well-articulated theoretical foundations. It is unclear how close he came to modern rights theory. For example, when (like other Greeks) he denied equal rights to non-citizens, especially slaves, did he mean to reject universal human rights or was he simply being inconsistent?

V. Rights in Roman Law

Many scholars have viewed rights as central to Roman law.[40] A recent translation of Justinian's *Institutes* begins, "Justice is an unswerving and perpetual determination to acknowledge all men's rights" (1.1).[41] Historians formerly took it for granted that Roman law was concerned with defining and protecting rights. Roman jurists divided the law into three parts – the laws of persons, of things, and of actions (1.2.12) – each of which was concerned with rights. The law of persons included the rights of a father over his children as well as the right to own, and to grant freedom to, slaves (1.3–8). The law of things involved important distinctions related to property rights. For example, Roman law distinguished between ownership of property and mere possession (4.6.1). Further, it distinguished between corporeal things (e.g., land, slaves, gold, etc.) and incorporeal things; the latter involve inheritance, usufruct, and contractual obligations. Even though what one inherits may be corporeal (e.g., a house), "the actual right of inheritance is incorporeal, as is the actual right to the use and fruits of a thing, and the right inherent in an obligation" (2.2.2). Finally, the law of actions involves juridical rights: "An action is nothing but a right (*ius*) to go to court to get one's due" (4.6). The Roman jurists distinguished between two kinds of action: *in personam*, against a particular individual who is

[40] Sections V and VI are based on Miller and Biondi 2007: 157–63. Permission granted by Springer Publishing.

[41] All translations of Justinian, *Institutes*, are by Birks and McLeod, 1987.

obligated to the plaintiff as a result of a contract or a tort (e.g., a claim of repayment of a debt), and *in rem*, against a defendant who is not under any kind of obligation to the plaintiff but is involved in a dispute with him over a thing (e.g., over ownership of a house). This is the source of the modern distinction between rights *in personam* and *in rem*.

Several Latin locutions correspond to the different senses of "rights" distinguished by Hohfeld:

Table II

Hohfeld	Latin
just claim	*ius*
liberty, privilege	*libera potestas, facultas*
authority	*dominius, auctoritas*
immunity, exemption	*immunitas*

It is instructive to compare Table II with Table I. Parallels between Greek and Latin legal terms are documented by the Edict of Milan in 313 C.E. of the Roman co-emperors. The original Latin text was recorded in Lactantius' *De mortibus persecutorum* 48, and a Greek translation is in Eusebius' *Ecclesiastical History* 10.5.1–14. In this edict the emperors Constantine and Licinius granted "both to Christians and to all men free power (*libera potestas* = *eleuthera hairesis*) to follow whatever religion each one wished." The emperors decided that "no one was to be denied the liberty (*facultas* = *exousia*) to follow the Christian worship or that religion which he felt to be suited to himself." Christians were granted "the free and unconditional power" (*libera atque absoluta potestas* = *eleuthera kai apolelumenē exousia*) of religion. Others, too, were granted this opportunity (*facultas* = *exousia*), so that "each individual may have the free opportunity (*libera facultas* = *exousia*) to choose and practice whatever form of worship he wishes." They also recognized that property belongs by right (*ius* = *to dikaion*) to Christian congregations and commanded restoration of such property to these bodies. The Edict of Milan thus illustrates the parallels between the Greek and Roman locutions for rights.

In spite of this evidence, legal historians caution that the ancient Romans did not view the legal order as essentially a structure of individual rights in the way that moderns do.[42] Going further, Michel Villey argues that individual rights play no role whatsoever in Roman law.[43]

[42] See Nicholas 1962: 100.

[43] Villey 1946 and 1953–54.

He contends that the word *ius* occurs only in the objective sense, never in the subjective sense. For example, when Justinian's *Institutes* begins, "Justice is an unswerving and perpetual determination to acknowledge all men's rights," the phrase "all men's rights" translates *ius suum cuique*. Here, Villey maintains, *ius* or "right" has the objective sense, meaning that legal justice results in a right or just state of affairs involving everyone, not that *a right* belongs to an individual subject. He also points out that in some instances *ius* does not correspond to a right, for example, when Gaius' *Institutes* 2.14 refers to the *ius* of a homeowner to take the overflow from a neighbor's gutter through his own property. In this case, according to Villey, *ius* refers to the entire rightful relationship involving both the homeowner and neighbor, rather than to the right of one of the parties to the dispute.[44]

Villey argues that the word *ius* came to refer to a subjective right only in the Middle Ages, when it was understood to denote a licit power by William of Ockham (*c.* 1285–1349). Along similar lines, Villey contends that the Roman term *dominium* (ownership) does not entail rights because ownership does not include the licit power to use one's property. For example, a will may leave to someone the bare ownership of an orchard, but to someone else a usufruct; here the usufructuary rather than the owner is permitted to consume the fruits of the orchard (Justinian, *Institutes* 2.4.1).

Though influential, Villey's arguments have met with objections, especially his radical dichotomy between subjective and objective right. Even if *ius* has an objective character, it can also be used in a subjective sense for someone's entitlement, as in *meum ius*, "my right." Michael Zuckert objects,

> [I]f one begins with right in the objective sense of "the right or just thing in itself," that is, the correct assignment or relation of things to persons, then the 'part' in that distribution that pertains to each readily becomes the basis for the assertion of a claim of the subjective right sort. From being "in the right" it is easy to move to "having a right."[45]

For example, in the overflow example, the *ius* might be understood to imply the right that a neighbor receive a stream or run-off to his buildings or site.

[44] Villey 1972 makes a similar claim about the Greek *dikaion* in Aristotle.

[45] Zuckert 1989: 74. Similar objections are raised by Pugliese 1954 and Kaser 1996.

Regarding Villey's claim that the idea of a right as a licit power emerged only with Ockham in the fourteenth century, it may be replied that the Romans already viewed a *ius* as an authorized exercise of a power: For example, "[o]ur authority (*potestas*) over our children is a right (*ius*) which only Roman citizens have" (Justinian, *Institutes* 1.9.2). The same goes for Villey's claim that *dominium* (mastery) does not imply licit power. For example, "Slaves are in the power of their masters (*in potestate dominorum*).... We ought not to abuse our rights (*nostro iure*)" (Gaius, *Institutes* 1.52–53). Brian Tierney remarks, "It is hard not to see here an assertion of the subjective *right* of the master consisting in his *power* over the slave who was under his *dominium*."[46] The distinction between mastery and usufruct, when it occurs, may be understood in terms of rights; for example, "The only person who can claim at law that he has a right (*ius*) to use and enjoy property is the man who has the usufruct of it. The master (*dominus*) of the estate cannot do so, as a man who has the mastery does not have a separate right (*ius*) of use and enjoyment" (Justinian, *Digest* 7.6.5 pr.).

Rights seem to have played an important role in ancient Roman law, even if it was not the dominant role of rights in modern law.

VI. Human Rights in Stoic Philosophy

Some scholars credit ancient Stoic philosophers with helping to lay the foundations for the modern theory of human rights. Phillip Mitsis argues that the Stoics "offer an account in which natural rights are bounded by natural law and grounded in a particular conception of a natural human *telos* and a natural impulse to community and social solidarity."[47] For example, Chrysippus (*c.* 280–207 B.C.E.) holds that all human beings are subject to "the universal law, which is right reason pervading everything and which is identical to Zeus, who is the director of the administration of existing things" (Diogenes Laertius 7.88). He describes natural law as follows: "Law is king of all things divine and human. It must preside over what is honorable and base, both as ruler and as guide, and in virtue of this it must be the standard of justice and injustice, prescribing to animals whose nature is political, what they should do, and prohibiting them from what they should not do."[48] Just

46 Tierney 1997: 17.

47 Mitsis 1999: 155.

48 *SVF* 3.314, trans. Long and Sedley 1987, 67R, with modifications.

as the law of a particular city defines the rights and duties of each of its citizens, so natural law defines the moral rights and duties of each citizen of the cosmos (*kosmopolitēs*). Mitsis claims that "the Stoics are the first thinkers in antiquity to develop a view that rights play that is natural in the stronger sense of being naturally attached to individuals by the mere fact that they are human beings and, as such, members of a natural human community."[49]

Richard Bauman also argues that the Roman idea of "human right" (*ius humanum*) is grounded in Stoic principles of benevolence (*humanitas*) and compassion (*clementia*) that require that individuals transcend their narrow self-interest.[50] For example, Seneca argues that we can achieve happiness only through a partnership of interests with other individuals. "No one can live happily who has regard to himself alone and transforms everything into a question of his own utility; you must live for your neighbor if you would live for yourself." He adds that this association (*societas*) "makes us mingle as humans with our fellow humans and judges that the human race has a certain right (*ius*) in common" (*Epistle* 48.3). Like Chrysippus, Seneca also argues that because all human beings are members of a single natural community, they have duties of justice and fairness to each other:

> Everything that you see, both divine and human, is one; we are the parts of one great body. Nature created us as relatives, for she created us from the same source and for the same end. She has endowed us with mutual love and sociability. She fashioned fairness and justice. According to her regulation it is worse to suffer than to inflict harm. Through her authority let our hands be prepared for what needs help. Let this verse be in your hearts and on your lips: "I am human; I regard nothing human as foreign to me." Let us have common ownership; our birth is in common. (*Epistle* 95.52–3; citing Terence, *Self-tormentor* 77)

The virtues of benevolence, justice, and fairness espoused in this passage may be viewed as foreshadowing modern concern with human rights.

Some scholars object, however, that Stoics could not have had a theory of human rights because they were primarily concerned with carrying out their duties, acting virtuously, and living according to

[49] Mitsis 1999: 162. See also Long 1997.

[50] Bauman 2000.

nature, rather than with recognizing the rights of others.[51] Mitsis replies, "A Stoic may be motivated to help someone by recognizing that such an action conforms to a duty enjoined by nature's law. But the object of that action is the benefit of the individual needing help."[52] Seneca offers the example of someone who obtains a magistracy by ransoming ten citizens out of a great number of captives. In this case the agent acts both for his own advantage and for the advantage of each captive he chooses to ransom (*De beneficiis* 6.13.3). Similarly, even if a Stoic acts justly because he is motivated by a sense of duty, the object of the just act is the other person's interest. By viewing the interests of others as the object of just acts, the Stoics cross the divide between duty and rights.

Another objection concerns slavery, which was a mainstay of the Roman economy and society. Slaves lacked rights and legal standing and were often maltreated and even brutalized. Spartacus, leader of a slave revolt in 73 B.C.E., is now celebrated as an early champion of human rights. It would seem that the Stoics would have condemned slavery if they were committed to human rights, but they did not. This is a complex and difficult issue. Seneca argues movingly for the humane treatment of slaves; for example, "Remember that he whom you call your slave sprang from the same stock and enjoys the same sky, and breathes, lives, and dies equally. Insofar as you can see him as freeborn, he can see you as a slave" (47.10). A slave is a victim of chance, and it is possible for us to find ourselves in the same situation as the person we despise. Seneca offers the following advice: "Behave toward your inferiors as you would want your superiors to behave toward you" (47.11). He recommends that slaves be treated in a kind and even friendly manner. We should evaluate slaves, like other human beings, on the basis of their character rather than their occupation. Even if someone is a slave, he may be free in his soul (*liber animo*) (47.17). Yet Seneca refrains from a sweeping critique of the Romans' inhumane treatment of slaves (cf. 47.11), and does not suggest that it is unjust for one human being to own another since all are equal by nature.

Similarly, though Epictetus taught that all men, free or slave, were "brothers by nature" and "children of Zeus" (*Discourses* 1.13.4), he did not condemn slavery (although he was once a slave himself). The Stoic acceptance of slavery may have been partly due to their view that

[51] See Sorabji 1993: 134–57. Burnyeat 1994 argues that the Greeks also placed the emphasis on duties rather than rights.

[52] Mitsis 1999: 168.

individuals are free in the strict sense only insofar as they are autonomous, or in control of their own beliefs and desires. Whether one is free depends on oneself alone and not on other people or external factors (1.19.7). Epictetus said, "Whoever wishes to be free, let him neither want anything, nor avoid anything, that is up to others; otherwise he is necessarily a slave" (*Encheiridion* 14.2). Hence, a manumitted slave will become no freer if he lacks autonomy and he will remain less free than a legal slave who is autonomous (*Discourses* 3.24.67–69, 4.1.33–40).

The Roman jurists expressed similar views. Ulpian declared that everyone would be born free by the natural law (Justinian, *Digest* 1.1.3), and Sabinus that "as far as concerns the natural law all men are equal" (50.17.32), and Florentinus called slavery "against nature" (1.5.4; cf. 1.3.12). However, "the jurists did not question the existence of the institution – most were slave-owners themselves."[53] The Romans did make reforms to ameliorate slavery. For example, the emperor Antoninus Pius (161–80), who was a Stoic, instituted legal curbs on cruelty to slaves, making "a man who kills his own slave without good grounds liable to the same punishment as one who kills someone else's slave," and compelling cruel masters to sell their slaves (*Institutes* 1.8.2). The Romans never abolished slavery, but the Stoic philosophers and jurists helped pave the way for the eventual condemnation of slavery.

VII. Rights in Ancient Judaism and Christianity

Nicholas Wolterstorff has recently argued, "The conception of justice as inherent [i.e., subjective] rights was not born in the fourteenth or seventeenth century; this way of thinking about justice goes back into the Hebrew and Christian Scriptures."[54] Two Hebrew words for justice, *mishpat* and *tsedeqa*, are contained in the proclamation, "Let justice roll down like waters, and rectitude like an ever-flowing stream" (Amos 5:24). Some scholars maintain that these terms refer to a judicial performance rather than to a just state of affairs.[55] Wolterstorff rejects this legalistic interpretation. In order for a judge to make a legally just decision, he must determine whether or not an accused person has violated

[53] Borkowski 1997, p. 92.

[54] Wolterstorff 2008: xii. Translations of the Bible are by Wolterstorff.

[55] O'Donovan 1996: 39.

the demands of *primary* justice, for example, by stealing the plaintiff's property.[56] 1 Kings 3:16–28 (a passage which Wolterstorff does not cite) seems to support his interpretation: Two prostitutes appear before King Solomon. One of them argues that the other's newborn baby died and she substituted it for the other's infant while she slept. Each woman claims, "The live baby is mine, the dead one is yours." Finally Solomon orders a sword and commands that the child be cut in two and half of it given to each woman. Overcome with compassion, the true mother offers to give up the baby if the king will spare its life, while the other insists that the baby be cut in two. The king awards the baby to the first woman, declaring, "She is its mother." The story concludes that all Israel was in awe of the king's verdict, "for they saw that he possessed wisdom from God to execute justice (*mishpat*)." The clear implication is that Solomon's wisdom enabled him to determine which woman made the just or rightful claim that the baby was hers.

Moreover, decrees are described as iniquitous and statutes as oppressive if they treat the needy unjustly and rob the poor of what is rightfully theirs (Is. 10:1–2). In one of the psalms Yahweh, the God of Israel, speaks to the gods of other nations in an imaginary council:

> How long will you judge unjustly
> and show partiality to the wicked?
> Give justice to the weak and the orphan;
> maintain the right of the lowly and the destitute.
> Rescue the weak and the needy;
> deliver them from the hand of the wicked. (Ps. 82:2–4)

Here Yahweh implies that his laws are morally superior to those of the heathen gods because his laws alone offer justice for the weak and defenseless.

Although this is evidence that the writers of the Hebrew Bible did not equate justice with mere obedience to legal conventions, it does not yet show that they recognized inherent rights (i.e., rights of persons). However, Wolterstorff argues, the existence of such rights is implicit in their writings. First it is implied that God has rights, because He is able to forgive wrongdoers and pardon all of their sins (cf. Ps. 79:9, 85:2, 103:2–3). One person is able to forgive another only if the former has been wronged by the latter and thus acquires certain rights of retribution, rights which one can forgo. Hence, argues Wolterstorff, "Israel's writers

[56] Wolterstorff 2008: 71–72.

presuppose . . . that God has the right to hold us accountable for doing justice," and that God has the right "against us to our obeying him when he exercises this prior right and does in fact hold us accountable."[57] Second, it is implied that human beings have rights because God made human beings in his image or likeness and gave them dominion over all the animals on earth (Gen. 1:26). Hence, as part of his covenant with Noah and his descendants God declares, "Whoever sheds the blood of a human, / by a human shall that person's blood be shed; / for in his own image / God made mankind" (Gen. 9:6). Wolterstorff argues that these themes are continued in the New Testament.[58] Jesus Christ quotes the prophet Isaiah, declaring that the Lord "has anointed me; he has sent me to announce good news to the poor, to proclaim release for prisoners and recovery of sight for the blind; to let the broken victims go free . . ." (Luke 4:18–19; cf. Is. 61:1–2, 58:6–7). As Richard Hays remarks, "By evoking these texts at the beginning of his ministry, Luke's Jesus declares himself as the Messiah who by the power of the Spirit will create a restored Israel in which justice and compassion for the people will prevail."[59] Jesus frequently expresses concern for the poor, the crippled, the blind, the lame, social outcasts, women, and Gentiles, and he advocates a kind of "social inversion" whereby the poor and powerless will be exalted and the rich and powerful will be humbled. In view of this, Wolterstorff contends that Jesus' commitment to justice is undeniable.

This interpretation is, however, related to controversial issues of translation. When the Hebrew Bible was translated into the Greek Septuagint (third and second centuries B.C.E.), the term *tsedeqa* was generally translated as *dikaiosunē*, and *mishpat* as *krisis*. In the King James Bible (1611 C.E.) *tsedeqa* and *dikaiosunē* were translated as "righteousness" and *mishpat* and *krisis* as "judgment." Most modern English translations have followed suit, though some recent translations have translated *mishpat* and *krisis* as "justice." Wolterstorff maintains that "righteousness" is misleading to present-day readers: "In everyday speech one seldom any more describes someone as *righteous*; if one does, the suggestion is that he is *self*-righteous. 'Justice,' by contrast, refers to an interpersonal situation; justice is present when persons are related to each other in a certain way."[60]

[57] Wolterstorff 2008: 93–94.

[58] Wolterstorff (2008, ch. 5) confines his interpretation to the Gospels and especially Luke.

[59] Hays 1996:116. Wolterstorff makes clear his debt to this book.

[60] Wolterstorff 2008: 111.

Wolterstorff suggests that human rights are implied by affirmations of the inherent worth of individuals: "Look at the birds of the air; they neither sow nor reap nor gather into barns; and yet your heavenly Father feeds them. Are you not of more value than they?" (Matt. 6:26, cf. 10:31, 12:11–12 and Luke 12:24) This implies, according to Wolterstorff, "the recognition of human beings as having worth and of that worth as grounding how they are to be treated."[61] Wolterstorff conjectures that this is ultimately the recognition that each human being is an image of God. Jesus describes the final judgment in which the Son of Man separates those destined for eternal life and those for eternal punishment on the basis of whether or not they cared for those in need. The Lord says, "Just as you did it to one of the least of these who are members of my family, you did it to me." And, "Just as you failed to do it for the least of these who are members of my family, you failed to do it for me" (Matt. 25:31–46).

Against this interpretation, it might be objected that Jesus advocates forgiveness over justice. When someone asks Jesus whether he should pardon seven times over someone who sins against him, Jesus replies that he should pardon him seventy-seven times (Matt. 18:21–22). Wolterstorff may be correct that "forgiveness presupposes that one has been deprived of that to which one has a right."[62] But the point of this objection is that we should not insist on justice in our dealings with others. If we ask God for mercy, we must be prepared to forgive others, because, "if you forgive others their trespasses, your heavenly Father will also forgive your trespasses" (Matt. 6:14–15, cf. Luke 6:37). Jesus warns that God will punish human beings on the basis of strict justice unless they themselves forgive others from their hearts (Matt. 18:35).

Moreover, if Jesus heals the sick because it is just to do so, this implies that the sick have a *right* or just claim against Jesus to be cared for. But Jesus makes a point of saying, "I have come to call not the just (*dikaioi*) but sinners." He also quotes the prophet Hosea: "I desire mercy not sacrifice" (Matt. 9:10–13; cf. Hosea 6:6). The basis for redemption seems to be not justice but mercy and grace grounded in God's unconditional love. Although the concept of rights may have a place in Christian ethics, it is debatable whether it has as central a place as for Greek thinkers like Aristotle and Demosthenes. Nevertheless, the Christian principle that every human being is worthy arguably

[61] Wolterstorff 2008: 130–31.
[62] Wolterstorff 2008: 130.

provided an important inspiration for the modern theory of human rights. Wolterstorff's path-breaking study invites further scholarly research on the possible place of rights in early Christian writings including the letters of Paul.

VIII. Conclusion

Undeniably there are deep differences between ancient and modern political views, but it is reasonable to recognize continuity as well as change in the history of political philosophy. Can the ultimate origins of rights be traced back to antiquity? This depends on how strictly rights are defined. If rights are understood as actionable claims of justice that individuals have against other members of the same community, it is hard to deny their presence in the legal systems of Greece and Rome. Both ancient Greek and Latin possess a sophisticated repertoire of locutions for legal relations that seem to correspond closely to modern rights locutions. There is also evidence that the Greeks understood a right in a subjective sense, that is, as belonging to an individual as a right holder. Some evidence has been considered for at least an implicit recognition of subjective rights in Jewish and Christian scriptures.

It is much harder to establish that ancient political theorists recognized the *rights of persons*. Though this has been claimed on behalf of Plato, the dominant view remains that Plato recognized at most *functional* rights, that is, rights to carry out tasks necessary for the city-state as a whole. There is a stronger case for rights of persons in Aristotle's political theory, but an individual possesses such rights only as a member of a city-state. Demosthenes seems to go further in asserting that individuals possess equal rights on the basis of a higher law. The Stoics go still further in adopting a cosmopolitan view that all human beings are naturally akin and should therefore treat each other humanely and justly. None of these ancient theorists go so far as to espouse *human rights* in the modern sense, since they all accept slavery.

It is noteworthy, however, that Aristotle mentions some theorists who argued that "all slavery is against nature" and merely based on convention. The critics offered the following syllogism: Any relation based on force rather than nature is unjust. Slavery is based on force rather than nature. Therefore, slavery is unjust (*Pol.* 1.3, 1253b20–23, cf. 1.5, 1254a17, 1.6, 1255a3). Aristotle does not name these early abolitionists, but one of them was probably Alcidamus, a Sophist in the fourth century B.C.E., who apparently condemned slavery on the basis of natural law in his *Messeniac Oration*. His argument was preserved by an anonymous medieval commentator: "God left everyone free; nature has made nobody a slave" (see Aristotle, *Rhetoric* 1.13, 1373b18, cf. *Pol.* 1.5, 1254a19). These critiques of slavery, though unfortunately rare, indicate that ancient political theory contained already a seed from which developed the modern theory of universal human rights.

Works Cited

Annas, J. 1976. "Plato's Republic and Feminism." *Philosophy* 51: 307–21.

Barker, E. 1906. *The Political Thought of Plato and Aristotle*. London.

Bauman, R. A. 2000. *Human Rights in Ancient Rome*. London.

Birks, P., and G. McLeod, trans. 1987. *Justinian's Institutes*. Ithaca, NY.

Borkowski, A. 1997. *Textbook on Roman Law*, 2nd ed. Oxford. 1997.

Brett, A. S. 1997. *Liberty, Right and Nature: Individual Rights in Later Scholastic Thought*. Ideas in Context. Cambridge.

Burnyeat, M. F. 1994. "Did the Greeks Have the Concept of Human Rights?" *Polis* 13: 1–11.

Cohen, D. 2006. "Democracy and Individual Rights in Athens." *Philosophical Inquiry* 27: 13–26.

Cooper, J. M. 1996. "Justice and Rights in Aristotle's Politics." *Review of Metaphysics* 49: 859–72.

Fornara, C. W., ed. and trans. 1977. *Archaic Times to the End of the Peloponnesian War*. Translated Documents of Greece and Rome 1. Baltimore, MD.

Grube, G. M. A. 1997. *Republic*, rev. C. D. C. Reeve. In *Plato: Complete Works*, ed. J. M. Cooper. Indianapolis, IN.

Hansen, M. H. 1991. *The Athenian Democracy in the Age of Demosthenes: Structure, Principles and Ideology*, trans. J. A. Cook. The Ancient World. Oxford.

Hays, R. B. 1996. *The Moral Vision of the New Testament: Community, Cross, New Creation*. San Francisco, CA.

Hohfeld, W. N. 1919. *Fundamental Legal Conceptions as Applied in Judicial Reasoning*. New Haven, CT.

Kaser, Max. 1996. *Das römische Zivilprozessrecht*, 2nd ed. Ed. K. Hackl. Rechtsgeschichte des Altertums, 10.3.4. München.

Keyt, D. 1991. "Aristotle's Theory of Distributive Justice." In *A Companion to Aristotle's Politics.*, ed. D. Keyt and F. D. Miller, Jr. Oxford.

Kraut, R. 1996. "Are There Natural Rights in Aristotle?" *Review of Metaphysics* 49: 755–74.

Long, A. A. 1997. "Stoic Philosophers on Persons, Property-ownership and Community." In *Aristotle and After*, ed. R. Sorabji. *BICS* Supplement 68. London.

Long, A. A., and D. N. Sedley. 1987. *The Hellenistic Philosophers*, 2 vols. Cambridge.

MacIntyre, A. 1981. *After Virtue: A Study in Moral Theory*. Notre Dame, IN.

Meiggs, R., and D. Lewis, ed. 1988. *Selections of Greek Historical Inscriptions to the End of the Fifth Century* B.C., rev ed. Oxford.

Miller, F. D., Jr. 1995. *Nature, Justice, and Rights in Aristotle's Politics*. Oxford.

1996. "Aristotle and the Origins of Natural Rights." *Review of Metaphysics* 49: 873–907.

2005. "Property Rights in Aristotle." In *Aristotle's Politics: Critical Essays*, ed. R. Kraut and S. Skultety. Critical Essays on the Classics. Lanham, MD.

2006. "Legal and Political Rights in Demosthenes and Aristotle." *Philosophical Inquiry* 27: 27–60.

Miller, F. D., and C.-A. Biondi, ed. 2007. *A Treatise of Legal Philosophy and General Jurisprudence*, vol. 6: *A History of the Philosophy of Law from the Ancient Greeks to the Scholastics*. Dordrecht.

Mitsis, P. 1999. "The Stoic Origin of Natural Rights." In *Topics in Stoic Philosophy*, ed. K. Ierodiakonou. Oxford.

Nicholas, B. 1962. *An Introduction to Roman Law*. Oxford.

O'Donovan, O. 1996. *The Desire of the Nations: Rediscovering the Roots of Political Theology*. Cambridge.

Popper, K. 1962. *The Open Society and Its Enemies*, 4th ed. Princeton, NJ.

Pugliese, G. 1953. "'Res corporales', 'res incorporales' e il problema del diritto soggettivo." In *Studi in onore di Vincenzo Arangio-Ruiz*, vol. III. Napoli.

Reid, C. J., Jr. 1991. "The Canonistic Contribution to the Western Rights Tradition: An Historical Inquiry." *Boston College Law Review* 33: 37–92.

Santas, G. X. 2006. "Justice, Law, and Women in Plato's Republic." *Philosophical Inquiry* 27: 91–103.

Schofield, M. 1996. "Sharing in the Constitution." *Review of Metaphysics* 49: 831–58.

2006. *Plato: Political Philosophy*. Founders of Modern Political and Social Thought. Oxford.

Schwenk, C. J. 1985. *Athens in the Age of Alexander: The Dated Laws and Decrees of "the Lykourgan Era" 388–322 B.C.* Chicago.

Sorabji, R. 1993. *Animal Minds and Human Morals: The Origins of the Western Debate*. Cornell Studies in Classical Philology, 54. Ithaca, NY.

Strauss, L. 1953. *Natural Right and History*. Chicago.

Tierney, B. 1997. *The Idea of Natural Rights: Studies on Natural Rights, Natural Law and Church Law 1150–1625*. Emory University Studies in Law and Religion. Atlanta, GA.

Tod, M. N. 1948. *A Selection of Greek Historical Inscriptions*, vol. II: *From 403 to 323 B.C.* Oxford.

Tuck, R. 1979. *Natural Rights Theories: Their Origin and Development*. Cambridge.

Villey, M. 1946. "L'idée du roit subjectif et les systèmes juridiques romains." *Revue historique du droit* 24–25: 201–28.

1953–54. "Les origines de la notion de droit subjectif." *Archives de philosophie du droit* 2: 201–27.

1964. "La genèse du droit subjectif chez Guillaume d'Occam." *Archives de philosophie du droit* 9: 97–127.

1972. "Bentham et le droit naturel classique." *Archives de philosophie du droit* 17: 423–31.

Vlastos, G. 1977. "The Theory of Social Justice in the Polis in Plato's Republic." In *Interpretations of Plato: A Swarthmore Symposium*, ed. H. F. North. Mnemosyne Supplementum 50. Leiden.

1978. "The Rights of Persons in Plato's Conceptions of the Foundations of Justice." In *Morals, Science and Society*, ed. H. T. Englehardt, Jr. and D. Callahan. Hastings-on-Hudson, NY. Reprinted in *Studies in Greek Philosophy*, vol. II: *Socrates, Plato, and Their Tradition* (Princeton, NJ, 1995).

1989. "Was Plato a Feminist?" *Times Literary Supplement* 4.485 (Mar. 17): 276, 288–89. Reprinted in *Studies in Greek Philosophy*, vol. II: *Socrates, Plato, and Their Tradition*. (Princeton, NJ, 1995).

Wolterstorff, N. 2008. *Justice: Rights and Wrongs*. Princeton, NJ.

Zeller, E. 1897. *Aristotle and the Earlier Peripatetics: Being a Translation from Zeller's "Philosophy of the Greeks,"* 2 vols. Trans. B. F. C. Costelloe and J. H. Muirhead. London.

Zuckert, M. 1989. "'Bringing Philosophy Down from the Heavens': Natural Right in the Roman Law." *Review of Politics* 51: 70–85.

12: The Emergence of Natural Law and the Cosmopolis

Eric Brown

Two Influential Metaphors

In his work *On Laws* (*De legibus*), Cicero seeks to imitate Plato and portray a discussion of the best laws, just as he imitated Plato when he offered a dialogue concerning the ideal state in *On the Commonwealth* (*De re publica*) (*Leg.* 1.15 and 2.14).[1] His discussants agree that laws should be based on a "science of right," and they seek to ground his account not in the Twelve Tables of Roman history – the traditional foundation of Roman laws – but on "deepest philosophy" (*Leg.* 1.17).

> Thus, the most learned men thought to proceed from law, as I am inclined to think is right if law is, as they define it, highest reason implanted in nature, which commands the things that ought to be done and prohibits the opposite. This reason, when made firm and complete in the mind of a human, is law (*Leg.* 1.18)

Here Cicero identifies right reason as a foundation for civic laws. Cicero seems to say (at least at first) that this right reason occurs not independent of human minds but only in the perfected reason of some humans; he goes so far as to identify the "mind and reason of the wise" as "the rule

[1] For these works, I cite Powell 2006, and translations are mine. Where Powell's arrangements of the fragments of *De re publica* depart from the widely reproduced numbering in Ziegler 1969 (e.g., in Zetzel 1999), I also refer to Ziegler's placement of the passage.

of right and wrong" (*Leg.* 1.19). Even if right reason does not occur in nature independent of human minds, however, there remains on this view a natural determinant of right and wrong, and human beings who perfect their reason have access to it. Cicero calls it "law" not because right reason is the literal sense of 'law' (Latin *lex*, Greek *nomos*), but because it determines right and wrong just as conventional laws were traditionally thought to do. In this way, he grounds his account of ideal civic laws in a metaphorical law of nature (*Leg.* 1.20).

This metaphor soon leads to another. As it happens, Cicero does not think that right reason emerges only in the minds of some humans; he believes that gods are responsible for nature's law and our capacity to recognize it. And this gets Cicero thinking. Since the gods govern nature and give human beings the power of reason to discover what is right and wrong, the gods seem, by this gift, to establish community with humans:

> Thus, since there is nothing better than reason and since reason exists in human and in god, the first fellowship of human with god is a fellowship of reason. But those who share reason must also share right reason. And since right reason is law, we must think that humans also have law in common with gods. In addition, those who share law must also share right, and those who share these things must also be thought to share the same political society. . . . Thus, this whole world now must be thought to be a single political society shared by gods and humans. (*Leg.* 1.23)

In short, the gods govern nature with the natural law of right reason, and because humans and gods share right reason, they also a share the metaphorical law and thereby a metaphorical political society. The universal "natural law" establishes a metaphorical "world-state" or "cosmopolis."

These metaphors are among the most influential ideas from ancient political thought.[2] Rationalizing medieval philosophers, none

[2] See also *Leg.* 1.33 and 42 and 2.8–13 and *Rep.* 1.16–29 (esp. 27) and 3.27 (33 in Ziegler 1969). Of these two texts, *On Laws* was the primary vehicle of transmission, as it appeared in eight printed editions of Cicero's works before 1600. *On the Commonwealth* was lost for hundreds of years until Cardinal Angelo Mai found large passages of it in a palimpsest in the Vatican library in 1820, although some of its references to natural law and the cosmopolis were known through others' quotations

with greater impact than Thomas Aquinas, embraced the idea of "natural law" because it joins the notion of God's plan to the idea that human reason can discover some important practical truths about God's plan. Early modern political theorists, such as Grotius, Pufendorf, Hobbes, and Locke, made regular appeal to natural law. Sometimes, though not always, these appeals to natural law brought with them cosmopolitan ideas, and the cosmopolis as a special metaphor noisily re-entered political discourse as an Enlightenment ideal. These metaphors are not of merely historical interest: some contemporary political thinkers identify themselves as natural law theorists or cosmopolitans.[3]

Cicero did not invent these metaphors; he drew them from earlier Greek philosophers. The "learned men" he cites for his doctrine of natural law are the Stoics, who defined law as "right reason" that provides "the standard of right and wrong, prescribing to naturally political animals the things that ought to be done and proscribing the things that ought not."[4] The Stoics also insisted that the cosmos is like a political society (a polis) shared by gods and human beings.[5] Moreover, although the Stoics are Cicero's direct source, both metaphors were around in some form before the Stoics gave them their own stamp.

In this chapter, I chart the emergence of these two metaphors in ancient Greece so as to lay bare the possibilities and challenges they present to political thought. My story is episodic, and it concentrates on the clearest evidence for the emergence of the central ideas that the two metaphors typically advance.

and paraphrases, including, for instance, *Rep.* 3.27 (33 in Ziegler 1969), which is a quotation from Lactantius, *Divine Institutions* 6.8.6–9.

[3] For contemporary natural law theory, see especially Finnis 1980, George 2001, Murphy 2001 and 2006, and the essays in Finnis 1991 and George 1994 and 2001a. For the burgeoning literature on contemporary cosmopolitanism, one might start with the essays in Nussbaum et al. 1996, Cheah and Robbins 1998, Pogge 2001, Grieff and Cronin 2002, and Vertovec and Cohen 2002. For brief introductions, see Murphy 2002 and Kleingeld and Brown 2006.

[4] For the formulaic definition, see Stobaeus 2.7.11d, 2.96.10–12 WH (WH = Wachsmuth and Hense) and 2.7.11i, 2.102.4–6 WH; Cicero, *Leg.* 1.18; Diogenes Laertius 7.88; and Alexander of Aphrodisias, *De fato* 207.5–21 Bruns. The slightly more elaborate expression I offer here is from the opening of Chrysippus' *On Law*, as quoted by Marcian 1 (SVF 3.314). ("SVF" refers to von Arnim 1903–1905. Most of the Stoic texts I cite can be found translated in vol. 1 of Long and Sedley 1987 or in Inwood and Gerson 1997, but the translations here are mine.)

[5] See Arius Didymus ap. Eusebius SVF 2.528; Cicero, *ND* 2.78 and 154; Cicero, *Fin.* 3.64; Cicero, *Parad.* 18; Clement SVF 3.327; and Plutarch, *Comm. not.* 1065e.

Conventional and Unconventional Norms

The core idea of natural law responds to a basic problem of politics. Political communities are constituted in part by the explicit and implicit norms that govern how members of the community behave. If these communal norms were complete and consistent, one might well take them to define what is just for the community so that justice requires only obedience to the norms. In this way, although perhaps because they were idealizing, classical Greek thinkers widely insisted that justice requires obedience to communal norms (*nomoi*, singular *nomos*, conventionally translated "law" or "custom"), and many of them held that the *nomoi* define what is just.[6]

But communal norms are never complete and consistent. Even apart from the difficulty of making a *complete* set of norms (see the fifth section of this chapter, Contesting the Law-likeness of Natural Norms), the norms that govern any real-world community are diverse in their origin and in their articulation. Some of them were made explicit by various legislators. Some remain implicit and emerge in a rich array of practices, including various religious ones. So it is not surprising that there was often tension among the *nomoi* the Greeks recognized. When there is such tension, to determine whether a particular action is right or wrong one must decide which norm has greater authority. One might then think that one of the norms is a recent convention, not deserving of the respect that the other is due. One might even think that one of the norms simply runs deeper than mere convention. This is the core idea of natural law theory: natural law must be an unconventional standard for right and wrong against which to measure convention.

This idea emerges dramatically in Sophocles' *Antigone*, which was first staged in or soon before 441 B.C.E.[7] Antigone's brothers Polyneices and Eteocles have recently died in battle after their power-sharing relationship had failed and Polyneices and his allies had attacked Eteocles and the Thebans. Their uncle Creon, now King of Thebes, has decreed that Polyneices must remain unburied while Eteocles receives full rites.

[6] See, for instance, the common opinions noted by Aristotle, *NE* 5.1 (= *EE* 4.1), 1129b11 and *Rhet.* 2.9, 1366b9–11, with Dover 1974: 185–86.

[7] I cite the text of Lloyd-Jones and Wilson 1990, but with few alterations I quote the translation of Wyckoff 1954. For a reading of the play that emphasizes its complex tensions, see Nussbaum 1986: 51–82. I here concentrate, instead, on how Antigone articulates natural law's core idea. Other early occasions in which divine laws are invoked (e.g., Sophocles, *Oedipus Tyrannos* 863–72) do not make the motivations or grounds for recognizing divine laws so clear.

But traditional religious norms call for Antigone and her sister Ismene to ensure proper burial for both brothers. There is, then, a conflict of norms, both of which demand obedience. Ismene thinks that nothing can be done (39–40, 90, 92), but Antigone insists that Creon does not have the authority to contravene traditional norms governing burial (cf. 48).

This is not a simple conflict between politics and religion. Creon rests his law on religious authority, too, by arguing that the gods would not want honor given to Polyneices (282–89), who unjustly made himself an enemy to his city (182–208). But Antigone, while rightly recognizing that Creon's decree is a law (*nomos*, 452, cf. 449 and 481), rejects Creon's interpretation of the gods' wishes: "For me it was not Zeus who made that order. / Nor did that Justice who lives with the gods below / mark out such laws to hold among mankind" (450–52). Without the gods on his side, Creon's authority would be sharply limited. So Antigone continues:

> Nor did I think your orders were so strong
> that you, a mortal man, could over-run
> the gods' unwritten and unfailing laws (*nomima*).
>
> Not today or yesterday, they always live,
> and no one knows their origin in time. (453–57)

When Antigone starkly contrasts Creon's mortal decree with the immortal norms of the gods, she assumes that the divine "laws" (*nomima*) outstrip the authority of civil laws such as Creon's decree.

Although Antigone appeals to unconventional norms to trump conventional ones, she does not invoke *natural* laws, and this proves to be problematic. The trouble is not that her unconventional norms are supposed to be *divine*. In the ancient world, the natural and the divine are not necessarily opposed, and if, in this context, one supposes that humans can discover in nature the norms that the gods are responsible for, such norms can and should be deemed natural.[8] But the trouble

[8] By focusing on whether the law in question is epistemologically natural – accessible to human beings studying nature – I do not mean to deny the significance of whether the law is metaphysically natural – dependent on nothing outside of nature for its existence. If a law is epistemically natural but metaphysically supernatural, then there is the chance for disputes over the interpretation of the law between those who claim to understand it via their study of nature and those who claim to understand it via their access to the gods. That dispute would not arise over a law that is both

is that Antigone offers no hint as to how humans can discover the unconventional norms naturally.

Antigone certainly claims to know the divine laws, but it does not seem that she gets her knowledge from inquiring into nature.[9] Rather, it seems that Antigone simply knows that the gods call for her to bury her brother, just as Teiresias knows that Creon has wronged the gods of the underworld who govern the dead (1074–75). This is problematic. If Antigone has no justification for her claim to know the divine laws, then her epistemic "authority" depends upon mere rhetorical force. That is, either her audience is persuaded by her claim – at least persuaded that there in fact is an unwritten divine law that conflicts with Creon's decree – or it is not. Antigone's ungrounded appeal to divine law encourages multiple interpreters of the divine to disagree, with tragic results.

There are two ways in which one might extract from Sophocles' play a way out of this tragic conflict. First, one might suppose that if civic laws and customs are supposed to answer to divine laws, as

epistemically and metaphysically natural. But if we reserve the title "natural law" for a law that is both epistemically and metaphysically natural, we will have to deny that there is any natural law theorist in antiquity and, even more perversely, that Aquinas is a natural law theorist. Hence, I focus on epistemic access.

9 Antigone does at one point appeal to some natural facts in the course of justifying herself. In lines that some readers (e.g., Jebb 1900: 164 and 258–63) have suspected to be interpolations and not original to Sophocles' play (contrast Griffith 1999: 277–79), Antigone says that she was right to flout the civic law and to bury her brother Polyneices but that she would not have been right to do the same for a husband or child (904–14). To explain this striking interpretation of the divine law, she appeals to two natural facts: a young woman who has lost a child can (usually) bear another and a young woman whose parents are dead cannot have another sibling. (She also notes that a woman who has lost a husband can remarry, but this is no natural fact, as it depends upon some elaborate conventions.) Antigone supposes that she has obligations to the family that her parents started and obligations to any family that she starts, and she assumes that once her parents are dead, she cannot find new (in this case, male) members of the former family to uphold her obligations to that family whereas she can find new (male) members of the latter family and then uphold her obligations to that family (cf. Herodotus 3.119). But she might have supposed otherwise about her family obligations without denying the natural facts. She might have supposed that she is obligated to each member of her family whether she could somehow produce another person in that relationship or not. After all, there might be harm to each unburied person, whether or not there could be another person similarly related to Antigone. So although Antigone takes natural facts to be relevant to her understanding of the divine laws, she cannot think that they determine that understanding because they do not determine her particular conception of family obligations.

Antigone insists, then ultimate political authority should be vested with those who have special authority in interpreting the divine. Perhaps power should lie with people such as Teiresias, who has a reputation for successful prophecy. One might even suppose that natural facts can tell who has special authority. After all, the facts about what Teiresias foretold and what actually ensued are natural, and they either do or do not support his authority to interpret the gods' unwritten laws. But this connection between facts and the divine law is indirect because the authority of the law's *interpreter* – not the content of the law – is inferred from certain easily observed facts. So although the factual grounding of Teiresias' authority would give *some* reason to believe that Teiresias is right about the divine laws, it would not establish that the divine law is natural, and it would leave the rest of us unable to know whether Teiresias' successful prophecies really signify special access to the divine laws. In this way, we would remain at the mercy of Teiresias and others who can persuade us that they have worked miracles or have successfully prophesied.

Creon might hint at a second way out of the conflict when he comes, eventually, to "fear that it is best to preserve the established laws (*nomoi*) to the end of life" (1113–14). Here Creon seems to say that the correct interpretation of the gods is the one that accords best with established tradition. This suggestion of deeply conservative politics has in its favor the thought that tradition represents the wisdom of many generations. But it is also plausible that humans over time have had the opportunity to learn from past mistakes and to improve their understanding of the world. Additionally, Creon's suggestion postpones some hard questions. If long-established *nomoi* are right, then what supported these *nomoi* before they were long established? What reasons did those who first established these *nomoi* have for establishing them? Did they look to nature in a way that we cannot? Did they have privileged access to the gods? Or did they actually invent the laws themselves and merely pretend that the laws were divine? Creon does not say.

In sum, Sophocles' *Antigone* offers the core idea of natural law, but its unwritten divine laws are not natural. The rhetoric of "divine laws" can be very powerful – especially from an authority or from a person with a reputation for miracles or prophecy, and especially if it accords with tradition. But in the absence of natural facts to ground the divine laws, there seem to be few good reasons for preferring one interpretation of them over another, or, indeed, for thinking that they exist at all.

Nature and Normative Authority

Even before Sophocles' *Antigone* was first staged, some philosophers sought a way of discovering divine standards of right and wrong in nature. Beginning in Miletus in the sixth century B.C.E., some Greeks – often called "inquirers into nature" (*phusiologoi*) by ancients and "pre-Socratics" by us – began to find rational order in the world, and they sought to explain this order by identifying nature's fundamental causes (Greek *archai*, Latin *principia*). These philosophers also suggested connections between the standards that govern the workings of the cosmos and the standards that ought to govern the workings of the city. They frequently used the language of justice to describe the orderly workings of nature,[10] and one of them also prominently invoked the language of law. Heraclitus, who was active in the late sixth and early fifth century B.C.E., introduced more clearly than anyone else the second core idea of natural law –that the unconventional standards of right and wrong are embedded in nature, discoverable by humans studying the natural world.[11]

Heraclitus takes the world to be a unified cosmos in which everything shares in a comprehensive account or reason (*logos*) (frr. 2 and 50; cf. frr. 30 and 113) that most humans fail to comprehend (frr. 1 and 34).[12] He links this logos to law: "Those who speak comprehendingly must base their strength on that which is comprehensive over all, as the city must base its strength on law (*nomos*), and even more strongly. For all human laws are nourished by a divine one. For it rules as far as it wills, and suffices for all, and is more than enough (fr. 114)." In the first sentence of this fragment, Heraclitus limits himself to an analogy: humans who want to speak with intelligence need to base their account on the universal logos (account or reason) just as a city that wants to flourish needs to base its strength on law. This analogy fits well with his insistence that understanding depends upon the universal logos (frr. 2 and 41) and his claim that "the people must fight on behalf of the

10 See, e.g., Anaximander fr. 1 DK (DK = Diels and Kranz 1951–52), Heraclitus fr. 94 DK, and Parmenides fr. 8.14–15 DK, with Vlastos 1947.

11 There are other more isolated suggestions of natural law among the Presocratics. See, e.g., Empedocles fr. 135 DK (quoted in n. 35 below).

12 I cite the fragments according to their presentation in Diels and Kranz 1951–52. My translations and interpretations are significantly indebted to Kahn 1979 (see esp. 117–18 for obvious borrowings), but when I use "comprehensive," "fail to comprehend," and (in the next fragment quoted above) "comprehendingly" to capture the wordplay of *xunos* and *axunetoi* and *xun noōi*, I owe a debt to Bury 1935: 72–73.

law as for the city wall" (fr. 44). But the second and third sentences of fragment 114 go beyond analogy and suggest that civic laws are based on a divine law.

To appreciate what is distinctive in Heraclitus' claim, consider what is not. The idea that human laws have divine origin or support was old news. After all, Antigone's fellow citizens agree with her that human laws should conform to the gods' wishes (*Antigone* 692–700). Hesiod had motivated this thought in the eighth century B.C.E.:

> This is the law (*nomos*) that Cronus' son [viz., Zeus] has established for human beings: that fish and beasts and winged birds eat one another, since there is no justice among them; but to human beings he has given justice, which turns out to be the best by far. For if someone who recognizes what is just is willing to speak out publicly, then far-seeing Zeus gives him wealth. But he who willfully swears a false oath, telling a lie in his testimony, is incurably hurt at the same time as he harms justice, and in later times his family is left more obscure; whereas the family of the man who keeps his oath is better in later times.[13]

Antigone simply extends this claim that because the gods gave humans the capacity for justice, they stand behind our norms of right and wrong. The claim also serves as the basis of Protagoras' Great Speech (Plato, *Protagoras* 320c–28d, esp. 321c–22d).

But Antigone, as we have seen, does not explain how to uncover the gods' norms in nature. And so far as Hesiod and Protagoras take it, the claim is compatible with the view that civic laws have merely conventional authority, for one might think that although Zeus gives humans the power of justice, humans realize justice through the laws that they invent. Hesiod insists that there is some defined content to the justice that Zeus gives to humans – it rules out lying, for example – but he does not suggest that Zeus has given humans a detailed legal code. Protagoras practically demands that Zeus' gift can be used to establish different codes of justice, if his Great Speech is supposed to cohere with his famous doctrine that "man is the measure" (esp. Plato, *Tht.* 152a). This relativist doctrine, according to which the wind is cool for me if it feels cool to me and is warm for you if it feels warm to you

[13] *Works and Days* 276–85. I follow closely the rendering of Most 2006 in translating the text in West 1978. See also Hesiod, *Theogony* 901–6.

(152b), implies that what is just in Athens might be unjust elsewhere (171d–72b).

Heraclitus, by contrast, grounds human laws in the single rational order of nature, and so rejects both conventionalism and relativism.[14] In fr. 114, he says that the source of human laws is something divine and sufficient that rules everything, which is to say that its source is the universal logos that determines how things happen (fr. 1). The whole fragment works like this. Heraclitus first compares the successful inquirer's dependence on the universal logos to the successful city's dependence on law, and then he identifies human law's dependence on the universal logos. Moreover, he supports the initial comparison by the identification that follows. Because the logos rules everything, human law takes its strength, its nourishment, from the logos, and because a city that takes its strength from law thereby takes its strength from the logos, a city depends on its law just as human understanding depends upon the logos.

Heraclitus, however, pulls up short of saying that the foundation for civic laws is a divine, natural *law*. He does not explicitly name the divine source of human laws, and his reticence is perhaps significant.[15]

[14] Some scholars, misled by fr. 102, miss this. (See, e.g., Strauss 1953: 93–94.) Diels extracted fr. 102 from this scholion on Homer's *Iliad*: "Heraclitus also says these things, that to god all things are fine and good and just, but humans have taken some things to be unjust, others just." But the language of this report and of its introduction marks it as a paraphrase, not a genuine fragment of Heraclitus' writing (see Kahn 1979: 183). Moreover, the scholiast is unlikely to have understood his point to involve conventionalism. The scholion concerns the opening sentence of *Iliad* 4, which has the gods drinking nectar from golden cups looking down at the city of Troy. The Homeric text, then, contrasts the experience of the divine or cosmic point of view with the human. This contrast does not require or otherwise suggest that human justice is merely conventional; it needs only the point that some human concerns do not matter to the divine or cosmic point of view. This point reminds the scholiast of a thought he associates with Heraclitus, namely, that the human concerns of justice and injustice do not touch the divine perspective because everything is good and just from the divine perspective. This thought might well be genuinely Heraclitean: Heraclitus could well think that at the cosmic level, the unity of opposites is simply good and just, so that the experience of injustice requires the more particular perspective of individual human beings. But whether the scholiast's paraphrase is accurate or not, it does not insist that Heraclitus adopted a conventionalist attitude toward justice, and given the clearly anti-conventionalist import of fr. 114, it would be perverse to read the scholiast's paraphrase that way.

[15] Nor, in fact, is he explicit about the nature of the law on which a city should base its strength: is it divine or human? My reading is neutral. Either way, Heraclitus ultimately means that a city should depend upon the logos, since (if it should depend

He elsewhere declares, "The only one wise thing is willing and unwilling to be called by the name of Zeus" (fr. 32). Accordingly, Heraclitus might believe that the universal logos that is fundamental to understanding and to human laws is and is not well characterized as "law." Reasons for such caution emerge in the fifth section of this chapter, Contesting the Law-likeness of Natural Norms.

Still, whatever one makes of Heraclitus' reticence, he clearly suggests the metaphor of natural law, for he affirms that there is a standard for human laws manifest in the order of the cosmos to be discovered by successful human inquiry. This has significant political implications: if there is such a standard, it would seem that laws should be made by those who can inquire successfully into nature or at least by those who can judge well the testimony of those who purport to have inquired successfully. This need not lead to anti-democratic inclinations, but Heraclitus is pessimistic about the abilities of most people. He says, "Nature loves to hide" (fr. 123), and he thinks that most human beings fail to grasp how things really are (e.g., frr. 1, 17, 34). So he would apparently favor rule by exceptional experts: "One is ten thousand, if he is best" (fr. 49, cf. 33 and 41). There is a straight line between this thought and Socrates' search for a political expert, Plato's dream of philosopher-rulers, Aristotle's preference for aristocracy, and the Stoic paradox that only the sage is a king. But if expertise is not so hard or, conversely, if it is so hard that no one can achieve it, then a natural law theorist might well argue for more democratic government.

Heraclitus' suggestion of a natural law also prompts some philosophical questions. He claims to offer an account of how the world is and suggests that this account is the proper source of human laws. But why should the rational order of the cosmos ground prescriptive laws instead of merely descriptive ones? And how, in particular, could the rational order of the *cosmos* ground norms for *human* behavior?

In the fragments of Heraclitus, the first of these questions simply does not arise. The rational principles that order the cosmos are also "divine" and "governing." They are never conceived as merely descriptive regularities. They are always prescriptive norms. For the ancients,

upon human law) human law depends upon the logos and (if it should depend upon divine law) divine law is the logos. Some readers (e.g., McKirahan 1994: 148) suppose that if Heraclitus means that a city should depend upon human laws, then he is flirting with conventionalism. I disagree. To say that a city must strengthen itself on human laws is not to say that it can strengthen itself on any and all human laws, especially when one goes on to insist that human laws take their strength from the divine source that orders the cosmos.

this assumption often rests in turn on another, deeper one. The world is ordered not just in a regular way, but in a good way.[16] So any laws that capture the way the world is also capture the way it should be. Humean worries about shifting from descriptive regularities to prescriptive laws fail to get off the ground in this environment and they continue to be grounded throughout antiquity. Those philosophers who denied that the cosmos is arranged in a good way – the atomists and their Epicurean heirs – also denied that it offers any rational principles to ground human norms.[17]

The fragments of Heraclitus do, however, admit of a response to the second question, and this response might even allay the worries that motivate the first. Heraclitus appears to believe that a human being can find within himself the universal logos that orders the cosmos (cf. fr. 45). His basic idea is proverbial: "it belongs to all human beings to know themselves and to be moderate (*sōphronein*)" (fr. 116). But the simplicity of this idea is deceptive. Given Heraclitus' standards of understanding, to know oneself and be moderate and so save one's thinking (*sō-phronein*) one must discover something more than private truths, which mark those who lack understanding (fr. 2); one must discover the universal logos on which intelligence depends (frr. 2, 41, 114). Heraclitus does not believe that self-examination suffices for understanding (fr. 35; cf. fr. 45), but he does make it clear that inquiry into the world is inseparable from self-examination. That is why Heraclitus, who expounds the universal logos (fr. 1), proclaims, "I searched into myself" (fr. 101).

If the rational principles that order the cosmos *also* order the human soul, then one might draw an intelligible connection between the rational principles of the cosmos and appropriate human behavior, for it is plausible that principles of psychology afford prescriptive norms. This is far from automatic because the way the human soul typically works provides no obvious grounds for asserting how it *should* work. But if principles of psychology can reveal not how human souls typically work but how human souls are put into (good) order, then no one makes a category mistake by inferring norms from psychology. Here lies a tantalizing promise of natural law: it is not impossible to imagine

16 It is not clear to what extent Heraclitus accepts this, but there is some reason to think that he does, given the connection (discussed below) between the order of the cosmos and the order of the soul, which he clearly takes to be good for a human being. See also fr. 102, discussed in n. 14 above.

17 The Epicureans get their norms from their account of *human* nature and not from the cosmos.

a science of human nature or psychology that tells us how human psychology functions well and poorly.

Of course, none of this is easy. It is far from clear what practical norms can be grounded in a science of psychology and entirely obscure how the rational order of the soul is supposed to be the same as or part of the rational order of the cosmos as a whole. Still, Heraclitus set the agenda by suggesting that the divine standard for human laws is discoverable by rational inquiry into the way the world and the soul work.[18] To consider the plausibility of this agenda, we can examine the two kinds of controversies it engendered.

Contesting the Norms of Nature

First, in fifth-century Greece, there was an explosion of contrasts between nature (*phusis*) and law or convention (*nomos*) that brought controversy concerning what nature recommends.[19]

Some appealed to natural law not to endorse moderation, as Heraclitus had, but to justify imperialist greed. Callicles, in Plato's *Gorgias*,[20] maintains that moderation and traditional justice are merely conventional values asserted by the many weak to check the powerful few (483a–c). Against the many, he asserts that it is in accordance with a "law of nature" that the powerful have more than the weak (483c–e).[21] Thucydides has some Athenian ambassadors appeal to something similar when they ask the Spartan colonists on Melos to surrender before the Athenian forces attack (5.84–116).[22] Like Callicles, Thucydides'

[18] For Heraclitus' influence on Plato, see Irwin 1977 and Menn 1995. See also the discussion in the next section. For Heraclitus' influence on the Stoics, see Long 1975–76 and Kahn 1979: esp. 5.

[19] The contrast between *nomos* and *phusis*, which Guthrie 1971: 21, calls "the most fundamental" feature of the fifth-century Sophists' outlook, has been much discussed. For a good recent contribution, see Barney 2006.

[20] I cite the text of Dodds 1959, and my translations are generally light revisions of Zeyl's, in Cooper 1997.

[21] Dodds 1959: ad 483e3, suggests that this might be the first occurrence of the phrase "law of nature" in Greek, since Plato has Callicles mark the phrase as strange with an interjection. Earlier surviving intimations of natural law, including Thucydides 5.105 (quoted below), do not conjoin *nomos* and *phusis* so closely in a single phrase.

[22] I cite the text of Jones 1900–2, and I quote, with some alteration, the translation of Warner 1954. I also agree with the scholarly consensus that Thucydides is liberally interpreting what the Athenians might have said so as to make a point he wants to make, since it is highly unlikely that the actual Athenian envoys would have given up all talk of justice. See, for example, Gomme, Andrewes, and Dover 1970: 161 and 164.

Athenians encourage their interlocutors to set aside conventional values, warning that the Melians will be destroyed by their conventional commitments (*nomima*) (esp. 5.105.4 with 111.3). Like Callicles, again, these ambassadors place traditional justice among the values to be set aside. But unlike Callicles, the Athenians set justice aside only because the relevant parties are greatly unequal (esp. 5.89 and 105.4), and they do not replace traditional justice with natural justice. Instead, they say, "It is a general necessity of nature to rule whatever one can," and they call this a "law (*nomos*)" that "we found already in existence" and that "we shall leave to exist forever among those who come after it" (5.105.1–2).

There is a difference between Callicles and Thucydides' Athenians, but it is often misunderstood. Because the Athenians ostentatiously set justice aside and do not replace ordinary justice with natural justice, many readers suppose that the Athenians appeal to something like a descriptive regularity rather than a prescriptive norm. So understood, whereas Callicles believes that it is just for the stronger to get more power, the Athenians think it is merely inevitable. The Athenians' rhetoric of "necessity" dupes these readers. The fact is that the Athenians' actions are not inevitable. There are anti-imperialists in Athens, but the Athenians *choose* to find their self-interest in conquering Melos and consequently *choose* to threaten the Melians with destruction. The reading also ignores the sentences that immediately precede and succeed the passage just quoted: "Nor do we think that that we will be left without the good will of the gods. . . . And therefore, so far as the gods are concerned, we see no good reason why we should fear being at a disadvantage" (5.105.1 and 105.3). The Athenians argue that they "must" conquer Melos in order to show that the gods permit their behavior.

This is their difference with Callicles. Callicles' natural law is fully prescriptive: it prescribes that the powerful should get more. Thucydides' Athenians, by contrast, appeal to a natural law to determine what is proscribed. Knowing that they want to conquer Melos, they need to be sure that this is permissible to the gods (and thus in their rational self-interest). Fortunately for them (but not so much for the Melians), they find a natural law that is remarkably permissive. (The Athenians do not even say what it proscribes. For their purposes, it is enough to say that it does not proscribe their proposed course in Melos.) So the difference here is between a law that prescribes – love your neighbor – and one that proscribes – do not murder. The latter sort of law does not determine exactly what behavior one should practice and is in this sense not fully prescriptive. But it is certainly prescriptive in the sense that it establishes standards for right and wrong.[23]

Despite this difference, both Callicles and Thucydides' Athenians find in nature a standard for assessing right and wrong human behavior and for justifying domination by the strong.[24] But that is just one side of a debate. Socrates opposes Callicles in Plato's *Gorgias*. He argues that one should pursue "organization and order" in one's soul, and he calls this psychological order justice and moderation or self-control (504d). Socrates even suggests his own notion of natural law to oppose Callicles' when he calls psychological order "law" (504d1–3).[25]

This debate raises questions about how one could determine what the natural norms are. To justify their finding, both Callicles and the Athenians appeal to how actual humans tend to behave and especially how whole peoples behave toward others (presumably because such behavior is less constrained by conventions). But there is little reason to suppose that the naturally common is the naturally normative. What if, as Socrates' inquiries suggest, we are all unwise about how to live?

[23] There will be objections to my reading of Thucydides. What if the Athenians address what the gods permit only because the Melians raised the question and not because they themselves take the gods seriously? It still does not follow that the Athenians are appealing to a merely descriptive natural law. What follows is that they are appealing to a normative law for merely *ad hominem* purposes. And what if, despite my claim to the contrary, the Athenians are arguing that the gods must permit their imperialist behavior because everyone really must, given the opportunity, pursue empire? The Athenians are still appealing to divine standards of right and wrong and judging their contents based on their study of nature.

[24] Compare Antiphon, and especially fr. 44 of his *Truth*, with Gagarin 2002 and Pendrick 2002. Antiphon does not explicitly invoke natural law, but he does argue against following convention.

[25] Plato's Socrates does not do much with this way of talking, and he probably goes for it here to heighten the contrast with Callicles. Also, although he says nothing in the *Gorgias* to encourage this reading, Socrates might mean that psychological order and harmony require agreement with conventional, civic laws. He elsewhere appears deeply devoted to obeying civic law, and he might well think that successfully ordering one's soul requires conformity with communal norms. (See Plato, *Ap.* 32a–c and *Cr. passim*, and Xenophon, *Mem.* 4.4, esp. 4.4.4. For the general thought, see also Anonymus Iamblichi 6.1. For discussion, see Balot 2006: 113–20.) Of course, if Socrates is attached to conventional laws, he might be attached to all and only those conventional laws that genuinely deserve the name 'law', and he might think that the only conventional laws that genuinely deserve the name 'law' are those that represent the natural law of psychological order. This way of defining conventional laws is familiar in the subsequent natural law tradition (see, e.g., Cicero, *Leg.* 2.11–13), and it is not entirely absent from Socratic texts. See Plato, *Hp. Ma.* 284a–85b and Pseudo-Plato, *Min.* 314e, and compare Plato, *Rep.* 422e and *Pol.* 293e.

Socrates therefore appeals instead to what is common among those who know what they are doing – the cobblers, shipbuilders, and other craftsmen – and argues that just as craftsmen seek to impart order and harmony to their products in order to make good products so too we should try to impart order and harmony to ourselves in order to be good people (*Gor.* 503e–4d).

Callicles also appeals briefly to animal behavior to support his claim that nature prescribes that the stronger get more (*Gor.* 483d3). But this kind of appeal, very common and easily parodied,[26] is vulnerable. One might appeal to cooperative animal behavior, as the Stoics would do (e.g., Cic., *Fin.* 3.62–63), or as Socrates does to a more abstract feature of animal life, namely the importance of order in the animal body (*Gor.* 506d5–8). Additionally, all such appeals are vulnerable to the objection that humans are or at least should be different from other animals.

Socrates suggests a third way of finding evidence of natural norms when he appeals, as Heraclitus had, to the geometric order and harmony of the whole cosmos (507e6–8a8). Unfortunately, Socrates makes no more clear than Heraclitus had how this sort of natural fact is relevant to norms for human behavior.

There remains one reason for Socrates to suppose that his conception of natural norms is superior to that of Callicles. He has his experiences of examining himself, Callicles, and many others. So far as he can tell, his views are consistent, and he can produce arguments for his contentious claims, whereas "no one I've ever met" can contradict his claims "without being ridiculous" (508e–9a, with 482a–c, quoting from 509a5–7). This includes Callicles, who contradicts himself several times in their conversation before he finally refuses to answer any more questions sincerely.[27]

In this way, Plato's *Gorgias* suggests a minimal test for an ethical theory in general and a natural law theory in particular: it must be coherent. The *Gorgias* also suggests that Socrates' ideas pass this test. So although the dialogue illustrates a debate about the content of natural norms, it also offers some promise for a particular approach to natural law. If Socrates is right about his experiences and if his experiences are telling, then perhaps human nature is so robust that it allows only one

[26] See, e.g., Herodotus 2.64 and the parody of Aristophanes, *Birds* 755–68. Diogenes of Sinope (discussed below) earns his nickname "the Cynic" ("Dog-like") from behavior that befits this trope.

[27] See Woolf 2000.

consistent theory of right and wrong, namely, that of Socrates. In the absence of a psychology that could justify the bold assumptions that underpin Socrates' claims about what makes an orderly soul possible, philosophers can do nothing but continue as they have. They must answer Heraclitus' call for self-examination, and they must see if he and Socrates are right to insist on moderation by testing what views are at least consistent. If Socrates' approach continues to pass the test and if the rivals continue to fail, the promise of a natural standard for right and wrong abides.

Contesting the Law-likeness of Natural Norms

Another set of controversies addresses more directly the propriety of the metaphor "natural law." Even if unconventional standards of right and wrong are discoverable by human study of nature, are they law-like enough to be called natural law? Moderns might worry that they fail to be law-like because they fail to have a legislator. But the ancients do not much worry about this, perhaps because the Greek *nomos* applies to conventions that arise gradually without any particular agents doing any particular convening.[28] Plato does, however, argue that natural norms cannot be fully law-like because right and wrong are not codifiable into exceptionless rules, and Aristotle and the Stoics provide divergent responses to the problem.

In Plato's *Statesman*, the Eleatic visitor expresses skepticism about civic laws.[29] He insists that ultimate authority should rest not with such laws but with a wise ruler (294a6–8), and to explain why, he notes,

> law could never accurately embrace what is best and most just for all at the same time, and so prescribe what is best, for the dissimilarities among human beings and their actions,

[28] Nor, as it happens, are ancient theological cosmologies friendly to the claim that god *made* natural law. Plato embraces the thought that the natural world is made by god, but not the thought that the norms governing the natural world are made by god. (Goodness exists independently of the creator in the *Timaeus*, probably because Plato continues to believe that although divine approval might attach to the right things, it does not make the right things right (*Eu.* 9a–11b).) Aristotle and the Stoics, on the other hand, deny that the world is created by a transcendent deity.

[29] For the *Statesman* (also known by its Latin title *Politicus*), I cite the text of Duke et al. 1995, and I follow closely the translation of Rowe, in Cooper 1997.

> and the fact that practically nothing in human affairs ever remains stable, prevent any sort of expertise whatsoever from making any simple decision in any sphere that covers all cases and will last for all time. (294a10–b6, cf. 294e–95b)

That is, fully law-like rules – general prescriptions and proscriptions – might capture what is right and wrong most of the time, for most people, in most circumstances. But right and wrong depend upon the particulars, and so even the best general laws will prescribe what is, in some special circumstances, wrong or proscribe what is, in some special circumstances, right. It would be better, then, to be ruled by someone who is wise and who can use his expertise itself as "law" (296e–97a). This is not to say that it would be better to live without laws. The Eleatic visitor recognizes the necessity of laws (294c–95a) and he acknowledges that the ideally wise ruler (at least in our time, as opposed to the age of Cronus [cf. 275c]) would make use of them (305e, 309d, 310a). But the wise ruler must be above the law, as the proper normative authority is not to be found in the generalizations of the laws but in reason or wisdom, which cannot be codified.[30]

This critique of laws suggests that any natural law would have to be less than fully law-like.[31] Anyone persuaded by Plato's critique but still drawn to the promise of natural law is faced with two main options. The first option is to forge ahead on the assumption that one can talk meaningfully of natural law despite its lack of full codifiability. The second is to scale back one's ambitions and to use the metaphor of natural law not for the standard for all right and wrong but only for more isolated, particular judgments.

[30] The roots of this critique are also evident in *Republic* 1, where Socrates impugns "returning what is owed" as a defining characteristic of justice on the grounds that in some circumstances, such as when one owes a weapon to a friend gone mad, it is not just to return what is owed (331c). The critique is also assumed in the *Laws* (text in vol. 5 of Burnet 1900–7). There, the Athenian concedes that it would be better to be ruled by one person's wisdom but argues that because this is not possible (875b–d; cf. 691c–d and 713c–d), the rule of law is the practicable best. Even still, the Athenian insists that laws should be made as regulations of reason (*nous*) (713e–15b, cf. 890d), and should be safeguarded by "men who are likened to reason (*nous*)" (965a1 with 960b–e and 961c).

[31] This might explain why Plato does not develop more fully a natural law theory of his own and why so many scholars have said so little about the explicit hints of natural law in Plato's dialogues. But see Maguire 1947, Morrow 1948, and Hall 1956: 201–5.

Aristotle takes the second of these options.[32] In the *Ethics* (*Nicomachean* 5.6–7 = *Eudemian* 4.6–7), Aristotle distinguishes between one part of political justice that holds by mere law and another that holds by nature. This is not the distinction between civic and natural law. Rather, it is the distinction between laws whose authority is *merely* conventional and those whose authority is natural. *Mere* law – *mere* convention – can make only what is naturally neither just nor unjust into something unjust (such as driving on a particular side of the road). Injustice so defined is (merely) legally unjust. But other laws articulate what is naturally just or unjust; they specify a justice that everywhere has the same force.

This might suggest that Aristotle wants to defend a robust conception of natural law with a broad set of general rules that everywhere have the same force. But it cannot be said that Aristotle develops this idea in the *Ethics*. First, Aristotle argues that the natural, including natural justice, is changeable (1134b24–30). It is unclear what exactly he means by this, but it seems to suggest local variations more than general rules that everywhere have the same force. Second, Aristotle does not explain how civic laws can articulate what is naturally just. He says that it is "clear" which laws are by nature and which merely by convention (1134b30–33), but as the debate between Callicles and Socrates shows, it is not clear.[33]

In the *Rhetoric*, Aristotle distinguishes between "particular" and "universal" laws (1.10, 1368b7–9; 1.13, 1373b4–6), where the former are established by a particular community for its members and the latter hold "by nature" (1.13, 1373b6). It is tempting to use this to illuminate the distinction between merely legal and natural justice so that merely legal justice is specified by particular laws whereas natural justice is specified by universal laws. But Aristotle says nothing explicitly

[32] For the *Ethics* and *Rhetoric*, I cite Bywater 1894 and Ross 1959, respectively, and my translations borrow from the renderings in Barnes 1984. With *NE* 5.7 (= *EE* 4.7), compare *Magna Moralia* 1.33, a text I set aside for now.

[33] Indeed, Yack 1993, esp. 140–49, asserts that Aristotle does not even say that there are natural standards of right and wrong. On his view, merely legal justice is derived "from agreements to designate as just or unjust actions about which we would otherwise be indifferent," and natural justice is derived "from judgments about the appropriate obligations to impose on members of political communities in particular situations" (144). I disagree. Natural justice has its force independent of human judgments: it "does not depend upon thinking this or that" (1134b19–20). The traditional interpretation – that Aristotle does mean to invoke natural standards for right and wrong – is developed with more optimism than I offer here by Miller 1991 (and Miller 1995: 74–79) and Kraut 2002: 125–32.

to encourage this reading.[34] He does, however, explicitly discuss natural law and even quotes Antigone twice (1.13, 1373b9–13; 1.15, 1375a33–b2).[35] Unfortunately, although he seems to approve of Antigone's appeal to unwritten laws (esp. 1.13, 1373b6–13), he does not explain why he thinks that these "unwritten laws" are genuine universal or natural laws. He certainly does not think that their being unwritten does the trick (despite the appearances at 1.10, 1368b7–9 and 1.15, 1375a27–b25), as he recognizes that particular laws can be unwritten (1.13, 1373b4–6). He simply assumes that Antigone's burial of Polyneices is an example of a naturally just action and so an action defined as just by a natural, universal law.

A wider view of Aristotle's discussion in the *Rhetoric* leaves two plain options to work out how to identify "universal," "natural" laws. The first is cynical. Since orators will appeal to universal or natural law whenever written, civic laws tell against their case and will argue against universal or natural laws whenever written, civic laws favor their case (1.15, 1375a27–b25), perhaps we should see these appeals as mere rhetorical devices. I doubt that Aristotle intends for his readers to take

34 Indeed, he seems to discourage it. In the *Ethics*, he insists that natural law can change (*EN* 5.7, 1134b24–34), but in the *Rhetoric*, he suggests otherwise (1.15, 1375a31–32). But one should not be discouraged. The *Rhetoric* passage is not in Aristotle's own voice: he is reporting what one "must say" if the written law is against one. (Even more obviously: in *Rhetoric* 1.13, it is Antigone and not Aristotle who says that the unwritten laws are eternal.) By contrast, when Aristotle endorses the idea of natural law in his own voice in *Rhetoric* 1.13, 1373b6–9, he does not say whether it is changeable or not.

35 In *Rhetoric* 1.13, he tries to give two other examples, but they fail to illuminate. He first quotes Empedocles fr. 135 DK (1373b14–17), but this mentions natural law without specifying its content ("But what is lawful for all extends continuously through the wide-ruling air and through the boundless light"). Then he notes a reference to natural law in Alcidamas' Messeniac Oration (1373b18), but he does not identify what Alcidamas said, at least not according to the surviving manuscripts. A scholiast suggests that he originally identified or meant to identify the following quotation: "God has set all men free, nature has made no man a slave." This would be a startling example for Aristotle to have used (or to have had in mind), given his belief that there are natural slaves (*Politics* 1.4–7). Of course, given his purposes in the *Rhetoric*, Aristotle need not be saying that each of these examples succeeds in pointing out a natural law; he could intend them merely as examples of rhetorical appeal to natural law (cf. 1.15, 1375a27–b8). But we still have little reason to suppose that the scholiast knew what passage in Alcidamas' speech Aristotle had in mind, and so I seriously doubt that Ross is right to print the scholion as though it reports Aristotle's original words, subsequently lost in the manuscripts.

this option, since he seems to endorse the reality of natural law (esp. 1.13, 1373b6–13).[36]

The second option is to take the contrast between "universal" and "particular" literally and to identify as universal those laws that are recognized by everyone, across all the various particular communities (see 1.10, 1368b8–9 and 1.13, 1373b6–9).[37] Unfortunately, this is problematic. First, how should we specify what counts as agreement and how much agreement is enough? Presumably, Aristotle does not mean that a universal law has to command full and immediate assent from literally every human being. Antigone's laws do not do that, at least as long as Creon thinks it right to leave Polyneices unburied. Perhaps he means that everyone must be disposed to assent eventually (as Creon does), under the right conditions, or that all but a few must be so disposed. But problems remain to specify the right conditions of assent or the principles that explain why some dissent is irrelevant. Second, and more problematically, why should one infer that something is natural from the fact that everyone accepts it? Cannot everyone be wrong? One might be tempted to think that Aristotle is trading the normative notion of natural law for an empirical observation of perfectly regular causal relations. On this view, it is not natural law that torturing babies for fun is wrong; it is natural law that humans find torturing babies

[36] Contrast Yack 1993: 144 and 146. Yack also doubts that the *Rhetoric*'s talk of "unchanging" natural law directly explains anything about the *Ethics*' changeable natural justice. But see n. 34 above.

[37] Cf. Xenophon, *Mem.* 4.4.19. Aristotle appears to assume that all universal, natural laws are unwritten (1.10, 1368b8–9 and 1.15, 1375a27–b25), even though he does not assume that all unwritten laws are universal and natural (1.13, 1373b4–6; contrast, perhaps, 1.10, 1368b7–9). This needs explaining if universal agreement is sufficient to make a law universal and natural. But Aristotle might think that there is never universal agreement on all the details of some *written* law, given natural variations among human communities. Hence, the universal, natural laws are unwritten. Note that they had better not be unwritten merely because they are so much more general than written laws, though, since they have to retain enough specificity to warrant the conclusion, e.g., that Antigone is right to bury Polyneices. It is, in fact, more plausible to think that they are unwritten because they are too particular. On this view, human beings can agree about some particular judgments of justice – and these are the "universal, natural laws" – but they cannot all agree on general judgments, since there are so many different ways in which we can generalize from the same set of particular judgments, let alone from various overlapping sets. Cf. Strauss 1953: 159–61. See also the remarks about Cicero and the Roman jurists below.

for fun to be wrong.[38] But this temptation should be resisted: Aristotle cannot duck the normative question so easily.

In sum, Aristotle shies away from developing an ambitious theory of natural law. He certainly recognizes the rhetorical power of the metaphor. But he does not invoke it in his own theorizing (in the *Ethics* and *Politics*), and when he does show some sympathy for it (in the *Rhetoric*), he leaves the ideas behind it undeveloped. In place of a natural standard of right and wrong for all civic laws and all human behavior, Aristotle offers natural law as a rhetorical device for some particular occasions concerning some particular laws and behavior, and he assigns this device the plausibility that depends upon taking widespread agreement as a sign of what is natural.[39]

The Stoics, by contrast, continue in the tradition of Heraclitus and Plato to insist that there is a natural standard for all civic laws and all human behavior, and they continue to apply the word "law" to this standard.[40] But at least the early Greek Stoics, like Aristotle (esp. *EN* 5.10 = *EE* 4.10), heed Plato's caution about exceptionless prescriptions or proscriptions. They recognize no exceptions to prescriptions of the tautologous form "act virtuously," but they accept no universal, non-tautologous prescriptions. On their view, it is generally appropriate to pursue, say, health, but sometimes inappropriate: "If healthy people had to serve a tyrant and by this be destroyed, while sick people were freed from service and so also freed from destruction, the sage would choose to be sick in this circumstance, rather than to be healthy" (Sextus, *M.* 11.66).[41] As the Stoics put it, pursuing health is generally appropriate,

38 Compare the "descriptive" reading of Thucydides 5.105.1–2, discussed in the third section of this chapter, Nature and Normative Authority. For descriptive natural law, see also Plato, *Tim.* 83e.

39 I here agree with Strauss' 1953: 146–63, broad distinction between the Socratic-Platonic-Stoic (I would add Heraclitean) and Aristotelian conceptions of natural right. On this view, Thomas Aquinas misunderstands the historical roots of his natural theory to the extent that he thinks of it as deeply Aristotelian. I also agree with Strauss 1953: 163–64, that the Thomistic conception of natural right is another thing altogether, although it is deeply influenced by the ancients.

40 For the Stoic conception of natural law, see Watson 1971; Striker 1986 and 1991: 248–61; Vander Waerdt 1989, 1994, and 2003; Schofield 1991; and Mitsis 1994 and 2003. My account in this section draws heavily on ideas that I develop more fully in Brown forthcoming.

41 Although the renegade Stoic Ariston of Chios used this example to argue that there is no general preference for health and no general distinctions of value to be drawn among conditions other than virtue, such as health, the example was not unwelcome to Chrysippus and orthodox Stoics as it makes the perfectly orthodox point I am describing.

and pursuing sickness is appropriate "in special circumstances (*kata peristasin*)" (see DL 7.109). Despite this, the Stoics make heavy appeal to law as right reason that pervades and organizes the cosmos, prescribing what one ought to do and proscribing what one ought not to do.[42]

Since they are insisting that right reason is *law* despite their awareness that it is not codifiable and so not fully law-like, the Stoics need some reason for sticking with the talk of natural law. One motivation is no doubt broadly Cynical. The Cynics were followers of Socrates who rejected conventional values of all sorts in favor of living in accordance with nature. Diogenes of Sinope, for example, was notorious for masturbating in the *agora*, which, though shocking, was only *conventionally* shocking (Plutarch, *Stoic. rep.* 1044b; DL 6.46 and 69). Like the Cynics and, for that matter, like Socrates, the Stoics called traditional values into question. Greeks traditionally cherished honor, wealth, and health, but Stoics insisted that these things do not matter to whether one is living well or poorly. At least some early Stoics also took their commitment to nature over convention to naughty, Cynical extremes: Zeno, the founder of Stoicism, and Chrysippus, its most prolific and ingenious expositor, both defended incest.[43] (Later Stoics, especially in Rome, recoiled and purged such Cynicism from the Stoa.) The metaphor of natural law (*nomos*) neatly serves Cynical aims because it wrests the traditional source of normativity (*nomos*) away from convention (which is how *nomoi* were traditionally recognized) and ties it exclusively to nature. That the metaphor also rings of paradox in the face of a sharp distinction between nature and law or convention (*nomos*) is just icing on the cake, since the Stoics, like Socrates, loved the way paradox stimulates thought.[44] That Plato and his Socrates had invoked the idea of calling right reason (wisdom) "law" would be something like the cherry on top (*Gor.* 504d, *Plt.* 297a).

The Stoics not only reclaimed the rhetoric of natural law as a standard for all right and wrong, but also made some progress toward justifying their particular account of what nature prescribes and proscribes. The Cynics on this score offered very little beyond what Callicles does.

[42] See the texts cited in n. 4 above.

[43] See especially Sextus: 3.245–46 = *M.* 11.191–92, citing Zeno and Chrysippus' *Republic*; and DL 7.188, citing Chrysippus' *On Republic*. The Stoics need not be endorsing incest quite generally; they could be defending it only in special circumstances (see Origen SVF 3.743). But Origen's testimony might (and I think likely does) reflect a later, well-scrubbed version of Stoicism and not the actual doctrine of Zeno and Chrysippus.

[44] See Brown 2006.

But the Stoics, to judge from the handbook summary of Cicero (in *De finibus* 3), offered a relatively sophisticated developmental psychology, starting with observation of infant behavior.[45] Their principal thought seems to have been that we *should* value what we *would* value had we developed naturally, without being corrupted by society and misleading appearances, and so they looked carefully into what constitutes natural development.

But they did not limit themselves to a study of human nature. Following Heraclitus, Socrates in the *Gorgias*, and several other Platonic dialogues, the earliest Stoics also believed that the pinnacle of human development requires agreeing with the harmonious organization of the cosmos.[46] That is, they maintained, first, that living well is living virtuously or with knowledge and that knowledge is psychological coherence, the reasoned agreement with oneself in the face of new experience and in the face of full Socratic examination.[47] But they also maintained that this coherence exists not just in the mind of any human being who has achieved wisdom but also, and more importantly (because, like Socrates, they do not recognize anyone who has achieved wisdom), in the rational order of the cosmos.

This gives them, like Socrates in the *Gorgias*, two routes to justify their account of what is natural. First, they have empirical evidence of what is natural. They have improved on this score by adding some sophisticated developmental psychology, but Stoic writings still leave empirical investigations very much in their infancy. Second, they also have their insistence that Stoic values – the Stoic account of what is prescribed and proscribed – are required for psychological coherence. This is open to continued investigation by Socratic examination and is, in its way, an empirical hypothesis. Either it is or it is not the case that

[45] Compare Cicero, *Fin.* 3.16–22 and Seneca, *Ep.* 121 with the undeveloped "appeal to the cradle" at Aristotle, *EN* 6.13 (= *EE* 5.13), 1144b4–6 and *Pol.* 1.5, 1254a23.

[46] See, e.g., DL 7.87–88 and Cleanthes' *Hymn to Zeus* (Stobaeus 1.1.12, 1.25.3–27.4 WH).

[47] For the identity of virtue and knowledge, see Stobaeus 2.7.5b, 2.58.9–11 WH and 2.7.5b4, 2.62.15–20 WH, and DL 7.90. All of the standard virtues are defined as forms of knowledge (*epistēmai*): see Stobaeus 2.7.5b1–2, 2.59.4–62.6 WH and DL 7.92–93. For the definition of knowledge as a cognitive grasp or system of cognitive grasps that is secure, firm, and unshakable by argument, see Stobaeus 2.7.5l, 2.73.19–74.1 WH; DL 7.47; Sextus, *M.* 7.151; Pseudo-Galen SVF 2.93; Philo SVF 2.95; and cf. Cicero, *Academica* 1.41–42, who attributes the account to Zeno of Citium, the founder of Stoicism. For a secondary definition of knowledge as a state of receiving impressions that is unshakable by argument, see Stobaeus 2.7.5l, 2.74.1–3 WH; DL 7.47; and Pseudo-Galen SVF 2.93.

psychological harmony requires the commitments of the Stoic sage. If it is, then there is, after all, a natural law in the right reason of the Stoic sage.

Of course, this natural law is not fully codifiable, given the Stoic caution about non-tautologous universal prescriptions.[48] But this does not mean that the Stoics take themselves to be using 'law' in a very loose metaphor. They have much to say about general rules in ethics. They emphasize the importance of such rules in moral education and advice.[49] And more importantly, although this point is contested, it seems likely that the Stoics appealed to general rules to explain how all the correct particular prescriptions and proscriptions cohere, since they say that all the virtues are share the same "theorems" (DL 7.125). On this view, right reason – which is virtue and natural law – comprises a wide range of rules all of which admit of exceptions, and it grasps how these *agree* in every particular judgment that it makes. In this way the Stoics demand a revised conception of law so that a fixed code of rules does not accurately capture the *form* of real law. Real law, instead, is just what reason sees, both in general (which tolerates exceptions) and in particular. There is no exhaustive codification of such law and no algorithm for applying its loose generalizations. But there is also no running from the explanation of prescriptions and proscriptions in light of a complex web of interlocking generalizations.

This conception of natural law can still serve as a standard for civic laws. But first, it would seem to allow a range of statutory codes, each of which is an appropriate interpretation of the general prescriptions and proscriptions that are most salient for its particular community. That fits the Stoic recommendation to engage in politics wherever one can in order to improve others' lives by bringing the life of the community closer to agreement with the law of right reason,[50] and their conception of civic laws as rules such as one would give in advice,

[48] The literature on the early Stoic conception of natural law (see n. 40 above) has been dominated by a dispute over whether Stoic natural law is codifiable or not. I here try to minimize the dispute.

[49] The fullest surviving discussion is Seneca, *Ep.* 94–95, but Seneca is drawing on a considerable earlier literature that is lost. The "paraenetic" or "perceptive" (from Greek and Latin words for "rule," respectively) branch of ethical philosophy that Seneca draws on (*Ep.* 95.1) is attested for the earliest Stoics (see Sextus, *M.* 7.12 on the renegade Ariston of Chios' rejection of the paraenetic branch, and cf. DL 7.84 on the part of ethics concerned with turning toward and away from appropriate actions).

[50] See esp. DL 7.121, with Brown forthcoming: chs. 7–10.

but with sanctions attached to help the advice take.[51] It also fits their "situationism" about politics – their recognition, for example, that the best regime for a community depends upon the particular composition of the community.[52]

It does not, however, fit Cicero's understanding of natural law in *On Laws*. He says, with the Stoics, that natural law is the same for all, but he also tries to offer a single best codification of that natural law. He admits that the codification cannot be complete (*Leg.* 2.18), but he does not suggest that an entirely different codification could be the best representation of natural law for a different community, just as his deeply Roman (see, e.g., *Leg.* 2.23–24) codification might be the best representation of natural law for Rome. This just shows that the metaphor of natural law retained its flexibility, and it meant something a bit different for Cicero than it did for the earliest Stoics.

The Stoics' comprehensive, unfolding conception of natural law is also ideally suited to serve as the metaphorical basis for civic laws that are conceived as a rich, open-ended body of thinking that includes interpretation of particulars. The fit between the Stoic ideal and Roman law is tight, which explains why the jurists included a trace of the philosophers' natural law as a fundamental element of Rome's *Corpus Iuris Civilis*.[53]

THE COSMOS AS A POLIS

Once one supposes that there is a law, right reason, governing the cosmos, it is natural to compare the cosmos to a well-ordered city. But the additional step is not mandatory for all conceptions of natural law. Aristotle conceives of natural law as something that holds *outside* of community (*Rhet.* 1.13, 1373b6–9), and Callicles' natural law does not

[51] See Seneca's defense of civic laws (*Ep.* 94.37) and the general report that the Stoic sage would make laws and educate (Stobaeus 2.7.11b, 2.94.7–20 WH).

[52] See, against Erskine 1990, Vander Waerdt 1991, and Brown forthcoming: §7.7.2.

[53] In Justinian's *Institutiones* (1.2.1, following Gaius, *Inst.* 1.1), the philosophers' natural law appears *not* as *ius naturale*, which is there said to govern animals and humans equally and to concern, e.g., sexual reproduction, but as *ius gentium*. But the jurist's definition of *ius gentium* conflates the Platonic-Stoic natural law as right reason with the law actually agreed to by all peoples: "That which natural reason has made between all human beings and holds among all peoples uniformly is called *ius gentium* because all peoples use this law." The same conflation is encouraged by Cicero, *Off.* 3.23 and 69, and by Aristotle, *Rhet.* 1.10, 1368b8–9 and 1.13, 1373b6–9 (discussed above).

establish a cosmic city. But if the natural law is right reason organizing the whole cosmos as law should organize a city, then the cosmos is like a city. This is the Stoic metaphor of the cosmopolis.[54] The ideas it expresses inherit their warrant from the Stoic defense of natural law: if Stoics have a plausible case for their account of a natural standard for right and wrong, they can use that case to defend their particularly cosmopolitan ideas. But what particular ideas are expressed by the metaphor of the cosmopolis that were not already advanced by the metaphor of natural law?

The great Stoic Chrysippus seems to have invoked the cosmopolis not directly for ethics or politics but for theology. He argued that since right reason made gods and wise human beings common citizens of the cosmos and since a city is made for the sake of its members, with everything in the city belonging to its citizens, the cosmos is made for the sake of gods and wise human beings, with everything in the cosmos belonging to gods and wise human beings. The cosmopolis is a premise in an argument for divine providence.[55]

Still, there is ethical and political import to this premise. The core idea that the cosmopolis expresses is of *community*. According to the standard ideology of the Greek city-state, the polis is the primary locus of the goods shared with other human beings. The metaphor of the cosmopolis calls this into question. Its negative import is that one's native city is *not* the appropriate locus of community and so not the source of so much normative authority. The positive import of the metaphor is that one does or should cultivate community with human beings outside of one's native city. This positive import can be articulated in elite or democratic terms, depending upon whether the community is conceived as a special achievement or a given feature of humanity. The evidence for the negative thesis is uncertain, but it would seem that Cynicizing Stoics incline toward it and Roman Stoics decline away from it.[56] The evidence concerning the positive thesis is much clearer. Chrysippus thinks that the cosmopolis is an elite community of the wise

[54] See n. 5. For Stoic cosmopolitanism, see Schofield 1991 and Brown forthcoming. For broader discussion of cosmopolitanism in ancient thought, see Baldry 1965.

[55] For the basic argument, see Cicero, *Nat. D.* 2.154 and Arius Didymus ap. Eusebius SVF 2.528. Unfortunately, both of these sources are a bit confused as to whether only the wise or all human beings are citizens of the cosmopolis. But the evidence for Chrysippus' elitist view is unambiguous: see Philodemus, *Piet.* 7.12–8.4 and Plutarch, *Comm. not.* 1065e–f. For discussion, see Brown forthcoming: §5.3–4.

[56] See Brown forthcoming: chs. 7–10. I argue that Chrysippus and Marcus Aurelius accept the negative thesis and that Cicero's *De officiis* and Seneca reject it.

by virtue of their expertise in the natural law, but later Stoics assume that all human beings are citizens of the cosmos by virtue merely of being subjects of the natural law.[57]

But these theses by themselves do not require belief in natural law, and they were far from unknown in the fifth and fourth centuries. Negative cosmopolitanism expressed itself in two main ways. Some, such as Anaxagoras, rejected obligations to their native polis in favor of contemplative withdrawal and were at least thought to have fancied this an attachment to the cosmopolis.[58] Others, such as Socrates and Diogenes the Cynic, rejected traditional political engagement in their native city in favor of an unusual sort of politics that they shared not just with native compatriots but also with foreigners. Insofar as these latter "negative cosmopolitans" embrace their mission of helping human beings as such, they also offer a clear example of positive cosmopolitanism.[59] There are other hints of this ethos among those who sought to follow nature instead of convention.[60]

Already it is clear that the ideas behind the metaphor of the cosmopolis tolerate a wide range of political commitments. They certainly

[57] For Chrysippus, see especially Philodemus, *Piet.* 7.12–8.4 and Plutarch, *Comm. not.* 1065e–f. For confused moves in a more democratic direction, see Cicero, *Nat. D.* 2.154 and Arius Didymus ap. Eusebius SVF 2.528. And for a perfectly democratic cosmopolis, see Cicero, *Fin.* 3.64. The democratic version is the one Cicero invokes at *De legibus* 1.23 (quoted in the first section of this chapter, Two Influential Metaphors), and the one that is prominent in the work of Roman Stoics (e.g., Seneca, *De otio* 4.1, and Marcus Aurelius 4.4).

[58] See the anecdote at DL 2.7. The anecdote might not be reliable evidence for Anaxagoras' attitudes, but it is certainly reliable evidence of at least a later ancient conception of the contemplative life.

[59] It is disputed whether Diogenes' cosmopolitanism (see, e.g., DL 6.63) is merely negative or also positive. Contrast Schofield 1991: 141–45, with Moles 1995, 1996, and 2000. (I favor Schofield's negative reading: see esp. DL 6.38, which expresses the negative cosmopolitanism of the homeless wanderer who is at home everywhere, for which see also Democritus fr. 247 DK and Euripides fr. 1047 TGF.) Socrates was recognized as a cosmopolitan by the later Stoic tradition: see the Stoics Musonius (fr. 9 [*That Exile is no Evil*] 42.1–2 Hense = Stobaeus 3.40.9, 3.749.2–3 Hense) and Epictetus (*Diss* 1.9.1) and the Stoicizing *Tusculan Disputations* of Cicero (5.108) and *De exilio* of Plutarch (600f–1a). Brown 2000 argues that Plato's Socratic dialogues give good cause for this interpretation. The Socratics in the Cyrenaic tradition also show at least negative cosmopolitanism. For Aristippus the Elder, see Xenophon, *Memorabilia* 2.1.13, and Plutarch, *On whether virtue can be taught* 2.439e, and for the later Cyrenaic Theodorus, see Diogenes Laertius 2.99 with 2.98, and compare Epiphanius, *Against heresies* 3.2.9.

[60] See, e.g., Hippias' remarks at Plato, *Prot.* 337c–d and Antiphon fr. 44 DK.

did for the Stoics. Many Stoics favored political engagement but argued that one should be willing to take up politics wherever one can best help people and not just in one's native city.[61] The political consequences here involve the spread of the Stoic ideology. Of course, the Stoic ideology is flexible because it insists that appropriate action fits its particular circumstances. But the ideal remains a worldwide agreement on a single, Stoic way of life manifested in a variety of separate communities.[62]

Empire is another way in which the Stoic metaphor of the cosmopolis could be put to political use. There is no good evidence that the earliest Greek Stoics favored this approach, despite the occasional assertion of Alexander the Great's influence.[63] But there are hints of a connection in Cicero's writings. In *On the Commonwealth*, Laelius appeals to Stoic natural law to defend justice against Philus' attacks. His invocation of natural law suggests the cosmopolis, as he stresses that one law joins all nations and says that "the person who does not obey it exiles himself."[64] But Laelius also defends Rome's imperialism in this same speech.[65] Given the fragmentary state of Cicero's text, it is impossible to know whether Laelius drew together his suggestion of a cosmopolis and his defense of empire, but he certainly made the connection possible. Cicero elsewhere embeds a defense of Roman imperialism in his Stoic theory of duties (*Off.* 1.34–38 and 2.26–27), joining together in close proximity praise for Rome's wars of expansion and insistence on the fellowship of all human beings with all human beings. And in *On Laws*, Cicero constructs an idealized version of the ancestral Roman laws to serve as a codification of natural law – exactly the law that is supposed to apply to all human beings. In neither of these texts, moreover, is there any explicit suggestion that Rome is the cosmopolis, and it is perhaps noteworthy that Cicero does not put the Stoic metaphor to this use more readily. But the connections between real-world imperialism and the doctrine of the cosmopolis are not difficult to make. The early

[61] See Brown forthcoming: chs. 7–10, where I argue that various Stoics disagree about whether one has special obligations to benefit native compatriots that must be balanced against one's reasons to emigrate.

[62] See the evidence for Zeno's *Republic*, including esp. Plutarch, *De Alex. fort.* 329a–b, with Brown forthcoming: ch. 6.

[63] On this, readers have been misled by Plutarch, *De Alex. fort.* 329a–b. See Badian 1958 and Baldry 1965: 113–27, against Tarn 1933 and 1948: 2.399–449.

[64] Cicero, *Rep.* 3.27 (33 in Ziegler 1969).

[65] Cicero, *Rep.* 3.21–26 (34–37 in Ziegler 1969).

Christians made them, and they cultivated a worldwide city of god as the cosmopolis of the wise.[66]

The Greek metaphors of natural law and the cosmopolis have exerted tremendous influence through Cicero's writings, Roman law, and Christianity, and many have found them irresistible. But a glance at their emergence is enough to show how flexible they are and how difficult it is to translate the metaphors in their richest, most suggestive form into persuasive non-metaphorical claims. These two lessons are related, and they encourage some skepticism. After all, flexibility gives these metaphors a specious semblance of power and plausibility if they are plausible but weak on some interpretations and powerful but much less plausible on others. Nevertheless, the bold claims that Heraclitus, Plato, and the Stoics made have not yet been shown false, and they have not lost their appeal. The skepticism called for is ancient: the skeptic keeps on inquiring.[67]

WORKS CITED

Arnim, H. von, ed. 1903–1905. *Stoicorum Veterum Fragmenta*, 3 vols. Leipzig.

Badian, E. 1958. "Alexander the Great and the Unity of Mankind." *Historia* 7: 425–44.

Baldry, H. C. 1965. *The Unity of Mankind in Greek Thought*. Cambridge.

Balot, R. K. 2006. *Greek Political Thought*. Oxford.

Barnes, J., ed. 1984. *The Complete Works of Aristotle: The Revised Oxford Translation*, 2 vols. Bollingen Series 71.2. Princeton, NJ.

Barney, R. 2006. "The Sophistic Movement." In *A Companion to Ancient Philosophy*, ed. M. L. Gill and P. Pellegrin. Blackwell Companions to Philosophy 31. Oxford.

Bobonich, C. 2002. *Plato's Utopia Recast: His Later Ethics and Politics*. Oxford.

Brown, E. 2000. "Socrates the Cosmopolitan." *Stanford Agora: An Online Journal of Legal Perspectives* 1: 74–87. http://agora.stanford.edu.

2006. "Socrates in the Stoa." In *A Companion to Socrates*, ed. S. Ahbel-Rappe and R. Kamtekar. Blackwell Companions to Philosophy 34. Oxford.

Forthcoming. *Stoic Cosmopolitanism*. Cambridge.

Burnet, J., ed. *Platonis Opera*, 5 vols. Oxford Classical Texts. Oxford.

Bury, R. B., ed. and trans. 1935. *Sextus Empiricus II: Against the Logicians*. Loeb Classical Library. Cambridge, MA.

Bywater, I., ed. 1894. *Aristotelis Ethica Nicomachea*. Oxford Classical Texts. Oxford.

Cheah, P., and B. Robbins, eds. 1998. *Cosmopolitics: Thinking and Feeling beyond the Nation*. Cultural Politics 14. Minneapolis, MN.

Cooper, J. M., ed. 1997. *Plato: Complete Works*. Indianapolis, IN.

[66] See *Ephesians* 2:20 and Augustine, *City of God*. The Christians also had a place for natural law (*Romans* 1:14), but theirs tends to be an especially otherworldly cosmopolis.

[67] I thank Steve Salkever and Jill Delston for their comments on an earlier draft.

Diels, H., and W. Kranz, eds. 1951–52. *Die Fragmente der Vorsokratiker*, 3 vols. 6th ed. Berlin.

Dodds, E. R. 1959. *Plato:* Gorgias. A revised text with introduction and commentary. Oxford.

Duke, E. A., W. F. Hicken, W. S. M. Nicoll, D. B. Robinson, and J. C. G. Strachan, eds. 1995. *Platonis Opera*, vol. 1. Oxford Classical Texts. Oxford.

Erskine, A. 1990. *The Hellenistic Stoa: Political Thought and Action*. Ithaca, NY.

Finnis, J. 1980. *Natural Law and Natural Rights*. Clarendon Law Series. Oxford.

ed. 1991. *Natural Law*, 2 vols. The International Library of Essays in Law and Legal Theory. New York.

Gagarin, M. 2002. *Antiphon the Athenian: Oratory, Law, and Justice in the Age of the Sophists*. Austin, TX.

George, R. P., ed. 1994. *Natural Law Theory: Contemporary Essays*. Oxford.

2001. *In Defense of Natural Law*. Oxford.

Ed. 2001a. *Natural Law, Liberalism, and Morality: Contemporary Essays*. Oxford.

Gomme, A. W., A. Andrewes, and K. J. Dover. 1970. *A Historical Commentary on Thucydides*, vol. IV: *Books V.25–VII*. Oxford.

Grieff, Pablo de, and C. Cronin, eds. 2002. *Global Justice and Transnational Politics: Essays on the Moral and Political Challenges of Globalization*. Cambridge, MA.

Griffith, M., ed. 1999. *Sophocles:* Antigone. Cambridge Greek and Latin Classics. Cambridge.

Guthrie, W. K. C. 1971. *A History of Greek Philosophy*, vol. 3, part 1: *The Sophists*. Cambridge.

Hall, J. 1956. "Plato's Legal Philosophy." *Indiana Law Journal* 31: 171–206.

Inwood, B., and L. Gerson, trans. 1997. *Hellenistic Philosophy: Introductory Readings*, 2nd ed. Indianapolis, IN.

Irwin, T. H. 1977. "Plato's Heracliteanism." *Philosophical Quarterly* 27: 1–13.

Jebb, R. C. 1900. *Sophocles: The Plays and Fragments*, part III: *The Antigone*, 3rd ed. Cambridge.

Jones, H. S., ed. 1900–2. *Thucydidis Historiae*, 2 vols. Oxford Classical Texts. Oxford.

Kahn, C. H. 1979. *The Art and Thought of Heraclitus: An Edition of the Fragments with Translation and Commentary*. Cambridge.

Kleingeld, P., and E. Brown. 2006. "Cosmopolitanism." In *The Stanford Encyclopedia of Philosophy* (Winter 2006 Edition), ed. E. N. Zalta. URL=<http://plato.stanford.edu/archives/win2006/entries/cosmopolitanism/>.

Klosko, G. 1988. "The Nocturnal Council in Plato's *Laws*." *Political Studies* 36: 74–88.

Kraut, R. 2002. *Aristotle: Political Philosophy*. Founders of Modern Political and Social Thought. Oxford.

Lloyd-Jones, H., and N. G. Wilson, eds. 1990. *Sophoclis Fabulae*. Oxford Classical Texts. Oxford.

Long, A. A. 1975–76. "Heraclitus and Stoicism." *Philosophia* (Athens) 5–6: 132–53. Reprinted in *Stoic Studies* (Cambridge, 1996).

Long, A. A., and D. N. Sedley. 1987. *The Hellenistic Philosophers*, 2 vols. Cambridge.

Maguire, J. P. 1947. "Plato's Theory of Natural Law." *Yale Classical Studies* 10: 151–78.

McKirahan, R. D., Jr. 1994. *Philosophy Before Socrates: An Introduction with Texts and Commentary*. Indianapolis, IN.

Menn, S. 1995. *Plato on God as Nous. Journal of the History of Philosophy Monograph Series.* Carbondale, IL.

Miller, F. D., Jr. 1991. "Aristotle on Natural Law and Justice." In *A Companion to Aristotle's Politics*, ed. D. Keyt and F. D. Miller, Jr. Oxford.

Jr. 1995. *Nature, Justice, and Rights in Aristotle's Politics*. Oxford.

Mitsis, P. 1994. "Natural Law and Natural Right in Post-Aristotelian Philosophy: The Stoics and Their Critics." *Aufstieg und Niedergang der römischen Welt* II.36.7: 4812–50.

2003. "The Stoics and Aquinas on Virtue and Natural Law." *Studia Philonica* 15: 35–53.

Moles, J. L. 1995. "The Cynics and Politics." In *Justice and Generosity: Studies in Hellenistic Social and Political Philosophy, Proceedings of the Sixth Symposium Hellenisticum*, ed. A. Laks and M. Schofield. Cambridge.

1996. "Cynic Cosmopolitanism." In *The Cynics: The Cynic Movement in Antiquity and Its Legacy*, ed. R. B. Branham and M.-O. Goulet-Cazé. Hellenistic Culture and Society 23. Berkeley, CA.

2000. "The Cynics." In *The Cambridge History of Greek and Roman Political Thought*, ed. C. Rowe and M. Schofield. Cambridge.

Morrow, G. R. 1948. "Plato and the Law of Nature." In *Essays in Political Theory Presented to George H. Sabine*, ed. M. R. Konvitz and A. E. Murphy. Ithaca, NY.

1993. *Plato's Cretan City: A Historical Interpretation of the Laws*. Princeton, NJ.

Most, G., ed. and trans. 2006. *Hesiod I: Theogony, Works and Days, Testimonia*. Loeb Classical Library. Cambridge, MA.

Murphy, M. C. 2001. *Natural Law and Practical Rationality*. Cambridge Studies in Philosophy and Law. Cambridge.

2002. "The Natural Law Tradition in Ethics." In *The Stanford Encyclopedia of Philosophy* (Winter 2002 Edition), ed. E. N. Zalta. http://plato.stanford.edu/archives/win2002/entries/natural-law-ethics/.

2006. *Natural Law in Jurisprudence and Politics*. Cambridge Studies in Philosophy and Law. Cambridge.

Nails, D. 2002. *The People of Plato: A Prosopography of Plato and Other Socratics*. Indianapolis, IN.

Nussbaum, M. C. 1986. *The Fragility of Goodness: Luck and Ethics in Greek Tragedy and Philosophy*. Cambridge.

Nussbaum, M. C., with respondents. 1996. *For Love of Country: Debating the Limits of Patriotism*, ed. J. Cohen. Boston.

Pendrick, G. J. 2002. *Antiphon the Sophist: The Fragments*. Edited with introduction, translation, and commentary. Cambridge Classical Texts and Commentaries 39. Cambridge.

Pogge, T. W., ed. 2001. *Global Justice*. Metaphilosophy 32.1/2. Oxford.

Powell, J. G. F., ed. 2006. *M. Tulli Ciceronis De re publica, De legibus, Cato Maior, De senectute, Laelius, De amicitia*. Oxford Classical Texts. Oxford.

Ross, W. D., ed. 1959. *Aristotelis Ars Rhetorica*. Oxford Classical Texts. Oxford.

Schofield, M. 1991. *The Stoic Idea of the City*. Cambridge.

Strauss, L. 1953. *Natural Right and History*. Chicago.

Striker, G. 1986. "Origins of the Concept of Natural Law." *Proceedings of the Boston Area Colloquium in Ancient Philosophy* 2: 79–94.

1991. "Following Nature: A Study in Stoic Ethics." *Oxford Studies in Ancient Philosophy* 9: 1–73.

Tarn, W. W. 1933. "Alexander the Great and the Unity of Mankind." *Proceedings of the British Academy* 19: 123–66.

1948. *Alexander the Great*, 2 vols. Cambridge.

Vander Waerdt, P. A. 1989. *The Stoic Theory of Natural Law.* Princeton University: Ph.D. dissertation.

1991. "Politics and Philosophy in Stoicism: A Discussion of A. Erskine, *The Hellenistic Stoa: Political Thought and Action.*" *Oxford Studies in Ancient Philosophy* 9: 185–211.

1994. "Zeno's *Republic* and the Origins of Natural Law." In *The Socratic Movement*, ed. P. A. Vander Waerdt. Ithaca, NY.

2003. "The Original Theory of Natural Law." *Studia Philonica* 15: 17–34.

Vertovec, S., and R. Cohen, ed. 2002. *Conceiving Cosmopolitanism: Theory, Context, and Practice*. Oxford.

Vlastos, G. 1947. "Equality and Justice in Early Greek Cosmologies." *Classical Philology* 42: 156–78.

Warner, R., trans. 1954. *Thucydides: The Peloponnesian War*. New York.

Watson, G. 1971. "The Natural Law and Stoicism." In *Problems in Stoicism*, ed. A. A. Long. London.

West, M. L., ed. 1978. *Hesiod: Works and Days*. Oxford.

Woolf, R. 2000. "Callicles and Socrates: Psychic (Dis)harmony in the *Gorgias*." *Oxford Studies in Ancient Philosophy* 18: 1–40.

Wyckoff, E., trans. 1954. *Sophocles:* Antigone. In *Sophocles I*, ed. D. Grene and R. Lattimore. The Complete Greek Tragedies. Chicago.

Yack, B. 1993. *The Problems of a Political Animal: Community, Justice, and Conflict in Aristotelian Political Thought*. Berkeley, CA.

Zetzel, J. E. G., ed. 1999. *Cicero:* On the Commonwealth *and* On the Laws. Cambridge Texts in the History of Political Thought. Cambridge.

Ziegler, K., ed. 1969. *M. Tulli Ciceronis Fasc. 39: De re publica*, 7th ed. Leipzig.

Select Bibliography

This list of works for further study is far from comprehensive, and is intended to supplement the bibliographies at the end of each chapter. It contains the editor's selection of books and articles that may prove helpful to readers – specialists and non-specialists alike – who wish to pursue further the themes and questions raised by the essays in this volume.

Works on General Questions in Greek Political Thought

Allen, D. 2000. *The World of Prometheus: The Politics of Punishing in Democratic Athens*. Princeton, NJ.

Arendt, H. 1958. *The Human Condition*. Chicago.

Balot, R. 2001. *Greed and Injustice in Classical Athens*. Princeton, NJ.

2006. *Greek Political Thought*. Oxford.

Euben, J. P. 1990. *The Tragedy of Political Theory: The Road Not Taken*. Princeton, NJ.

Nussbaum, M. 1986. *The Fragility of Goodness: Luck and Ethics in Greek Tragedy and Philosophy*. Cambridge.

Ober, J. 1989. *Mass and Elite in Democratic Athens: Rhetoric, Ideology, and the Power of the People*. Princeton, NJ.

1998. *Political Dissent in Democratic Athens: Intellectual Critics of Popular Rule*. Martin Classical Lectures. Princeton, NJ.

Saxonhouse, A. W. 1992. *Fear of Diversity: The Birth of Political Science in Ancient Greek Thought*. Chicago.

Strauss, L. 1953. *Natural Right and History*. Chicago.

1964. *The City and Man*. Chicago.

Williams, W. 1993. *Shame and Necessity*. Berkeley, CA.

Works on Particular Authors, Genres, or Schools

Berger, H., Jr. 1987. "Levels of Discourse in Plato's Dialogues." In *Literature and the Question of Philosophy*, ed. A. J. Cascardi. Baltimore, MD.

Bobonich, C. 2002. *Plato's Utopia Recast: His Later Ethics and Politics*. Oxford.

Bolotin, D. 1987. "Thucydides." *In History of Political Philosophy*, 3rd ed., ed. L. Strauss and J. Cropsey. Chicago.

Brann, E. 2002. *Homeric Moments: Clues to Delight in Reading* The Odyssey *and* The Iliad. Philadelphia, PA.

Bruehl, C. 1987. "Xenophon." *In History of Political Philosophy*, 3rd ed., ed. L. Strauss and J. Cropsey. Chicago.

Burger, R. 2008. *Aristotle's Dialogue With Socrates: On the* Nicomachean Ethics. Chicago.

Clark, S. R. L. 1975. *Aristotle's Man: Speculations upon Aristotelian Anthropology*. Oxford.

Collins, S. D. 2006. *Aristotle and the Rediscovery of Citizenship*. Cambridge.

Davis, M. 1996. *The Politics of Philosophy: A Commentary on Aristotle's Politics*. Lanham, MD.

Euben, J. P., ed.1986. *Greek Tragedy and Political Theory*. Berkeley, CA.

Ferrari, G. R. F., ed. 2007. *The Cambridge Companion to Plato's* Republic. Cambridge.

Frank, J. 2005. *A Democracy of Distinction: Aristotle and the Work of Politics*. Chicago.

Griswold, C., ed. 2002. *Platonic Writings/Platonic Readings*. University Park, PA.

Howland, J. 1998. *The Paradox of Political Philosophy: Socrates' Philosophic Trial*. Lanham MD.

Kraut, R. 2002. *Aristotle: Political Philosophy*. Oxford.

Kullmann, W. 1991. "Man as a Political Animal in Aristotle." In *A Companion to Aristotle's Politics*, ed. David Keyt and Fred D. Miller, Jr. Oxford.

Mara, G. M. 1997. *Socrates' Discursive Democracy: Logos and Ergon in Platonic Political Philosophy*. Albany, NY.

Miller, F. D., Jr. 1995. *Nature, Justice, and Rights in Aristotle's Politics*. Oxford.

Monoson, S. S. 2000. *Plato's Democratic Entanglements: Athenian Politics and the Practice of Philosophy*. Princeton, NJ.

Mulgan, R. G. 1977. *Aristotle's Political Theory: An Introduction For Students of Political Theory*. New York.

Murdoch, I. 1971. *The Sovereignty of Good*. New York.

Nails, D. 2002. *The People of Plato: A Prosopography of Plato and Other Socratics*. Indianapolis, IN.

Nichols, M. P. 1992. *Citizens and Statesmen: A Study of Aristotle's* Politics. Lanham, MD.

Nightingale, N. 1995. *Genres in Dialogue: Plato and the Construct of Philosophy*. Cambridge.

Orwin, C. 1994. *The Humanity of Thucydides*. Princeton, NJ.

Salkever, S. 1990. *Finding the Mean: Theory and Practice in Aristotelian Political Philosophy*. Princeton, NJ.

Saxonhouse, A. W. 1976. "The Philosopher and the Female in the Political Thought of Plato." *Political Theory* 4: 195–212.

Saxonhouse, A. W. 1998. "Democracy, Equality, and *Eidê:* A Radical View from Book 8 of Plato's *Republic*." *American Political Science Review* 92: 273–83.

Schofield, M. 1999. *The Stoic Idea of the City*. Chicago.

Smith, T. W. 2001. *Revaluing Ethics: Aristotle's Dialectical Pedagogy*. Albany, NY.

Wallach, J. R. 2001. *The Platonic Political Art: A Study of Critical Reason and Democracy*. University Park, PA.

Yack, B. 1993. *The Problems of a Political Animal: Community, Justice, and Conflict in Aristotelian Political Thought*. Berkeley, CA.

Zuckert, C. H. 1996. *Postmodern Platos: Nietzsche, Heidegger, Gadamer, Strauss, Derrida*. Chicago.

Index